Efficient
C/C++
Programming

**Smaller,
Faster,
Better**

2nd Edition

LIMITED WARRANTY AND DISCLAIMER OF LIABILITY

Efficient
C/C++
Programming

Smaller, Faster, Better

2 **nd Edition**

Steve Heller
Chrysalis Software Corporation
Baldwin, New York

AP PROFESSIONAL
Boston   San Diego   New York
London   Sydney   Tokyo   Toronto

The previous edition of this book was titled
Large Problems, Small Machines

All brand names and product names mentioned in
this book are trademarks or registered trademarks
of their respective companies.

AP PROFESSIONAL
955 Massachusetts Avenue, Cambridge, MA 02139

An Imprint of ACADEMIC PRESS, INC.
A Division of HARCOURT BRACE & COMPANY

United Kingdom Edition published by
ACADEMIC PRESS LIMITED
24–28 Oval Road, London NW1 7DX

Library of Congress Cataloging-in-Publication Data

Heller, Steve, 1949 Apr. 17-
    Efficient C/C++ programming : smaller, faster, better / Steve
Heller. -- 2nd ed.
        p. cm.
    Includes bibliographical references and index.
    ISBN 0-12-339095-8
    1. C (Computer program language) 2. C++ (Computer program
language) I. Title.
    QA76.73.C15H45 1994   94-27488
    005.13--dc20   CIP

Printed in the United States of America
94 95 96 97 98 IP 9 8 7 6 5 4 3 2 1

I would like to dedicate this book to my beautiful and brilliant wife, Judy Schwartz, whose encouragement and example set me on the tortuous path to writing for publication.

Contents

Table of Listings

Chapter 1

Chapter 2

Chapter 3

Chapter 4

Chapter 5

Chapter 6

Chapter 7

Foreword

If you were to ask a typical CS graduate how much he or she knows about programming, the most honest possible answer would be, "Theoretically, I know a lot."

Theoretically.

Ask the same student how fast a given piece of code is, and the student is likely to say, "Theoretically, pretty damned fast."

Well, how fast, *really*? Nine out of ten programmers wouldn't have a clue. What, me profile? I'm a software *engineer*. I don't do profilers.

Ahhh, me. There's book learning, and then there's learning by tearing your hair out. Book learning is beautiful in that crystalline, organized sense. (You can also cram for its tests.) The other type of learning is lots more painful, and (as I discovered a little too late) you eventually run out of hair. Problem is, that's the only way you really can be sure you *know* something, and not just "theoretically."

Part of the problem is that book learning follows the advance of the state of the art reluctantly, if at all. We used to be able to gauge code performance in practical terms by looking up opcodes in a reference and counting machine cycles. Most of us who "book learned" prior to 1980 learned it that way, and it worked, too—on the 8080 CPU under CP/M.

Time marches on. The 8080 is in a museum under a bell jar. Count cycles today and your code will make a fool of you by refusing to come anywhere close to your cycle count. There are things like prefetch queues, primary and secondary caches, pipelines, address generation interlocks and—sheesh!—superscalar execution. No amount of analysis under a microscope will allow you to predict with any accuracy how a given sequence of instructions will perform. Ya gotta go in there and *look* at it.

This is one reason why I like Steve Heller's work. He doesn't just dish out conventional wisdom without commentary. (He doesn't, in fact, do *anything* without commentary.) He's one of the very rare practitioners of what I genuinely consider software engineering who does dirty his hands with profilers, and who knows what works, what doesn't, and how fast. Not just theoretically. For real.

Let me give you a f'rinstance. For years now, interpreters have existed under a cloud, condemned as ancient artifacts from an era when memory was hideously expensive and had to be conserved at all costs. We now have cheap memory—so what the hey, climb every mountain, unroll every loop, and if you end up with a four megabyte executable, drop another SIMM in the jukebox and keep on rockin'.

The catch is that we now have abundant, cheap, *slow* memory—and our CPUs are getting faster lots faster than our memory is getting faster. That's why CPU manufacturers have begun putting superfast cache memory right on the CPU die. Otherwise, our superfast CPUs would spend all their time tapping their feet waiting for code and data to come in from creaky-slow RAM.

So what we have is a few thousand bytes of superfast cache, and limitless megabytes of superslow RAM. Steve caught on quickly to the implication: That interpreters can now actually beat in-line code in many cases, because an interpreter can be wedged entirely inside that cache, where they can interpret at speed without sitting around waiting for RAM. The books have only recently been preaching that interpreters are slow, ancient and useless—and now, like loud ties, they're back, whether you like them or not.

For if you're genuinely concerned about efficient code, it doesn't matter what you like or don't like. It only matters what works.

You'll find that attitude again and again throughout this book: What's good is what works, and works efficiently; that is, without spending either space or cycles to no clear gain. Steve is not afraid to create a data structure that bows to the inevitable peccadilloes of the underlying hardware, if doing so will make it a more efficient data structure. The aforementioned spreadsheet interpreter (see Chapter 5) is a superb example. It's an algorithm, yes, but it was brought to life with the express intent that it run efficiently on clock-multiplied Intel processors—primarily the 486/DX2.

Hey, if you want portability, *be prepared to pay for it.*

So let me make a few suggestions: Read this book, from start to finish, and while doing so set aside any preconceived notions you may have about "beautiful" code, or portable code, or lord knows, fast code. (Recursion, for example, is "beautiful." It's also dangerous, and *slow.*) Also, don't just look at the code. Load it, compile it, run it, *understand* it—not just as code, but as an element of a larger system that includes—rather than willfully ignores—the underlying hardware.

Once you do that, you will have learned a lot.

Not just theoretically. For real and for all time.

—Jeff Duntemann KG7JF

Preface

Imagine that you are about to finish a relatively large program, one that has taken a few weeks or months to write and debug. Just as you are putting the finishing touches on it, you discover that it is either too slow or runs out of memory when you feed it a realistic set of input data. You sigh, and start the task of optimizing it.

But why optimize? If your program doesn't fit in memory, you can just get more memory; if it is too slow, you can get a faster processor.

I have written *Efficient C/C++ Programming* because I believe that this common attitude is incorrect, and that a knowledge of optimization is essential to a professional programmer. One very important reason is that we often have little control over the hardware on which our programs are to be run. In this situation, the simplistic approach of adding more hardware is not feasible.

Efficient C/C++ Programming provides working programmers and those who intend to be working programmers with a practical, real-world approach to program optimization. Many of the optimization techniques presented are derived from my reading of academic journals that are, sadly, little known in the programming community. This book also draws on my 25 years of experience as a programmer in diverse fields of application, during which I have become increasingly concerned about the amount of effort spent in reinventing optimization techniques rather than applying those already developed.

The first question you have to answer is whether your program needs optimization at all. If it does, you have to determine what part of the program is the culprit, and what resource is being overused. Chapter 1 indicates a method of attack on these problems, as well as a real-life example.

I am always happy to receive correspondence from readers. If you wish to contact me, please send email to "stheller@pipeline.com" on the Internet, or write to the following address:

Chrysalis Software Corporation
P.O. Box 0335
Baldwin, NY 11510

Acknowledgments

I would like to thank the following readers of my manuscript who graciously volunteered their services in response to my pleas for help on the Internet: Bruce E. Wilson, Dave Voorhis, Raymond Erdey, Randall T. Long, David Arnstein, David Loo, Shane McRoberts, and Pete Humphrey. The following colleagues of mine also answered the call and deserve the same thanks: William Miller, Joe Koplik, Brian Zaino, and Dave Schleifer.

Special thanks are also due Bob Sosin, who was involved with the first edition and therefore should have known better, and Mike Mohle, who escaped involvement in the first edition but couldn't get out of it this time. Of course, I couldn't forget Jeff Duntemann, author of one of the most laudatory forewords I've ever had the privilege to read.

Finally, let me acknowledge my editor, Chuck Glaser of AP Professional, whose unfailing support saw this project through the arduous process of publication.

CHAPTER 1

Let's Get Small (and Fast)

Introduction to Optimization

Definition: Optimization is the art and science of modifying a working computer program so that it makes more efficient use of one or more scarce resources, primarily memory, disk space, or time.
Corollary (The First Law of Optimization): The speed of a nonworking program is irrelevant.

ALGORITHMS DISCUSSED

`Radix40` Data Representation, Lookup Tables[1]

Deciding Whether to Optimize

Suppose you have written a program to calculate mortgage payments; the yearly run takes ten minutes. Should you spend two hours to double its speed? Probably not, since it will take twenty-four years to pay back the original investment of time at five minutes per year.[2] On the other hand, if you run a program for three hours every

---

1. If you don't have the time to read this book in its entirety, you can turn to figures 8.1–8.5 in Chapter 8 to find the algorithms best suited to your problem.

2. Actually, you will never be ahead; five minutes saved 23 years from now is not as valuable as five minutes spent now. This is analogous to the lottery in which you win a million dollars, but the prize is paid as one dollar a year for a million years!

working day, even spending thirty hours to double its speed will pay for itself in only twenty working days, or about a month. Obviously the latter is a much better candidate for optimization. Usually, of course, the situation is not nearly so unambiguous: even if your system is overloaded, it may not be immediately apparent which program is responsible.[3]

My general rule is not to optimize a program that performs satisfactorily. If you (or the intended users) don't become impatient while waiting for it to finish, don't bother. Of course, if you just feel like indulging in some recreational optimization, that's another matter.

Why Optimization Is Necessary

Assuming that our programs are too big, or too slow, why don't we just add more memory or a faster processor? If that isn't possible today, then the next generation of processors should be powerful enough to spare us such concerns.

Let's examine this rather widely held theory. Although the past is not an infallible guide to the future, it is certainly one source of information about what happens when technology changes. A good place to start is to compare the computers of the late1970's with those of the mid-1990's.

The first diskette-based computer I ever owned was a Radio Shack TRS-80 Model III™, purchased in 1979.[4] It had a 4 MHz Z80™ processor, 48 Kbytes of memory, and Basic™ in ROM. The diskettes held about 140 Kbytes apiece. Among the programs that were available for this machine were word processors, assemblers, debuggers, data bases, and games. While none of these were as advanced as the ones that are available today on 80x86 or 680x0 machines, most of the basic functions were there.

The i486™ machines of today have at least 100 times as much memory and 200 times as much disk storage and are at least 100 times as fast. Therefore, according to this theory, we should no longer need to worry about efficiency.

Recently, however, several of the major microcomputer software companies have had serious performance problems with new software releases of both application programs and system programs, as they attempted to add more and more features to those available in the previous versions.[5] This illustrates what I call the Iron Law of Programming: whenever more resources are made available, a more ambitious project

---

3. This is especially true on a multiuser system.

4. My previous computer was also a Radio Shack computer, but it had only a cassette recorder/player for "mass storage"!

5. Microsoft is the most prominent example at the moment; the resource consumption of Windows NT™ is legendary, and Visual C++ isn't exactly a speed demon even on a big, fast machine.

is attempted. This means that optimal use of these resources is important no matter how fast or capacious the machine.

Why Optimization Is Often Neglected

In view of this situation, why has optimization of application programs not gained more attention? I suspect that a major reason is the tremendous and continuing change in the relative costs of programming time and computer hardware. To illustrate this, let us examine two situations where the same efficiency improvement is gained, but the second example occurs after twenty years of technological improvement.

In the early 1970's a programmer's starting salary was about $3 per hour, and an hour of timesharing connect time cost about $15. Therefore, if a program originally took one hour to run every day, and the programmer spent a week to reduce this time by 20%, in about eight weeks the increased speed would have paid for the programmer's time.

In the mid-1990's, the starting salary is in the vicinity of $12 per hour, and if we assume that the desktop computer costs $4000 and is amortized over three years, the weekly cost of running the unoptimized program is about $3. Holding the other assumptions constant, the optimization payback time is about fifteen years![6]

This long-term trend seems to favor hardware solutions for performance problems over the investment of programming effort. However, the appropriate strategy for performance improvement of a program depends on how much control you have over the hardware on which the program will run. The less control you have over the hardware, the greater the advantage of software solutions to performance problems, as illustrated by the situations below.

Considering a Hardware Solution

While every optimization problem is different, here are some general guidelines that can help you decide whether adding hardware to help you with your performance problems makes sense.

1. If you are creating a system that includes both software and hardware, and you can improve the functioning of the program, ease maintenance, or speed up develop-

---

6. This example is actually quite conservative. The program that took one hour to run on a timesharing terminal would probably take much less than that on a current desktop computer; we are also neglecting the time value of the savings, as noted above.

ment at a small additional expense for extra hardware resources, you should almost certainly do so.

A few years ago, I was involved in a classic example of this situation. The project was to create a point-of-sale system, including specialized hardware and programs, that tied a number of terminals into a common database. Since the part of the database that had to be accessed rapidly could be limited to about 1 $1/2$ megabytes, I suggested that we put enough memory in the database server machine to hold the entire database. That way, the response time would be faster than even a very good indexing system could provide, and the programming effort would be greatly reduced. The additional expense came to about $150 per system, which was less than 3% of the price of the system. Of course, just adding hardware doesn't always mean that no software optimization is needed. In this case, as you will see below, adding the hardware was only the beginning of the optimization effort.

2. If you are writing programs for your own use on one computer, and you can afford to buy a machine powerful enough to perform adequately, then you might very well purchase such a machine rather than optimizing the program.[7]

3. If you are writing a program that will be running on more than one computer, even if it is only for internal use at your company, the expense and annoyance of requiring the other users to upgrade their computers may outweigh the difficulty of optimization.

4. If your program is to run on many computers at your company, it is almost always a good idea to try to optimize it rather than to require all those users to upgrade their hardware.

5. If your program is to be sold in the open market to run on standard hardware, you must try to optimize it. Otherwise, the users are likely to reject the program.

An excellent example of what happens when you try to make a number of users upgrade their computers is the dismal sales record (as of this writing) of the Windows NT™ operating system.

In order to get any reasonable performance under the initial version of Windows NT, you need at least 24 megabytes of memory and a 486/66 processor. Since almost no users have this amount of RAM, the sales of this program have been very disappointing. The next version of Windows NT is supposed to be able to run reasonably well on "only" 16 megabytes; perhaps this will make this operating system more popular, but the jury is still out.

---

7. Of course, if your old machine is more than two or three years old, you might want to replace it anyway, just to get the benefit of the improved technology available today.

Categories of Optimization

There are two broad categories of optimization: using a better algorithm, and improving the implementation of the algorithm we are already using. Generally, we should replace an algorithm by a better one as soon as possible, as this usually does not hinder understanding or later modification of the program. An example is the use of a distribution counting sort (see Chapter 3) in preference to Quicksort. Of course, if we employ these efficient algorithms from the start of our programming effort, then we are not optimizing in the strict sense of our definition (changing a working program to make it more efficient). However, the end result is still a better program than we would have obtained otherwise.[8]

The second category of optimization is the modification of the implementation of an existing algorithm (for example, by rewriting a portion of the code in assembly language; see Chapter 4). This type of modification often has the unfortunate side effect of making the algorithm much harder to understand or modify in the future; it also impairs portability among different hardware and software architectures. Therefore, such an optimization should be postponed until the last possible moment, in order to reduce its negative effects on the development and maintenance of the program. This is an application of the First Law of Optimization: don't try to optimize a program (in the strict sense of modifying an existing program) until it is working correctly.

Finding the Critical Resource

It may seem obvious that, before you can optimize a program, you have to know what is making it inefficient. Of course, if you run out of memory or disk space while executing the program, this determination becomes much simpler.

Depending on which language and machine you are using, there may be "profiling" tools available which allow you to determine where your program is spending most of its time. These, of course, are most useful when the problem is CPU time, but even if that is not the problem, you may still be able to find out that, e.g., your program is spending 95% of its time in the disk reading and/or writing routines. This is a valuable clue to where the problem lies.

However, even if no profiler is available for your system, it isn't hard to gather some useful information yourself. One way to do this is to insert a call to a system timer routine (such as `clock()` in ANSI C) at the beginning of the segment to be timed and another call at the end of the segment and subtract the two times. Depending on the resolution of the timer, the length of the routine, and the speed of

---

8. Perhaps this could be referred to as optimizing the design.

your processor, you may have to execute the segment more than once to gather any useful information. This is illustrated in the real-life example below.

Determining How Much Optimization Is Needed

Sometimes your task is simply to make the program run as fast (or take as little memory) as possible. In this case, you must use the most effective optimization available, regardless of the effort involved. However, you often have (or can get) a specific target, such as a memory budget of 1.4 megabytes for your data. If you can achieve this goal by relatively simple means, it would be a waste of your time to try to squeeze the last few kilobytes out of the data by a fancier compression algorithm. In fact, it may be worse than a waste of time; the simpler algorithm may also have other desirable characteristics (other than its raw performance).

A good example of such a simple algorithm is the `Radix40` data compression method (see Chapter 2, listings 2.4 and 2.5), which is, on average, considerably less effective at reducing the size of a data file than a number of other data compression algorithms. On the other hand, it is quite fast, requires very little storage, and always produces the same amount of output for the same amount of input, which means that its compression efficiency can be calculated exactly in advance. The (statistically) more effective routines such as those using arithmetic coding take more memory and more time, and they generally produce different amounts of output for a given amount of input (depending on what has gone before), so that their compression efficiency cannot be predicted exactly. (In fact, in rare circumstances, they produce output that is larger than the input.) This context dependence also means that they are more difficult to use in applications where random access to compressed data is needed.

The moral is that you should use the simplest algorithm that will meet your needs. If you can define your needs precisely, you probably won't have to implement as sophisticated an algorithm to solve your problem, which will leave you more time to work on other areas that need improvement.

A Real-Life Example

The point-of-sale database program I mentioned earlier is an excellent example of the fact that optimization rarely follows a straight-line path. The first problem was the speed of access to the database by multiple users. Since the software is supplied with specialized hardware, it was reasonable to solve this problem by adding enough memory to hold the portion of the database that requires rapid access. My employer determined that 15,000 invoice records and 5000 customer records would be sufficient, resulting in a memory requirement of about 1.25 megabytes. The expense of this amount of memory was within reason.

Unfortunately, that part of memory (**conventional** memory) which allows normal program access is limited to 640 kilobytes on IBM-compatible systems running the MS-DOS operating system. While our actual hardware allowed for more memory, it could be referenced only as **expanded** memory, which cannot be allocated as simply as conventional memory.

Luckily, the problem of using expanded memory for data storage has been addressed by libraries of routines which allow any particular 16 Kbyte "page" of expanded memory to be loaded when the data in it are required.[9] Storing the records in expanded memory solved the speed problem by eliminating excessive disk I/O.

However, the amount of expanded memory required was very close to the total available. In the very likely event of adding even a single field to the record definition, there would not be enough room for all the records. Therefore, I had to consider ways to reduce the space taken by these records.

The makeup of the database is important to the solution of this new problem. It consists almost entirely of 15,000 invoice records of approximately 35 bytes each and 5000 customer records of approximately 145 bytes each. Fortunately, the majority of the fields in the customer record contained only uppercase alphabetic characters, numeric digits, a few special characters ("."., ",", and "-"), and spaces. This limited character set allows the use of `Radix40` compression, which packs three characters into two bytes. (See Chapter 2 for more details on this algorithm).

However, the time required to convert these fields from ASCII to `Radix40` representation seemed excessive. Some testing disclosed that converting 5000 records containing 6 fields of 12 characters each from ASCII to `Radix40` on a 33 MHz i386 took about 40 seconds![10] Although the most common operations in this system do not require wholesale conversion, it is required in such cases as importing an old-style database into this new system, and such inefficiency was unacceptable. So my space problem had become a speed problem again.

I resolved to improve the speed of this conversion (from 1300 microseconds/12 character string) as much as was practical, before proposing further hardware upgrades to the system. The first problem was to determine which operation was consuming the most CPU time. Examination of the code (listing 1.3), disclosed that the `toupper` function was being called for every character in the string, every

---

9. If you have a similar problem, you might want to try the package I used, called PowerSTOR. It can be obtained from Acme Software, P.O. Box 40734, Portland, OR 97240.

10. This is worse than it may sound; the actual hardware on which the system runs is much slower than the i386 development machine I was using at the time.

time the character was being examined (lines 84–89). This seemed an obvious place to start.

The purpose of writing the loop in this way was to avoid making changes to the input string; after all, it was an input variable. However, a more efficient way to leave the input string unaltered was to make a copy of the input string and convert the copy to uppercase, as indicated in listing 1.4, lines 68–70. This reduced the time to 650 microseconds/12 character string, but I suspected that more savings were possible.

Another possible area of improvement was to reduce the use of dynamic string allocation to get storage for the copy of the string to be converted to uppercase. In my application, most of the strings would be less than 100 characters, so I decided to allocate room for a string of 99 characters (plus the required null at the end) on the stack and to call the dynamic allocation routine only if the string was larger than that (see listing 1.5, lines 71–74). However, this change didn't affect the time significantly, so I removed it.

I couldn't see any obvious way to increase the speed of this routine further, until I noticed that if the data had about the same number of occurrences of each character, the loop to figure out the code for a single character would be executed an average of 20 times per character! Could this be dispensed with?

Yes, by allocating 256 bytes for a table of conversion values. Then I could index into the table rather than searching the string of legal values (see listing 1.6, line 115). Timing this version revealed an impressive improvement: 93 microseconds/12 character string. This final version is 14 times the speed of the original.[11]

The use of a profiler would have reduced the effort needed to determine the major causes of the inefficiency. Even without such an aid, attention to which lines were being executed most frequently enabled me to remove the major bottlenecks in the conversion to `Radix40` representation. It is no longer a significant part of the time needed to access a record.

Summary

In this chapter, I have given some guidelines and examples of how to determine whether optimization is required and how to apply your optimization effort effectively. In the next chapter we will start to examine the algorithms and other solutions that you can apply once you have determined where your program needs improvement.

---

11. I also changed the method of clearing the result array to use `memset` rather than a loop, in line 74 of the same routine.

Listing 1.1 *radtest.h: include file for Radix40 routines*

```
1
2    /****keyword-flag*** "%v %f %n" */
3    /* "4 20-Aug-92,21:05:02 RADTEST.H" */
4
5
6    #define STRING_LENGTH 12
7
8    #define REPS 30000
9
10   extern char legal_chars[40];
11
12   extern unsigned weights[3];
13
14   int ascii_to_radix40_1(unsigned *radix40_data, unsigned char *ascii_data, int max_chars);
15
16   int ascii_to_radix40_2(unsigned *radix40_data, unsigned char *ascii_data, int max_chars);
17
18   int ascii_to_radix40_3(unsigned *radix40_data, unsigned char *ascii_data, int max_chars);
19
20   int ascii_to_radix40_4(unsigned *radix40_data, unsigned char *ascii_data, int max_chars);
```

Listing 1.2 *radix40.h: include file for Radix40 routines*

```
 1
 2   /****keyword-flag*** "%v %f %n" */
 3   /* "3 20-Aug-92,22:57:02 RADIX40.H" */
 4
 5
 6   #define CPW 3 /* characters per word in Radix40 code */
 7
 8   #define S_OKAY 0
 9   #define S_ILLEGAL 1
10
11   #define HYPHEN 2
12   #define ILLEGAL 0x80
13   #define IL (HYPHEN|ILLEGAL)
14   /* this is the code for a -, but with the illegal flag set */
15   /* it is used in the conversion table to indicate that a character is invalid */
16
17
18   typedef unsigned Radix40;
19
20   int radix40_to_ascii(unsigned char *ascii_data, Radix40 *radix40_data,int max_chars);
21
22   int ascii_to_radix40(Radix40 *radix40_data, unsigned char *ascii_data, int max_chars);
```

Listing 1.3 *ascrad1.c: Radix40 test program #1*

```
 1   /****keyword-flag*** "%v %f %n" */
 2   /* "9 20-Aug-92,23:05:12 ASCRAD1.C" */
 3
 4   #include <stdio.h>
 5   #include <string.h>
 6   #include <alloc.h>
 7   #include <time.h>
 8   #include <ctype.h>
 9   #include "radix40.h"
10   #include "radtest.h"
11
12   main()
13   {
14     int i;
15     unsigned char test[STRING_LENGTH+1] = "Radix40 Test";
16     Radix40 temp[STRING_LENGTH];
17     unsigned char test2[STRING_LENGTH+1];
18     clock_t start, end;
19
20     start = clock();
21     for (i = 0; i < REPS; i ++)
22         ascii_to_radix40_1(temp,test,STRING_LENGTH);
23     end = clock();
24     printf("Timer ticks for version 1: %d\n",end-start);
25
26     radix40_to_ascii(test2,temp,STRING_LENGTH);
27     if (stricmp((char *)test2,(char *)test) != 0)
28         printf("Match 1 failed\n");
29
30     return(0);
31   }
32
33   int ascii_to_radix40_1(radix40_data,ascii_data,max_chars)
34   unsigned *radix40_data;
35   unsigned char *ascii_data;
36   int max_chars;
37   /* this routine converts a null-terminated ascii character string */
38   /* to radix 40 representation.  The allowable characters are: */
39   /* A-Z, 0-9, period, comma, hyphen, and space.  If any illegal characters */
40   /* are detected, they will be converted to hyphens, and the return value */
41   /* will be S_ILLEGAL. */
42   /* Lowercase letters will be upper-cased without error indication. */
43   /* The radix40 value will be padded with blanks to a multiple of three */
44   /* characters. If the number of characters in the ascii string is > max_chars */
45   /* only max_chars will be converted, and the return value will be S_ILLEGAL. */
46   /* If no error is detected, the return value will be S_OKAY. */
47   {
48     int i;
49     int j;
50     int ascii_length;
```

Listing 1.3 *ascrad1.c: Radix40 test program #1 (continued)*

```
 51    int result;
 52    int conversion_status;
 53    int words_to_convert;
 54    int words_to_clear;
 55    int cycle;
 56    unsigned current_word_index;
 57
 58    result = S_OKAY;
 59    ascii_length = strlen((char *)ascii_data);
 60    if (ascii_length > max_chars)
 61        {
 62        ascii_length = max_chars;
 63        result = S_ILLEGAL;
 64        }
 65
 66    words_to_convert = ascii_length / 3;
 67    if (ascii_length % 3 != 0)
 68        words_to_convert ++;
 69
 70    words_to_clear = max_chars / 3;
 71    if (max_chars % 3 != 0)
 72        words_to_clear ++;
 73
 74    for (i = 0; i < words_to_clear; i ++)
 75        radix40_data[i] = 0; /* this blanks out the output string */
 76
 77    current_word_index = -1;
 78    cycle = 0;
 79    for (i = 0; i < ascii_length; i ++)
 80        {
 81        if (cycle == 0)
 82            current_word_index ++;
 83        conversion_status = 0;
 84        for (j = 0; j < 40; j ++)
 85            if (legal_chars[j] == toupper(ascii_data[i]))
 86                {
 87                conversion_status = 1;
 88                break;
 89                }
 90        if (conversion_status == 0)
 91            {
 92            result = S_ILLEGAL;
 93            j = HYPHEN; /* code for hyphen */
 94            }
 95        radix40_data[current_word_index] += weights[cycle] * j;
 96        cycle = (cycle + 1) % 3;
 97        }
 98
 99    return(result);
100    }
```

Listing 1.4 *ascrad2.c: Radix40 test program #2*

```
 1    /****keyword-flag*** "%v %f %n" */
 2    /* "9 13-Mar-93,8:26:02 ASCRAD2.C" */
 3
 4    #include <stdio.h>
 5    #include <string.h>
 6    #include <alloc.h>
 7    #include <time.h>
 8    #include <ctype.h>
 9    #include "radix40.h"
10    #include "radtest.h"
11
12    main()
13    {
14      int i;
15      unsigned char test[STRING_LENGTH+1] = "Radix40 Test";
16      Radix40 temp[STRING_LENGTH];
17      unsigned char test2[STRING_LENGTH+1];
18      clock_t start, end;
19
20      start = clock();
21      for (i = 0; i < REPS; i ++)
22          ascii_to_radix40_2(temp,test,STRING_LENGTH);
23      end = clock();
24      printf("Timer ticks for version 2: %d\n",end-start);
25
26      radix40_to_ascii(test2,temp,STRING_LENGTH);
27      if (stricmp((char *)test2,(char *)test) != 0)
28          printf("Match 2 failed\n");
29
30      return(0);
31    }
32
33
34    int ascii_to_radix40_2(radix40_data,ascii_data,max_chars)
35    unsigned *radix40_data;
36    unsigned char *ascii_data;
37    int max_chars;
38    /* this routine converts a null-terminated ascii character string */
39    /* to radix 40 representation.  The allowable characters are: */
40    /* A-Z, 0-9, period, comma, hyphen, and space.  If any illegal characters */
41    /* are detected, they will be converted to hyphens, and the return value */
42    /* will be S_ILLEGAL. */
43    /* Lowercase letters will be upper-cased without error indication. */
44    /* The radix40 value will be padded with blanks to a multiple of three */
45    /* characters. If the number of characters in the ascii string is > max_chars */
46    /* only max_chars will be converted, and the return value will be S_ILLEGAL. */
47    /* If no error is detected, the return value will be S_OKAY. */
48    {
49      int i;
50      int j;
```

Listing 1.4 *ascrad2.c: Radix40 test program #2 (continued)*

```
51      int ascii_length;
52      int result;
53      int conversion_status;
54      int words_to_convert;
55      int words_to_clear;
56      int cycle;
57      unsigned current_word_index;
58      unsigned char *temp_ascii_data;
59
60      result = S_OKAY;
61      ascii_length = strlen((char *)ascii_data);
62      if (ascii_length > max_chars)
63          {
64          ascii_length = max_chars;
65          result = S_ILLEGAL;
66          }
67
68      temp_ascii_data = malloc(ascii_length+1);
69      for (i = 0; i < ascii_length+1; i ++)
70          temp_ascii_data[i] = toupper(ascii_data[i]);
71
72      words_to_convert = ascii_length / 3;
73      if (ascii_length % 3 != 0)
74          words_to_convert ++;
75
76      words_to_clear = max_chars / 3;
77      if (max_chars % 3 != 0)
78          words_to_clear ++;
79
80      for (i = 0; i < words_to_clear; i ++)
81          radix40_data[i] = 0; /* this blanks out the output string */
82
83      current_word_index = -1;
84      cycle = 0;
85      for (i = 0; i < ascii_length; i ++)
86          {
87          if (cycle == 0)
88              current_word_index ++;
89          conversion_status = 0;
90          for (j = 0; j < 40; j ++)
91              if (legal_chars[j] == temp_ascii_data[i])
92                  {
93                  conversion_status = 1;
94                  break;
95                  }
96          if (conversion_status == 0)
97              {
98              result = S_ILLEGAL;
99              j = HYPHEN; /* code for hyphen */
100             }
```

Listing 1.4 *ascrad2.c: Radix40 test program #2 (continued)*

```
101            radix40_data[current_word_index] += weights[cycle] * j;
102            cycle = (cycle + 1) % 3;
103            }
104
105     free(temp_ascii_data);
106     return(result);
107  }
```

Listing 1.5 *ascrad3.c: Radix40 test program #3*

```
 1   /****keyword-flag*** "%v %f %n" */
 2   /* "9 13-Mar-93,8:27:28 ASCRAD3.C" */
 3
 4   #include <stdio.h>
 5   #include <string.h>
 6   #include <alloc.h>
 7   #include <time.h>
 8   #include <ctype.h>
 9   #include "radix40.h"
10   #include "radtest.h"
11
12   main()
13   {
14     int i;
15     unsigned char test[STRING_LENGTH+1] = "Radix40 Test";
16     Radix40 temp[STRING_LENGTH];
17     unsigned char test2[STRING_LENGTH+1];
18     clock_t start, end;
19
20     start = clock();
21     for (i = 0; i < REPS; i ++)
22         ascii_to_radix40_3(temp,test,STRING_LENGTH);
23     end = clock();
24     printf("Timer ticks for version 3: %d\n",end-start);
25
26     radix40_to_ascii(test2,temp,STRING_LENGTH);
27     if (stricmp((char *)test2,(char *)test) != 0)
28         printf("Match 3 failed\n");
29
30     return(0);
31   }
32
33
34   #define STACK_DATA_SIZE 100
35
36   int ascii_to_radix40_3(radix40_data,ascii_data,max_chars)
37   unsigned *radix40_data;
38   unsigned char *ascii_data;
39   int max_chars;
40   /* this routine converts a null-terminated ascii character string */
41   /* to radix 40 representation.  The allowable characters are: */
42   /* A-Z, 0-9, period, comma, hyphen, and space.  If any illegal characters */
43   /* are detected, they will be converted to hyphens, and the return value */
44   /* will be S_ILLEGAL. */
45   /* Lowercase letters will be upper-cased without error indication. */
46   /* The radix40 value will be padded with blanks to a multiple of three */
47   /* characters. If the number of characters in the ascii string is > max_chars */
48   /* only max_chars will be converted, and the return value will be S_ILLEGAL. */
49   /* If no error is detected, the return value will be S_OKAY. */
50   {
```

Listing 1.5 *ascrad3.c: Radix40 test program #3 (continued)*

```
51    int i;
52    int j;
53    int ascii_length;
54    int result;
55    int conversion_status;
56    int words_to_convert;
57    int words_to_clear;
58    int cycle;
59    unsigned current_word_index;
60    unsigned char *temp_ascii_data;
61    unsigned char stack_ascii_data[STACK_DATA_SIZE];
62
63    result = S_OKAY;
64    ascii_length = strlen((char *)ascii_data);
65    if (ascii_length > max_chars)
66        {
67        ascii_length = max_chars;
68        result = S_ILLEGAL;
69        }
70
71    if (ascii_length < STACK_DATA_SIZE)
72        temp_ascii_data = stack_ascii_data;
73    else
74        temp_ascii_data = malloc(ascii_length+1);
75
76    for (i = 0; i < ascii_length+1; i ++)
77        temp_ascii_data[i] = toupper(ascii_data[i]);
78
79    words_to_convert = ascii_length / 3;
80    if (ascii_length % 3 != 0)
81        words_to_convert ++;
82
83    words_to_clear = max_chars / 3;
84    if (max_chars % 3 != 0)
85        words_to_clear ++;
86
87    for (i = 0; i < words_to_clear; i ++)
88        radix40_data[i] = 0; /* this blanks out the output string */
89
90    current_word_index = -1;
91    cycle = 0;
92    for (i = 0; i < ascii_length; i ++)
93        {
94        if (cycle == 0)
95            current_word_index ++;
96        conversion_status = 0;
97        for (j = 0; j < 40; j ++)
98            if (legal_chars[j] == temp_ascii_data[i])
99                {
100               conversion_status = 1;
```

Listing 1.5 *ascrad3.c: Radix40 test program #3 (continued)*

```
101                    break;
102                        }
103            if (conversion_status == 0)
104                {
105                result = S_ILLEGAL;
106                j = HYPHEN; /* code for hyphen */
107                }
108            radix40_data[current_word_index] += weights[cycle] * j;
109            cycle = (cycle + 1) % 3;
110                }
111
112    if (ascii_length >= STACK_DATA_SIZE)
113            free(temp_ascii_data);
114
115    return(result);
116    }
```

Listing 1.6 *ascrad4.c: Radix40 test program #4*

```
 1    /****keyword-flag*** "%v %f %n" */
 2    /* "8 13-Mar-93,8:28:38 ASCRAD4.C" */
 3
 4    #include <stdio.h>
 5    #include <string.h>
 6    #include <time.h>
 7    #include "radix40.h"
 8    #include "radtest.h"
 9
10    main()
11    {
12      int i;
13      unsigned char test[STRING_LENGTH+1] = "Radix40 Test";
14      Radix40 temp[STRING_LENGTH];
15      unsigned char test2[STRING_LENGTH+1];
16      clock_t start, end;
17
18      start = clock();
19      for (i = 0; i < REPS; i ++)
20          ascii_to_radix40_4(temp,test,STRING_LENGTH);
21      end = clock();
22      printf("Timer ticks for version 4: %d\n",end-start);
23
24      radix40_to_ascii(test2,temp,STRING_LENGTH);
25      if (stricmp((char *)test2,(char *)test) != 0)
26          printf("Match 4 failed\n");
27
28      return(0);
29    }
30
31     /* this is the code for a -, but with the illegal flag set */
32
33    unsigned char lookup_chars[256] =
34    {IL, IL, IL, IL, IL, IL, IL, IL,/* 00 */
35    IL, IL, IL, IL, IL, IL, IL, IL, /* 08 */
36    IL, IL, IL, IL, IL, IL, IL, IL, /* 10 */
37    IL, IL, IL, IL, IL, IL, IL, IL, /* 18 */
38     0, IL, IL, IL, IL, IL, IL, IL, /* 20 */
39    IL, IL, IL, IL,  1,  2,  3, IL, /* 28 */
40     4,  5,  6,  7,  8,  9, 10, 11, /* 30 */
41    12, 13 ,IL, IL, IL, IL, IL, IL, /* 38 */
42    IL, 14, 15, 16, 17, 18, 19, 20, /* 40 */
43    21, 22, 23, 24, 25, 26, 27, 28, /* 48 */
44    29, 30, 31, 32, 33, 34, 35, 36, /* 50 */
45    37, 38, 39, IL, IL, IL, IL, IL, /* 58 */
46    IL, 14, 15, 16, 17, 18, 19, 20, /* 60 */
47    21, 22, 23, 24, 25, 26, 27, 28, /* 68 */
48    29, 30, 31, 32, 33, 34, 35, 36, /* 70 */
49    37, 38, 39, IL, IL, IL, IL, IL, /* 78 */
50    IL, IL, IL, IL, IL, IL, IL, IL, /* 80 */
51    IL, IL, IL, IL, IL, IL, IL, IL, /* 88 */
```

Listing 1.6 *ascrad4.c: Radix40 test program #4 (continued)*

```
52   IL, IL, IL, IL, IL, IL, IL, IL, /* 90 */
53   IL, IL, IL, IL, IL, IL, IL, IL, /* 98 */
54   IL, IL, IL, IL, IL, IL, IL, IL, /* A0 */
55   IL, IL, IL, IL, IL, IL, IL, IL, /* A8 */
56   IL, IL, IL, IL, IL, IL, IL, IL, /* B0 */
57   IL, IL, IL, IL, IL, IL, IL, IL, /* B8 */
58   IL, IL, IL, IL, IL, IL, IL, IL, /* C0 */
59   IL, IL, IL, IL, IL, IL, IL, IL, /* C8 */
60   IL, IL, IL, IL, IL, IL, IL, IL, /* D0 */
61   IL, IL, IL, IL, IL, IL, IL, IL, /* D8 */
62   IL, IL, IL, IL, IL, IL, IL, IL, /* E0 */
63   IL, IL, IL, IL, IL, IL, IL, IL, /* E8 */
64   IL, IL, IL, IL, IL, IL, IL, IL, /* F0 */
65   IL, IL, IL, IL, IL, IL, IL, IL};/* F8 */
66
67   int ascii_to_radix40_4(radix40_data,ascii_data,max_chars)
68   unsigned *radix40_data;
69   unsigned char *ascii_data;
70   int max_chars;
71   /* this routine converts a null-terminated ascii character string */
72   /* to radix 40 representation.  The allowable characters are: */
73   /* A-Z, 0-9, period, comma, hyphen, and space.  If any illegal characters */
74   /* are detected, they will be converted to hyphens, and the return value */
75   /* will be S_ILLEGAL. */
76   /* Lowercase letters will be upper-cased without error indication. */
77   /* The radix40 value will be padded with blanks to a multiple of three */
78   /* characters. If the number of characters in the ascii string is > max_chars */
79   /* only max_chars will be converted, and the return value will be S_ILLEGAL. */
80   /* If no error is detected, the return value will be S_OKAY. */
81   {
82     int i;
83     int j;
84     int ascii_length;
85     int result;
86     int words_to_convert;
87     int words_to_clear;
88     int cycle;
89     unsigned current_word_index;
90
91     result = S_OKAY;
92     ascii_length = strlen((char *)ascii_data);
93     if (ascii_length > max_chars)
94         {
95         ascii_length = max_chars;
96         result = S_ILLEGAL;
97         }
98
99     words_to_convert = ascii_length / 3;
100    if (ascii_length % 3 != 0)
101        words_to_convert ++;
102
```

Listing 1.6 *ascrad4.c: Radix40 test program #4 (continued)*

```
103      words_to_clear = max_chars / 3;
104      if (max_chars % 3 != 0)
105          words_to_clear ++;
106
107      memset(radix40_data,0,words_to_clear*sizeof(Radix40));
108
109      current_word_index = -1;
110      cycle = 0;
111      for (i = 0; i < ascii_length; i ++)
112          {
113          if (cycle == 0)
114              current_word_index ++;
115          j = lookup_chars[ascii_data[i]];
116          if (j & 0x80)
117              {
118              j = j & 0x7f;
119              result = S_ILLEGAL;
120              }
121          radix40_data[current_word_index] += weights[cycle] * j;
122          cycle = (cycle + 1) % 3;
123          }
124
125      return(result);
126  }
127
128
```

Listing 1.7 *radasc.c: radix40 to ascii conversion*

```
1    /****keyword-flag*** "%v %f %n" */
2    /* "7 13-Mar-93,8:29:50 RADASC.C" */
3
4    #include <stdio.h>
5    #include <string.h>
6    #include "radix40.h"
7
8
9    char legal_chars[40] = " ,-.0123456789ABCDEFGHIJKLMNOPQRSTUVWXYZ";
10
11   unsigned weights[3] = {1600, 40, 1};
12
13   int radix40_to_ascii(unsigned char *ascii_data, Radix40 *radix40_data, int max_chars)
14   /* this routine converts a radix 40 character string */
15   /* to ascii representation.  Trailing blanks will be deleted. */
16   {
17     int i;
18     int ascii_length;
19     int new_ascii_length;
20     int words_to_convert;
21     int cycle;
22     unsigned current_word_index;
23     unsigned current_word;
24     unsigned current_char;
25
26     ascii_length = max_chars;
27
28     words_to_convert = ascii_length / 3;
29     if (ascii_length % 3 != 0)
30         words_to_convert ++;
31
32     for (i = 0; i < max_chars + 1; i ++)
33         ascii_data[i] = 0; /* this nulls out the output string */
34
35     current_word_index = -1;
36     cycle = 0;
37     for (i = 0; i < ascii_length; i ++)
38         {
39         if (cycle == 0)
40             {
41             current_word_index ++;
42             current_word = radix40_data[current_word_index];
43             }
44         current_char = current_word / weights[cycle];
45         current_word -= current_char * weights[cycle];
46
47         ascii_data[i] = legal_chars[current_char];
48         cycle = (cycle + 1) % 3;
49         }
50
```

Listing 1.7 *radasc.c: radix40 to ascii conversion (continued)*

```
51      new_ascii_length = strlen((char *)ascii_data);
52      for (i = new_ascii_length - 1; i >= 0; i --)
53          {
54          if (ascii_data[i] != ' ')
55              break;
56          ascii_data[i] = 0;
57          }
58
59      return(S_OKAY);
60  }
61
62
63
```

2

Hash, Cache, and Crunch

A Supermarket Price Lookup System

ALGORITHMS DISCUSSED
Hash Coding, Radix40 Data Representation, BCD Data Representation, Caching

Introduction

In this chapter we will use a supermarket price lookup system to illustrate how to save storage by using a restricted character set and how to speed up access to records by employing **hash coding** (or "scatter storage") and **caching** (or keeping copies of recently accessed records in memory). We will look items up by their UPC (Universal Product Code), which is printed in the form of a "bar code" on virtually all supermarket items other than fresh produce. We will emphasize rapid retrieval of prices, as maintenance of such files is usually done after hours, when speed would be less significant.

Up the Down Staircase

To begin, let us assume that we can describe each item by the information in the structure definition in figure 2.1.

Figure 2.1 *Item information*

```
typedef struct {
        char upc[10];
        char description[21];
        float price;
        } ItemRecord;
```

One solution to our price-retrieval problem would be to create a file with one record for each item, sorted by UPC code. This would allow us to use a binary search to locate the price of a particular item. How long would it take to find a record in such a file containing 10,000 items?

To answer this question, we have to analyze the algorithm of the binary search in some detail. We start the search by looking at the middle record in the file. If the key we are looking for is greater than the key of the middle record, we know that the record we are looking for must be in the second half of the file (if it is in the file at all). Likewise, if our key is less than the one in the middle record, the record we are looking for must be in the first half of the file (again, if it is there at all). Once we have decided which half of the file to examine next, we look at the middle record in that half and proceed exactly as we did previously. Eventually, either we will find the record we are looking for or we will discover that we can no longer divide the segment we are looking at, as it has only one record (in which case the record we are looking for is not there).

Probably the easiest way to figure out the average number of accesses that would be required to find a record in the file is to start from the other end of the problem: how many records could be found with one access? Obviously, only the middle record. With another access, we could find either the record in the middle of the first half of the file or the record in the middle of the second half. The next access adds another four records, in the centers of the first, second, third, and fourth quarters of the file. In other words, each added access doubles the number of added records that we can find.

Figure 2.2 shows the calculation of the average number of accesses for a 10,000 item file. Notice that each line represents twice the number of records as the one above, with the exception of line 14. The entry for that line (1809) is the number of 14-access records needed to reach the capacity of our 10,000 record file. As you can see, the average number of accesses is approximately 12.4 per record. Therefore, at a typical hard disk speed of 12 milliseconds per access, we would need almost 150 milliseconds to look up an average record using a binary search. While this lookup time might not seem excessive, remember that a number of checkout terminals would probably be attempting to access the database at the same time, and the waiting time could become noticeable. We might also be concerned about the amount of wear on the disk mechanism that would result from this approach.

Figure 2.2 *Binary search statistics*

Number of accesses		Number of records newly accessible	Total accesses to find all records	Total records accessible
1	x	1	1	1
2	x	2	4	3
3	x	4	12	7
4	x	8	32	15
5	x	16	80	31
6	x	32	192	63
7	x	64	448	127
8	x	128	1024	255
9	x	256	2304	511
10	x	512	5120	1023
11	x	1024	11264	2047
12	x	2048	24576	4095
13	x	4096	53248	8191
14	x	1809	25326	10000
		———	———	
		10000	123631	

Average number of accesses per record = 12.3631 accesses/record

Some Random Musings

Before we try to optimize our search, let us define some terms. There are two basic categories of storage devices, distinguished by the access they allow to individual records. The first type is **sequential access;**[12] in order to read record 1000 from a sequential device, we must read records 1 through 999 first, or at least skip over them. The second type is **direct access**; on a direct access device, we can read record 1000 without going past all of the previous records. However, only some direct access devices allow nonsequential accesses without a significant time penalty; these are called **random access** devices.[13]

Unfortunately, disk drives are direct access devices, but not random access ones. The amount of time it takes to get to a particular data record depends on how close the read/write head is to the desired position; in fact, sequential reading of data may be more than ten times as fast as random access.

Is there a way to find a record in a large file with an average of about one nonsequential access? Yes; in fact, there are several such methods, varying in complexity. They are all variations on **hash coding**, or address calculation; as you will see, such

---

12. Tape drives are the most commonly used sequential access devices.

13. There is one random access device that we all use: RAM, which stands for random access memory.

methods actually can be implemented quite simply, although for some reason they have acquired a reputation for mystery.

Hashing It Out

Let's start by considering a linear or sequential search. That is, we start at the beginning of the file and read each record in the file until we find the one we want (because its key is the same as the key we are looking for). If we get to the end of the file without finding a record with the key we are looking for, the record isn't in the file. This is certainly a simple method, and indeed is perfectly acceptable for a very small file, but it has one major drawback: the average time it takes to find a given record increases every time we add another record. If the file gets twice as big, it takes twice as long to find a record, on the average. So this seems useless.

Divide and Conquer

But what if, instead of having one big file, we had many little files, each with only a few records in it? Of course, we would need to know which of the little files to look in, or we wouldn't have gained anything. Is there any way to know that?

Let's see if we can find a way. Suppose that we have 1000 records to search through, keyed by telephone number. To speed up the lookup, we have divided the records into 100 subfiles, averaging 10 numbers each. We can use the last two digits of the telephone number to decide which subfile to look in (or to put a new record in), and then we have to search through only the records in that subfile. If we get to the end of the subfile without finding the record we are looking for, it's not in the file. That's the basic idea of hash coding.

But why did we use the last two digits, rather than the first two? Because they will probably be more evenly distributed than the first two digits. Most of the telephone numbers on your list probably fall within a few telephone exchanges near where you live (or work). For example, my telephone book contains mostly 867, 868, 622, and 623 numbers. Therefore, if I were to use the first two digits for this hash coding scheme, I would end up with two big subfiles (numbers 86 and 62) and 98 small ones, thus negating most of the benefit of dividing the file. You see, even though the average subfile size would still be 10, about 90% of the records would be in the two big subfiles, which would have perhaps 450 records each. Therefore, the average search for 90% of the records would require reading 225 records, rather than the five we were planning on. That is why it is so important to get a reasonably even distribution of the data records in a hash-coded file.

Figure 2.3 *Hashing with subfiles, initialized file*

Subfile #				
0	I 0000000	I 0000000	I 0000000	I 0000000
1	I 0000000	I 0000000	I 0000000	I 0000000
2	I 0000000	I 0000000	I 0000000	I 0000000
3	I 0000000	I 0000000	I 0000000	I 0000000
4	I 0000000	I 0000000	I 0000000	I 0000000
5	I 0000000	I 0000000	I 0000000	I 0000000
6	I 0000000	I 0000000	I 0000000	I 0000000
7	I 0000000	I 0000000	I 0000000	I 0000000
8	I 0000000	I 0000000	I 0000000	I 0000000
9	I 0000000	I 0000000	I 0000000	I 0000000

Unite and Rule

It is inconvenient to have 100 little files lying around, and the time required to open and close each one as we need it makes this implementation inefficient. But there's no reason we couldn't combine all of these little files into one big one and use the hash code to tell us where we should start looking in the big file. That is, if we have a capacity of 1000 records, we could use the last two digits of the telephone number to tell us which "subfile" we need of the 100 "subfiles" in the big file (records 0–9, 10–19, 20–29, ..., 980–989, 990–999). To help visualize this, let's look at a smaller example: 10 subfiles having a capacity of four telephone numbers each and a hash code consisting of just the last digit of the telephone number (figure 2.3).

In order to use a big file rather than a number of small ones, we have to make some changes to our algorithm. When using many small files, we had the end-of-file indicator to tell us where to add records and where to stop looking for a record; with one big file subdivided into small subfiles, we have to find another way to handle these tasks.

Knowing When to Stop

One way is to add a "valid-data" flag to every entry in the file, which is initialized to "I" (for invalid) in the entries in figure 2.3, and set each entry to "valid" (indicated by

Figure 2.4 *Hashing with distinct subfiles*

Subfile #

0	I 0000000	I 0000000	I 0000000	I 0000000
1	V 9876541	V 2323231	V 9898981	I 0000000
2	V 2345432	I 0000000	I 0000000	I 0000000
3	I 0000000	I 0000000	I 0000000	I 0000000
4	I 0000000	I 0000000	I 0000000	I 0000000
5	I 0000000	I 0000000	I 0000000	I 0000000
6	I 0000000	I 0000000	I 0000000	I 0000000
7	I 0000000	I 0000000	I 0000000	I 0000000
8	I 0000000	I 0000000	I 0000000	I 0000000
9	I 0000000	I 0000000	I 0000000	I 0000000

a "V" in that same position) as we store data in it. Then if we get to an invalid record while looking up a record in the file, we know that we are at the end of the subfile and therefore the record is not in the file (figure 2.4).

For example, if we are looking for the number "9898981", we start at the beginning of subfile 1 in figure 2.4 (because the number ends in 1), and examine each record from there on. The first two entries have the numbers "9876541" and "2323231", which don't match, so we continue with the third one, which is the one we are looking for. But what if we were looking for "9898971"? Then we would go through the first three entries without finding a match. The fourth entry is "I 0000000", which is an invalid entry. This is the marker for the end of this subfile, so we know the number we are looking for isn't in the file.

Now let's add another record to the file with the phone number "1212121". As before, we start at the beginning of subfile 1, since the number ends in 1. The first three records are already in use, so we can't use them. The fourth (and last) record in the subfile is available, so we store our new record there, resulting in the situation in figure 2.5.

However, what happens if we look for "9898971" in the above situation? We start out the same way, looking at records with phone numbers "9876541", "2323231", "9898981", and "1212121". But we haven't gotten to an invalid record yet. Can we stop before we get to the first record of the next subfile?

Figure 2.5 *Hashing with merged subfiles*

Subfile #

0	I 0000000	I 0000000	I 0000000	I 0000000
1	V 9876541	V 2323231	I 9898981	I 1212121
2	V 2345432	I 0000000	I 0000000	I 0000000
3	I 0000000	I 0000000	I 0000000	I 0000000
4	I 0000000	I 0000000	I 0000000	I 0000000
5	I 0000000	I 0000000	I 0000000	I 0000000
6	I 0000000	I 0000000	I 0000000	I 0000000
7	I 0000000	I 0000000	I 0000000	I 0000000
8	I 0000000	I 0000000	I 0000000	I 0000000
9	I 0000000	I 0000000	I 0000000	I 0000000

Handling Subfile Overflow

To answer that question, we have to see what would happen if we had added another record that belonged in subfile 1. There are a number of possible ways to handle this situation, but most of them are appropriate only for memory-resident files. As I mentioned above, reading the next record in a disk file is much faster than reading a record at a different place in the file. Therefore, for disk-based data, the most efficient place to put "overflow" records is in the next open place in the file, which means that adding a record with phone number "1234321" to this file would result in the arrangement in figure 2.6.[14]

So the answer is that we can't stop before the beginning of the next subfile, because the record we are looking for might have overflowed to the next subfile, as "1234321" just did. Where can we stop? Well, we know that the record we are looking for is somewhere between the beginning of the subfile it belongs in and the next invalid record, since we go to the next subfile only when the one we are trying to

---

14. In general, the "next open place" is not a very good place to put an overflow record if the hash table is kept in memory rather than on the disk; the added records "clog" the table, leading to slower access times. A linked list approach is much better for tables that are actually memory resident. Warning: this does not apply to tables in virtual memory, where linked lists provide very poor performance. For more discussion on overflow handling, see the dynamic hashing algorithm in Chapter 7.

Figure 2.6 *Hashing with overflow between subfiles*

Subfile #

0	I 0000000	I 0000000	I 0000000	I 0000000
1	V 9876541	V 2323231	I 9898981	I 1212121
2	V 2345432	V 1234321	I 0000000	I 0000000
3	I 0000000	I 0000000	I 0000000	I 0000000
4	I 0000000	I 0000000	I 0000000	I 0000000
5	I 0000000	I 0000000	I 0000000	I 0000000
6	I 0000000	I 0000000	I 0000000	I 0000000
7	I 0000000	I 0000000	I 0000000	I 0000000
8	I 0000000	I 0000000	I 0000000	I 0000000
9	I 0000000	I 0000000	I 0000000	I 0000000

use is filled up. Therefore, if we get to an invalid record, we know that the record could not be stored later in the file, since the current subfile is not filled up yet; this means that we can stop looking when we get to the first invalid record.

Some Drawbacks of Hashing

This points out one of the drawbacks of standard disk-based hashing (SDBH). We cannot delete a record from the file simply by setting the invalid flag in that record; if we did, any record which overflowed past the one we deleted would become inaccessible, as we would stop looking when we got to the invalid record. For this reason, invalid records must be only those that have never been used and therefore can serve as "end-of-subfile" markers.

While we're on the topic of drawbacks of SDBH, we ought to note that as the file gets filled up, the maximum length of a search increases, especially an unsuccessful search. That is because adding a record to the end of a subfile that has only one invalid entry left results in "merging" that subfile and the next one, so that searches for entries in the first subfile have to continue to the next one. In our example, when we added "1212121" to the file, the maximum length of a search for an entry in sub-file 1 increased from four to seven, even though we had added only one record. With a reasonably even distribution of hash codes (which we don't have in our example), this problem is usually not serious until the file gets to be about 80% full.

While this problem would be alleviated by increasing the capacity of the file as items are added, unfortunately SDBH does not allow such incremental expansion, since there would be no way to use the extra space; the subfile starting positions can't be changed after we start writing records, or we won't be able to find records we have already stored. Of course, one way to overcome this problem is to create a new file with larger (or more) subfiles, read each record from the old file and write it to the new one. What we will do in our example is simply to make the file 25% bigger than needed to contain the records we are planning to store, which means the file won't get more than 80% full.

Another problem with SDBH methods is that they are not well suited to storage of variable-length records; the address calculation used to find a "slot" for a record relies on the fact that the records are of fixed length.

Finally, there's the ever-present problem of coming up with a good hash code. Unfortunately, unless we know the characteristics of the input data precisely, it's theoretically possible that all of the records will generate the same hash code, thus negating all of the performance advantages of hashing. Although this is unlikely, it makes SDBH an inappropriate algorithm for use in situations where a maximum time limit on access must be maintained.

When considering these less-than-ideal characteristics, we should remember that other search methods have their own disadvantages, particularly in speed of lookup. All in all, the disadvantages of such a simply implemented access method seem rather minor in comparison with its benefits, at least for the current application. In addition, recent innovations in hashing have made it possible to improve the flexibility of SDBH methods by fairly simple changes. For example, the use of "last-come, first-served" hashing, which stores a newly added record exactly where the hash code indicates, greatly reduces the maximum time needed to find any record; it also makes it possible to determine for any given file what that maximum is, thus removing one of the barriers to using SDBH in a time-critical application.[15]

Even more recently, a spectacular advance in the state of the art has made it possible to increase the file capacity incrementally, as well as to delete records efficiently. Chapter 7 provides a C++ implementation of this remarkable innovation in hashing.

Caching out Our Winnings

Of course, even one random disk access takes a significant amount of time, from the computer's point of view. Wouldn't it be better to avoid accessing the disk at all?

---

15. For a description of "last-come, first-served" hashing, see Patricio V. Poblete and J. Ian Munro, "Last-Come-First-Served Hashing", in *Journal of Algorithms* 10, 228–248, or my article "Galloping Algorithms", in *Windows Tech Journal*, 2(February 1993), 40–43.

While that would result in the fastest possible lookup, it would require us to have the entire database in memory, which is usually not feasible. However, if we had some of the database in memory, perhaps we could eliminate some of the disk accesses.

A **cache** is a portion of a large database that we want to access, kept in a type of storage that can be accessed more rapidly than the type used to store the whole database. For example, if your system has an optical disk which is considerably slower than its hard disk, a portion of the database contained on the optical disk may be kept on the hard disk. Why don't we just use the hard disk for the whole database? The optical disk may be cheaper per megabyte, it may have more capacity, or the removability and long projected life span of the optical diskettes may be the major reason. Of course, our example of a cache uses memory to hold a portion of the database that is stored on the hard disk, but the principle is the same: memory is more expensive than disk storage, and with certain computers, it may not be possible to install enough memory to hold a copy of the entire database even if price were no object.

If a few items account for most of the transactions, the use of a cache speeds up access to those items, since they are likely to be among the most recently used records. This means that if we keep a number of the most recently accessed records in memory, we can reduce the number of disk accesses significantly. However, we have to have a way to locate items in the cache quickly: this problem is very similar to a hash-coded file lookup, except that we have more freedom in deciding how to handle overflows, where the entry we wish to use is already being used by another item. Since the cache is only a copy of data that is also stored elsewhere, we don't have to be so concerned about what happens to overflowing entries; we can discard them if we wish to, since we can always get fresh copies from the disk.

The simplest caching lookup algorithm is a direct-mapped cache. That means each key corresponds to one and only one entry in the cache. In other words, overflow is handled by overwriting the previous record in that space with the new entry. The trouble with this method is that if two (or more) commonly used records happen to map to the same cache entry, only one of them can be in the cache at one time. This requires us to go back to the disk repeatedly for these conflicting records. The solution to this problem is to use a multiway associative cache. In this algorithm, each key corresponds to a **cache line**, which contains more than one entry. In our example, it contains eight entries. Therefore, if a number of our records have keys that map to the same line, up to eight of them can reside in the cache simultaneously. How did I decide on an eight-way associative cache? By trying various cache sizes until I found the one that yielded the greatest performance.

The performance of a disk caching system is defined by its hit ratio, or the proportion of accesses to the disk that are avoided by using the cache. In order to estimate the performance of this caching algorithm, we have to quantify our assumptions. I have written a program to generate test keys in which 20% of the items account for 80% of the database accesses (listing 2.7), along with another that initializes the database (listing 2.8), and a third to read the test keys and look them up (listing 2.9). The results of this simulation indicated that, using an eight-way associative cache, approx-

Figure 2.7 *Line size effects*

Line size	Hit ratio[16]
1	.34
2	.38
4	.42
8	.44
16	.43

imately 44% of the disk accesses that would be needed in a noncached system could be eliminated.

Figure 2.7 shows the results of my experimentation with various line sizes. The line size is defined by the constant `MAPPING_FACTOR` in "superm.h" (listing 2.1, line 38).

Heading for The Final Lookup

Now that we have added a cache to our optimization arsenal, only three more changes are necessary to reach the final lookup algorithm that we will implement. The first is to shrink each of the subfiles to one entry. That is, we will calculate a record address rather than a subfile address when we start trying to add or look up a record. This tends to reduce the length of the search needed to find a given record, as each record (on average) will have a different starting position, rather than a number of records having the same starting position, as is the case with longer subfiles.

The second change is that, rather than having a separate flag to indicate whether a record position in the file is in use, we will create an "impossible" key value to mean that the record is available. Since our key will consist only of decimal digits (compressed to two digits per byte), we can set the first digit to 0xf (the hex representation for 15), which cannot occur in a genuine decimal number. This will take the place of our "invalid" flag, without requiring extra storage in the record.

Finally, we have to deal with the possibility that the search for a record will encounter the end of the file, because the last position in the file is occupied by another record. In this case, we will wrap around to the beginning of the file and keep looking. In other words, position 0 in the file will be considered to follow immediately after the last position in the file.

Saving Storage

Now that we have decided on our lookup algorithm, we can shift our attention to reducing the amount of storage required for each record in our supermarket price

---

16. This is a direct-mapped cache.

lookup program. Without any special encoding, the disk storage requirements for one record would be 35 bytes (10 for the UPC, 21 for the description, and 4 for the price). For a file of 10,000 items, this would require 350 Kbytes; allowing 25% extra space to prevent the hashing from getting too slow means that the file would end up taking up about 437 Kbytes. For this application, disk storage space would probably not be a problem unless the central computer had only floppy disk drives; however, the techniques we will use to reduce the file size are useful in many other applications as well. Also, searching a smaller file is likely to be faster, because the heads have to move a shorter distance on the average to get to the record where we are going to start our search.

If you look back at figure 2.1, you will notice that the upc field is ten characters long. Using the ASCII code for each digit, which is the usual representation for character data, takes one byte per digit or 10 bytes in all. I mentioned above that we would be using a limited character set to reduce the size of the records. UPC codes are limited to the digits 0 through 9; if we pack two digits into one byte, by using four bits to represent each digit, we can cut that down to five bytes for each UPC value stored. Luckily, this is quite simple, as you will see when we discuss the BCD conversion code below. The other data compression method we will employ is to convert the item descriptions from strings of ASCII characters, limited to the sets 0–9, A–Z, and the special characters comma, period, minus, and space, to Radix40 representation, mentioned in Chapter 1. The main difference between Radix40 conversions and those for BCD is that in the former case we need to represent 40 different characters, rather than just the 10 digits, and therefore the packing of data must be done in a slightly more complicated way than just using four bits per character.

The Code

Now that we have covered the optimizations that we will use in our price lookup system, it's time to go through the code that implements these algorithms. This specific implementation is set up to handle a maximum of FILE_CAPACITY items, defined in "superm.h" (listing 2.1, line 12).[17] Each of these items, as defined in the ItemRecord structure on lines 24–29 of the same file, has a price, a description, and a key, which is the UPC code. The key would be read in by a bar-code scanner in a real system, although our test program will read it in from the keyboard.

---

17. While we can increase the maximum number of records in the file by increasing FILE_CAPACITY, we would also have to reduce the cache size as a fraction of the file size (line 12) if the file is to be made much larger, or we would run out of memory fairly quickly.

Some User-Defined Types

Several of the fields in the `ItemRecord` structure definition require some explanation. The `upc` field is defined as a `BCD` (binary-coded decimal) value of ASCII_KEY_SIZE digits (contained in BCD_KEY_SIZE bytes), as described in lines 16–17. The `description` field is defined as a `Radix40` field of DESCRIPTION_WORDS in size; each of these words contains three `Radix40` characters.

A `BCD` value is stored as two digits per byte, each digit being represented by a four-bit code between 0000(0) and 1001(9). Routine `ascii_to_BCD` in "bcdconv.c" (listing 2.5, lines 30–62) converts a decimal number, stored as ASCII digits, to a `BCD` value by extracting each digit from the input argument and subtracting the code for '0' from the digit value; `BCD_to_ascii` (lines 10–28) does the opposite.

A UPC code is a ten-digit number between 0000000000 and 9999999999, which unfortunately is too large to fit in a long integer of 32 bits. Of course, we could store it in ASCII, but that would require 10 bytes per UPC code. So BCD representation saves five bytes per item compared to ASCII.

A `Radix40` field, as mentioned above, stores three characters (from a limited set of possibilities) in 16 bits. This algorithm (like some other data compression techniques) takes advantage of the fact that the number of bits required to store a character depends on the number of distinct characters to be represented[18]. The BCD routines described above are an example of this approach. In this case, however, we need more than just the 10 digits. If our character set can be limited to 40 characters (think of a `Radix40` value as a "number" in base 40), we can fit three of them in 16 bits, because 40^3 is less than 2^{16}.

Line 13 in "radix40.c" (listing 2.6) defines the characters that can be expressed in this implementation of `Radix40`.[19] Line 15 defines the variable `weights`, which contains the multipliers to be used to construct a two-byte `Radix40` value from the three characters that we wish to store in it.

As indicated in the comment in lines 101-110, the routine `ascii_to_radix40` converts a null-terminated ASCII character string to `Radix40` representation. After some initialization and error checking in lines 121–137, the main loop begins by incrementing the index to the current word being constructed, after every third character is translated. It then (line 145) translates the current ASCII character by indexing into the `lookup_chars` table. Any character that translates to a value with its high bit set is an illegal character and is converted to a hyphen; the result flag is changed to `S_ILLEGAL` if this occurs.

In line 151, the character is added into the current output word after being multiplied by the power of 40 that is appropriate to its position. The first character in a word is represented by its position in the `legal_chars` string. The second character

---

18. The arithmetic coding data compression algorithm covered in Chapter 4, however, does not restrict the characters that can be represented; rather, it takes advantage of the differing probabilities of encountering each character in a given situation.

19. Note that this `legal_chars` array must be kept in synchronization with the `lookup_chars` array defined in lines 66–98.

is represented by 40 times that value and the third by 1600 times that value, as you would expect for a base-40 number.

The complementary routine `radix40_to_ascii` decodes each character unambiguously, as you can see in lines 48–50. First, the current character is extracted from the current word by dividing by the weight appropriate to its position; then the current word is updated so the next character can be extracted. Finally, the ASCII value of the character is looked up in the `legal_chars` array.

Preparing to Access the Price File

Now that we have examined the user-defined types used in the `ItemRecord` structure, we can go on to the `PriceFile` structure, which is used to keep track of the data for a particular price file.[20] The best way to learn about this structure is to follow the program as it creates, initializes, and uses it. The function **main**, in file "superm.c" (listing 2.2, lines 12–39), after checking that it was called with the correct number of arguments, calls the `initialize_price_file` routine in file "suplook.c" (listing 2.3, lines 13–67) to set up the PriceFile structure.

The routine `initialize_price_file` allocates storage for and initializes the `PriceFile` structure, which is used to control access to the price file. This structure contains pointers to the file, to the array of cached records that we have in memory, and to the array of record numbers of those cached records. As we discussed earlier, the use of a cache can reduce the amount of time spent reading records from the disk by maintaining copies of a number of those records in memory, in the hope that they will be needed again. Of course, we have to keep track of which records we have cached, so that we can tell whether we have to read a particular record from the disk or can retrieve a copy of it from the cache instead.

When execution starts, we don't have any records cached; therefore, we initialize each entry in these arrays to an "invalid" state (the key is set to INVALID_BCD_VALUE). If `file_mode` is set to CLEAR_FILE, we write such an "invalid" record to every position in the price file as well, so that any old data left over from a previous run is erased.

Now that access to the price file has been set up, we can call the **process** routine (listing 2.2, lines 43–174). This routine allows us to enter items and/or look up their prices and descriptions, depending on the value of **mode**.

First, let's look at entering a new item (INPUT_MODE). We must get the UPC code, the description, and the price of the item. The UPC code is converted to BCD, the description to `Radix40`, and the price to `unsigned`. Then we call `write_record` (listing 2.3, lines 254–276) to add the record to the file.

In order to write a record to the file, `write_record` calls `lookup_record_number` to determine where the record should be stored so that we can retrieve it quickly later.

---

20. There could theoretically be more than one active at one time, although our example program uses only one.

Since the operations required by `lookup_record_number` and `lookup_record` (which returns a pointer to the record rather than its number) are virtually identical, they are implemented as calls to a common routine: `lookup_record_and_number` (lines 71–223).

After a bit of setup code, the first thing we do in `lookup_record_and_number` is find out whether the record we want is already in the cache, in which case we don't have to search the file for it (lines 97–121). To do this, we call `compute_cache_hash` (lines 327–337), which in turn calls `compute_hash` to do most of the work of calculating the hash code (lines 295–309). This may look mysterious, but it's actually pretty simple. After clearing the hash code we are going to calculate, it enters a loop that first shifts the old hash code one (decimal) place to the left, end around, then adds the low four bits of the next character from the key to the result. When it finishes this loop, it returns to the caller, in this case `compute_cache_hash`. How did I come up with this algorithm?

Making a Hash of Things

Well, as you will recall from our example of looking up a telephone number, the idea of a hash code is to make the most of variations in the input data, so that there will be a wide distribution of "starting places" for the records in the file. If all the input values produced the same hash code, we would end up with a linear search again, which would be terribly slow. In this case, our key is a UPC code, which is composed of decimal digits. If each of those digits contributes equally to the hash code, we should be able to produce a fairly even distribution of hash codes, which are the starting points for searching through the file for each record. As we noted earlier, this is one of the main drawbacks of hashing: the difficulty of coming up with a good hashing algorithm. After analyzing the nature of the data, you may have to try a few different algorithms with some test data, until you get a good distribution of hash codes. However, the effort is usually worthwhile, since you can often achieve an average of slightly over one disk access per lookup (assuming that several records fit in one physical disk record).

Meanwhile, back at `compute_cache_hash`, we convert the result of `compute_hash`, which is an `unsigned` value, into an index into the cache. This is then returned to `lookup_record_number` as the starting cache index. As mentioned above, we are using an eight-way associative cache, in which each key can be stored in any of eight entries in a **cache line**. The routine `compute_starting_cache_hash` (listing 2.3, lines 340–343) returns the index to the first entry in the line, and `compute_ending_cache_hash` (lines 346–349) returns one more than the index to the last entry in the line (because the standard C loop control goes from the first value up to one less than the ending value).

We compare the key in each entry to the key that we are looking for, and if they are equal, we have found the record in the cache. In this event, we set the value of the record_number argument to the file record number for this cache entry, and return with the status set to FOUND.

Otherwise, the record isn't in the cache, so we will have to look for it in the file; if we find it, we will need a place to store it in the cache. So, in line 124, we pick a "random" entry in the line (cache_replace_index) by calculating the remainder after dividing the number of accesses we have made by the MAPPING_FACTOR. This will generate an entry index between 0 and the highest entry number, cycling through all the possibilities on each successive access, thus not favoring a particular entry number.

However, if the line has an invalid entry (where the key is INVALID_BCD_VALUE), we should use that one, rather than throwing out a real record that might be needed later. Therefore, in lines 127–135, we search the line for such an empty entry, and if we are successful, we set cache_replace_index to its index.

Next, we calculate the place to start looking in the file, via compute_file_hash (lines 313–323), which is very similar to compute_cache_hash except that it uses the FILE_SIZE constant in "superm.h" (listing 2.1, line 14) to calculate the index rather than the CACHE_SIZE constant, as we want a starting index in the file rather than in the cache. As we noted above, this is another of the few drawbacks of this hashing method: that the size of the file must be decided in advance, rather than being adjustable as data is entered. The reason is that to find a record in the file, we must be able to calculate its approximate position in the file in the same manner as it was calculated when the record was stored. The calculation of the hash code is designed to distribute the records evenly throughout a file of known size; if we changed the size of the file, we wouldn't be able to find records previously stored. Of course, different files can have different sizes, as long as we know the size of the file we are operating on currently: the size doesn't have to be an actual constant as it is in our example, but it does have to be known in advance for each file.

Searching the File

Now we're ready to start looking for our record in the file at the position specified by starting_file_index. Therefore, we enter a loop that searches from this starting position toward the end of the file, looking for a record with the correct key. First we set the file pointer to the first position to be read, using position_record (listing 2.3, lines 352–361), then read the record at that position. If its key is the one we are looking for, our search is successful. On the other hand, if the record is invalid, then the record we are looking for is not in the file; when we add records to the file, we start at the position given by starting_file_index and store our new record in the first invalid record we find.[21] Therefore, no record can overflow past an invalid record, as the invalid record would have been used to store the overflow record.

---

21. Of course, we might also find a record with the same key as the one we are trying to add, but this is an error condition, since keys must be unique.

In either of these cases, we are through with the search, so we break out of the loop. On the other hand, if the entry is neither invalid nor the record we are looking for, we keep looking through the file until either we have found the record we want, we discover that it isn't in the file by encountering an invalid record, or we run off the end of the file. In the last case we start over at the beginning of the file (listing 2.3, lines 182–223).

If we have found the record, we copy it to the cache entry we selected in lines 124–135 and copy its record number into the list of record numbers in the cache so that we'll know which record we have stored in that cache position. Then we return to the calling routine, **write_record,** with the record we have found. If we have determined that the record is not in the file, then we obviously can't read it into the cache, but we do want to keep track of the record number where we stopped, since that is the record number that will be used for the record if we write it to the file.

To clarify this whole process, let's make a file with room for only nine records by changing **FILE_SIZE** to 6 in "superm.h" (listing 2.1, line 14). After adding a few records, a dump looks like figure 2.8.

Let's add a record with the key "23232" to the file. Its hash code turns out to be 3, so we look at position 3 in the file. That position is occupied by a record with key "121212", so we can't store our new record there. The next position we examine,

Figure 2.8 *Initial condition*

```
Position   Key            Data
   0.      INVALID
   1.      INVALID
   2.      0000098765:MINESTRONE:245
   3.      0000121212:OATMEAL, 1 LB.:300
   4.      INVALID
   5.      INVALID
   6.      0000012345:JELLY BEANS:150
   7.      INVALID
   8.      0000099887:POPCORN:99
```

Figure 2.9 *After adding "milk" record*

```
Position   Key            Data
   0.      INVALID
   1.      INVALID
   2.      0000098765:MINESTRONE:245
   3.      0000121212:OATMEAL, 1 LB.:300
   4.      0000023232:MILK:128
   5.      INVALID
   6.      0000012345:JELLY BEANS:150
   7.      INVALID
   8.      0000099887:POPCORN:99
```

number 4, is invalid, so we know that the record we are planning to add is not in the file. (Note that this is the exact sequence we follow to look up a record in the file as well). We use this position to hold our new record. The file now looks like figure 2.9.

Looking up our newly added record follows the same algorithm. The hash code is still 3, so we examine position 3, which has the key "121212". That's not the desired record, and it's not invalid, so we continue. Position 4 does match, so we have found our record. Now let's try to find some records that aren't in the file.

If we try to find a record with key "98789", it turns out to have a hash code of 8. Since that position in the file is in use, but with a different key, we haven't found our record. However, we have encountered the end of the file. What next?

Wrapping Around at EOF

In order to continue looking for this record, we must start over at the beginning of the file. That is, position 0 is the next logical position after the last one in the file. As it happens, position 0 contains an invalid record, so we know that the record we want isn't in the file.[22]

In any event, we are now finished with lookup_record_and_number. Therefore, we return to lookup_record_number, which returns the record number to be used to write_record (listing 2.3, line 264), along with a status value of FILE_FULL, FOUND, or NOT_IN_FILE (which is the status we want). FILE_FULL is an error, as we cannot add a record to a file that has reached its capacity. So is FOUND, in this situation, as we are trying to add a new record, not look one up. In either of these cases, we simply return the status to the calling routine, process in "superm.c" (listing 2.2, line 121), which gives an appropriate error message and continues execution.

However, if the status is NOT_IN_FILE, write_record continues by positioning the file to the record number returned by lookup_record_number, writing the record to the file, and returns the status NOT_IN_FILE to process, which continues execution normally.

That concludes our examination of the input mode in process. The lookup mode is very similar, except that it uses lookup_record (listing 2.3, lines 227–237) rather than lookup_record_number, since it wants the record to be returned, not just the record number. The lookup mode, of course, also differs from the entry mode in that it expects the record to be in the file, and displays the record data when found.

After process terminates when the user enters "*" instead of a code number to be looked up or entered, main finishes up by calling terminate_price_file (lines 279–288), which closes the price file and returns. All processing complete, main exits to the operating system.

---

22. If we were adding a new record with this key rather than trying to find one, we would use position 0.

Summary

In this chapter, we have covered ways to save storage by using a restricted character set and to gain rapid access to data by an exact key, using hash coding and caching. In the next chapter we will see how to use bitmaps, strip files, and distribution sorting to speed up the process of extracting and rearranging information by criteria that can be specified at run-time.

Problems

1. What modifications to the program would be needed to add the following capabilities?

   a. Deleting records

   b. Handling a file that becomes full, as an off-line process

   c. Keeping track of the inventory of each item

2. How could hash coding be applied to tables in memory?

3. How could caching be applied to reduce the time needed to look up an entry in a table in memory?

   (You can find suggested approaches to problems in Chapter 8).

Listing 2.1 *superm.h: supermarket pricing include file*

```
 1
 2    /****keyword-flag*** "%v %f %n" */
 3    /* "8 31-Aug-91,13:36:46 SUPERM.H" */
 4
 5
 6    #include "radix40.h"
 7    #include "bcdconv.h"
 8    #include <string.h>
 9    #define DESCRIPTION_WORDS 7
10    #define DESCRIPTION_CHARS (CPW*DESCRIPTION_WORDS)
11
12    #define FILE_CAPACITY 1000
13
14    #define FILE_SIZE ((unsigned)(FILE_CAPACITY*1.25))
15
16    #define BCD_KEY_SIZE 5
17    #define ASCII_KEY_SIZE (BCD_KEY_SIZE*2)
18
19    #define INVALID_BCD_VALUE 0xFF
20    #define DELETED_BCD_VALUE 0xFE
21
22    #define INVALID_RECORD_NUMBER 0xFFFF
23
24    typedef struct
25    {
26      BCD upc[BCD_KEY_SIZE];
27      Radix40 description[DESCRIPTION_WORDS];
28      unsigned price;
29    } ItemRecord;
30
31    typedef struct
32    {
33      FILE *dos_file_stream;
34      ItemRecord **item_cache;
35      unsigned *file_record_number;
36    } PriceFile;
37
38    #define MAPPING_FACTOR 8   /* how many slots can be used by any one record */
39
40    #define APPROXIMATE_CACHE_SIZE (max(FILE_CAPACITY*.20,MAPPING_FACTOR))
41
42    #define CACHE_SIZE \
43    ((unsigned)(APPROXIMATE_CACHE_SIZE/MAPPING_FACTOR)*MAPPING_FACTOR)
44
45    #define QUESTIONABLE 0
46    #define FOUND 1
47    #define NOT_IN_FILE 2
48    #define FILE_FULL 3
49
50    #define INPUT_MODE 0
```

Listing 2.1 *superm.h: supermarket pricing include file (continued)*

```
51    #define LOOKUP_MODE 1
52
53    #define CLEAR_FILE 0
54    #define KEEP_FILE 1
55
56    unsigned compute_hash(char *key_value);
57    unsigned compute_file_hash(char *key_value);
58    unsigned compute_cache_hash(char *key_value);
59    int lookup_record(FILE *price_file, char *ascii_key_value,
60    ItemRecord **item_record);
61    int lookup_record_number(FILE *price_file, char *ascii_key_value,
62    unsigned *record_number);
63    int write_record(FILE *price_file, ItemRecord new_record);
64    unsigned compute_starting_cache_hash(unsigned cache_index);
65    unsigned compute_ending_cache_hash(unsigned cache_index);
66    FILE *initialize_price_file(char *price_file_name, int file_mode);
67    void terminate_price_file(FILE *price_file);
68    void position_record(FILE *price_file, unsigned record_number);
69    int lookup_record_and_number(FILE *price_file, char *ascii_key_value,
70    ItemRecord **item_record, unsigned *record_number);
71
```

Listing 2.2 *superm.c: supermarket pricing main program*

```
1
2    /****keyword-flag*** "%v %f %n" */
3    /* "3 14-Aug-91,7:04:32 SUPERM.C" */
4
5
6    #include <stdio.h>
7    #include <stdlib.h>
8    #include "superm.h"
9
10   void process(FILE *price_file);
11
12   void main(int argc, char *argv[])
13   {
14     FILE *price_file;
15     char price_file_name[100];
16     char answer[100];
17     int file_mode;
18
19     if (argc < 2)
20         {
21         printf("Usage: superm price_file\n");
22         exit(1);
23         }
24
25     strcpy(price_file_name,argv[1]);
26
27     printf("Do you want to clear the file?\n");
28     gets(answer);
29     if (toupper(answer[0]) == 'Y')
30         file_mode = CLEAR_FILE;
31     else
32         file_mode = KEEP_FILE;
33
34     price_file = initialize_price_file(price_file_name,file_mode);
35
36     process(price_file);
37
38     terminate_price_file(price_file);
39   }
40
41
42
43   void process(FILE *price_file)
44   {
45     ItemRecord *item_record_ptr;
46     ItemRecord new_record;
47     char ascii_code_number[100];
48     int status;
49     char upc[11];
50     char description[100];
51     float price;
```

Listing 2.2 *superm.c: supermarket pricing main program (continued)*

```
52      int i;
53      char *result;
54      char out_line[81];
55      int mode;
56      int old_mode;
57      char temp_string[100];
58      char temp2[100];
59      int field_length;
60
61      mode = INPUT_MODE;
62      old_mode = LOOKUP_MODE;
63
64      for (i = 0; ; i ++)
65          {
66          if (mode == INPUT_MODE)
67              {
68              if (old_mode != INPUT_MODE)
69                  {
70                  printf("Now in INPUT mode.\n");
71                  old_mode = INPUT_MODE;
72                  }
73              printf("Please enter code number,\n");
74              printf("ENTER to switch to lookup mode,\n");
75              printf("or * to terminate the program.\n");
76              gets(temp_string);
77              if (strcmp(temp_string,"*") == 0)
78                  break;
79              if (strlen(temp_string) == 0)
80                  {
81                  mode = LOOKUP_MODE;
82                  continue;
83                  }
84              field_length = strlen(temp_string);
85              if (field_length > ASCII_KEY_SIZE)
86                  {
87                  printf("UPC code is a maximum of %d characters\n",ASCII_KEY_SIZE);
88                  continue;
89                  }
90              else if (field_length < ASCII_KEY_SIZE)
91                  {
92                  memset(temp2,0,ASCII_KEY_SIZE+1);
93                  memset(temp2,'0',ASCII_KEY_SIZE-field_length);
94                  strcat(temp2,temp_string);
95                  strcpy(temp_string,temp2);
96                  }
97              ascii_to_BCD(new_record.upc,temp_string,ASCII_KEY_SIZE);
98
99              printf("Please enter description: ");
100             gets(temp_string);
101             field_length = strlen(temp_string);
102             if (field_length > DESCRIPTION_CHARS)
```

Listing 2.2 *superm.c: supermarket pricing main program (continued)*

```
103                             {
104                             printf("Description is a maximum of %d characters\n",
105                             DESCRIPTION_CHARS);
106                             continue;
107                             }
108                     ascii_to_radix40(new_record.description,temp_string,
109                     DESCRIPTION_CHARS);
110
111                     printf("Please enter price: ");
112                     gets(temp_string);
113                     price = atof(temp_string);
114                     if (price > 655.35)
115                             {
116                             printf("Price too large - limit is $655.35\n");
117                             continue;
118                             }
119                     new_record.price = (unsigned)(100*price);
120
121                     status = write_record(price_file,new_record);
122                     if (status == FILE_FULL)
123                             {
124                             printf("Cannot add entry for item #%s to file\n",
125                             new_record.upc);
126                             break;
127                             }
128                     else if (status == FOUND)
129                             printf("Item #%s already in file\n",new_record.upc);
130                     }
131             else
132                     {
133                     if (old_mode != LOOKUP_MODE)
134                             {
135                             printf("Now in LOOKUP mode.\n");
136                             old_mode = LOOKUP_MODE;
137                             }
138                     printf("Please enter code number: ");
139                     gets(temp_string);
140                     if (strcmp(temp_string,"*") == 0)
141                             break;
142                     if (strlen(temp_string) == 0)
143                             {
144                             mode = INPUT_MODE;
145                             continue;
146                             }
147                     field_length = strlen(temp_string);
148                     if (field_length > ASCII_KEY_SIZE)
149                             {
150                             printf("UPC code is a maximum of %d characters\n",ASCII_KEY_SIZE);
151                             continue;
152                             }
153                     else if (field_length < ASCII_KEY_SIZE)
```

Listing 2.2 *superm.c: supermarket pricing main program (continued)*

```
154                        {
155                        memset(temp2,0,ASCII_KEY_SIZE+1);
156                        memset(temp2,'0',ASCII_KEY_SIZE-field_length);
157                        strcat(temp2,temp_string);
158                        strcpy(temp_string,temp2);
159                        }
160                    strcpy(ascii_code_number,temp_string);
161                    status = lookup_record(price_file,ascii_code_number,&item_record_ptr);
162                    if (status == FOUND)
163                        {
164                        BCD_to_ascii(upc,&item_record_ptr->upc[0],ASCII_KEY_SIZE);
165                        radix40_to_ascii(description,&item_record_ptr->description[0],
166                        DESCRIPTION_CHARS);
167                        price = item_record_ptr->price;
168                        printf("%s:%s:%u\n",upc,description,price);
169                        }
170                    else if (status == NOT_IN_FILE)
171                        printf("Item #%s not found\n",ascii_code_number);
172                    }
173            }
174    }
175
176
```

Listing 2.3 *suplook.c: supermarket pricing main program*

```
1
2    /****keyword-flag*** "%v %f %n" */
3    /* "8 31-Aug-91,22:31:04 SUPLOOK.C" */
4
5
6    #include <stdio.h>
7    #include <stdlib.h>
8    #include "superm.h"
9
10   long lookup_count = 0;      /* for hit ratio calculation */
11   long hit_count = 0;         /* same here */
12
13   FILE *initialize_price_file(char *price_file_name, int file_mode)
14   {
15     PriceFile *price_file;
16     FILE *dos_file_stream;
17     ItemRecord **temp_cache_ptr;
18     ItemRecord *temp_cache_data;
19     unsigned i;
20     ItemRecord dummy_record;
21     unsigned *temp_record_number_ptr;
22
23     price_file = malloc(sizeof(PriceFile));
24
25     dos_file_stream = fopen(price_file_name,"r+b");
26     if (dos_file_stream == NULL)
27         dos_file_stream = fopen(price_file_name,"w+b");
28     if (dos_file_stream == NULL)
29         {
30         printf("Can't open price file %s.\n",price_file_name);
31         exit(1);
32         }
33
34     price_file->dos_file_stream = dos_file_stream;
35
36     temp_cache_ptr = (ItemRecord **)calloc(CACHE_SIZE, sizeof(ItemRecord *));
37     temp_cache_data = (ItemRecord *)calloc(CACHE_SIZE, sizeof(ItemRecord));
38
39     memset(&dummy_record,0,sizeof(ItemRecord));
40     dummy_record.upc[0] = (unsigned char)INVALID_BCD_VALUE;
41
42     for (i = 0; i < CACHE_SIZE; i ++)
43         {
44         temp_cache_ptr[i] = temp_cache_data ++;
45         *(temp_cache_ptr[i]) = dummy_record;
46         }
47
48     price_file->item_cache = temp_cache_ptr;
49
50     temp_record_number_ptr = (unsigned *)calloc(CACHE_SIZE, sizeof(unsigned));
51
```

Listing 2.3 *suplook.c: supermarket pricing main program (continued)*

```c
52      for (i = 0; i < CACHE_SIZE; i ++)
53          temp_record_number_ptr[i] = INVALID_RECORD_NUMBER;
54
55      price_file->file_record_number = temp_record_number_ptr;
56
57      if (file_mode == CLEAR_FILE)
58          {
59          for (i = 0; i < FILE_SIZE; i ++)
60              {
61              position_record(dos_file_stream,i);
62              fwrite(&dummy_record,1,sizeof(ItemRecord),dos_file_stream);
63              }
64          }
65
66      return((FILE *)price_file);
67   }
68
69
70
71   int lookup_record_and_number(FILE *price_file, char *ascii_key_value,
72   ItemRecord **item_record, unsigned *record_number)
73   {
74     unsigned starting_cache_index;
75     ItemRecord *temp_cache_data;
76     ItemRecord temp_file_data;
77     PriceFile *temp_price_file;
78     int status;
79     unsigned starting_file_index;
80     FILE *dos_file_stream;
81     unsigned current_file_index;
82     unsigned start_looking_in_cache;
83     unsigned stop_looking_in_cache;
84     int i;
85     unsigned cache_replace_index;
86     BCD *bcd_key_value;
87   static unsigned longest_search = 0;
88     unsigned current_search;
89
90     bcd_key_value = malloc(strlen(ascii_key_value));
91
92     lookup_count ++;
93
94     temp_price_file = (PriceFile *)price_file;
95     dos_file_stream = temp_price_file->dos_file_stream;
96
97     starting_cache_index = compute_cache_hash(ascii_key_value);
98
99     ascii_to_BCD(bcd_key_value,ascii_key_value,ASCII_KEY_SIZE);
100
101    status = QUESTIONABLE;
102
```

Listing 2.3 *suplook.c: supermarket pricing main program (continued)*

```
103     start_looking_in_cache = compute_starting_cache_hash(starting_cache_index);
104     stop_looking_in_cache = compute_ending_cache_hash(starting_cache_index);
105     for (i = start_looking_in_cache; i < stop_looking_in_cache; i ++)
106         {
107         temp_cache_data = temp_price_file->item_cache[i];
108         if (memcmp(&temp_cache_data->upc,bcd_key_value,BCD_KEY_SIZE) == 0)
109             {
110             status = FOUND;
111             hit_count ++;
112             break;
113             }
114         }
115
116     if (status == FOUND)
117         {
118         *item_record = temp_cache_data;
119         *record_number = temp_price_file->file_record_number[i];
120         free(bcd_key_value);
121         return(status);
122         }
123
124     cache_replace_index = start_looking_in_cache +
125     (lookup_count % MAPPING_FACTOR);
126
127     for (i = start_looking_in_cache; i < stop_looking_in_cache; i ++)
128         {
129         temp_cache_data = temp_price_file->item_cache[i];
130         if (temp_cache_data->upc[0] == INVALID_BCD_VALUE)
131             {
132             cache_replace_index = i; /* use an invalid entry, if there is one */
133             break;
134             }
135         }
136
137     starting_file_index = compute_file_hash(ascii_key_value);
138
139     for (current_file_index = starting_file_index;
140     current_file_index < FILE_SIZE; current_file_index ++)
141         {
142         position_record(price_file,current_file_index);
143         fread(&temp_file_data,1,sizeof(ItemRecord),dos_file_stream);
144         if (temp_file_data.upc[0] == INVALID_BCD_VALUE)
145             {
146             status = NOT_IN_FILE;
147             break;
148             }
149         if (memcmp(&temp_file_data.upc,bcd_key_value,BCD_KEY_SIZE) == 0)
150             {
151             status = FOUND;
152             break;
153             }
```

Listing 2.3 *suplook.c: supermarket pricing main program (continued)*

```
154            }
155
156        current_search = current_file_index - starting_file_index;
157        if (current_search > longest_search)
158             longest_search = current_search;
159
160        temp_cache_data = temp_price_file->item_cache[cache_replace_index];
161
162        if (status == FOUND)
163             {
164             memcpy(temp_cache_data,&temp_file_data,sizeof(ItemRecord));
165             temp_price_file->file_record_number[cache_replace_index] =
166             current_file_index;
167             *item_record = temp_cache_data;
168             *record_number = current_file_index;
169             free(bcd_key_value);
170             return(status);
171             }
172        else if (status == NOT_IN_FILE)
173             {
174             temp_price_file->file_record_number[cache_replace_index] =
175             current_file_index;
176             *item_record = temp_cache_data;
177             *record_number = current_file_index;
178             free(bcd_key_value);
179             return(NOT_IN_FILE);
180             }
181
182        for (current_file_index = 0; current_file_index < starting_file_index;
183        current_file_index ++)
184             {
185             position_record(price_file,current_file_index);
186             fread(&temp_file_data,1,sizeof(ItemRecord),dos_file_stream);
187             if (temp_file_data.upc[0] == INVALID_BCD_VALUE)
188                  {
189                  status = NOT_IN_FILE;
190                  break;
191                  }
192             if (memcmp(&temp_file_data.upc,bcd_key_value,BCD_KEY_SIZE) == 0)
193                  {
194                  status = FOUND;
195                  break;
196                  }
197             }
198
199        if (status == FOUND)
200             {
201             memcpy(temp_cache_data,&temp_file_data,sizeof(ItemRecord));
202             temp_price_file->file_record_number[cache_replace_index] =
203             current_file_index;
204             *item_record = temp_cache_data;
```

Listing 2.3 *suplook.c: supermarket pricing main program (continued)*

```
205          *record_number = current_file_index;
206          free(bcd_key_value);
207          return(status);
208          }
209    else if (status == NOT_IN_FILE)
210          {
211          temp_price_file->file_record_number[cache_replace_index] =
212          current_file_index;
213          *item_record = temp_cache_data;
214          *record_number = current_file_index;
215          free(bcd_key_value);
216          return(NOT_IN_FILE);
217          }
218    else
219          {
220          free(bcd_key_value);
221          return(FILE_FULL);
222          }
223  }
224
225
226
227  int lookup_record(FILE *price_file, char *ascii_key_value,
228  ItemRecord **item_record)
229  {
230    int status;
231    unsigned record_number;
232
233    status = lookup_record_and_number(price_file, ascii_key_value,
234    item_record, &record_number);
235
236    return(status);
237  }
238
239
240
241  int lookup_record_number(FILE *price_file, char *ascii_key_value,
242  unsigned *record_number)
243  {
244    int status;
245    ItemRecord *item_record;
246
247    status = lookup_record_and_number(price_file, ascii_key_value,
248    &item_record, record_number);
249
250    return(status);
251  }
252
253
254  int write_record(FILE *price_file, ItemRecord new_record)
255  {
```

Listing 2.3 *suplook.c: supermarket pricing main program (continued)*

```
256      PriceFile *temp_price_file;
257      FILE *dos_file_stream;
258      int status;
259      unsigned record_number;
260      char ascii_key_value[ASCII_KEY_SIZE+1];
261
262      BCD_to_ascii(ascii_key_value,new_record.upc,ASCII_KEY_SIZE);
263
264      status = lookup_record_number(price_file,ascii_key_value,&record_number);
265
266      if (status == FILE_FULL || status == FOUND)
267          return(status);
268
269      temp_price_file = (PriceFile *)price_file;
270      dos_file_stream = temp_price_file->dos_file_stream;
271
272      position_record(price_file,record_number);
273      fwrite(&new_record,1,sizeof(ItemRecord),dos_file_stream);
274
275      return(NOT_IN_FILE);
276  }
277
278
279  void terminate_price_file(FILE *price_file)
280  {
281    FILE *dos_file_stream;
282    PriceFile *temp_price_file;
283
284    temp_price_file = (PriceFile *)price_file;
285
286    dos_file_stream = temp_price_file->dos_file_stream;
287    fclose(dos_file_stream);
288  }
289
290
291  #define UINT_MAX ((unsigned)-1)
292  #define HASH_DIVISOR (UINT_MAX / 10)
293
294
295  unsigned compute_hash(char *key_value)
296  {
297      int i;
298      unsigned hash_code;
299      unsigned hash_divisor;
300
301      hash_code = 0;
302      for (i = 0; i < ASCII_KEY_SIZE; i ++)
303          {
304          hash_code = ((hash_code * 10) + (hash_code / HASH_DIVISOR));
305          hash_code += (key_value[i] & 15);
306          }
```

Listing 2.3 *suplook.c: supermarket pricing main program (continued)*

```
307
308      return(hash_code);
309    }
310
311
312
313    unsigned compute_file_hash(char *key_value)
314    {
315      unsigned hash_code;
316      unsigned file_index;
317
318      hash_code = compute_hash(key_value);
319
320      file_index = hash_code % FILE_SIZE;
321
322      return(file_index);
323    }
324
325
326
327    unsigned compute_cache_hash(char *key_value)
328    {
329      unsigned hash_code;
330      unsigned cache_index;
331
332      hash_code = compute_hash(key_value);
333
334      cache_index = hash_code % CACHE_SIZE;
335
336      return(cache_index);
337    }
338
339
340    unsigned compute_starting_cache_hash(unsigned cache_index)
341    {
342      return((cache_index/MAPPING_FACTOR)*MAPPING_FACTOR);
343    }
344
345
346    unsigned compute_ending_cache_hash(unsigned cache_index)
347    {
348      return((cache_index/MAPPING_FACTOR)*MAPPING_FACTOR+MAPPING_FACTOR);
349    }
350
351
352    void position_record(FILE *price_file, unsigned record_number)
353    {
354      PriceFile *temp_price_file;
355      FILE *dos_file_stream;
356
357      temp_price_file = (PriceFile *)price_file;
```

Listing 2.3 *suplook.c: supermarket pricing main program (continued)*

```
358
359     dos_file_stream = temp_price_file->dos_file_stream;
360     fseek(dos_file_stream,sizeof(ItemRecord)*(long)record_number,SEEK_SET);
361  }
362
363
```

Listing 2.4 *bcdconv.h: BCD conversion include file*

```
 1
 2   /****keyword-flag*** "%v %f %n" */
 3   /* "1 8-Jul-90,11:27:18 BCDCONV.H" */
 4
 5
 6   typedef unsigned char BCD;
 7
 8   char *BCD_to_ascii(char *ascii_value, BCD *bcd_value, int ascii_length);
 9   BCD *ascii_to_BCD(BCD *bcd_value, char *ascii_value, int ascii_length);
10
```

Listing 2.5 *bcdconv.c: conversions to/from BCD*

```
1
2    /****keyword-flag*** "%v %f %n" */
3    /* "4 20-Oct-91,9:54:42 BCDCONV.C" */
4
5
6    #include <stdio.h>
7    #include <stdlib.h>
8    #include "superm.h"
9
10   char *BCD_to_ascii(char *ascii_value, BCD *bcd_value, int ascii_length)
11   {
12     int i;
13     int j;
14     int temp_bcd;
15     int temp_digit;
16
17     j = 0;
18     for (i = 0; i < ascii_length/2; i ++)
19         {
20         temp_bcd = bcd_value[i];
21         temp_digit = temp_bcd >> 4;
22         ascii_value[j++] = temp_digit + '0';
23         temp_digit = temp_bcd & 15;
24         ascii_value[j++] = temp_digit + '0';
25         }
26     ascii_value[ascii_length] = 0;
27     return(ascii_value);
28   }
29
30   BCD *ascii_to_BCD(BCD *bcd_value, char *ascii_value, int ascii_length)
31   {
32     int i;
33     int j;
34     int temp_bcd;
35     int temp_digit;
36     int temp_ascii_digit;
37
38     j = 0;
39     for (i = 0; i < ascii_length/2; i ++)
40         {
41         temp_ascii_digit = ascii_value[j++];
42         if (temp_ascii_digit < '0' || temp_ascii_digit > '9')
43             {
44             printf("Invalid ascii to BCD conversion: input char = %c\n",
45             temp_ascii_digit);
46             exit(1);
47             }
48         temp_bcd = (temp_ascii_digit & 15) << 4;
49
50         temp_ascii_digit = ascii_value[j++];
51         if (temp_ascii_digit < '0' || temp_ascii_digit > '9')
```

Listing 2.5 *bcdconv.c: conversions to/from BCD (continued)*

```
52                  {
53                  printf("Invalid ascii to BCD conversion: input char = %c\n",
54                  temp_ascii_digit);
55                  exit(1);
56                  }
57          temp_bcd += temp_ascii_digit & 15;
58          bcd_value[i] = temp_bcd;
59          }
60
61      return(bcd_value);
62  }
```

Listing 2.6 *radix40.c: conversions to/from Radix40 representation*

```
 1
 2    /****keyword-flag*** "%v %f %n" */
 3    /* "3 7-Nov-90,20:29:54 RADIX40.C" */
 4
 5
 6    #include <stdio.h>
 7    #include <stdio.h>
 8    #include <string.h>
 9    #include <alloc.h>
10    #include <time.h>
11    #include "radix40.h"
12
13    char legal_chars[40] = " ,-.0123456789ABCDEFGHIJKLMNOPQRSTUVWXYZ";
14
15    unsigned weights[3] = {1600, 40, 1};
16
17    int radix40_to_ascii(unsigned char *ascii_data, Radix40 *radix40_data,int max_chars)
18    /* this routine converts a radix 40 character string */
19    /* to ascii representation.  Trailing blanks will be deleted. */
20    {
21      int i;
22      int j;
23      int ascii_length;
24      int new_ascii_length;
25      int words_to_convert;
26      int cycle;
27      unsigned current_word_index;
28      unsigned current_word;
29      unsigned current_char;
30
31      ascii_length = max_chars;
32
33      words_to_convert = ascii_length / 3;
34      if (ascii_length % 3 != 0)
35          words_to_convert ++;
36
37      memset(ascii_data,0,max_chars+1);
38
39      current_word_index = -1;
40      cycle = 0;
41      for (i = 0; i < ascii_length; i ++)
42          {
43          if (cycle == 0)
44              {
45              current_word_index ++;
46              current_word = radix40_data[current_word_index];
47              }
48          current_char = current_word / weights[cycle];
49          current_word -= current_char * weights[cycle];
50          ascii_data[i] = legal_chars[current_char];
51          cycle = (cycle + 1) % 3;
```

Listing 2.6 *radix40.c: conversions to/from Radix40 representation (continued)*

```
52           }
53
54      new_ascii_length = strlen(ascii_data);
55      for (i = new_ascii_length - 1; i >= 0; i —)
56           {
57           if (ascii_data[i] != ' ')
58                break;
59           ascii_data[i] = 0;
60           }
61
62      return(S_OKAY);
63    }
64
65
66    char lookup_chars[256] =
67    {IL, IL, IL, IL, IL, IL, IL, IL,/* 00 */
68    IL, IL, IL, IL, IL, IL, IL, IL, /* 08 */
69    IL, IL, IL, IL, IL, IL, IL, IL, /* 10 */
70    IL, IL, IL, IL, IL, IL, IL, IL, /* 18 */
71     0, IL, IL, IL, IL, IL, IL, IL, /* 20 */
72    IL, IL, IL, IL,  1,  2,  3, IL, /* 28 */
73     4,  5,  6,  7,  8,  9, 10, 11, /* 30 */
74    12, 13 ,IL, IL, IL, IL, IL, IL, /* 38 */
75    IL, 14, 15, 16, 17, 18, 19, 20, /* 40 */
76    21, 22, 23, 24, 25, 26, 27, 28, /* 48 */
77    29, 30, 31, 32, 33, 34, 35, 36, /* 50 */
78    37, 38, 39, IL, IL, IL, IL, IL, /* 58 */
79    IL, 14, 15, 16, 17, 18, 19, 20, /* 60 */
80    21, 22, 23, 24, 25, 26, 27, 28, /* 68 */
81    29, 30, 31, 32, 33, 34, 35, 36, /* 70 */
82    37, 38, 39, IL, IL, IL, IL, IL, /* 78 */
83    IL, IL, IL, IL, IL, IL, IL, IL, /* 80 */
84    IL, IL, IL, IL, IL, IL, IL, IL, /* 88 */
85    IL, IL, IL, IL, IL, IL, IL, IL, /* 90 */
86    IL, IL, IL, IL, IL, IL, IL, IL, /* 98 */
87    IL, IL, IL, IL, IL, IL, IL, IL, /* A0 */
88    IL, IL, IL, IL, IL, IL, IL, IL, /* A8 */
89    IL, IL, IL, IL, IL, IL, IL, IL, /* B0 */
90    IL, IL, IL, IL, IL, IL, IL, IL, /* B8 */
91    IL, IL, IL, IL, IL, IL, IL, IL, /* C0 */
92    IL, IL, IL, IL, IL, IL, IL, IL, /* C8 */
93    IL, IL, IL, IL, IL, IL, IL, IL, /* D0 */
94    IL, IL, IL, IL, IL, IL, IL, IL, /* D8 */
95    IL, IL, IL, IL, IL, IL, IL, IL, /* E0 */
96    IL, IL, IL, IL, IL, IL, IL, IL, /* E8 */
97    IL, IL, IL, IL, IL, IL, IL, IL, /* F0 */
98    IL, IL, IL, IL, IL, IL, IL, IL};/* F8 */
99
100   int ascii_to_radix40(Radix40 *radix40_data, unsigned char *ascii_data, int max_chars)
101   /* this routine converts a null-terminated ascii character string */
102   /* to radix 40 representation.  The allowable characters are: */
```

Listing 2.6 *radix40.c: conversions to/from Radix40 representation (continued)*

```
103    /* A-Z, 0-9, period, comma, hyphen, and space.  If any illegal characters */
104    /* are detected, they will be converted to hyphens, and the return value */
105    /* will be S_ILLEGAL. */
106    /* Lowercase letters will be upper-cased without error indication. */
107    /* The radix40 value will be padded with blanks to a multiple of three */
108    /* characters. If the number of characters in the ascii string is > max_chars */
109    /* only max_chars will be converted, and the return value will be S_ILLEGAL. */
110    /* If no error is detected, the return value will be S_OKAY. */
111    {
112      int i;
113      unsigned char j;
114      int ascii_length;
115      int result;
116      int words_to_convert;
117      int words_to_clear;
118      int cycle;
119      unsigned current_word_index;
120
121      result = S_OKAY;
122      ascii_length = strlen(ascii_data);
123      if (ascii_length > max_chars)
124          {
125          ascii_length = max_chars;
126          result = S_ILLEGAL;
127          }
128
129      words_to_convert = ascii_length / 3;
130      if (ascii_length % 3 != 0)
131          words_to_convert ++;
132
133      words_to_clear = max_chars / 3;
134      if (max_chars % 3 != 0)
135          words_to_clear ++;
136
137      memset(radix40_data,0,words_to_clear*sizeof(Radix40));
138
139      current_word_index = -1;
140      cycle = 0;
141      for (i = 0; i < ascii_length; i ++)
142          {
143          if (cycle == 0)
144              current_word_index ++;
145          j = lookup_chars[ascii_data[i]];
146          if (j & ILLEGAL)
147              {
148              j = HYPHEN ; /* make it a hyphen */
149              result = S_ILLEGAL; /* and remember that it was illegal */
150              }
151          radix40_data[current_word_index] += weights[cycle] * j;
152          cycle = (cycle + 1) % 3;
153          }
```

Listing 2.6 *radix40.c: conversions to/from Radix40 representation (continued)*

```
154
155     return(result);
156   }
157
158
```

Listing 2.7 stestgen.c: generates test code file

```
1
2    /****keyword-flag*** "%v %f %n" */
3    /* "3 16-May-92,8:50:36 STESTGEN.C" */
4
5
6    #include <stdio.h>
7    #include <stdlib.h>
8    #include "superm.h"
9
10   void process(FILE *in_file, FILE *out_file);
11
12   void main(int argc, char *argv[])
13   {
14     FILE *in_file;
15     FILE *out_file;
16
17     if (argc < 3)
18         {
19         printf("Usage: stestgen in_code_file out_code_file\n");
20         exit(1);
21         }
22
23     in_file = fopen(argv[1],"r+");
24     out_file = fopen(argv[2],"w+");
25
26     process(in_file,out_file);
27
28     fclose(in_file);
29     fclose(out_file);
30   }
31
32
33
34   void process(FILE *in_file,FILE *out_file)
35   {
36     ItemRecord *item_record_ptr;
37     unsigned record_number;
38     char *ascii_code_number[FILE_CAPACITY];
39     int status;
40     char upc[11];
41     char description[100];
42     unsigned price;
43     int i;
44     char *result;
45     int selection_range;
46     char temp_code_number[100];
47     int random_value;
48     int file_capacity;
49
50     for (i = 0; i < FILE_CAPACITY; i ++)
51         {
```

Listing 2.7 *stestgen.c: generates test code file (continued)*

```
52            ascii_code_number[i] = malloc(ASCII_KEY_SIZE+1);
53            result = fgets(temp_code_number,100,in_file);
54            if (result == NULL)
55                break;
56            temp_code_number[ASCII_KEY_SIZE] = 0;
57            strcpy(ascii_code_number[i],temp_code_number);
58            }
59
60     file_capacity = FILE_CAPACITY; /* for easier debugging */
61
62     for (i = 0; i < FILE_CAPACITY; i ++)
63         {
64         random_value = random(file_capacity);
65         if (random_value < (long)file_capacity * 80 / 100)
66             {
67             /* usually pick one in first 20% */
68             selection_range = (long)file_capacity * 20 / 100;
69             record_number = random(selection_range);
70             }
71         else
72             {
73             selection_range = (long)file_capacity * 80 / 100;
74             record_number = random(selection_range) +
75             (long)file_capacity * 20 / 100;
76             }
77         fputs(ascii_code_number[record_number],out_file);
78         fputs("\n",out_file);
79         }
80     }
```

Listing 2.8 *supinit.c: supermarket pricing file initialization*

```
1
2    /****keyword-flag*** "%v %f %n" */
3    /* "8 16-May-92,8:50:32 SUPINIT.C" */
4
5
6    #include <stdio.h>
7    #include <stdlib.h>
8    #include "superm.h"
9
10   FILE *initialize(char *price_file_name);
11   void process(FILE *price_file,char *source_file_name, char *list_file_name);
12   void terminate(FILE *price_file);
13
14   void main(int argc, char *argv[])
15   {
16     FILE *price_file;
17
18     if (argc < 4)
19         {
20         printf("Usage: supinit source_file price_file list_file\n");
21         exit(1);
22         }
23
24     price_file = initialize(argv[2]);
25
26     process(price_file,argv[1],argv[3]);
27
28     terminate(price_file);
29   }
30
31
32   #define MAX_DESCRIPTIONS 100
33   #define MAX_DESC_LENGTH 100
34
35   FILE *initialize(char *price_file_name)
36   {
37     PriceFile *price_file;
38     FILE *dos_file_stream;
39     ItemRecord **temp_cache_ptr;
40     ItemRecord *temp_cache_data;
41     unsigned i;
42     ItemRecord dummy_record;
43     unsigned *temp_record_number_ptr;
44
45     price_file = malloc(sizeof(PriceFile));
46
47     memset(&dummy_record,0,sizeof(ItemRecord));
48     dummy_record.upc[0] = (unsigned char)INVALID_BCD_VALUE;
49
50     dos_file_stream = fopen(price_file_name,"w+b");
51     if (dos_file_stream == NULL)
```

Listing 2.8 *supinit.c: supermarket pricing file initialization (continued)*

```
52              {
53              printf("Can't open price file %s.\n",price_file_name);
54              exit(1);
55              }
56
57      price_file->dos_file_stream = dos_file_stream;
58
59      temp_cache_ptr = (ItemRecord **)calloc(CACHE_SIZE, sizeof(ItemRecord *));
60      temp_cache_data = (ItemRecord *)calloc(CACHE_SIZE, sizeof(ItemRecord));
61
62      for (i = 0; i < CACHE_SIZE; i ++)
63              {
64              temp_cache_ptr[i] = temp_cache_data ++;
65              *(temp_cache_ptr[i]) = dummy_record;
66              }
67
68      price_file->item_cache = temp_cache_ptr;
69
70      temp_record_number_ptr = (unsigned *)calloc(CACHE_SIZE, sizeof(unsigned));
71
72      for (i = 0; i < CACHE_SIZE; i ++)
73              temp_record_number_ptr[i] = (unsigned)-1;
74
75      price_file->file_record_number = temp_record_number_ptr;
76
77      return((FILE *)price_file);
78  }
79
80
81  void process(FILE *price_file,char *source_file_name, char *list_file_name)
82  {
83      unsigned i;
84      int j;
85      int k;
86      unsigned record_number;
87      FILE *source_file_stream;
88      FILE *list_file_stream;
89      char *item_description[MAX_DESCRIPTIONS];
90      char description[MAX_DESC_LENGTH];
91      char *desc_status;
92      int desc_count;
93      ItemRecord dummy_record;
94      PriceFile *temp_price_file;
95      FILE *dos_file_stream;
96      BCD bcd_code_number[BCD_KEY_SIZE];
97      char ascii_code_number[ASCII_KEY_SIZE+1];
98      char *lf_pos;
99      int status;
100     ItemRecord *item_record_ptr;
101
102     temp_price_file = (PriceFile *)price_file;
```

Listing 2.8 *supinit.c: supermarket pricing file initialization (continued)*

```
103      dos_file_stream = temp_price_file->dos_file_stream;
104
105      memset(&dummy_record,0,sizeof(ItemRecord));
106      dummy_record.upc[0] = (unsigned char)INVALID_BCD_VALUE;
107
108      for (i = 0; i < FILE_SIZE; i ++)
109          {
110          position_record(price_file,i);
111          fwrite(&dummy_record,1,sizeof(ItemRecord),dos_file_stream);
112          }
113
114      source_file_stream = fopen(source_file_name,"r");
115      if (source_file_stream == NULL)
116          {
117          printf("Can't open source file %s.\n",source_file_name);
118          exit(1);
119          }
120
121      list_file_stream = fopen(list_file_name,"w");
122      if (list_file_stream == NULL)
123          {
124          printf("Can't open list file %s.\n",list_file_name);
125          exit(1);
128      for (i = 0; i < MAX_DESCRIPTIONS; i ++)
129          {
130          desc_status = fgets(description,MAX_DESC_LENGTH,source_file_stream);
131          if (desc_status == NULL)
132              break;
133          item_description[i] = malloc(strlen(description)+1);
134          lf_pos = strchr(description,'\n');
135          *lf_pos = 0;
136          strcpy(item_description[i],description);
137          }
138
139      desc_count = i;
140
141      for (i = 0; i < FILE_CAPACITY; i ++)
142          {
143          j = i % desc_count;
144          k = i / desc_count;
145
146          sprintf(description,"%s #%d",item_description[j],k);
147          ascii_to_radix40(&dummy_record.description[0],description,
148          DESCRIPTION_CHARS);
149
150          sprintf(ascii_code_number,"%0101d",(long)10000*random(desc_count)+i);
151          ascii_to_BCD(&dummy_record.upc[0],ascii_code_number,ASCII_KEY_SIZE);
152
153          fprintf(list_file_stream,"%s %s\n",ascii_code_number,description);
154
155          dummy_record.price = 100*j+k;
```

Listing 2.8 *supinit.c: supermarket pricing file initialization (continued)*

```
156
157              status = lookup_record_number(price_file,ascii_code_number,
158              &record_number);
159
160         if (status == NOT_IN_FILE)
161              {
162              position_record(price_file,record_number);
163              fwrite(&dummy_record,1,sizeof(ItemRecord),dos_file_stream);
164              }
165         else if (status == FILE_FULL)
166              {
167              printf("Cannot add entry for item #%s to file\n",ascii_code_number);
168              break;
169              }
170         else if (status == FOUND)
171              printf("Item #%s already in file\n",ascii_code_number);
172         }
173
174   fclose(dos_file_stream);
175
176   }
177
178
179   void terminate(FILE *price_file)
180   {
181   FILE *dos_file_stream;
182   PriceFile *temp_price_file;
183
184   temp_price_file = (PriceFile *)price_file;
185
186   dos_file_stream = temp_price_file->dos_file_stream;
187   fclose(dos_file_stream);
188   }
189
190
```

Listing 2.9 *supert.c: supermarket pricing main program*

```
 1
 2    /****keyword-flag*** "%v %f %n" */
 3    /* "9 16-May-92,8:50:36 SUPERT.C" */
 4
 5
 6    #include <stdio.h>
 7    #include <stdlib.h>
 8    #include "superm.h"
 9
10    void process(FILE *price_file, FILE *UPC_file);
11
12    extern long lookup_count;
13    extern long hit_count;
14
15    void main(int argc, char *argv[])
16    {
17      FILE *price_file;
18      FILE *UPC_file;
19
20      if (argc < 3)
21          {
22          printf("Usage: supert price_file code_file\n");
23          exit(1);
24          }
25
26      price_file = initialize_price_file(argv[1],KEEP_FILE);
27      UPC_file = fopen(argv[2],"r+");
28
29      setvbuf(UPC_file,NULL,_IOFBF,32000);
30
31      process(price_file,UPC_file);
32
33      terminate_price_file(price_file);
34
35      fclose(UPC_file);
36      printf("Hit rate: %3.2f\n",((float)hit_count/(float)lookup_count));
37    }
38
39
40
41    void process(FILE *price_file,FILE *UPC_file)
42    {
43      ItemRecord *item_record_ptr;
44      unsigned record_number;
45      char ascii_code_number[100];
46      int status;
47      char upc[11];
48      char description[100];
49      int i;
50      char *result;
51      char out_line[81];
```

Listing 2.9 *supert.c: supermarket pricing main program (continued)*

```
52
53      for (i = 0; ; i ++)
54          {
55          result = fgets(ascii_code_number,100,UPC_file);
56          if (result == NULL)
57              break;
58          ascii_code_number[10] = 0;
59          status =lookup_record(price_file,ascii_code_number,&item_record_ptr);
60
61          if (status == FOUND)
62              {
63              BCD_to_ascii(upc,&item_record_ptr->upc[0],ASCII_KEY_SIZE);
64              radix40_to_ascii(description,&item_record_ptr->description[0],
65              DESCRIPTION_CHARS);
66  /*          printf("%s:%s:%u\n",upc,description,item_record_ptr->price); */
67              }
68          else if (status == NOT_IN_FILE)
69              printf("Item #%s notfound\n",ascii_code_number);
70          }
71
72  }
73
74
```

Strips, Bits, And Sorts

A Mailing List System

ALGORITHMS DISCUSSED
The Distribution Counting Sort, Strip Files, Bitmaps

Introduction

In this chapter we will use a selective mailing list system to illustrate rapid access to and rearrangement of information selected by criteria specified at runtime. Our example will allow us to select customers of a retail store by the amount they have spent in the current calendar year and by the last time they have been in the store. This would be very useful for a retailer who wants to send coupons to lure back the (possibly lost) customers who have spent more than $100 this year but who haven't been in for 30 days. The labels for the letters should be produced in ZIP code order, to take advantage of the discount for presorted mail.

A First Approach

To begin, let us assume that the information we have about each customer can be described by the structure definition in figure 3.1.

A straightforward approach would be to store all of this information in a disk file, with one `DataRecord` record for each customer. In order to construct a selective

Figure 3.1 *Customer information*

```
typedef struct
{
char last_name[LAST_NAME_LENGTH+1];
char first_name[FIRST_NAME_LENGTH+1];
char address1[ADDRESS1_LENGTH+1];
char address2[ADDRESS2_LENGTH+1];
char city[CITY_LENGTH+1];
char state[STATE_LENGTH+1];
char zip[ZIP_LENGTH+1];
int date_last_here;
int dollars_spent;
} DataRecord;
```

mailing list, we read through the file, testing each record to see whether it meets our criteria. We extract the sort key (ZIP code) for each record that passes the tests of amount spent and last transaction date, keeping these keys and their associated record numbers in memory. After reaching the end of the file, we sort the keys (possibly with a heapsort or Quicksort) and rearrange the record numbers according to the sort order, then reread the selected records in the order of their ZIP codes and print the address labels.

It may seem simpler just to collect records in memory as they meet our criteria. However, the memory requirements of this approach might be excessive if a large percentage of the records are selected. The customer file of a retail store is often fairly large, with 5000 or more 100-byte records quite common; in this situation a one-pass approach might require as much as 500 Kbytes of memory for storing the selected records.

However, if we keep only the keys of the selected records in memory and print the label for each customer as his record is reread on the second pass, we never have to have more than one record in memory at a time. In our example, the length of the key (ZIP code) is nine bytes and the record number is two bytes long, so that 5000 selected records would require only 55 Kbytes. This is a much more reasonable memory budget, considering that we also need memory for the operating system and our program code and working storage for the sort.

Even so, there is no reason to allocate all the storage we might ever need in advance, and every reason not to. We'd like the program to run in the minimum memory possible, so that it would be useful even on a machine with limited memory or one that is loaded up with network drivers and memory-resident utilities.

A linked list is a fairly simple way to allocate memory as needed, but we must be careful to use this method efficiently. Allocating a new block of storage for each record that matches our criteria would be very wasteful, as extra control storage is needed to keep track of each allocation. In MS-DOS, each allocation requires at least 16 bytes of control storage, so 5000 allocations would use about 80 Kbytes just for the control storage![23]   This problem is easy to solve; we will allocate storage for a number of records at once, 100 in our example, which reduces that 80 Kbyte overhead to less than 1 Kbyte.[24]

Saving Storage with Bitmaps

Let's start our optimization by trying to reduce the memory we need for each selected record during this first pass through the file.   One possibility is to convert the ZIP codes to `Radix40` representation to save memory.   Unfortunately, such data is not suitable for sorting.

However, there is another way for us to save memory during the first pass: using a **bitmap** to keep track of the records that match our criteria. A bitmap is an array of bits that can be used to record one characteristic of a number of items, as long as that characteristic can be expressed as yes/no, true/false, present/absent, or some similar pair of opposites.   In this case, all we want to remember is whether each record was selected.   So if we allocate a bitmap with one bit for each possible record number, we can clear the whole bitmap at the start (indicating we haven't selected any records yet) and then set the bit for each record number we select.   When we get done with the selection, we will know how many records were selected, so we can allocate storage for the record numbers we need to sort.   Then we can go through the bitmap, and every time we find a bit that is set, we will add the corresponding record number to the end of the list to be passed to the sort.

Of course, we could use an array of bytes, one per record, instead of a bitmap, which would not require us to write bit access routines.   However, the bitmap requires only one-eighth as much as storage as an array of bytes, which can result in considerable savings with a big array.   In our example, with a 5000-record file, a bitmap with one bit per record would occupy less than 1 Kbyte, whereas an equivalent byte array would occupy 5 Kbytes.   While this difference may not be significant in the present case, larger files produce proportionally larger savings.

As with almost everything, there is a drawback to the use of bitmaps; they usually require more time to access than byte arrays.   This is especially true for those machines (such as the 8086) that do not have an instruction set designed for easy access to individual bits.   Even on machines like the 68020 and its successors, which do have good bit manipulation instructions, compiler support for these functions may be poor (although in this case we could obtain good performance by writing some assembly language routines).   However, since CPU time is unlikely to be the limiting

---

23. Other operating systems have similar overhead when allocating many small blocks of memory; Windows 3.1™, for example, has even more overhead for each allocation, and there is a further limit of 8192 blocks of dynamically allocated memory in the entire system.

24. 50 blocks of 100 records, at 16 bytes of overhead per block, yields an overhead of 50*16, or 800 bytes.

factor while we are reading records from our input file, this extra processing time is probably unimportant in our case.

Increasing Processing Speed

Now that we have reduced the memory requirements for the first pass, is there any way to speed up the program? It seems that, during the first pass, our main target must be to reduce the time it takes to read through the file, since the disk is much slower than the processor.

One way to do this is to use a larger **disk buffer**, so that the operating system can make fewer physical disk accesses. The default buffer size under MS-DOS is quite small, less than 1 Kbyte; if we increase the buffer size, the number of disk accesses is decreased proportionately until an entire track of the disk is being read in one operation. My experimental results indicate that, in our mailing list program, we can increase the speed of the first pass by about 40% by increasing the buffer size to 32 Kbytes.

Of course, this does not speed up the entire program by 40%; on a test case that selects a small portion of the file, the first pass takes about 3 seconds before we increase the buffer size to 32 Kbytes, and about 2 seconds after. The time needed to execute the entire program decreases from about 5 seconds to about 4 seconds, so we have achieved an overall increase in speed of about 20%.

The Law of Diminishing Returns

This brings up an important point. Let's suppose that we could approximately double the speed of the first pass from its current 2 seconds to 1 second. What effect would this have on the overall program speed? The overall time would now be 3 seconds, so we would achieve an speed increase of about 30%. If we doubled the speed of the first pass again (to .5 seconds), the overall time would be 2.5 seconds, for a further increase of about 20% over the previous version. At this point, even the largest theoretically possible increase in speed (i.e., eliminating the first pass completely) would bring the overall time to 2 seconds, about a 25% further improvement in overall speed for this incredible feat.

The general rule is that *successive improvements in the speed or memory consumption of a particular part of the program yield less and less overall improvement.* On reflection, the reason is obvious: we select a part of the program to optimize because it is one of the most significant consumers of some resource, which in the current example is input/output time. But the greater our success in optimizing that part, the smaller the proportion of that resource it uses, so the less benefit we get from each succeeding improvement. Therefore, as our optimization effort proceeds, we have to keep reevaluating which portions of the program have the most potential for gain.

That is not to say that our overall performance could not benefit from further optimization of pass one. After all, it would still account for 2 seconds out of 4, or 50% of the time required to execute the entire program. What other optimizations can we employ?

The next optimization is to read a number of records at once and then process each one of them without having to call the operating system for each one separately. This produces about a 5% improvement in the pass one time, for an overall improvement of about 2% in our small test case. Have we reached the bottom of the barrel?

Strip Mining

Surprisingly, the answer is a resounding NO. In fact, we can speed up pass one by a further 450%! That is a speed-up worth attaining, since in our example it would increase the overall speed by about 95%. But how is it possible to read through the whole file so much more quickly?

We can't. The trick here is that we don't have to read the whole file, just the part that we need to determine whether each record satisfies the criteria of our search. We have to read part of every record in the file, but not all of every record. One way to do this would be to position the file to the beginning of each record and just read the part of the record we want, but that would be much slower than reading the entire file, since we would lose the benefit of having a large buffer by reading such a small amount at once. Our solution is to make the file into a **strip file**. This kind of file consists of several strips, each of which holds the information for several fields of each record in the original file. Suppose the original file looks like figure 3.2.

Then the strips of the strip file might look like figures 3.3 and 3.4.

With this division of the data, we can get all the information we need for the selection process by reading the 14-byte records in strip one rather than the 98-byte records of the original file (see figure 3.5). This reduces the amount of data we have to read from the disk by a factor of 7 and speeds up pass one of the program by almost that amount (5.5 to 1).

Figure 3.2: *Normal file*

Last Name	First Name	Street Address	Extra Address	City	State	ZIP Code	Date	Amount Spent
Jones	John	123 Main	Apt. 2B	NY	NY	91234	9/1/90	100
Smith	Robert	456 2nd.	3rd Fl.	Phila.	PA	90909	9/5/90	200

Now that pass one has been reduced to a small part of the total processing time, we should turn our attention to the next segment of the program, the sort.

Sorting Speed

Surely we should use one of the commonly used sorts (Quicksort, heapsort, etc.). After all, the conventional wisdom is that even the fastest sorting algorithm takes time proportional to $n*\log(n)$. That is, if sorting 1000 items takes 1 second, sorting 1,000,000 items would take at least 2000 seconds, using an optimal sorting algo-

Figure 3.3 *Strip one*

ZIP Code	Date	Amount Spent
91234	9/1/90	100
90909	9/5/90	200

Figure 3.4 *Strip two*

Last Name	First Name	Street Address	Extra Address	City	State
Jones	John	123 Main	Apt.2B	NY	NY
Smith	Robert	456 2nd.	3rd Fl.	Phila.	PA

Figure 3.5 *Strip definitions*

```
typedef struct
{
char last_name[LAST_NAME_LENGTH+1];
char first_name[FIRST_NAME_LENGTH+1];
char address1[ADDRESS1_LENGTH+1];
char address2[ADDRESS2_LENGTH+1];
char city[CITY_LENGTH+1];
char state[STATE_LENGTH+1];
} DataRecord;

typedef struct
{
char zip[ZIP_LENGTH+1];
int date_last_here;
int dollars_spent;
} KeyRecord;
```

rithm. Since these commonly used algorithms all have average times proportional to this best case, it seems that all we have to do is select the one best suited for our particular problem.

This is a common misconception; in fact, only sorts that require comparisons among keys have a lower bound proportional to $n*\log(n)$. The distribution counting sort we are going to use takes time proportional to n, not $n*\log(n)$, so that if it takes 1 second to sort 1000 items, it would take 1000 seconds to sort 1,000,000 items, not 2000 seconds.[25] Moreover, this sort is quite competitive with the commonly used sorts even for a few hundred items, and it is easy to code as well. For some applications, however, its most valuable attribute is that its timing is data independent. That is, the sort takes the same amount of time to execute whether the data items are all the same, all different, already sorted, in reverse order, or randomly shuffled. This is particularly valuable in real-time applications, where knowing the average time is not sufficient.[26]

Actually, this sort takes time proportional to the number of keys multiplied by the length of each key. The reason that the length of the keys is important is that a distribution sort actually treats each character position of the sort keys as a separate "key"; these keys are used in order from the least to the most significant. Therefore, this method actually takes time proportional to $n*m$, where n is the number of keys and m is the length of each key. However, in most real-world applications of sorting, the number of items to be sorted far exceeds the length of each item, and additions to the list take the form of more items, not lengthening of each one. If we had a few very long items to sort, this sort would not be as appropriate.

You're probably wondering how fast this distribution sort really is. To quantify its performance relative to Quicksort, which is one of the most commonly used sorts, I have written a sample program called "sorttest.c" (listing 3.7) that applies both Quicksort and the distribution counting sort to a number of ten-character strings. The Quicksort implementation is the one from the Borland C library, and as is standard with the C `qsort` function, it requires the user to supply the address of a function that will compare the items to be sorted. It is entirely possible to write a Quicksort routine that has the calls to the comparison routine included within it, rather than needing this indirect method to call the routine. Since the purpose here is to compare the sorting algorithms, not the overhead added by convenience factors such as a user-

---

25. A description of this sort can be found in Donald Knuth's book *The Art of Computer Programming*, vol. 3. Reading, Massachusetts: Addison-Wesley, 1968. Every programmer should be aware of this book, since it describes a great number of generally applicable algorithms. Unfortunately, due to its early date of publication, these algorithms are described in an assembly language for a hypothetical machine, rather than in an immediately usable form, but it is quite valuable nonetheless.

26. However, distribution counting is not suitable for use where the data will be kept in virtual memory. See my article "Galloping Algorithms", in *Windows Tech Journal*, 2(February 1993), 40–43, for details on this limitation.

defined comparison routine, I used the Borland Turbo Profiler™ program to ascertain what part of the execution time was accounted for by the qsort routine itself and the time in the strcmp routine actually used to compare the strings. The overhead added by the calls from qsort to the sort_function routine is not included, even though it adds to the elapsed time needed to perform the sort.[27]

I discovered that the qsort routine required approximately 285 msec to sort 1000 (randomly generated) strings of ten characters each. My version of the distribution counting sort, which I call Megasort, took only 99 msec to sort the same 1000 ten-character strings, which is 2.9 times as fast. For 4000 such strings, qsort required 1700 msec as compared to 430 msec for Megasort, a speed advantage of 4 to 1, which continues to increase as the number of items to be sorted grows. Shorter keys are handled even more efficiently with a distribution sort; for example, sorting 4000 two- byte strings requires about 1250 msec using qsort, and about 90 msec using Megasort, an advantage in speed of almost 14 to 1 for the distribution sort.

You're probably wondering how such increases in performance can be achieved with a simple algorithm. It's time to satisfy your curiosity.

The Distribution Counting Sort

The basic method used is to make one pass through the keys for each character position in the key, in order to discover how many keys have each possible ASCII character in the character position that we are currently considering, and another pass to actually rearrange the keys. As a simplified example, suppose that we have ten keys to be sorted and we want to sort only on the first letter of each key (see figure 3.6).

The first pass consists of counting the number of keys that begin with each letter. In this example, we have three keys that begin with the letter 'A', five that begin with the letter 'B', and two that begin with the letter 'C'. Since 'A' is the lowest character we have seen, the first key we encounter that starts with an 'A' should be the first key in the result array, the second key that begins with an 'A' should be the second key in the result array, and the third 'A' key should be the third key in the result array, since all of the 'A' keys should precede all of the 'B' keys. The next keys in sorted order will be the ones that start with 'B'; therefore, the first key that we encounter that starts with a 'B' should be the fourth key in the result array, the second through fifth 'B' keys should be the fifth through eighth keys in the result array, and the 'C' keys should be numbers nine and ten in the result array, since all of the 'B' keys should precede the 'C' keys. Figure 3.7 illustrates this relationship.

If we rearrange the keys in the order indicated by their new indexes, we arrive at the situation shown in figure 3.8.

---

27. Elimination of this calling overhead biases the comparison slightly toward Quicksort; however, this small advantage is completely overwhelmed by the difference in inherent efficiency of the two algorithms.

Figure 3.6 *Unsorted keys*

1	bicycle
2	airplane
3	anonymous
4	cashier
5	bottle
6	bongos
7	antacid
8	competent
9	bingo
10	bombardier

Figure 3.7 *Counts and pointers*

```
Counts                  Starting indexes

A    B    C             A      B      C
3    5    2             1      4      9


Key           Old       New       Explanation
              Index     Index
Bicycle        1          4       The first B goes to position 4.
Airplane       2          1       The first A goes to position 1.
Anonymous      3          2       The second A goes after the first.
Cashier        4          9       The first C goes to position 9.
Bottle         5          5       The second B goes after the first.
Bongos         6          6       The third B goes after the second.
Antacid        7          3       The third A goes after the second.
Competent      8         10       The second C goes after the first.
Bingo          9          7       The fourth B goes after the third.
Bombardier    10          8       The fifth B goes after the fourth.
```

Multicharacter Sorting

Of course, we usually want to sort on more than the first character. As we noted earlier, each character position is actually treated as a separate key; that is, the pointers to the keys are rearranged to be in order by whatever character position we are currently sorting on. With this in mind, let's take the case of a two character string; once we can handle that situation, the algorithm doesn't change significantly when we add more character positions.

We know that the final result we want is for all the A's to come before all the B's, which must precede all the C's, etc., but within the A's, the AA's must come before the AB's, which have to precede the AC's, etc. Of course, the same applies to keys starting with B and C: the BA's must come before the BB's, etc. How can we manage this?

Figure 3.8 *After the sort on the first character*

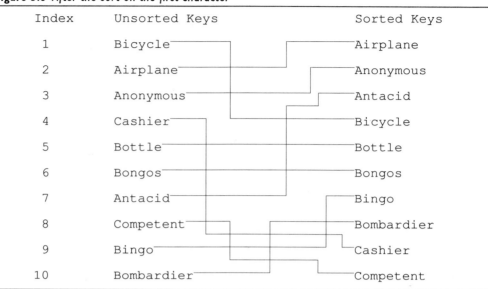

Index	Unsorted Keys	Sorted Keys
1	Bicycle	Airplane
2	Airplane	Anonymous
3	Anonymous	Antacid
4	Cashier	Bicycle
5	Bottle	Bottle
6	Bongos	Bongos
7	Antacid	Bingo
8	Competent	Bombardier
9	Bingo	Cashier
10	Bombardier	Competent

We already know that we are going to have to sort the data separately on each character position, so let's work backward from what the second sort needs as input. When we are getting ready to do the second (and final) sort, we need to know that all the AA's precede all the AB's, which precede all the AC's, etc., and that all the BA's precede the BB's, which precede the BC's. The same must be true for the keys starting with C, D, and any other letter. The reason that the second sort will preserve this organization of its input data is that it moves keys with the same character at the current character position from input to output in order of their previous position in the input data. Therefore, any two keys that have the same character in the current position (both A's, B's, C's, etc.) will maintain their relative order in the output. For example, if all of the AA's precede all of the AB's in the input, they will also do so in the output, and similarly for the BA's and BB's. This is exactly what we want. Notice that we don't care at this point whether the BA's are behind or ahead of the AB's, as arranging the data according to the first character is the job of the second sort (which we haven't done yet). But how can we ensure that all the AA's precede the AB's, which precede the AC's, etc. in the input? By sorting on the second character position!

For example, suppose we are sorting the following keys: AB, CB, BA, BC, CA, BA, BB, CC. We start the sort by counting the number of occurrences of each character in the second position of each key (the less significant position). There are three A's, three B's, and two C's. Since A is the character closest to the beginning of the alphabet, the first key that has an A in the second position goes in the first slot of the output. The second and third keys that have an A in the second position follow the first

Figure 3.9 *Less significant character sort*

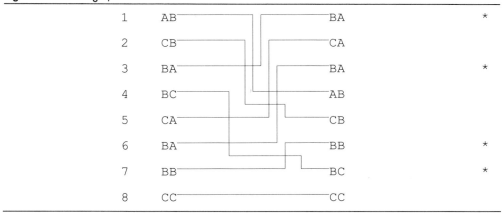

one. Those that have a B in the second position are next, in output positions 4, 5, and 6. The C's bring up the rear, producing the situation in figure 3.9.

After this first sort (on the second character position), all of the keys that have an A in the second position are ahead of all of the keys that have a B in the second position, which precede all those that have a C in the second position. Therefore, all AA keys precede all AB keys, which precede all AC keys, and the same is true for BA, BB, BC and CA, CB, and CC as well. This is the exact arrangement of input needed for the second sort.

Now we are ready for the second, and final, sorting operation. We start by counting the number of occurrences of each character in the first, or more significant, position. There is one A in this position, along with four B's, and three C's. Starting with the lowest character value, the key that has an A in this position ends up in the first slot of the output. The B's follow, starting with the second slot. Remember that the keys are already in order by their second, or less significant, character, because of our previous sort. This is important when we consider the order of keys that have the same first character. In figure 3.9, the asterisks mark the keys that start with B.[28] They are in order by their second character, since we have just sorted on that character. Therefore, when we rearrange the keys by their first character position, those that have the same first character will be in order by their second character as well, since we always move keys from the input to the output in order of their position in the input. That means that the B records have the same order in the output that they had in the input, as you can see in figure 3.10.

This may seem like a lot of work to sort a few strings. However, the advantage of this method when we have many keys to be sorted is that the processing for each pass is extremely simple, requiring only a few machine instructions per byte handled (less than 30 on the 80x86 family).

---

28. Of course, we could just as well have used the keys that start with any other character.

Figure 3.10 *More significant character sort*

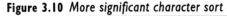

1	BA	AB
2	CA	BA
3	BA	BA
4	AB	BB
5	CB	BC
6	BB	CA
7	BC	CB
8	CC	CC

On the Home Stretch

Having finished sorting the keys, we have only to retrieve the records we want from the input file in sorted order and write them to the output file. In our example, this requires reading records from strip two and writing the required data into an output record. But how do we know which records we need to read and in what order?

The sort routine requires more than just the keys to be sorted. We also have to give it a list of the record numbers to which those keys correspond, so that it can rearrange that list in the same way that it rearranges the keys. Then we can use the rearranged list of record numbers to retrieve the records in the correct order, which completes the task of our program.

The Code

Now we're ready to look at the implementation of these algorithms. Function `main` (in file "mail.c", listing 3.5, lines 20–73) begins by checking the number of arguments with which it was called, and exits with an informative message if there aren't enough. Otherwise, it constructs the key (first strip) and data (second strip) file names and opens the files for binary input. Then it calls the `initialize` routine at lines 76–89 to set up the selection criteria according to input arguments 3 through 6 (minimum spent, maximum spent, earliest last-here date, and latest last-here date). Now we are ready to call `process` (lines 91–210) to select the records that meet those criteria.

The first order of business in `process` is to set up the buffering for the key and data files (lines 91–210). It is important to note that we are using a large buffer for the key file and a small one (one record) for the data file. What is the reason for this discrepancy?

Determining the Proper Buffer Size

Since we are going to read every record in the key file in physical order, a large buffer is very helpful in reducing the number of physical disk accesses needed. As I mentioned above, using a buffer of 32 Kbytes reduces the time needed to read this file by about 40%.

This analysis, however, does not apply to the data file. In this case, using a bigger buffer for the data file would actually reduce performance, since reading a large amount of data at once is helpful only if you are going to use the data that you are reading.[29] The speed of our disk accessing algorithm is based on the fact that we have to read a particular data record (from strip two) only after that record has satisfied our selection criteria (which we can determine by reading the corresponding key file record from strip one). When we do read the data records, it will be in order of their ZIP codes, forcing us to move to a different position in the data file for each record rather than reading them consecutively. Using a big buffer in this situation would mean that most of the data in the buffer would be irrelevant.

Preparing to Read the Key File

Continuing in **process**, we calculate the number of records in the key file (lines 121–124), which determines how large our record selection bitmap should be. Then we call the macro **allocate_bitmap**, defined in "bitfunc.h" (listing 3.8, line 11) to allocate storage for the bitmap. Of course, each byte of a bitmap can store eight bits, so the macro divides the number of bits we need by eight and adds one byte to the result. The extra byte is to accommodate any remainder after the division by eight.

Now that we have allocated our bitmap, we can read through the key file and select the records that meet our criteria (listing 3.5, lines 128–165). After initializing our counts of "items read" and "found" to zero, we are ready to start reading records. Of course, we could calculate the number of times through the loop rather than continue until we run off the end of the input file, since we know how many records there are in the file. However, since we are processing records in batches, the last of which is likely to be smaller than the rest, we might as well take advantage of the fact that when we get a short count of **items_read,** the operating system is telling us that we have reached the end of the file.

---

29. There are some situations where this is not strictly true. For example, suppose we want to read a large fraction of the records in a file in physical order, and the records are only a few hundred bytes or less. In that case, it is almost certainly faster to read them all with a big buffer and skip the ones we aren't interested in. The gain from reading large chunks of data at once is likely to outweigh the time lost in reading some unwanted records.

Reading the Key File

The first thing we do in the "infinite" loop is to read a set of `processing_batch` records (to avoid the overhead of calling the operating system to read each record). Now we are ready to process one record at a time in the inner loop (lines 134–161). Of course, we want to know whether the record we are examining meets our selection criteria, which are whether the customer has spent at least `min_spent`, no more than `max_spent,` and has last been here between `min_date` and `max_date` (inclusive). If the record fails to meet any of these criteria, we skip the remainder of the processing for this record via "continue". However, let's suppose that a record passes these four tests.

In that case, we increment `items_found.` Then we want to set the bit in the found bitmap that corresponds to this record. To do this, we need to calculate the current record number, by adding the number of records read before the current processing batch (`total_items_read`) and the entry number in the current batch (`i`). Now we are ready to call `setbit` (listing 3.9, lines 6–27).

Setting a Bit in a Bitmap

The `setbit` routine is quite simple. Since there are eight bits in a byte, we have to calculate which byte we need to access (line 13) and which bit within that byte (line 15). Once we have calculated these two values, we can retrieve the appropriate byte from the bitmap (line 17).

In order to set the bit we are interested in, we need to create a "mask" to isolate that bit from the others in the same byte. This code, in line 19, may seem mysterious, but all we are doing is generating a value that has a 1 in the same position as the bit we are interested in and 0 in all other positions. Therefore, after we perform a "logical or" operation of the mask and the byte from the bitmap (line 21), the resulting value, stored back into the bitmap, will have the desired bit set.

This `setbit` routine also returns a value indicating the value of the bit before we set it (lines 23–23). Thus, if we want to know whether we have actually changed the bit from off to on, we don't have to make a call to `testbit` before the call to `setbit`; we can use the return value from `setbit` to determine whether the bit was set before we called `setbit`. This would be useful, for example, in an application where the bitmap was being used to allocate some resource, such as a printer, which cannot be used by more than one process at a time. The routine would call `setbit` and, if that bit had already been set, would return an error indicating that the resource was not available.

Now we have a means of keeping track of which records have been selected. However, we also need to save the ZIP code for each selected record for our sort. Unfortunately, we don't know how many records are going to be selected until we select them. This is easily dealt with in the case of the bitmap, which is so economical of storage that we can comfortably allocate a bit for every record in the file; ZIP codes, which take ten bytes apiece, pose a more difficult problem. We need a method of allocation which can provide storage for an unknown number of ZIP codes.

Allocate as You Go

Of course, we could use a simple linked list. In that approach, every time we found a record that matches our criteria, we would allocate storage for a ZIP code and a pointer to the next ZIP code. However, this consumes storage very rapidly, as additional memory is required to keep track of every allocation of storage. When very small blocks of ten bytes or so are involved, the overhead can easily exceed the amount of storage actually used for our purposes, so that allocating 5000 14-byte blocks can easily take 150 Kbytes or more, rather than the 70 Kbytes that we might expect.

To avoid this inefficiency, we can allocate larger blocks that can accommodate a number of ZIP codes each, and keep track of the addresses of each of these larger blocks so that we can retrieve individual ZIP codes later. That is the responsibility of lines 148–156.

To understand how this works, let's look back at lines 113–114, which set `current_zip_block` to -1 and `current_zip_entry` to `ZIP_BLOCK_ENTRIES`. This initialization ensures that the code in the "if" will be executed for the first selected record. We start by incrementing `current_zip_block` (to zero, in this case) and setting `current_zip_entry` to zero, to start a new block. Then we allocate storage for a new block of ZIP codes (`zip_block`) and set up pointers to each one (`temp_zip_pointer`) so that we can copy the ZIP codes from the keys as we select each record.

Once that bookkeeping is out of the way, we can copy the ZIP code for the current record into the ZIP block via the `temp_zip_pointer` pointer array and increment which pointer in the array will be used next (`current_zip_entry`).

Now we're at the end of the processing for one record in a processing batch. Once all the records in the batch have been processed, we fall off the end of the inner loop at line 161. At this point, we can add the number of items we have read in this batch to `total_items_read`. If we have read less than a full batch, we must have reached the end of the file, so we are finished with this phase of processing (at line 165).

Getting Ready to Sort

Now that we have all the information needed to sort the keys, we can read the records in ZIP code order. However, the sort routine, `Megasort` (listing 3.6) requires that information in a different form. Looking at the parameters for this routine, on lines 10–11, we see that the data to be sorted are described by an array of string pointers (`unsigned char **PtrArray`), whereas what we have is a number of blocks of ZIP codes. The record numbers, which the sort routine will rearrange according to the order of the ZIP codes, must be passed as an array of unsigned values (`unsigned *RecNums`), rather than as the bitmap in which they are stored by our search routine.

To set up the first argument to `Megasort`, we need to produce an array of pointers to each of the ZIP codes we have stored in the blocks, which we do in listing 3.22 on lines 167–180.

We start by allocating a block of ZIP code pointers (`zip_pointer`) that can hold all the pointers we will need (`items_found`). Then, for each block of ZIP codes we have created (`zip_block[i]`), we calculate the address of each ZIP code in the block and store it in an entry of our `zip_pointer` array.

That takes care of the pointers to the ZIP codes. Now we have to turn the bitmap into an array of record numbers to be rearranged. That is the task of lines 182-191. First we allocate the array of unsigned values, with `items_found` entries. Then we call `testbit` (listing 3.9, lines 54–73) for every record number in the file, and every time we find a bit set, we store that record number in the next available space in the `record_number` array. The `testbit` routine is very similar to `setbit`, described above. The difference is that we don't want to set the bit, but to find out whether it is already set; therefore, we don't modify the bitmap array. Now we are finally ready to call `Megasort` (listing 3.6).

The Megasort Routine

The main variables involved are the `BucketCount` array, which keeps track of the number of strings that have each character in the current sorting position (the number of A's, B's, etc.), and the `BucketPosition` array, which maintains the current position in the output array for each possible character (where the next A string should go, the next B string, etc.). We also have to allocate storage to the `TempPtrArray` variable for a copy of the pointers to the strings, and to the `TempRecNums` variable for a copy of the record numbers to be rearranged. All of this setup code having been executed between lines 27 and 41, the main sorting loop is ready to go.

You may be surprised to see how few lines of code are involved in the main loop. If we disregard blank lines and those that contain only a starting or ending brace, only 17 lines contain any executable code. Yet in many common applications this simple algorithm will outperform all of the complex methods favored by the computer science textbooks.

The outer loop is executed once for each character position in the sort. That is, if we are sorting a number of ten-character strings, it will be executed ten times. Its role is to select which character of the strings to be sorted will be used in the current pass through the strings. The reason that the loop index i decreases for each pass through the loop was discussed above: each character position is treated as a separate "key", so we have to sort on the least significant "key" first and work our way up to the most significant one. Each pass of this sort leaves strings in the same order as they were in before the current pass if they have the same character in the current position.

The first operation in the main loop is to use the **memset** routine to clear the **BucketCount** array, which maintains the counts for each possible ASCII character code (line 43). In the first pass through the input data (lines 45–49) we step through **PtrArray**, selecting the ith character as the current character to be sorted from each element of the array. The ASCII value of that character, m, is used to select the element of **BucketCount** to be incremented, so that when we reach the end of the pointer array, we will know the number of strings that have that character in the current position being sorted.

Once all the counts have been accumulated, we can use that information to fill in the **BucketPosition** array, which indicates the next available slot for each possible character position (lines 51–53). This serves the function of directing traffic from the input pointer array **PtrArray** to the output one, **TempPtrArray**. Each element in the **BucketPosition** array corresponds to the next output position to be used in **TempPtrArray** for a given character. For example, suppose that the lowest character in the current position of the array to be sorted is 'A', and there are five strings that have an 'A' in the current position. In that case, the initial value of **BucketPosition['A']** would be 0, and the initial value of **BucketPosition['B']** would be 5, since the first 'A' key should go into output slot 0 and the first 'B' key should go into output slot 5.

After filling in the **BucketPosition** array, we are ready to rearrange the pointers to the keys by copying these pointers into the temporary array **TempPtrArray**. That is done in the second inner loop through all the keys (lines 55-61). First, we calculate the appropriate index into the **BucketPosition** array by retrieving the character from the input string, as in the first inner loop above. Then we use that index to retrieve the appropriate element of the **BucketPosition** array, which we will use to copy both the key pointer and the record number of the current record into the output arrays, **TempPtrArray** and **TempRecNums**, respectively.

Then we increment the element of **BucketPosition** that we have used, because the next key that has that particular character in the current position should go in the next position of the output. In our example, after the first 'A' key has been copied into the output array, **BucketPosition['A']** would be incremented to 1, meaning that the next 'A' key should go into output slot 1. Similarly, after the first 'B' key has been copied into the output array, **BucketPosition['B']** would be incremented to 6, meaning that the next 'B' key should go into output slot 6.

After copying all of the pointers from **PtrArray** into **TempPtrArray**, and all of the record numbers from **RecNums** into **TempRecNums** in sorted order, we copy them back into the original arrays for use in the next sorting pass, if there is one, or as the final result if we are done.

Finishing Up

When we are done with the sort, we can return the sorted keys and record numbers to **process** (listing 3.5, at line 196), so that we can retrieve and print the first and last name and the ZIP code for each customer in order by their ZIP codes. This task is accomplished in lines 198–201. We then free the dynamic storage used in the routine and return to the main program, which calls `terminate` to close the files, then exits.

Performance

You may be wondering how much performance improvement we have obtained by using strip files and distribution sorting in our example program, "mail.c". In order to answer this question, I have written another program, "mailx.c" (listing 3.2), which is identical to "mail.c", with the exception of these two optimizations. Unlike our earlier comparison of `qsort` with the distribution sort, where we excluded the overhead of calling the comparison routine, the following profiles indicate the total time actually needed to execute the programs.

These execution profiles consist of information extracted from the output of Borland's Turbo Profiler™, during runs which resulted in the selection of 2948 records out of 4573 in the input file.

The profile in figure 3.11 represents the results of executing "mailx.exe". Approximately 99% of the execution time is accounted for by the six lines listed. These are, in order: the call to `qsort` to sort the records by their ZIP codes; the `fread` call that reads each selected data record for printing; the `fprintf` call to write the results to the output file; the `fread` call to read records for selection on the first pass; the call to `fseek` to position to the next selected record in ZIP code order during the second pass; and the call to `fclose` to close the output file, which flushes the output buffer.

The profile in figure 3.12 represents the results of executing "maily.exe", which is the mailing list program after implementing strip files and the distribution counting sort. At that point, over 94% of the total time was accounted for by the six lines listed. These are, in order: the `fread` call that reads each selected data record for printing;[30] the `fprintf` call to write the results to the output file; the call to `fseek` to position to the next selected record in ZIP code order during the second pass; the call to `fclose` to close the output file, which flushes the output buffer; the `fread` call to read records for selection on the first pass; and the call to `Megasort` to sort the records by their ZIP codes.

I admit that when I first saw the above result, it didn't seem that there was much more to be gained from further attempts at optimization, as over 80% of the remaining time used by the program consisted of positioning the input file to the selected records

---

30. You may wonder why this operation takes only a third as much time as the corresponding line in the previous profile. The reason is that the `Megasort` routine does not move records around that are already in the right relative order, which many of them are; `qsort` causes much more head motion by rearranging such records.

Figure 3.11 *Profile of mailx.exe*

```
Turbo Profiler  Version 1.1  Sun Aug 25 21:26:00 1991
Program: C:\OPT\MAIL\MAILX.EXE
Total time: 66.248 sec

#MAILX#187      41.861 sec  63% (qsort)
#MAILX#195      15.018 sec  22% (fread pass 2)
#MAILX#196      4.4277 sec   6% (fprintf)
#MAILX#136      1.9892 sec   2% (fread pass 1)
#MAILX#193      1.7190 sec   2% (fseek)
#MAILX#213      0.5838 sec  <1% (fclose)
```

Figure 3.12 *Profile of maily.exe*

```
Turbo Profiler  Version 1.1  Sun Aug 25 20:59:15 1991
Program: C:\OPT\MAIL\MAILY.EXE
Total time: 13.330 sec

#MAILY#203      5.3817 sec  40% (fread pass 2)
#MAILY#205      4.2302 sec  31% (fprintf)
#MAILY#202      1.7095 sec  12% (fseek)
#MAILY#222      0.6134 sec   4% (fclose)
#MAILY#137      0.3700 sec   2% (fread pass 1)
#MAILY#197      0.2791 sec   2% (Megasort)
```

in order of their ZIP codes, reading the records, and writing formatted output to the output file. None of these operations seemed to be a good candidate for further optimization other than by rewriting the library routines that they employ, which is beyond the scope of this book. However, I was wrong, as you can see by the profile of the final version of "mail.exe", in figure 3.13.

Approximately 92% of the time is accounted for by the six lines listed, which are the same lines as in "maily.exe", although in a different order. What is the magic responsible for this additional 45% speedup after everything seemed to have been wrung out of the program?

The only changes from "maily.exe" to "mail.exe" were opening the output file with the "b" modifier (binary mode, rather than text mode, which is the default) in line 59, and the corresponding addition of a carriage return character before the line feed when writing each line to the customer list file in line 201. Those two tiny changes decreased the time needed to write the output file from 4.23 seconds to 0.662 seconds, an increase in speed for that operation of 6.4 to 1. It seems to me that such a large variance in performance from such a small change should be noted in the Borland C manual, but it isn't.

Figure 3.13 *Profile of mail.exe*

```
Turbo Profiler  Version 1.1  Sun Aug 25 20:53:43 1991
Program: C:\OPT\MAIL\MAIL.EXE
Total time: 9.1708 sec

#MAIL#203    5.1765 sec    56%  (fread pass 2)
#MAIL#202    1.7299 sec    18%  (fseek)
#MAIL#205    0.6617 sec     7%  (fprintf)
#MAIL#137    0.3698 sec     4%  (fread pass 1)
#MAIL#197    0.2792 sec     3%  (Megasort)
#MAIL#222    0.1971 sec     2%  (fclose)
```

Finally, we are prepared to determine how much all our efforts have gained. We have managed to increase the speed of the program by a factor of 66.2/9.17, or 7.2 to 1, more than enough to spell the difference between success and failure in many commercial projects.

For the record, all of the above profiles were run on a 33-MHz i386 with a 28-msec disk drive, with software disk caching disabled. Of course, the relative speed improvement would probably be different on a differently configured computer: I achieved an increase in speed of almost 10 to 1 on a 12-MHz 80286-based computer with a 23-msec disk drive, with software disk caching disabled. However, the improvement is likely to be substantial on any machine.

Back to the Future

The above was originally written in 1992, for the first edition of this book. Since that edition was published, I have discovered that the version of `qsort` in Borland C++ 2.0, current at that time, was defective; it therefore does not fairly represent the inherent characteristics of the Quicksort algorithm. Therefore, when preparing the current edition, I decided to run experiments similar to those described above, to see how the overall times would come out. Of course, my home machine no longer has a i386 CPU, as it did then; rather it is a 486/66DX2 with a 12-msec hard disk. These runs select 3513 records out of 4730 in the input files, but I assumed this fairly minor difference would be overwhelmed by the improvement in my hardware resources. Imagine my surprise when the profile in figure 3.14 turned up for "mailx.exe".

The `qsort` problem has certainly been fixed; even multiplying the new time by 5 to take account of the much faster CPU speed of my new machine, it's about 40 times as fast as the old version. But what could possibly cause the `fread` time to more than double?

The first thing to check is whether the final "mail.exe" exhibits the same strange behavior. The profile is shown in figure 3.15. This is even worse: the fread time is seven times what it was before! I was really at a loss; my hard disk is supposed to be over twice as **fast** as the old one, not many times slower.

As often happens, after putting the problem out of my mind for a few hours, my "background task" came up with the answer: it must be the composition of the data. The original data came from a business with a very local clientele, so that most of the records had one of a few ZIP codes; in addition, most of the ZIP codes weren't even filled in but were left blank. However, I had foolishly not saved the original data and therefore had to make up a new set to use for my tests; I generated these new test records from a national telephone directory CD/ROM, so their ZIP codes were scattered all over the place.

To test this theory, I modified my test data generator to produce test data that more closely resembled the original; about 55% of the records have a blank ZIP code, and 3/4 of the rest share one of three ZIP codes. Only 11% of the records have the ZIP codes from the CD/ROM data. As you can see from figure 3.16, the results of this test of "mailx.exe" are much more reasonable.

The same is true for my test of "mail.exe" (figure 3.17).

Here's another interesting point to be gleaned from these profiles: the great difference in speed between "binary" output and "text" output that we saw in Borland

Figure 3.14 *New profile of mailx.exe*

```
Turbo Profiler   Version 2.1   Thu May 05 23:14:46 1994
Program: C:\OPT\MAIL\MAILX.EXE
Total time: 40.723 sec

#MAILX#195        37.622 sec   93%  (fread pass 2)
#MAILX#196        0.9075 sec    2%  (fprintf)
#MAILX#193        0.8181 sec    1%  (fseek)
#MAILX#136        0.7352 sec    1%  (fread pass 1)
#MAILX#187        0.1987 sec   <1%  (qsort)
```

Figure 3.15 *New profile of mail.exe*

```
Turbo Profiler   Version 2.1   Thu May 05 20:47:10 1994
Program: C:\OPT\MAIL\MAIL.EXE
Total time: 38.016 sec

#MAIL#203         36.262 sec   95%  (fread pass 2)
#MAIL#202         0.8062 sec    2%  (fseek)
#MAIL#205         0.5118 sec    1%  (printf)
#MAIL#137         0.1314 sec   <1%  (fread pass 1)
#MAIL#197         0.1191 sec   <1%  (Megasort)
```

Figure 3.16 *New profile of mailx.exe with comparable data composition*

```
Turbo Profiler  Version 2.1  Thu May 05 23:10:41 1994
Program: C:\OPT\MAIL\MAILX.EXE
Total time: 14.272 sec

#MAILX#195        11.272 sec   81%  (fread pass 2)
#MAILX#196         0.9637 sec    6%  (fprintf)
#MAILX#193         0.8122 sec    5%  (fseek)
#MAILX#136         0.7439 sec    5%  (fread pass 1)
#MAILX#187         0.0423 sec   <1%  (qsort)
```

Figure 3.17 *New profile of mail.exe with comparable data composition*

```
Turbo Profiler  Version 2.1  Thu May 05 08:15:08 1994
Program: C:\OPT\MAIL\MAIL.EXE
Total time: 6.5987 sec

#MAIL#203          4.9025 sec   76%  (fread pass 2)
#MAIL#202          0.7850 sec   12%  (fseek)
#MAIL#205          0.4315 sec    6%  (fprintf)
#MAIL#137          0.1408 sec    2%  (fread pass 1)
#MAIL#197          0.1185 sec    1%  (Megasort)
```

C++ 2.0 has been reduced significantly. Text output is only about twice as slow as binary, rather than the 6 to 1 ratio previously obtaining.

Finally, you will notice one rather ironic fact; according to the profiler, in this latest comparison, qsort is almost three times as fast as Megasort! However, the disk accesses in "mail.exe" take much less time than those in "mailx.exe", since Megasort doesn't rearrange records that were in the correct order in the input file; this effect completely swamps the relatively minor extra CPU time needed to do the sort. As a result, we have still accomplished a speed increase of over 2 to 1. Is there a moral to this story?

Moral Support

Actually, there are several. The first might be that it's possible that a well-respected compiler vendor can overlook very serious performance problems in its libraries. When this happens, it's very helpful to have another way to get our problem solved.

Another moral might be that the characteristics of an algorithm can contribute to the performance of the final program in unexpected ways. We originally turned to Megasort to remedy performance deficits in qsort, but even after qsort was fixed, we were better off using Megasort, as it does not rearrange records that are already in order in the input file.

Yet another lesson to be drawn from this example is that what at first seems to be a significant speed improvement can be virtually insignificant in the final product. I anticipated that speeding up pass one by "strip mining" would be an major contributor to the performance increase of the final version, but in our final results it contributed .6 seconds of the performance improvement of 7.7 seconds, or about 8% of the time reduction. The reason for this misjudgment is that I did not realize how much of the time would go to random reads of the input file in pass two, since my original test program selected so few records.

The common thread of all of these lessons is that no matter how carefully you plan a programming task, the unexpected is very likely to occur. You have to be willing to examine all your preconceptions and discard them if necessary in the face of new evidence. Perhaps this willingness, along with the ability to handle the unexpected when it occurs, is the difference between a novice and an expert.

Summary

In this chapter, we have covered the use of a bitmap to keep track of one attribute of a number of records, sorting via the distribution counting sort, and how to gain rapid access to data according to criteria specified at runtime, by searching a strip file. In the next chapter we will see how to use assembly language to speed up the operation of the arithmetic coding method of data compression.

Problems

What modifications to the distribution counting sort would be needed to:

1. Arrange the output in descending order rather than ascending order?

2. Make only one pass through the data for each character position, rather than two as at present?

3. Add the ability to handle integer or floating-point data rather than character data?

4. Add the ability to handle variable-length strings as keys?

(You can find suggested approaches to problems in Chapter 8).

Listing 3.1 *mailx.h: mailing list include file*

```
1
2   /****keyword-flag*** "%v %f %n" */
3   /* "6 20-Aug-92,20:38:26 MAILX.H" */
4
5
6   #include <string.h>
7
8   #define DATA_FIELD_COUNT 9
9   #define BATCH_SIZE 100
10  #define ZIPBLOCK_COUNT 150
11  #define ZIP_BLOCK_ENTRIES 100
12
13  #define MAX_ASCII_FIELD_LENGTH 15
14
15  #define LAST_NAME_LENGTH 15
16  #define FIRST_NAME_LENGTH 9
17  #define ADDRESS1_LENGTH 15
18  #define ADDRESS2_LENGTH 15
19  #define CITY_LENGTH 12
20  #define STATE_LENGTH 2
21  #define ZIP_LENGTH 9
22
23  #define ASCII_DATE_LENGTH 10
24  #define ASCII_CENTS_LENGTH 10
25
26  #define BINARY_DATE_LENGTH 2
27  #define BINARY_DOLLARS_LENGTH 2
28
29  typedef struct
30  {
31    char last_name[LAST_NAME_LENGTH+1];
32    char first_name[FIRST_NAME_LENGTH+1];
33    char address1[ADDRESS1_LENGTH+1];
34    char address2[ADDRESS2_LENGTH+1];
35    char city[CITY_LENGTH+1];
36    char state[STATE_LENGTH+1];
37    char zip[ZIP_LENGTH+1];
38    int date_last_here;
39    int dollars_spent;
40  } DataRecord;
41
42  typedef struct
43  {
44    int min_spent;
45    int max_spent;
46    int min_date;
47    int max_date;
48  } CustomerSelection;
49
50  typedef struct
51  {
```

Listing 3.1 *mailx.h: mailing list include file (continued)*

```
52      char zip[ZIP_LENGTH+1];
53      unsigned record_number;
54  } ZipRecord;
55
56  void Megasort(unsigned char **PtrArray, unsigned *RecNums, int KeyLength,
57  unsigned ArraySize );
58
```

Listing 3.2 *mailx.c: mailing list program*

```
1
2     /****keyword-flag*** "%v %f %n" */
3     /* "10 12-May-92,19:23:14 MAILX.C" */
4
5
6     #include <stdio.h>
7     #include <stdlib.h>
8     #include "mailx.h"
9     #include "bitfunc.h"
10    #include "date.h"
11
12    extern unsigned _stklen = 32000;
13
14    int data_field_length[DATA_FIELD_COUNT] = {15,9,15,15,12,2,9};
15    char *data_field_name[DATA_FIELD_COUNT] = {"LAST NAME", "FIRST NAME",
16    "ADDRESS1","ADDRESS2","CITY","STATE","ZIP"};
17
18    CustomerSelection initialize(char *min,char *max,char *start,char *end);
19    void process(FILE *customer_data_file, FILE *customer_list_file,
20    CustomerSelection customer_selection);
21    void terminate(FILE *customer_data_file, FILE *customer_list_file);
22
23    void main(int argc, char *argv[])
24    {
25      FILE *customer_data_file;
26      FILE *customer_list_file;
27      char customer_data_file_name[100];
28      char customer_list_file_name[100];
29      CustomerSelection customer_selection;
30
31      if (argc < 6)
32          {
33          printf("Usage: mailx customer_file min max start end\n");
34          exit(1);
35          }
36
37      strcpy(customer_data_file_name,argv[1]);
38      strcat(customer_data_file_name,".dat");
39      strcpy(customer_list_file_name,argv[1]);
40      strcat(customer_list_file_name,".lst");
41
42      customer_data_file = fopen(customer_data_file_name,"rb");
43
44      if (customer_data_file == NULL)
45          {
46          printf("Cannot open file %s.\n",customer_data_file_name);
47          exit(1);
48          }
49
50      customer_list_file = fopen(customer_list_file_name,"w");
51
```

Listing 3.2 *mailx.c: mailing list program (continued)*

```
52    if (customer_list_file == NULL)
53        {
54        printf("Cannot open file %s.\n",customer_list_file_name);
55        exit(1);
56        }
57
58    setvbuf(customer_list_file, NULL, _IOFBF, 32000);
59
60    customer_selection = initialize(argv[2],argv[3],argv[4],argv[5]);
61
62    process(customer_data_file, customer_list_file, customer_selection);
63
64    terminate(customer_data_file, customer_list_file);
65  }
66
67
68  CustomerSelection initialize(char *min,char *max,char *start,char *end)
69  {
70    CustomerSelection temp_selection;
71
72    temp_selection.min_spent = atoi(min);
73
74    temp_selection.max_spent = atoi(max);
75
76    temp_selection.min_date = date_string_to_days(start);
77
78    temp_selection.max_date = date_string_to_days(end);
79
80    return(temp_selection);
81  }
82
83
84  int sort_function(const void *a, const void *b)
85  {
86    return(strcmp(*(char **)a,*(char **)b));
87  }
88
89  void process(FILE *customer_data_file, FILE *customer_list_file,
90  CustomerSelection customer_selection)
91  {
92    int i;
93    unsigned k;
94    unsigned zip_block_start;
95    unsigned zip_count;
96    unsigned zip_entry;
97    unsigned items_read;
98    unsigned total_items_read;
99    DataRecord search_record[BATCH_SIZE];
100   DataRecord data_record;
101   long data_file_length;
102   long data_file_count;
```

Listing 3.2 *mailx.c: mailing list program (continued)*

```
103    char *found;
104    ZipRecord *temp_zip_pointer[ZIP_BLOCK_ENTRIES];
105    ZipRecord **zip_pointer;
106    ZipRecord *zip_block[ZIP_BLOCK_COUNT];
107    unsigned items_found;
108    char *file_buffer;
109    int processing_batch = BATCH_SIZE;
110    int current_zip_block = -1;
111    int current_zip_entry = ZIP_BLOCK_ENTRIES;
112
113    fseek(customer_data_file, 0L, SEEK_END);
114    data_file_length = ftell(customer_data_file);
115    fseek(customer_data_file, 0L, SEEK_SET);
116
117    data_file_count = data_file_length / sizeof(DataRecord);
118    fseek(customer_data_file, 0L, SEEK_SET);
119
120    file_buffer = calloc(32000,1);
121    setvbuf(customer_data_file, file_buffer, _IOFBF, 32000);
122
123    found = allocate_bitmap(data_file_count);
124
125    items_found = 0;
126    total_items_read = 0;
127    for (;;)
128        {
129        items_read = fread(search_record, sizeof(DataRecord), processing_batch,
130        customer_data_file);
131        for (i = 0; i < items_read; i ++)
132            {
133            if (search_record[i].dollars_spent < customer_selection.min_spent)
134                continue;
135            if (search_record[i].dollars_spent > customer_selection.max_spent)
136                continue;
137            if (search_record[i].date_last_here < customer_selection.min_date)
138                continue;
139            if (search_record[i].date_last_here > customer_selection.max_date)
140                continue;
141
142            items_found ++;
143            setbit(found,(long)(i+total_items_read));
144
145            if (current_zip_entry == ZIP_BLOCK_ENTRIES)
146                {
147                current_zip_block ++;
148                current_zip_entry = 0;
149                zip_block[current_zip_block] = (ZipRecord *)
150                calloc(ZIP_BLOCK_ENTRIES,sizeof(ZipRecord));
151                for (k = 0; k < ZIP_BLOCK_ENTRIES; k ++)
152                    temp_zip_pointer[k] = zip_block[current_zip_block] + k;
```

Listing 3.2 *mailx.c: mailing list program (continued)*

```
153                             }
154
155                     memcpy(&temp_zip_pointer[current_zip_entry]->zip,
156                     search_record[i].zip,ZIP_LENGTH+1);
157                     temp_zip_pointer[current_zip_entry]->record_number =
158                     i+total_items_read;
159                     current_zip_entry ++;
160                     }
161             total_items_read += items_read;
162             if (items_read != processing_batch)
163                 break;
164             }
165
166      zip_pointer = (ZipRecord **)calloc(items_found,sizeof(ZipRecord *));
167      zip_block_start = 0;
168      for (i = 0; i <= current_zip_block; i ++)
169          {
170          if (i < current_zip_block)
171                  zip_count = ZIP_BLOCK_ENTRIES;
172          else
173                  zip_count = items_found-zip_block_start;
174          for (zip_entry = 0; zip_entry < zip_count; zip_entry ++)
175                  {
176                  zip_pointer[zip_block_start+zip_entry] = zip_block[i] + zip_entry;
177                  }
178          zip_block_start += zip_entry;
179          }
180
181      qsort(zip_pointer,items_found,sizeof(ZipRecord *),sort_function);
182
183      setvbuf(customer_data_file, file_buffer, _IOFBF, sizeof(DataRecord));
184
185      for (i = 0; i < items_found; i ++)
186          {
187          fseek(customer_data_file,
188          (long)(zip_pointer[i]->record_number)*(long)sizeof(DataRecord),SEEK_SET);
189          fread(&data_record, sizeof(DataRecord), 1, customer_data_file);
190          fprintf(customer_list_file,"%s %s %s\n",data_record.first_name,
191          data_record.last_name,zip_pointer[i]->zip);
192          }
193
194      free(file_buffer);
195      free(found);
196      free(zip_pointer);
197      for (i = 0; i <= current_zip_block; i ++)
198          free(zip_block[i]);
199
200  }
201
202
```

Listing 3.2 *mailx.c: mailing list program (continued)*

```
203
204    void terminate(FILE *customer_data_file, FILE *customer_list_file)
205    {
206      fclose(customer_data_file);
207      fclose(customer_list_file);
208    }
209
210
```

Listing 3.3 *mail.h: mailing list include file*

```
 1
 2    /****keyword-flag*** "%v %f %n" */
 3    /* "6 20-Aug-92,20:37:40 MAIL.H" */
 4
 5
 6    #include <string.h>
 7
 8    #define DATA_FIELD_COUNT 6
 9    #define BATCH_SIZE 100
10    #define ZIP_BLOCK_COUNT 150
11    #define ZIP_BLOCK_ENTRIES 100
12
13    #define MAX_ASCII_FIELD_LENGTH 15
14
15    #define LAST_NAME_LENGTH 15
16    #define FIRST_NAME_LENGTH 9
17    #define ADDRESS1_LENGTH 15
18    #define ADDRESS2_LENGTH 15
19    #define CITY_LENGTH 12
20    #define STATE_LENGTH 2
21    #define ZIP_LENGTH 9
22
23    #define ASCII_DATE_LENGTH 10
24    #define ASCII_CENTS_LENGTH 10
25
26    #define BINARY_DATE_LENGTH 2
27    #define BINARY_DOLLARS_LENGTH 2
28
29    typedef struct
30    {
31      char last_name[LAST_NAME_LENGTH+1];
32      char first_name[FIRST_NAME_LENGTH+1];
33      char address1[ADDRESS1_LENGTH+1];
34      char address2[ADDRESS2_LENGTH+1];
35      char city[CITY_LENGTH+1];
36      char state[STATE_LENGTH+1];
37    } DataRecord;
38
39    typedef struct
40    {
41      char zip[ZIP_LENGTH+1];
42      int date_last_here;
43      int dollars_spent;
44    } KeyRecord;
45
46    typedef struct
47    {
48      int min_spent;
49      int max_spent;
50      int min_date;
51      int max_date;
```

Listing 3.3 *mail.h: mailing list include file (continued)*

```
52    } CustomerSelection;
53
54    typedef struct
55    {
56      char zip[ZIP_LENGTH+1];
57    } ZipRecord;
58
59    void Megasort(unsigned char **PtrArray, unsigned *RecNums, int KeyLength,
60    unsigned ArraySize);
61
```

Listing 3.4 *maily.c: mailing list program*

```
1
2     /****keyword-flag*** "%v %f %n" */
3     /* "3 12-May-92,19:30:10 MAILY.C" */
4
5
6     #include <stdio.h>
7     #include <stdlib.h>
8     #include "mail.h"
9     #include "bitfunc.h"
10    #include "date.h"
11
12    extern unsigned _stklen = 32000;
13
14    CustomerSelection initialize(char *min,char *max,char *start,char *end);
15    void process(FILE *customer_key_file, FILE *customer_data_file,
16    FILE *customer_list_file, CustomerSelection customer_selection);
17    void terminate(FILE *customer_key_file, FILE *customer_data_file,
18    FILE *customer_list_file);
19
20    void main(int argc, char *argv[])
21    {
22      FILE *customer_key_file;
23      FILE *customer_data_file;
24      FILE *customer_list_file;
25      char customer_key_file_name[100];
26      char customer_data_file_name[100];
27      char customer_list_file_name[100];
28      CustomerSelection customer_selection;
29
30      if (argc < 6)
31          {
32          printf("Usage: mail customer_file min max start end\n");
33          exit(1);
34          }
35
36      strcpy(customer_key_file_name,argv[1]);
37      strcat(customer_key_file_name,".key");
38      strcpy(customer_data_file_name,argv[1]);
39      strcat(customer_data_file_name,".dat");
40      strcpy(customer_list_file_name,argv[1]);
41      strcat(customer_list_file_name,".lst");
42
43      customer_key_file = fopen(customer_key_file_name,"rb");
44
45      if (customer_key_file == NULL)
46          {
47          printf("Cannot open file %s.\n",customer_key_file_name);
48          exit(1);
49          }
50
51      customer_data_file = fopen(customer_data_file_name,"rb");
```

Listing 3.4 *maily.c: mailing list program (continued)*

```
52
53    if (customer_data_file == NULL)
54        {
55        printf("Cannot open file %s.\n",customer_data_file_name);
56        exit(1);
57        }
58
59    customer_list_file = fopen(customer_list_file_name,"w");
60
61    if (customer_list_file == NULL)
62        {
63        printf("Cannot open file %s.\n",customer_list_file_name);
64        exit(1);
65        }
66
67    customer_selection = initialize(argv[2],argv[3],argv[4],argv[5]);
68
69    process(customer_key_file, customer_data_file, customer_list_file,
70    customer_selection);
71
72    terminate(customer_key_file, customer_data_file, customer_list_file);
73    }
74
75
76    CustomerSelection initialize(char *min,char *max,char *start,char *end)
77    {
78      CustomerSelection temp_selection;
79
80      temp_selection.min_spent = atoi(min);
81
82      temp_selection.max_spent = atoi(max);
83
84      temp_selection.min_date = date_string_to_days(start);
85
86      temp_selection.max_date = date_string_to_days(end);
87
88      return(temp_selection);
89    }
90
91    void process(FILE *customer_key_file, FILE *customer_data_file,
92    FILE *customer_list_file, CustomerSelection customer_selection)
93    {
94      int i;
95      unsigned k;
96      unsigned zip_block_start;
97      unsigned zip_count;
98      unsigned zip_entry;
99      unsigned list_index;
100     unsigned items_read;
101     unsigned total_items_read;
102     KeyRecord key_record[BATCH_SIZE];
```

Listing 3.4 *maily.c: mailing list program (continued)*

```
103    DataRecord data_record;
104    long key_file_length;
105    int key_file_count;
106    char *found;
107    ZipRecord *temp_zip_pointer[ZIP_BLOCK_ENTRIES];
108    ZipRecord **zip_pointer;
109    ZipRecord *zip_block[ZIP_BLOCK_COUNT];
110    unsigned *record_number;
111    unsigned items_found;
112    int processing_batch = BATCH_SIZE;
113    int current_zip_block = -1;
114    int current_zip_entry = ZIP_BLOCK_ENTRIES;
115
116    setvbuf(customer_key_file, NULL, _IOFBF, 32000);
117    setvbuf(customer_list_file, NULL, _IOFBF, 32000);
118
119    setvbuf(customer_data_file, NULL, _IOFBF, sizeof(DataRecord));
120
121    fseek(customer_key_file, 0L, SEEK_END);
122    key_file_length = ftell(customer_key_file);
123    fseek(customer_key_file, 0L, SEEK_SET);
124    key_file_count = (unsigned)(key_file_length / sizeof(KeyRecord));
125
126    found = allocate_bitmap(key_file_count);
127
128    items_found = 0;
129    total_items_read = 0;
130    for (;;)
131        {
132        items_read = fread(key_record, sizeof(KeyRecord), processing_batch,
133        customer_key_file);
134        for (i = 0; i < items_read; i ++)
135            {
136            if (key_record[i].dollars_spent < customer_selection.min_spent)
137                continue;
138            if (key_record[i].dollars_spent > customer_selection.max_spent)
139                continue;
140            if (key_record[i].date_last_here < customer_selection.min_date)
141                continue;
142            if (key_record[i].date_last_here > customer_selection.max_date)
143                continue;
144
145            items_found ++;
146            setbit(found,(long)(i+total_items_read));
147
148            if (current_zip_entry == ZIP_BLOCK_ENTRIES)
149                {
150                current_zip_block ++;
151                current_zip_entry = 0;
152                zip_block[current_zip_block] = (ZipRecord *)
153                calloc(ZIP_BLOCK_ENTRIES,sizeof(ZipRecord));
```

Listing 3.4 *maily.c: mailing list program (continued)*

```
154                  for (k = 0; k < ZIP_BLOCK_ENTRIES; k ++)
155                      temp_zip_pointer[k] = zip_block[current_zip_block] + k;
156                  }
157
158              memcpy((char *)temp_zip_pointer[current_zip_entry],key_record[i].zip,
159              ZIP_LENGTH+1);
160              current_zip_entry ++;
161              }
162          total_items_read += items_read;
163          if (items_read != processing_batch)
164              break;
165          }
166
167      zip_pointer = (ZipRecord **)calloc(items_found,sizeof(ZipRecord *));
168      zip_block_start = 0;
169      for (i = 0; i <= current_zip_block; i ++)
170          {
171          if (i < current_zip_block)
172              zip_count = ZIP_BLOCK_ENTRIES;
173          else
174              zip_count = items_found-zip_block_start;
175          for (zip_entry = 0; zip_entry < zip_count; zip_entry ++)
176              {
177              zip_pointer[zip_block_start+zip_entry] = zip_block[i] + zip_entry;
178              }
179          zip_block_start += zip_entry;
180          }
181
182      record_number = (unsigned *)calloc(items_found,sizeof(int));
183      list_index = 0;
184      for (i = 0; i < key_file_count; i ++)
185          {
186          if (testbit(found,i))
187              {
188              record_number[list_index] = i;
189              list_index ++;
190              }
191          }
192
193      Megasort((char **)zip_pointer, record_number, ZIP_LENGTH, items_found);
194
195      for (i = 0; i < items_found; i ++)
196          {
197          fseek(customer_data_file,(long)record_number[i]*(long)sizeof(DataRecord),
198          SEEK_SET);
199          fread(&data_record, sizeof(DataRecord), 1, customer_data_file);
200          fprintf(customer_list_file,"%s %s %s\n",data_record.first_name,
201          data_record.last_name,zip_pointer[i]);
202          }
203
204      free(found);
```

Listing 3.4 *maily.c: mailing list program (continued)*

```
205      free(zip_pointer);
206      for (i = 0; i <= current_zip_block; i ++)
207            free(zip_block[i]);
208
209   }
210
211
212
213   void terminate(FILE *customer_key_file, FILE *customer_data_file,
214   FILE *customer_list_file)
215   {
216     fclose(customer_key_file);
217     fclose(customer_data_file);
218     fclose(customer_list_file);
219   }
220
221
```

Listing 3.5 *mail.c: mailing list program*

```
 1
 2    /****keyword-flag*** "%v %f %n" */
 3    /* "15 13-Mar-93,9:29:34 MAIL.C" */
 4
 5
 6    #include <stdio.h>
 7    #include <stdlib.h>
 8    #include "mail.h"
 9    #include "bitfunc.h"
10    #include "date.h"
11
12    extern unsigned _stklen = 32000;
13
14    CustomerSelection initialize(char *min,char *max,char *start,char *end);
15    void process(FILE *customer_key_file, FILE *customer_data_file,
16    FILE *customer_list_file, CustomerSelection customer_selection);
17    void terminate(FILE *customer_key_file, FILE *customer_data_file,
18    FILE *customer_list_file);
19
20    void main(int argc, char *argv[])
21    {
22      FILE *customer_key_file;
23      FILE *customer_data_file;
24      FILE *customer_list_file;
25      char customer_key_file_name[100];
26      char customer_data_file_name[100];
27      char customer_list_file_name[100];
28      CustomerSelection customer_selection;
29
30      if (argc < 6)
31          {
32          printf("Usage: mail customer_file min max start end\n");
33          exit(1);
34          }
35
36      strcpy(customer_key_file_name,argv[1]);
37      strcat(customer_key_file_name,".key");
38      strcpy(customer_data_file_name,argv[1]);
39      strcat(customer_data_file_name,".dat");
40      strcpy(customer_list_file_name,argv[1]);
41      strcat(customer_list_file_name,".lst");
42
43      customer_key_file = fopen(customer_key_file_name,"rb");
44
45      if (customer_key_file == NULL)
46          {
47          printf("Cannot open file %s.\n",customer_key_file_name);
48          exit(1);
49          }
50
51      customer_data_file = fopen(customer_data_file_name,"rb");
```

Listing 3.5 *mail.c: mailing list program (continued)*

```
52
53      if (customer_data_file == NULL)
54          {
55          printf("Cannot open file %s.\n",customer_data_file_name);
56          exit(1);
57          }
58
59      customer_list_file = fopen(customer_list_file_name,"wb");
60
61      if (customer_list_file == NULL)
62          {
63          printf("Cannot open file %s.\n",customer_list_file_name);
64          exit(1);
65          }
66
67      customer_selection = initialize(argv[2],argv[3],argv[4],argv[5]);
68
69      process(customer_key_file, customer_data_file, customer_list_file,
70      customer_selection);
71
72      terminate(customer_key_file, customer_data_file, customer_list_file);
73  }
74
75
76  CustomerSelection initialize(char *min,char *max,char *start,char *end)
77  {
78      CustomerSelection temp_selection;
79
80      temp_selection.min_spent = atoi(min);
81
82      temp_selection.max_spent = atoi(max);
83
84      temp_selection.min_date = date_string_to_days(start);
85
86      temp_selection.max_date = date_string_to_days(end);
87
88      return(temp_selection);
89  }
90
91  void process(FILE *customer_key_file, FILE *customer_data_file,
92  FILE *customer_list_file, CustomerSelection customer_selection)
93  {
94      int i;
95      unsigned k;
96      unsigned zip_block_start;
97      unsigned zip_count;
98      unsigned zip_entry;
99      unsigned list_index;
100     unsigned items_read;
101     unsigned total_items_read;
102     KeyRecord key_record[BATCH_SIZE];
```

Listing 3.5 *mail.c: mailing list program (continued)*

```
103     DataRecord data_record;
104     long key_file_length;
105     int key_file_count;
106     char *found;
107     ZipRecord *temp_zip_pointer[ZIP_BLOCK_ENTRIES];
108     ZipRecord **zip_pointer;
109     ZipRecord *zip_block[ZIP_BLOCK_COUNT];
110     unsigned *record_number;
111     unsigned items_found;
112     int processing_batch = BATCH_SIZE;
113     int current_zip_block = -1;
114     int current_zip_entry = ZIP_BLOCK_ENTRIES;
115
116     setvbuf(customer_key_file, NULL, _IOFBF, 32000);
117     setvbuf(customer_list_file, NULL, _IOFBF, 32000);
118
119     setvbuf(customer_data_file, NULL, _IOFBF, sizeof(DataRecord));
120
121     fseek(customer_key_file, 0L, SEEK_END);
122     key_file_length = ftell(customer_key_file);
123     fseek(customer_key_file, 0L, SEEK_SET);
124     key_file_count = (unsigned)(key_file_length / sizeof(KeyRecord));
125
126     found = allocate_bitmap(key_file_count);
127
128     items_found = 0;
129     total_items_read = 0;
130     for (;;)
131         {
132         items_read = fread(key_record, sizeof(KeyRecord), processing_batch,
133         customer_key_file);
134         for (i = 0; i < items_read; i ++)
135             {
136             if (key_record[i].dollars_spent < customer_selection.min_spent)
137                 continue;
138             if (key_record[i].dollars_spent > customer_selection.max_spent)
139                 continue;
140             if (key_record[i].date_last_here < customer_selection.min_date)
141                 continue;
142             if (key_record[i].date_last_here > customer_selection.max_date)
143                 continue;
144
145             items_found ++;
146             setbit(found,(long)(i+total_items_read));
147
148             if (current_zip_entry == ZIP_BLOCK_ENTRIES)
149                 {
150                 current_zip_block ++;
151                 current_zip_entry = 0;
152                 zip_block[current_zip_block] = (ZipRecord *)
153                 calloc(ZIP_BLOCK_ENTRIES,sizeof(ZipRecord));
```

Listing 3.5 *mail.c: mailing list program (continued)*

```
154                    for (k = 0; k < ZIP_BLOCK_ENTRIES; k ++)
155                            temp_zip_pointer[k] = zip_block[current_zip_block] + k;
156                    }
157
158                memcpy((char *)temp_zip_pointer[current_zip_entry],key_record[i].zip,
159                ZIP_LENGTH+1);
160                current_zip_entry ++;
161                }
162            total_items_read += items_read;
163            if (items_read != processing_batch)
164                break;
165            }
166
167        zip_pointer = (ZipRecord **)calloc(items_found,sizeof(ZipRecord *));
168        zip_block_start = 0;
169        for (i = 0; i <= current_zip_block; i ++)
170            {
171            if (i < current_zip_block)
172                zip_count = ZIP_BLOCK_ENTRIES;
173            else
174                zip_count = items_found-zip_block_start;
175            for (zip_entry = 0; zip_entry < zip_count; zip_entry ++)
176                {
177                zip_pointer[zip_block_start+zip_entry] = zip_block[i] + zip_entry;
178                }
179            zip_block_start += zip_entry;
180            }
181
182        record_number = (unsigned *)calloc(items_found,sizeof(int));
183        list_index = 0;
184        for (i = 0; i < key_file_count; i ++)
185            {
186            if (testbit(found,i))
187                {
188                record_number[list_index] = i;
189                list_index ++;
190                }
191            }
192
193        Megasort((unsigned char **)zip_pointer, record_number, ZIP_LENGTH,
194        items_found);
195
196        for (i = 0; i < items_found; i ++)
197            {
198            fseek(customer_data_file,(long)record_number[i]*(long)sizeof(DataRecord),
199            SEEK_SET);
200            fread(&data_record, sizeof(DataRecord), 1, customer_data_file);
201            fprintf(customer_list_file,"%s %s %s\r\n",data_record.first_name,
202            data_record.last_name,zip_pointer[i]);
203            }
204
```

Listing 3.5 *mail.c: mailing list program (continued)*

```
205      free(found);
206      free(zip_pointer);
207      for (i = 0; i <= current_zip_block; i ++)
208          free(zip_block[i]);
209
210   }
211
212
213
214   void terminate(FILE *customer_key_file, FILE *customer_data_file,
215   FILE *customer_list_file)
216   {
217     fclose(customer_key_file);
218     fclose(customer_data_file);
219     fclose(customer_list_file);
220   }
221
222
```

Listing 3.6 *megac.c: distribution sorting program*

```
1
2    /****keyword-flag*** "%v %f %n" */
3    /* "7 20-Aug-92,20:35:12 MEGAC.C" */
4
5
6    #include <stdio.h>
7    #include <stdlib.h>
8    #include <mem.h>
9
10   void Megasort(unsigned char **PtrArray, unsigned *RecNums, int KeyLength,
11   unsigned ArraySize)
12   {
13
14     unsigned char  m;
15     int    cum;
16     int    i, j;
17
18     int    BucketCount [ 256 ];
19     int    BucketPosition[ 256 ];
20     unsigned char  **TempPtrArray;
21     unsigned *TempRecNums;
22
23   /* either 0 or 1 element means no sorting required */
24     if (ArraySize < 2)
25         return;
26
27     TempPtrArray = (unsigned char **) malloc ( sizeof(unsigned char *) * ArraySize);
28     if ( TempPtrArray == NULL )
29         {
30         printf( "out of memory\n" );
31         exit( 1 );
32         }
33     TempRecNums = (unsigned *) malloc ( sizeof(unsigned) * ArraySize );
34
35     if (TempRecNums  == NULL )
36         {
37         printf( "out of memory\n" );
38         exit( 1 );
39         }
40
41     for (i = KeyLength-1; i >= 0; i- )
42         {
43         memset(BucketCount,0,256*sizeof(int));
44
45         for (j = 0; j < ArraySize; j++ )
46             {
47             m = PtrArray[ j ][ i ];
48             ++BucketCount[m];
49             }
50
51         BucketPosition[0] = 0;
```

Listing 3.6 *megac.c: distribution sorting program (continued)*

```
52           for (cum = 1; cum < 256; cum++ )
53                BucketPosition[ cum ] = BucketCount[ cum-1 ] + BucketPosition[ cum-1 ];
54
55           for (j = 0; j < ArraySize; j++ )
56                {
57                m = PtrArray[j][i];
58                TempPtrArray[BucketPosition[m]] = PtrArray[j];
59                TempRecNums[BucketPosition[m]] = RecNums[j];
60                ++BucketPosition[m];
61                }
62
63           memcpy(PtrArray,TempPtrArray,ArraySize*sizeof(unsigned char *));
64           memcpy(RecNums,TempRecNums,ArraySize*sizeof(int));
65           }
66
67      free(TempPtrArray);
68      free(TempRecNums);
69      }
```

Listing 3.7 *sorttest.c: test sorting program*

```
1
2    /****keyword-flag*** "%v %f %n" */
3    /* "3 13-Mar-93,9:24:56 SORTTEST.C" */
4
5
6    #include <stdio.h>
7    #include <stdlib.h>
8    #include <string.h>
9
10   void Megasort(unsigned char **PtrArray, unsigned *RecNums, int KeyLength,
11   unsigned ArraySize);
12
13   int sort_function(const void *a, const void *b);
14
15
16   main(int argc,char *argv[])
17   {
18     int i;
19     int j;
20     char **string;
21     int *recnum;
22     int sort_count;
23     int string_length;
24     char *string1;
25     char *string2;
26     int loop_count;
27
28     if (argc < 3)
29         {
30         printf("Usage: sorttest sort-count string-length\n");
31         exit(0);
32         }
33     sort_count = atoi(argv[1]);
34     string_length = atoi(argv[2]);
35     string = (char **)calloc(sort_count,sizeof(char *));
36     recnum = (int *)calloc(sort_count,sizeof(int));
37     for (i = 0; i < sort_count; i ++)
38         {
39         string[i] = calloc(string_length+1,1);
40         for (j = 0; j < string_length; j ++)
41             string[i][j] = (rand() % 26) + 97;
42         recnum[i] = i;
43         }
44
45     if (sort_count <= 4000)
46         qsort(string[0],sort_count,16,sort_function);
47
48     Megasort(string,recnum,string_length,sort_count);
49   }
50
51   int sort_function(const void *a, const void *b)
```

Listing 3.7 *sorttest.c: test sorting program (continued)*

```
52    {
53      return(strcmp(a,b));
54    }
```

Listing 3.8 *bitfunc.h: bitmap header file*

```
 1
 2   /****keyword-flag*** "%v %f %n" */
 3   /* "2 12-May-92,19:23:14 BITFUNC.H" */
 4
 5
 6
 7   int setbit(char *bitmap,unsigned long element);
 8   int clearbit(char *bitmap,unsigned long element);
 9   int testbit(char *bitmap,unsigned long element);
10
11   #define allocate_bitmap(x) calloc((unsigned)(x/8+1),1)1
```

Listing 3.9 *bitfunc.c: bitmap functions*

```
 1
 2    /****keyword-flag*** "%v %f %n" */
 3    /* "3 12-May-92,19:07:48 BITFUNC.C" */
 4
 5
 6    int setbit(char *bitmap,unsigned long element)
 7    {
 8      unsigned bytenumber;
 9      int bitnumber;
10      int byte;
11      int mask;
12
13      bytenumber = (unsigned)(element / 8);
14
15      bitnumber = (unsigned)(element % 8);
16
17      byte = bitmap[bytenumber];
18
19      mask = 1 << bitnumber;
20
21      bitmap[bytenumber] |= mask;
22
23      if (mask & byte)
24          return(1);
25      else
26          return(0);
27    }
28
29
30    int clearbit(char *bitmap,unsigned long element)
31    {
32      unsigned bytenumber;
33      int bitnumber;
34      int byte;
35      int mask;
36
37      bytenumber = (unsigned)(element / 8);
38
39      bitnumber = (unsigned)(element % 8);
40
41      byte = bitmap[bytenumber];
42
43      mask = 1 << bitnumber;
44
45      bitmap[bytenumber] &= ~mask;
46
47      if (mask & byte)
48          return(1);
49      else
50          return(0);
51    }
```

Listing 3.9 *bitfunc.c: bitmap functions (continued)*

```
52
53
54    int testbit(char *bitmap,unsigned long element)
55    {
56      unsigned bytenumber;
57      int bitnumber;
58      int byte;
59      int mask;
60
61      bytenumber = (unsigned)(element / 8);
62
63      bitnumber = (unsigned)(element % 8);
64
65      byte = bitmap[bytenumber];
66
67      mask = 1 << bitnumber;
68
69      if (mask & byte)
70          return(1);
71      else
72          return(0);
73    }
```

4

Cn U Rd Ths Qkly?

A Data Compression Utility

TOPICS DISCUSSED
Huffman Coding, Arithmetic Coding, Lookup Tables,
Assembly Language Enhancements

Introduction

In this chapter we will examine the Huffman coding and arithmetic coding methods of data compression and develop an implementation of the latter algorithm. The arithmetic coding algorithm allows a tradeoff among memory consumption and compression ratio; our emphasis will be on minimum memory consumption, on the assumption that the result would eventually be used as embedded code within a larger program.

We will also be applying one of the most powerful methods of improving the efficiency of a given algorithm: recoding critical areas of the program in assembly language. While the exact details of this enhancement are specific to machines based on the 80x86 architecture, the principles that we will use to focus our effort are generally applicable.

Huffman Coding

Huffman coding is widely recognized as the most efficient method of encoding characters for data compression. This algorithm is a way of encoding different characters in different numbers of bits, with the most common characters encoded in the fewest bits. For example, suppose we have a message made up of the letters 'A', 'B', and 'C', which can occur in any combination. Figure 4.1 shows the relative frequency of each of these letters and the Huffman code assigned to each one.

The codes are determined by the frequencies: as mentioned above, the letter with the greatest frequency, 'C', has the shortest code, of one bit. The other two letters, 'A' and 'B', have longer codes. On the other hand, the simplest code to represent any of three characters would use two bits for each character. How would the length of an encoded message be affected by using the Huffman code rather than the fixed-length one?

Let's encode the message "CABCCABC" using both codes. The results are shown in figure 4.2.

Here we have saved one-fourth of the bits required to encode this message; often, the compression can be much greater. Since we ordinarily use an eight-bit ASCII code to represent characters, if one of those characters (such as carriage return or line feed) accounts for a large fraction of the characters in a file, giving it a short code of two or three bits can reduce the size of the file noticeably.

Let's see how arithmetic coding[31] would encode the first three characters of the same message, "CAB".

Figure 4.3 is the first of several figures which contain the information needed to determine how arithmetic coding would encode messages of up to three characters

Figure 4.1 *Huffman Code Table*

Letter	Frequency	Huffman Code	Fixed-length Code
A	1/4	00	00
B	1/4	01	01
C	1/2	1	10

Figure 4.2 *Huffman vs. fixed-length coding*

Letter	Huffman Code	Fixed-length Code
C	1	10
A	00	00
B	01	10
C	1	10
C	1	01
A	00	00
B	01	01
C	1	10
Total bits used	12	16

31. I. H. Witten, R. M. Neal, and J. G. Cleary. "Arithmetic Coding for Data Compression," *Commun. ACM* 30(6), 520–540 (June 1987).

Figure 4.3 *One-character messages*

Message	Freq.	Cum. Freq.	Codes	Previous Output	Current Output	Output So Far
A	16	16	000000(0)-001111(15)	None	00	00
B	16	32	010000(16)-011111(31)	None	01	01
* C	32	64	100000(32)-111111(63)	None	1	1

from an alphabet consisting of the letters 'A', 'B', and 'C', with frequencies of 1/4, 1/4, and 1/2, respectively. The frequency of a message composed of three characters chosen independently is the product of the frequencies of those characters. Since the lowest common denominator of these three fractions is 1/4, the frequency of any three-character message will be a 3 multiple of (1/4) , or 1/64. For example, the frequency of the message "CAB" will be (1/2)*(1/4)*(1/4), or 1/32 (=2/64). For this reason, we will express all of the frequency values in terms of 1/64ths.

Thus, the "Freq." column signifies the expected frequency of occurrence of each message, in units of 1/64; the "Cum. Freq." column accumulates the values in the first column; the "Codes" column indicates the range of codes that can represent each message;[32] the "Previous Output" column shows the bits that have been output before the current character was encoded; the "Current Output" column indicates what output we can produce at this point in the encoding process; and the "Output So Far" column shows the cumulative output for that message, starting with the first character encoded.

As the table indicates, since the first character happens to be a 'C', then we can output "1", because all possible messages starting with 'C' have codes starting a "1". Let's continue with figure 4.4 to see the encoding for a two-character message.

After encoding the first two characters of our message, "CA", our cumulative output is "100", since the range of codes for messages starting with "CA" is from "100000" to "100111"; all these codes start with "100". The whole three-character message is encoded as shown in figure 4.5.

We have generated exactly the same output from the same input as we did with Huffman coding. So far, this seems to be an exercise in futility; is arithmetic coding just another name for Huffman coding?

---

32. This column is derived from the "Cum. Freq." column; it represents the range of codes that has been allocated to messages that begin with the characters in the "Message So Far" column. For example, messages beginning with the character 'A' have a cumulative frequency of 16/64. This means that messages that start with that letter have codes between the cumulative frequency of the previous message (in this case 0, since this is the first message) and 15/64. Similarly, since messages beginning with the letter 'B' have a cumulative frequency of 32/64, codes for such messages must lie between 16/64, which is the cumulative frequency of the previous entry, and 31/64

Figure 4.4 *Two-character messages*

Message	Freq.	Cum. Freq.	Codes	Previous Output	Current Output	Output So Far
AA	4	4	000000(00)-000011(03)	00	00	0000
AB	4	8	000100(04)-000111(07)	00	01	0001
AC	8	16	001000(08)-001111(15)	00	1	001
BA	4	20	010000(16)-010011(19)	01	00	0100
BB	4	24	010100(20)-010111(23)	01	01	0101
BC	8	32	011000(24)-011111(31)	01	1	011
* CA	8	40	100000(32)-100111(39)	1	00	100
CB	8	48	101000(40)-101111(47)	1	01	101
CC	16	64	110000(48)-111111(63)	1	1	11

Figure 4.5 *Three-character messages*

Message	Freq.	Cum. Freq.	Codes	Previous Output	Current Output	Output So Far
AAA	1	1	000000(00)-000000(00)	0000	00	000000
AAB	1	2	000001(01)-000001(01)	0000	10	000001
AAC	2	4	000010(02)-000011(03)	0000	1	00001
ABA	1	5	000100(04)-000100(04)	0001	00	000100
ABB	1	6	000101(05)-000101(05)	0001	01	000101
ABC	2	8	000110(06)-000111(07)	0001	1	00011
ACA	2	10	001000(08)-001001(09)	001	00	00100
ACB	2	12	001010(10)-001011(11)	001	01	00101
ACC	4	16	001100(12)-001111(15)	001	1	0011
BAA	1	17	010000(16)-010000(16)	0100	00	010000
BAB	1	18	010001(17)-010001(17)	0100	01	010001
BAC	2	20	010010(18)-010011(19)	0100	1	01001
BBA	1	21	010100(20)-010100(20)	0101	00	010100
BBB	1	22	010101(21)-010101(21)	0101	01	010101
BBC	2	24	010110(22)-010111(23)	0101	1	01011
BCA	2	26	011000(24)-011001(25)	011	00	01100
BCB	2	28	011010(26)-011111(27)	011	01	01101
BCC	4	32	011100(28)-011111(31)	011	1	0111
CAA	2	34	100000(32)-100001(33)	100	00	10000
* CAB	2	36	100010(34)-100011(35)	100	01	10001
CAC	4	40	100100(36)-100111(39)	100	1	1001
CBA	2	42	101000(40)-101001(41)	101	00	10100
CBB	2	44	101010(42)-101011(43)	101	01	10101
CBC	4	48	101100(44)-101111(47)	101	1	1011
CCA	4	52	110000(48)-110011(51)	11	00	1100
CCB	4	56	110100(52)-110111(55)	11	01	1101
CCC	8	64	110000(56)-111111(63)	11	1	111

Figure 4.6 *Suboptimal Huffman code table*

Letter	Frequency	Huffman Code	Fixed-length Code
A	3/4	0	0
B	1/4	1	1

These two algorithms provide the same compression efficiency only when the frequencies of the characters to be encoded happen to be representable as integral powers of 1/2, as was the case in our examples so far; however, consider the frequency table shown in figure 4.6.

Using Huffman coding, there is no way to assign theoretically optimal codes to characters with such a frequency distribution.[33] Since the shortest possible Huffman code is one bit, the best we can do is to assign a one-bit code to each character, although this does not reflect the difference in their frequencies. In fact, Huffman coding can never provide any compression at all with a two-character alphabet.

However, such a situation is handled very well indeed by arithmetic compression. To see how, we will start by asking a fundamental question: what is a bit?

Half a Bit Is Better than One

A bit is the amount of information required to specify an alternative that has a frequency of 50%; two bits can specify alternatives that have a frequency of 25%, and so forth. For example, the toss of a coin can result in either heads or tails, each of which can be optimally represented by a one-bit code; similarly, if a chance event has four equally likely outcomes, we can express each possible result most economically with two bits. On the other hand, as we have seen in our discussion of Huffman codes, we can have a number of alternatives that are not equally likely; in that case, we assign longer codes for those alternatives that are less likely. However, the shortest possible code in Huffman coding is one bit, which is assigned to an outcome with a frequency of one-half.

The general formula for the optimal length of a code specifying a particular outcome with frequency f is "$\log_2 (1/f)$". In our previous examples, an outcome with a frequency of .5 should have a code length of $\log_2 (1/(1/2))$ or 1 bit. Similarly, if an outcome has a frequency of .25 it should have a code length of $\log_2 (1/(1/4))$, or two bits.

But what if one of the possible outcomes has a frequency greater than one-half? Logically, we should use less than one bit to specify it. For example, if we have a data file in which 84% of the characters are spaces, we can calculate the appropriate number of bits in the code for that character as $\log_2 (1/(.84))$, or approximately .25 bits. If the remaining 255 characters all have equal frequencies, each of these frequencies is .0627%, so that our formula reduces to $\log_2 (1/(.0627))$, or approximately 10.63 bits each. This would result in an average code length of (.84)*(.25) + (.16)*10.63, or 1.91 bits per character. By contrast, a Huffman code would require (.84)*1 + (.16)*9, or 2.28 bits per character. If we were compressing a 250-Kbyte file

---

33. For that matter, a similar problem occurs when we have three characters of equal frequency; the characters have to end up with different code lengths in a Huffman code, even though their frequencies are equal.

with such characteristics, using Huffman codes would produce a 71-Kbyte file, whereas arithmetic coding would result in a 60-Kbyte file, about a 20% difference between these two approaches.[34]

Getting a Bit Excited

Of course, we can't output a code of less than one bit. However, we can use a set of one or more bits to represent more than one character in the same message. This is why the statement that Huffman coding is the most efficient way to represent characters is true, but misleading; if our messages contain more than one character each, we may be able to combine the codes for a number of characters while consuming a fractional number of bits for some characters.

To make this clearer, let's go through the encoding of a three-character message, "ABA", from a two-character alphabet in which the letter 'A' accounts for three-fourths of all the characters and the letter 'B' the remaining one-fourth. The situation after we see the first character is shown in figure 4.7.

If the first character were a 'B', then we could output "11", because all possible messages starting with 'B' have codes starting with those two bits. However, what can we output when the first character is an 'A'?

Figure 4.7 *The first character*

Message So Far	Freq.	Cum. Freq.	Codes	Previous Output	Current Output	Output So Far
* A	48	48	000000(0)-101111(47)	None	None	None
B	16	64	110000(48)-111111(63)	None	11	11

Figure 4.8 *The second character*

Message So Far	Freq.	Cum. Freq.	Codes	Previous Output	Current Output	Output So Far
AA	36	36	000000(0)-100011(35)	None	None	None
* AB	12	48	100100(36)-101111(47)	None	10	10
BA	12	60	110000(48)-111011(59)	11	None	11
BB	4	64	111100(60)-111111(63)	11	11	1111

---

34. As we will see later, there are commonly occurring situations which have even more lop-sided distributions than this, when the context in which each character is seen is taken into account; for example, following a carriage return in a DOS-formatted text file, the next character is almost certain to be a line feed. In such cases, we can use much less than one-fourth of a bit to represent a line feed character following a carriage return and gain far more efficiency compared to Huffman coding.

Figure 4.9 *The third character*

Message So Far	Freq.	Cum. Freq.	Codes	Previous Output	Current Output	Output So Far
AAA	27	27	000000(0)-011010(26)	None	0	0
AAB	9	36	011011(27)-100011(35)	None	None	None
* ABA	9	45	100100(36)-101100(44)	10	None	10
ABB	3	48	101101(45)-101111(47)	10	11	1011
BAA	9	57	110000(48)-111000(56)	11	None	11
BAB	3	60	111001(57)-111011(59)	11	10	1110
BBA	3	63	111100(60)-111110(62)	1111	None	1111
BBB	1	64	111111(63)-111111(63)	1111	11	111111

Nothing! We don't know whether the first bit of our encoded message will be a 0 or a 1; that depends on what happens next. Remember, messages starting with the letter 'A' can have codes starting with 00 through 10, or three-fourths of all possible codes. An 'A' gives us somewhat less than 1/2 bit of information, not nearly enough to produce any output by itself. Now let's look at figure 4.8 for the information needed to encode the next character.

We have two bits of output, since all the codes for messages starting with "AB" have the initial bits "10".[35] Let's continue with figure 4.9 for the third (and last) character of our message.

We have still produced only two bits of output from our three-character message, "ABA". The best we could do with Huffman coding is three bits. However, this is not the extreme case; if we were encoding the most frequent message, "AAA", we would have only a "0" bit.[36]

A Character Study

This algorithm will work nicely if we happen to know in advance what the frequencies of all the possible characters will be, but how do we acquire this information? If our program reads an input file and writes an output file, we can go through the input file once, counting the number of times a given character appears, build the table of frequencies, and then make a second pass using this table to do the actual encoding. However, this is not possible when we are compressing data as it is being

---

35. Notice that if we were encoding "AA", we still wouldn't have even the first bit!

36. The second most frequent message, "AAB", is a special case, which we will see again later. Although it occupies only nine of the 64 possible message positions, some of those nine start with a 0 and some with a 1; therefore, we don't know the first bit to be output. However, we do know that the code for messages beginning with "AAB" starts with either "011" or "100"; as we continue encoding characters, eventually we will have enough information to decide which. At that point, we will be able to output at least those first three bits.

generated, as there is then no input file to be analyzed. This might seem to be an insurmountable obstacle.

Luckily, it is not; calculating the character frequencies as we encode yields about the same compression efficiency as precalculation—and in some cases even better efficiency! The reason for this surprising result is that most files (or sets of data) are not uniform throughout, but rather exhibit local variations in the frequency of a given character or set of characters. Calculating the frequencies on the fly often produces a better match for these changing characteristics.

Therefore, our approach is as follows. Every character is initially assumed to have the same frequency of occurrence. After each character is read and encoded, its entry in the table of frequencies is increased to reflect our having seen it. The next time we encode it, its encoding will account for the fact that we have seen it before.

That may seem quite simple for the sender, but not for the receiver. If the encoding table is being modified as we go, how does the receiver keep in step?

The receiver has the same initial table as the transmitter; each character has the same expected frequency of occurrence. Then, as the receiver decodes each character, it updates its copy of the frequency table. This also explains why we increase a character's frequency after we encode it, rather than before; until the receiver decodes the character, it cannot update the frequency of that character's occurrence.[37]

Keeping It in Context

In our implementation, we achieve a large improvement in compression efficiency by using the context in which a character occurs when estimating its frequency of occurrence. It should be apparent that the frequency of a given character appearing in a message at a given point is quite dependent on the previous context. For example, in English text, a "q" is almost certain to be followed by a "u", at least if we exclude articles about software such as DESQview! Ideally, therefore, the amount of information needed to encode a "u" following a "q" should be very small. The same principle, of course, applies to the encoding of a line feed following a carriage return in text files where this is a virtual certainty.

On the other hand, the amount of storage required to keep track of a large amount of previous context can become excessive.[38] Even one character of previous context requires the construction of 256 tables of frequencies, one for each possible previous character. A direct extension of the approach given in the reference in footnote 38 would require over 300 Kbytes of storage for these tables.

We will apply a number of space-saving methods to reduce the above storage requirement by about 90%, to approximately 35 Kbytes, while still achieving good data-compression performance in most cases.

---

37. A consequence of this approach is that we cannot decompress data in any order other than the one in which it was compressed, which prevents direct access to records in compressed files. This limitation is the subject of one of the problems at the end of this chapter.

38. A. Moffat. "Word-based Text Compression," *Software — Practice and Experience,* 19(2), 185–198 (February 1989).

Conspicuous Nonconsumption

In order to achieve such a reduction in memory consumption, we must avoid storing anything that can be recalculated, such as the cumulative frequencies of all possible characters.[39] We must also dispense with the use of a self-organizing table that attempts to speed up encoding and decoding by moving more frequently used characters toward the front of the table, as is done in the reference in footnote 31.

However, we must provide as large a dynamic range of frequencies as possible: the larger the ratio between the highest frequency and the lowest, the greater the possible efficiency. The greatest dynamic range is needed when one character always occurs in a particular context, such as line feed after carriage return. Assuming that we must be able to encode any of the 256 possible one-byte values, the algorithm limits the possible dynamic range to approximately one-fourth of the range of an unsigned value.[40] For maximum compression efficiency we therefore need 256 tables of 256 two-byte entries each, consuming a total of 128 Kbytes.[41] When I first implemented this algorithm, I saw no way to reduce this significantly.

Then early one morning, I woke up with the answer. We need some very large frequency values and some very small ones, but surely not every one in between. Why not use a code to represent one of a number of frequency values? These values would be spaced out properly to get as close as possible to optimal compression efficiency, but each would be represented by a small index, rather than literally.

How small an index? First I considered using an eight-bit index. But that still would require 64 Kbytes for a complete 256x256 table. Maybe a smaller index would help. But wouldn't that impose an unreasonable processing time penalty?

Amazingly enough, we can use a four-bit index with no time penalty: in fact, processing is actually faster than with a byte index! This seemingly magical feat is accomplished by one of my favorite time-saving methods: the lookup table.

You see, a significant amount of the CPU time needed to encode a symbol is spent in a loop that computes the necessary portion of the cumulative frequency table for the current context. If each frequency value occupied one byte, we would have to execute that loop once for every index in the table up to the ASCII value of the character whose cumulative frequency we are trying to compute. However, since we have packed two indexes into one byte, we can accumulate two indexes worth of frequency values with one addition, thus reducing the number of times the loop has to be executed by approximately 50%.

Each execution of the loop translates a pair of indexes contained in one byte into a total frequency value that is the sum of their individual frequency values by using the byte as an index into a 256-word table, which has one entry for each possible

39. This is the column labeled "Cum. Freq." in figures 4.3–4.5 and 4.7–4.9.

40. For compilers which produce two-byte `unsigned`s, the maximum cumulative frequency is 16,383 if we wish to avoid the use of `long` arithmetic. This limits the dynamic range to 16,128 for the one common character and 1 for each of the other characters.

41. Theoretically, we could use 14 bits per entry, but the CPU time required to encode or decode would be greatly increased by packing and unpacking frequencies stored in that way.

combination of two indexes. This table (the `both_weights` table) is calculated once at the start of the program.

Once we have determined the frequency of occurrence assigned to the character to be encoded, we can decide how many bits we can send and what their values are.

Receiving the Message

The receiver uses almost the same code as the sender, with two main exceptions. First, the receiver reads the input one bit at a time and outputs each character as soon as it is decoded, just the reverse of the sender. Second, rather than knowing how many frequency entries we have to accumulate in advance as the sender does, we have to accumulate them until we find the one that corresponds to the range we are trying to interpret. The latter situation reduces the efficiency of our loop control, which accounts for much of the difference in speed between encoding and decoding.

The Code

The `main` function in "encode.c" (listing 4.3) opens the input and output files and sets up buffers to speed up input and output. Then it calls `start_model` (listing 4.5, lines 42–72). This routine starts out by initializing the `upgrade_threshold` array, which is used to determine when to promote a character to the next higher frequency index value. As noted above, these values are not consecutive, so that we can use a four-bit index rather than literal values; this means that we have to promote a character only once in a while rather than every time we see it, as we would do with literal frequency values. How do we decide when to do this?

A pseudorandom approach seems best: we can't use a genuine random number to tell us when to increment the index, because the receiver would have no way of reproducing our decisions when decoding the message. My solution is to keep a one-byte hash total of the ASCII codes for all the characters that have been sent (`char_total`) and to increment the index in question whenever `char_total` is greater than the corresponding value stored in the `upgrade_threshold` array. That threshold value is calculated so that the probability of incrementing the index is inversely proportional to the gap between frequency values in the translation table.[42] If, for example, each frequency value in the translation table were twice the previous value, there would be a 1/2 probability of incrementing the index each time a character was encountered.

---

42. The last entry in the `upgrade_threshold` array is set to 255, which prevents the index from being increased beyond 15, the maximum value that can be stored in a four-bit value; `char_total`, being an `unsigned char` variable, cannot exceed 255.

After we finish initializing the `upgrade_threshold` array, we set `char_total` to 0, in preparation for accumulating our hash total.

The next operation in `start_model` (lines 56–58) generates the `both_weights` table. As we discussed above, this table allows us to translate from a pair of frequency values (or weights) to the total frequency to which they correspond. We calculate it by generating every possible pair and adding them together to fill in the corresponding table entry. The values in the `translate` table are defined in listing 4.2, line 43. How did I generate these values?

A Loose Translation

It wasn't easy. I knew that I wanted to allow the largest possible dynamic range, which means that the lowest value has to be 1 and the highest value has to be close to the maximum that can be accommodated by the algorithm (16,128). The reason I chose a top value lower than that maximum value is that if the highest value were 16,128, then the occurrence of *any* character other than the preferred one would cause the total frequency to exceed the allowable maximum, with the result that the table of frequencies would be recalculated to reduce the top value to the next lower step. This would greatly reduce the efficiency of the compression for this case. That accounts for the lowest and highest values. What about the ones in between?

Initially, I decided to use a **geometric progression**, much like the tuning of a piano; in such a progression, each value is a fixed multiple of the one before it. However, I found that I achieved better compression on a fairly large sample of files by starting the progression with the second value at 16 and ending with the next to the last at 1024. Why is this so?

The reason for leaving a big gap between the lowest frequency and the second lowest one is that many characters *never* occur in a particular situation. If they occur once, they are likely to recur later. Therefore, setting the next-to-the-lowest frequency to approximately one-tenth of 1% of the maximum value improves the efficiency of the compression. I have also found through experimentation that the compression ratio is improved if the first time a character is seen, it is given a frequency of about six-tenths of 1%, which requires an initial index of 7. Lower initial frequencies retard adaptation to popular new characters, and higher ones overemphasize new characters that turn out to be unpopular in the long run.

The reason to leave a large gap between the next-to-highest frequency and the highest one is that most of the time, a very skewed distribution has exactly one extremely frequent character. It is rare to find several very high-frequency characters that have about the same frequency. Therefore, allowing the highest frequency to approach the theoretical maximum produces the best results.

Of course, these are only empirical findings. If you have samples that closely resemble the data that you will be compressing, you can try modifying these frequency values to improve the compression.

Getting in on the Ground Floor

Continuing in `start_model`, in lines 60–66 we initialize `NO_OF_CHARS` `frequency_info` tables, one for every possible character. Each of these tables will store the frequencies for characters that follow a particular character. If we start to encode the string "This is a test", the first character, 'T', will be encoded using the table for character 0 (a null); this is arbitrary, since we haven't seen any characters before this one. Then the 'h' will be encoded using the table for 'T'; the 'i' will be encoded with the table for 'h', and so forth. This approach takes advantage of the context dependence of English text; as we noted before, after we see a 'q', the next character is almost certain to be a 'u', so we should use a very short code to represent a 'u' in that position.

However, our initialization code contains no information about the characteristics of English text (or any other kind of data for that matter). We assign the same frequency (the lowest possible) to every character in every frequency table. As discussed above, the encoding program will learn the appropriate frequencies for each character in each table as it processes the input data. At the end of the initialization for each table, we set its `total_freq` value to the translation of the lowest frequency, multiplied by the number of index pairs in the table. This value is needed to calculate the code that corresponds to each character, and recalculating it every time we access the table would be time-consuming.

The last operation in `start_model` (lines 68–69) initializes the `char_translation` array, which is used to translate the internal representation of the characters being encoded and decoded to their ASCII codes.[43] Then we return to line 30 in "encode.c".

Gentlemen, Start Your Output

The next operation in `main` is to call `start_outputing_bits` (listing 4.6, lines 127–132). Of course, we can't send individual bits to the output file; we have to accumulate at least one byte's worth. Whenever we have some bits to be output, we will store them in `buffer`; since we haven't encoded any characters yet, we set it to 0. In order to keep track of how many more bits we need before we can send `buffer` to the output file, we set `bits_to_go` to eight; then we return to `main`.

The next thing we do in `main` is to call `start_encoding` (listing 4.6, lines 37–43). This is a very short routine, but it initializes some of the most important variables in the program; `low`, `high`, and `bits_to_follow`. The first two of these keep track of the range of codes for the current message; at this point we know nothing about the message, so they are set to indicate the widest possible range of mes-

---

43. Although this array is not used in the initial version of our program, we will see near the end of this chapter how it contributes to our optimization effort.

sages, from 0 to TOP_VALUE, which is defined in "arith.h" (listing 4.1, line 10). In our current implementation, with 16-bit code values, TOP_VALUE evaluates to 65535.[44] The third variable, bits_to_follow, keeps track of the number of bits that have been deferred for later output. This is used where the range of possible codes for the current message includes codes that start with 0 and some that start with 1; as we have seen already, in such a situation we're not ready to send out any bits yet. After initializing these variables, we return to main.

The Main Loop

Upon returning to main, we need to do one more initialization before we enter the main loop of our program, which is executed once for each character in the input file. At line 32, we set oldch to 0. This variable controls the context in which we will encode each character. Since we haven't seen any characters as yet, it doesn't really matter which frequency table we use, as long as the decoding program selects the same initial table.

The first operation in the main loop is to get the character to be encoded, via getc. If we have reached the end of the file, we break out of the loop. Otherwise, at line 38, we call encode_symbol (listing 4.6, lines 45–114) to place the representation of the current character in the output stream. This routine takes two parameters: ch, the character to be encoded, and oldch, which determines the frequency table to be used for this encoding. As we have noted above, selecting a frequency table based upon the previous character encoded provides far better compression efficiency, as the frequency of occurrence of a particular character is greatly affected by the character that precedes it.

encode_symbol

Although encode_symbol is a short routine, it is the subtlest function in this chapter; fortunately, you can use this algorithm effectively without going through the explanation below. The version here closely follows the reference in footnote 31; if you are really interested in the details of operation of this routine, I strongly advise you to study that reference very carefully in conjunction with the explanation here.

To clarify this algorithm, we will work through a somewhat simplified example as we examine the code. For ease in calculation, we will set TOP_VALUE to 255, or 11111111 binary, rather than 65535 as in the actual program; as a result, high will start out at 255 as well.   We will also use a single, constant frequency table

---

44. To fully understand the function of low and high, we must wait until we examine encode_symbol (listing 4.6, lines 45–114). For now, let's just say that they indicate the current state of our knowledge about the message being encoded; the closer together they are, the more bits we are ready to output.

(figure 4.10) containing only four entries rather than selecting a 256-entry table according to the previous character and modifying it as we see each character, so our `translate` and `both_weights` tables (figures 4.11 and 4.12, respectively) will be adjusted correspondingly. Instead of ASCII, we will use the codes from 0 (for 'A') to 3 (for 'D') in our example message.

As we begin `encode_symbol`, we establish `temp_freq_info` as a pointer to the structure containing the current frequency table. Next, we set `freq_ptr` to the address of the frequency table itself and `total_freq` to the stored total frequency in the frequency structure; as we will see shortly, `total_freq` is used to determine what fraction of the frequency range is accounted for by the particular character being encoded. The final operation before entering the frequency accumulation loop is to set `prev_cum` to 0. This variable is used to keep track of the cumulative frequency of all characters up to but not including the one being encoded; this is used to determine the position of the character being encoded as a part of the entire range of possibilities.

Figure 4.10 *Sample frequency table*

Character	Frequency code
A,B	00010011 (1,3)
C,D	00000010 (0,2)

Figure 4.11 *Sample translate table*

Index	Value
0	1
1	2
2	8
3	52

Figure 4.12 *Sample both_weights table*

First Index	Second Index 0	1	2	3
0	2	3	9	53
1	3	4	10	54
2	9	10	16	60
3	53	54	60	104

ON THE RIGHT FREQUENCY

Now we are ready to enter the frequency accumulation loop (lines 63–68). The reason we need this loop is that, as we saw before, we cannot afford to keep the cumulative frequency tables in memory; they would occupy hundreds of kilobytes of memory. Instead, we calculate the cumulative frequency for each character being encoded, as we need it. The `total_freq` variable, however, we do maintain from one encoding to the next; recalculating it would require us to go all the way through the frequency table for each character, even if we are encoding a character with a low ASCII code. Since we are saving the total frequency with the table, we have to accumulate the frequencies only up to the ASCII code of the character we are encoding.

Let's see how this loop accumulates the frequencies of all the characters up to the character we want to encode. The first interesting item is that the loop executes only half as many times as the value of the character being encoded, since we are packing two 4-bit indexes into each byte of the frequency table. So the first statement in the loop retrieves one of these pairs of indexes from the frequency table and increments the pointer to point to the next pair. Then we index into the `both_weights` table with the index pair we just retrieved and set `total_pair_weight` to that entry in the table. The `both_weights` table is the key to translating two 4-bit indexes into a total frequency. Each entry in the table is the sum of the frequency values that correspond to the two indexes that make up the byte we use to index into the table. Finally, we add `total_pair_weight` to `prev_cum`, which is accumulating all of the frequencies.

> In our example, the first letter of our message is 'D', which has a `symbol` value of 3. Using the `frequency` table in figure 4.10, we execute the statements in the loop once. First, we set `current_pair` to the first entry in the `frequency` table, 00010011, which indicates that the frequency code for 'A' is 1 (0001 binary) and the frequency code for 'B' is 3 (0011 binary). Then we set `total_pair_weight` to entry (1,3) from the `both_weights` table, the sum of the frequencies to which this pair of indexes corresponds; its value is 54. The last statement in the loop adds this value to `prev_cum`, which was set to 0 before the loop was started.

The next section of code, lines 69–84, finishes the accumulation of the cumulative frequencies of the character to be encoded and the previous character, for both of the possible alignments of the character we are encoding and the previous character. If the target character has an even ASCII code, we already have the correct value for `prev_cum`; to calculate `cum`, the frequency accumulation for the current character, we need the first index from the next byte, which is stored in the high half of the byte. So we pick up `current_pair`, shift its high index down, and use it to retrieve the corresponding weight from the `both_weights` table. Then we add that frequency value to `prev_cum` to calculate `cum`.

On the other hand, if the target character has an odd ASCII code, we need to update both `prev_cum` and `cum`. First, we add the total weights for the last two characters to `prev_cum`, which results in `cum`. Then we translate the high half of the `current_pair` and add that to `prev_cum`.

> In our example, the code of the first character is 3, so we need to update both `prev_cum` and `cum`. The value of `current_pair` is (0,2). Looking in the `both_weights` table, we set `total_pair_weight` to the translation of that pair, which is 9. Then cum is calculated as the sum of `prev_cum` and `total_pair_weight`, or 63. Then we extract the high part of `current_pair`, 0, which translates to 1; we add this amount to `prev_cum`, setting it to 55. This means that the code range associated with character "D" starts at 55 and ends slightly before 64, a range of 9 positions out of the total of 64. This will allow us to send out slightly less than three bits for this character, as we will narrow the range by a factor of more than 7.

HOME ON THE RANGE

Now that we have calculated the cumulative frequencies of the current character and the previous character, we are ready to narrow the range of frequencies that correspond to our message. First we have to calculate the previous range of frequencies for our message (line 86). Then we apply the transformations on lines 87 and 88 to calculate the new range of the message.

The purpose of `low` and `high` is to delimit the frequency interval in which the current message falls; `range` is just the size of the frequency interval extending from the old value of `low` to the old value of `high`, inclusive.

> In our example, the old value of `low` is 0 and the old value of `high` is 255. Therefore, the formula for `range`, `(long)(high-low)+1`, produces 256, which is its maximum value. This makes sense, as we have not yet used the information from the first character of our message.

The new values of `low` and `high` represent the narrowing of the previous range due to the frequency of the new character. We calculate the new value of high, which represents the high end of the new range of frequencies for our message after the most recent character is added to the message.[45]

---

45. Actually, the top end of the range of frequencies for the message is just below `high+1`; even the authors of the reference in footnote 31, which is the source of the original version of this algorithm, admit that this is confusing!

Similarly, the new value of `low` represents the low end of the range of frequencies for our message after the most recent character is added to the message.

In our example, `low` is still 0, `range` is 256, `cum` is 63, and `total_freq` is 63. The expression to calculate `high` is `low + (range * cum) / total_freq - 1`. Therefore, `high` is calculated as 0+(256*63)/63–1, or 255. This means that the new range of frequencies for our message ends slightly below 256. Next, we recalculate `low`. Its value is still 0 so far, `range` is 256, `prev_cum` is 55, and `total_freq` is 63. The expression to calculate `low` is `low + (range * prev_cum)/total_freq`. Therefore, we calculate the new value of `low` as 0+(256*55)/63, or 223. This means that the new range of frequencies for our message begins at 223.

A Bit of All Right

Now we are finally ready to start sending bits out. The loop starting at line 90 extracts as many bits as possible from the encoding of the message so far, and widens the range correspondingly to allow the encoding of more characters. In order to understand this code, we need to look at the table of possible initial bits of `high` and `low`, which is given in figure 4.13.

The entries in this table could use some explanation. The first two columns contain all the possible combinations of the first two bits of `low` and `high`; we know that `low` cannot be greater than `high`, since these two values delimit the range of codes for the message being compressed. If `low` ever became greater than `high`, it would be impossible to encode any further characters. The "Action" column indicates what, if anything, we can output now. Clearly, if `low` and `high` have the same first bit, we can output that bit. The entries labeled "Next" indicate that since the separation between the values of `low` and `high` is at least one-fourth of the total range of values (0–TOP_VALUE), we can encode at least one more character now; this is the reason for the limit on the total frequency of all characters.

Figure 4.13 *Possible initial code bits*

Low	High	Action
00	00	0
00	01	0
00	10	Next
00	11	Next
01	01	0
01	10	Defer
01	11	Next
10	10	1
10	11	1
11	11	1

The entry "Defer" means that we can't do any output now; however, when we do have output, we will be able to emit at least the first two bits of the result, since we know already that these bits are either "01" or "10". As we will see shortly, this condition is indicated by a nonzero value for `bits_to_follow`.

TESTING: ONE, TWO, THREE

The first test, at line 92, determines whether the highest frequency value allocated to our message is less than one-half of the total frequency `range`. If it is, we know that the first output bit is 0, so we call the `bit_plus_follow_0` macro (lines 16–24) to output that bit. Let's take a look at that macro.

First we call `output_0`, which adds a 0 bit to the output buffer and writes it out if it is full. Then, in the event that `bits_to_follow` is greater than 0, we call `output_1` and decrement `bits_to_follow` until it reaches 0. Why do we do this?

The reason is that `bits_to_follow` indicates the number of bits that could not be output up till now because we didn't know the first bit to be produced ("deferred" bits). For example, if the range of codes for the message had been 011 through 100, we would be unable to output any bits until the first bit was decided. However, once we have enough information to decide that the first bit is 0, we can output three bits, "011". The value of `bits_to_follow` would be 2 in that case, since we have two deferred bits. Of course, if the first bit turns out to be 1, we would emit "100" instead. The reason that we know that the following bits must be the opposite of the initial bit is that the only time we have to defer bits is when the code range is split between codes starting with 0 and those starting with 1; if both `low` and `high` started with the same bit, we could send that bit out.

> The values of HALF, FIRST_QTR, and THIRD_QTR are all based on TOP_VALUE (listing 4.24). In our example, FIRST_QTR is 64, HALF is 128, and THIRD_QTR is 192. The current value of `high` is 255, which is more than HALF, so we continue with our tests.

Assuming that we haven't obtained the current output bit yet, we continue at line 94, which tests the complementary condition. If `low` is greater than or equal to HALF, we know that the entire frequency range allocated to our message so far is in the top half of the total frequency range; therefore, the first bit of the message is 1. If this occurs, we output a 1 via `bit_plus_follow_1`. The next two lines reduce `high` and `low` by HALF, since we know that both are above that value.

> In our example, `low` is 223, which is more than HALF. Therefore, we can call `bit_plus_follow_1` to output a 1 bit. Then we adjust both `low` and `high` by subtracting HALF, to account for the 1 bit we have just produced; `low` is now 95 and `high` is 127.

If we haven't passed either of the tests to output a 0 or a 1 bit, we continue at line 100, where we test whether the range is small enough but in the wrong position to provide output at this time. This is the situation labeled "Defer" in figure 4.13. We know that the first two bits of the output will be either 01 or 10; we just don't know which of these two possibilities it will be. Therefore, we defer the output, incrementing `bits_to_follow` to indicate that we have done so; we also reduce both `low` and `high` by `FIRST_QTR`, since we know that both are above that value. If this seems mysterious, remember that the encoding information we want is contained in the differences between `low` and `high`, so we want to remove any redundancy in their values.[46]

If we get to line 107, we still don't have any idea what the next output bit(s) will be. This means that the range of frequencies corresponding to our message is still greater than 50% of the maximum possible frequency;[47] we must have encoded an extremely frequent character, since it hasn't even contributed one bit! If this happens, we break out of the output loop; obviously, we have nothing to declare.

In any of the other three cases, we now have arrived at line 109, with the values of `low` and `high` guaranteed to be less than half the maximum possible frequency. Therefore, we shift the values of `low` and `high` up one bit to make room for our next pass through the loop. One more detail: we increment `high` after shifting it because the range represented by `high` actually extends almost to the next frequency value; we have to shift a 1 bit in rather than a 0 to keep this relationship.

> In our example, `low` is 95 and `high` is 127, which represents a range of frequencies from 95 to slightly less than 128. The shifts give us 190 for `low` and 255 for `high`, which represents a range from 190 to slightly less than 256. If we hadn't added 1 to `high`, the range would have been from 190 to slightly less than 255.

ROUND AND ROUND AND ROUND IT GOES

Since we have been over the code in this loop once already, we can continue directly with the example. We start out with `low` at 190 and `high` at 255. Since `high` is not less than `HALF` (128), we proceed to the second test, where `low` turns out to be greater than `HALF`. So we call `bit_plus_follow_1` again as on the first loop and then reduce both `low` and `high` by `HALF`, producing 62 for `low` and 127 for `high`. At the bottom of the loop, we shift a 0 into `low` and a 1 into `high`, resulting in 124 and 255, respectively.

On the next pass through the loop, `high` is not less than `HALF`, `low` isn't greater than or equal to `HALF`, and `high` isn't less than `THIRD_QTR` (192), so we hit the `break` and exit the loop. We have sent two bits to the output buffer.

---

46. In our example, we don't execute this particular adjustment.

47. The proof of this is left to the reader as an exercise; see the problems at the end of the chapter.

We are finished with `encode_symbol` for this character. Now we will start processing the next character of our example message, which is 'B'. This character has a symbol value of 1, as it is the second character in our character set. First, we set `prev_cum` to 0. The frequency accumulation loop at lines 63–68 will not be executed at all, since `symbol/2` evaluates to 0; we fall through to the adjustment code starting at line 69 and select the odd path after the `else`, since the symbol code is odd. We set `current_pair` to (1,3), since that is the first entry in the frequency table. Then we set `total_pair_weight` to the corresponding entry in the `both_weights` table, which is 54. Next, we set `cum` to 0 + 54, or 54. The high part of the current pair is 1, so `high_half_weight` becomes entry 1 in the `translate` table, or 2; we add this to `prev_cum`, which becomes 2 as well.

Now we have reached line 86. Since the current value of `low` is 124 and the current value of `high` is 255, the value of `range` becomes 131. Next, we recalculate `high` as 124 + (131*54)/63 – 1, or 235. The new value of `low` is 124 + (131*2)/63, or 128. We are ready to enter the output loop.

First, `high` is not less than `HALF`, so the first test fails. Next, `low` is equal to `HALF`, so the second test succeeds. Therefore, we call `bit_plus_follow_1` to output a 1 bit; it would also output any deferred bits that we might have been unable to send out before, although there aren't any at present. We also adjust `low` and `high` by subtracting `HALF`, to account for the bit we have just sent; their new values are 0 and 107, respectively.

Next, we proceed to line 109, where we shift `low` and `high` up, injecting a 0 and a 1, respectively; the new values are 0 for `low` and 215 for `high`. On the next pass through the loop we will discover that these values are too far apart to emit any more bits, and we will break out of the loop and return to the main function.

We could continue with a longer message, but I imagine you get the idea. So let's return to line 39 in `main` (listing 4.3).[48]

update_model

The next function called is `update_model` (listing 4.5, lines 42–72), which adjusts the frequencies in the current frequency table to account for having seen the most recent character. The arguments to this routine are `symbol`, the internal value of the character just encoded, and `oldch`, the previous character encoded, which indicates the frequency table that was used to encode that character. What is the internal value of the character? In the current version of the program, it is the same as the ASCII code of the character; however, near the end of the chapter we will employ an opti-

---

48. You may be wondering what happened to the remaining information contained in `low` and `high`. Rest assured that it will not be left twisting in the wind; there is a function called `done_encoding` that makes sure that all of the remaining information is encoded in the output stream.

mization that involves translating characters from ASCII to an internal code to speed up translation.

This function starts out by adding the character's ASCII code to `char_total`, a hash total which is used in our simple pseudorandom number generator to decide when to upgrade a character's frequency to the next frequency index code (line 86). We use the `symbol_translation` table to get the ASCII value of the character before adding it to `char_total`; this is present for compatibility with our final version which employs character translation.

The next few lines (88–90) initialize some variables: `old_weight_code`, which we set when changing a frequency index code or "weight code", so that we can update the frequency total for this frequency table; `temp_freq_info`, a pointer to the frequency table structure for the current character; and `freq_ptr`, the address of the frequency table itself.

Next, line 91 computes the index into the frequency table for the weight code we want to examine. If we find that this symbol is in the high part of that byte in the frequency table, we execute the code at lines 93–106. This starts by setting `temp_freq` to the high four bits of the table entry. If the result is 0, this character has the lowest possible frequency value; we assume that this is because it has never been encountered before and set its frequency index code to `INIT_INDEX`. Then we update the `total_freq` element in the frequency table.

However, if `temp_freq` is not 0, we have to decide whether to upgrade this character's frequency index code to the next level. The probability of this upgrade is inversely proportional to the ratio of the current frequency to the next frequency; the larger the gap between two frequency code values, the less the probability of the upgrade.[49] So we compare `char_total` to the entry in `upgrade_threshold`; if `char_total` is greater, we want to do the upgrade, so we record the previous frequency code in `old_weight_code` and add `HIGH_INCREMENT` to the byte containing the frequency index for the current character. We have to use `HIGH_INCREMENT` rather than 1 to adjust the frequency index, since the frequency code for the current character occupies the high four bits of its byte.

Of course, the character is just as likely to be in the low part of its byte; in that case, we execute the code from lines 108 to 121, which corresponds exactly to the above code. In either case, we follow up at lines 123–127 by testing whether a frequency index code was incremented. If it was, we add the difference between the new code and the old one to the `total_freq` entry in the current frequency table, unless the character previously had a frequency index code of 0; in that case, we have already adjusted the `total_freq` entry.

OVER THE TOP

The last operation in `update_symbol` is to make sure that the total of all frequencies in the frequency table does not exceed the limit of `MAX_FREQUENCY`; if that

---

49. See the discussion on pages 132–133.

were to happen, more than one character might map into the same value between high and low, so that unambiguous decoding would become impossible. Therefore, if temp_total_freq exceeds MAX_FREQUENCY, we have to reduce the frequency indexes until this is no longer the case. The while loop starting at line 130 takes care of this problem.

First, we initialize temp_total_freq to 0, as we will use it to accumulate the frequencies as we modify them. Then we set freq_ptr to the address of the first entry in the frequency table to be modified. Now we are ready to step through all the bytes in the frequency table; for each one, we test whether both indexes in the current byte are 0. If so, we can't reduce them, so we just add the frequency value corresponding to the translation of two 0 indexes (BOTH_WEIGHTS_ZERO) to temp_total_freq.

Otherwise, we copy the current index pair into freq. If the high index is nonzero (line 141), we decrement it. Similarly, if the low index is nonzero, we decrement it. After handling either or both of these cases, we add the translation of the new index pair to temp_total_freq. After we have processed all of the index values in this way, we retest the while condition, and when temp_total_freq is no longer out of range, we store it back into the frequency table and return to the main program.

THE HOME STRETCH

Finally, we have returned to line 40 in main (listing 4.3). Here, we copy ch to oldch, so that the current character will be used to select the frequency table for the next character to be encoded, and continue in the main loop until all characters have been processed.

When we reach EOF in the input file, the main loop terminates; we use encode_symbol to encode EOF_SYMBOL, which tells the receiver to stop decoding. Then we call done_encoding (listing 4.6, lines 116–124) and done_outputing_bits (listing 4.6, lines 116–124) to flush any remaining information to the output file. Finally, we close the input and output files and exit.

Finding the Bottlenecks

Now that we have developed a working version of our program, let's see how much more performance we can get by the use of assembly language in the right places. The first step is to find out where those places are.

These routines account for about 94% of the total execution time of the program. As you can see from the profile in figure 4.14, the vast majority of the CPU time is spent in the encode_symbol routine. So let's see which lines of that routine are the most expensive.

The profile in figure 4.15 indicates that the vast majority of the time in the `encode_symbol` routine is spent on just five lines![50] These lines, which can be divided into two groups, are obvious candidates for assembly language replacement.

Dead Slow Ahead

Since we've already discussed the code at lines 63–68 (the frequency accumulation loop), let's start with the other group, which calculates the new upper and lower bounds after encoding the current character (figure 4.16).

Figure 4.14 *Profile of encode.exe, no assembly language*

```
Turbo Profiler   Version 1.1   Mon Aug 26 20:51:43 1991
Program: C:\OPT\COMPRESS\ENCODE.EXE[51]
Total time: 4.4027 sec

_encode_symbol    2.7700 sec   66%
_main             0.4357 sec   10%
_update_model     0.3741 sec    8%
_output_1         0.2901 sec    6%
_output_0         0.2781• sec   6%
```

Figure 4.15 *Profile of arenc module of encode.exe, no assembly language*

```
Turbo Profiler   Version 1.1   Mon Aug 26 20:48:42 1991
Program: C:\OPT\COMPRESS\ENCODE.EXE
Total time: 18.791 sec

#ARENC#68    4.3426 sec   24%
#ARENC#70    4.3362 sec   23%
#ARENC#69    4.3280 sec   23%
#ARENC#89    0.6551 sec    3%
#ARENC#90    0.6521 sec    3%
```

Figure 4.16 *One of the main culprits in arenc.c*

```
high = low + (range * cum)/total_freq-1;
low = low + (range * prev_cum)/total_freq;
```

50. The percentages cannot be taken literally, since the profiling program has too much overhead to accurately profile individual lines of code.

51. As you will see, the total times for the profiles that track individual lines are considerably longer than those that track only whole routines. This is due to the extra overhead of profiling at such a low level. Only profiles that operate at the same level should be compared.

Figure 4.17 *A little test program*

```
main()
{
    unsigned range;
    unsigned cum;
    unsigned total_freq;
    unsigned high;

    range = 16384;
    cum = 4;
    total_freq = 8;
    high = range * cum / total_freq;
    printf("%u\n",high);
}
```

What these two lines are doing is something that is extremely inefficient in Borland C; they are multiplying two `unsigned` values to get a `long` value, which is then divided by another `unsigned` value to get an `unsigned` result. The reason that this is so inefficient is that the C language makes no provision for "mixed-mode" arithmetic. To see what this implies, let's look at the program in figure 4.17.

What result should we get from this program? I vote for "8192", as that is the correct answer according to the normal laws of arithmetic. However, what we actually get is 0! The reason for this absurd result is that the Borland C compiler insists that the product of two `unsigned` values must be `unsigned`, not `unsigned long`. The relevant portion of the assembly language translation of our little test program is shown in figure 4.18.

The problem is the translation of the line "`high = range * cum / total_freq;`". The first two assembly language statements are fine: the first loads `ax` with `range` and the second multiplies it by `cum`, the result going into `dx` and `ax` (which we can tell by reading the 80x86 manual). So far, so good. The third statement, "`xor dx,dx`", is the culprit. It is clearing the high part of our result variable. Although the multiply instruction actually produces the intermediate value we want, the compiler replaces the high word of the result with 0! The rest of the translation of the C line is fine, dividing the intermediate value by `total_freq` and then storing the result in `si`, which is the equivalent of `high`, but the damage has been done. Note that the compiler actually had to generate an extra instruction to produce an incorrect result. If the `xor dx,dx` instruction were omitted, we would get the result we intended.

Getting the Correct Answer, Slowly

Of course, there *is* a way to multiply two `unsigned` values and divide the result by an `unsigned` value, producing the correct `unsigned` result. The key is to change

Figure 4.18 *The assembly language translation*

```
; main()
;
; {
;       unsigned range;
;       unsigned cum;
;       unsigned total_freq;
;       unsigned high;
;
;       range = 16384;
;
  mov   word ptr [bp-2],16384
;
;       cum = 4;
;
  mov   word ptr [bp-4],4
;
;       total_freq = 8;
;
  mov   word ptr [bp-6],8
;
;       high = range * cum / total_freq;
;
  mov   ax,word ptr [bp-2]
  imul  word ptr [bp-4]
  xor   dx,dx
  div   word ptr [bp-6]
  mov   word ptr [bp-8],ax
;
;       printf("%u\n",high);
;
  push  word ptr [bp-8]
  mov   ax,offset DGROUP:s

  push  ax
  call  near ptr _printf
  pop   cx
  pop   cx
;
; }
;
```

`range` from an `unsigned` variable to a `long` one, as it is in listing 4.6. This forces all arithmetic involving `range` to use `long` operations rather than the `unsigned` ones.[52] The program now produces the correct answer, 8192.

52. Strictly speaking, `range` should really be an `unsigned long` rather than just a `long`; however, since the maximum value of `cum` is less than 16384, the result will never exceed the range of a `long`.

However, getting the correct answer is not always enough; our goal is a correct program that is also as fast as possible. While the speed of `long` addition and subtraction is only moderately reduced from that of the corresponding `unsigned` operations, the routines used to do `long` multiplication and (especially) `long` division are extremely slow. To quantify this, I have written a slightly larger test program which executes the C statement `c = a * b / d;` and the equivalent assembly language statements one million times each (listing 4.7). In each case, the final result is an `unsigned` value, but the intermediate value is a `long`. The assembly language code is 34 times as fast as the C code!

Actually, I've simplified a bit; `range` has to be a `long` anyway, since its maximum value is 65,536, or one greater than the highest possible `unsigned` value. However, we can handle this as a special case, and still get almost all of the theoretically possible speed-up. Let's look at the code for this optimization.

Some Assembly Is Required

As you can see in listing 4.8, lines 114–118 take care of the possibility that `range` is actually 65,536. In the very likely event that it isn't, we proceed directly to the assembly language version.

The first part of the assembly language code (lines 121–123) simply loads the variables that will be accessed more than once into registers, for faster access.[53] Then we copy the value of `range` (in `bx`) into `ax`, since one of the arguments to the multiply instruction `mul` is always `ax` or `al`: the other is the argument to the instruction (`cum`, in this case). The reason that we have to say "`mul word ptr cum`" is that the `mul` instruction can multiply either two bytes or two words. The `word ptr` modifier tells it to multiply `ax` by the word starting at the address `cum`, rather than multiplying `al` by the byte at that address.

The 32-bit result of this multiply instruction goes into `dx` (the high 16 bits) and `ax` (the low 16 bits). This is convenient, since the next instruction, the `div` (divide) instruction, divides whatever is in `dx` and `ax` by its argument, in this case the `cx` register, which has a copy of `total_freq` in it.[54] The result, `range*cum/total_freq`,

---

53. Perhaps I should explain how we can load `range`, a `long` variable, into a 16-bit register. On the 80x86, the low part of a `long` has the same address as the `long` itself does; portability is not a problem here since assembly language is not portable to other processors in any event. Therefore, by using the `word ptr` modifier, we can access the low part of `range` as though it were the whole variable; since we have already eliminated the possibility that the value of `range` was 65,536, the low part of `range` actually contains the entire value.

54. The reason that we don't need to (and can't) specify `word ptr` here is that the second argument, `cx`, is a 16-bit register; specifying such a 16-bit register automatically selects the proper form for the `div` instruction.

is stored in ax. Next, we subtract one, and then add the value of low, which is held in si. The result is moved into high.

I'm sure you can follow the code to calculate the new value of low, as it is a virtual duplicate of the above. Figure 4.19 shows the performance improvement we get from this fairly small amount of assembly language.

As you can see, we have increased the overall speed by 84%. While we have doubled the speed of the encode_symbol function, it still accounts for almost five-eighths of the total time taken by all our routines. Let's zoom in for a closer look at encode_symbol, whose profiling results are indicated in figure 4.20.

As I mentioned in the discussion of the algorithm, a significant amount of the CPU time needed to encode a symbol is spent in the loop at lines 91–96 in listing 4.8. According to the above results, about 74% of the time spent in encode_symbol can be attributed to these few lines, even though we have packed two indexes into each byte. This looks like a good place to continue our optimization.

Unlike our first foray into assembly language code, however, our second venture (listing 4.10, lines 99–122) is not an exact transcription of what the compiler should have produced from our C code. In this case, there is no one operation that is ridiculously slow; it's just that we have to execute these few lines so many times. Unfortunately, executing a few instructions repeatedly in a loop tends to be inefficient on the 80x86 family of processors (at least up through the i386). The explanation for this requires some discussion of the compromises inherent in microprocessor hardware.

Figure 4.19 *Assembly language enhancements multiply/divide*

```
Turbo Profiler  Version 1.1  Mon Aug 26 20:59:45 1991
Program: C:\OPT\COMPRESS\ENCODE1.EXE
Total time: 2.3904 sec

_encode_symbol    1.3577 sec    62%
_main             0.4163 sec    19%
_update_model     0.3557 sec    16%
_start_model      0.0408 sec     1%
```

Figure 4.20 *Profile of arenc module of encode1.exe, after first assembly language enhancements*

```
Turbo Profiler  Version 1.1  Mon Aug 26 21:45:54 1991
Program: C:\OPT\COMPRESS\ENCODE1.EXE
Total time: 16.113 sec

#ARENC1#95        3.8799 sec    25%
#ARENC1#97        3.8691 sec    25%
#ARENC1#96        3.7685 sec    24%
```

Memories Are Made of This

My home computer has a 33-MHz i386 processor. According to the instruction timing manual, a fast instruction such as an `add reg,immediate` takes two clock cycles, or 60 nanoseconds (nsec). However, since the main memory in my machine runs at about 80 nsec, if the processor had to load this instruction as it came to it, the load would take longer than the instruction execution! Of course, this would greatly reduce the effective speed of the machine.

There are a number of ways to lessen this problem. One is to use memory that is as fast as the microprocessor, or 30 nsec. Unfortunately, using such memory as the main memory of a microcomputer is prohibitively expensive, although it is possible to use some very fast memory as a memory cache, which holds the most recently used data in the hope that they will be accessed again in the near future. Even if they are found in the cache, however, the processor would still spend much of its time loading instructions rather than executing them. Therefore, the designers have added a separate "bus unit", operating in parallel with the "execution unit". The bus unit spends its time prefetching as many future instructions as possible so that the execution unit will not have to wait while its next instruction is fetched.

However, the bus unit can't predict with certainty what instructions should be prefetched, as that may depend on the result of conditional instructions such as `jz` (jump if zero) and `loop` (jump if `cx` is not zero); it simply prefetches the instructions following the one currently being executed.[55] While this scheme works nicely in the case of a long string of instructions with no jumps, it is not very useful when we have a loop consisting of a few instructions and a jump back to the beginning of the loop. In this case, the prefetch queue is constantly being invalidated and reloaded, which takes many memory cycles; in the meantime, the execution unit cannot run at full speed.

How do we get around this? We use a technique called **loop unrolling**.[56]

Loop, De-loop

The basic idea of unrolling a loop is that as more operations are performed in one pass through the loop, the loop overhead becomes less significant.[57] Let's look at the initialization code in lines 99–103. First, we clear `bx`, which will be used to index

---

55. The problem of incorrect prediction of the prefetch path becomes increasingly more significant as the processor speeds continue to increase. As a result, some newer processors such as the Pentium™ have "branch prediction" hardware that keeps track of the results of each conditional branch and prefetches based on that knowledge, rather than continuing blindly along the path of increasing memory addresses.

56. The value of this technique is quite dependent on the exact implementation of the processor; please see the discussion on pages 154–155.

57. While this technique could also be applied to the C version of the program, the improvement in performance would probably not be very great, since the number of instructions in the loop is considerably greater in the C version; the greatest speed improvement occurs when very short loops are unrolled.

into the table of weights, and set **cx** to the number of entries that we will accumulate. Then we shift **cx** one place to the right, to calculate the number of pairs of entries we will accumulate at two per byte, and clear **dx**, which will accumulate our total. Then we set **si** to the address[58] of the beginning of the **freq_ptr** table, which is where the relative frequency indexes are stored.

Now, at line 104, we test whether we need to execute our loop at all. If the number of pairs of entries to be processed is 0 (that is, the symbol being encoded had a value of 0 or 1), we just skip to the end of the loop. So far, all of this is quite similar to the code generated by the C compiler. Here is where we start the loop unrolling operation.

The first step is to divide the number of pairs of weights by two (line 105), as we are going to load two pairs at once in our loop. If the result comes out even (the **carry** flag is not set), we can enter the main body of the loop, which processes two pairs of weights for each pass through the loop.

Odd Man Out

However, if we have an odd pair of weights to process, we will handle that first, which is the province of lines 107–110. This sequence starts with a **lodsb**, which loads the next pair of weights into **al** and increments the pointer to the next pair of weights. The pair of weights is then copied to **bl**, with the result that **bx** is the entry number in the **both_weights** table.

Now we have to convert an entry number into an address. Since there are two bytes in each entry, that requires multiplying the entry number by two and adding it to the address of the beginning of the **both_weights** table. The word at the resulting address can then be stored in our running total of weights. One way to do this is the following sequence:

```
2    xor  bh,bh ;     clear the high part of the index register
2    mov  bl,al    ;get the entry number
2    add  bx,bx    ;multiply by two
4    mov  dx,both_weights[bx]; move the entry to the accumulator
--
10   cycles total time (i386)
```

However, this is not the best we can do. The only reason that we have to clear **bh** each time before we load **bl** is that **bh** might be nonzero due to our doubling

---

58. Strictly speaking, this is not an address, but the "offset" of the beginning of the **freq_ptr** table. This is a consequence of the segmented architecture of the 80x86 line of processors, a full discussion of which is outside the scope of this book. However, in all memory models we will be using, global data such as the **freq_ptr** table are stored in one segment, which is always pointed to by the **ds** segment register. A similar rule applies to local data, which are always accessible via the **ss** register. These rules, together with the Borland C compiler's support for in-line assembly language, mean that when dealing with global data or data declared in the current routine, we can ignore the segmented nature of the processor in our in-line assembly code.

of bx. Another way to have the effect of doubling bx without actually changing it is the following:

```
2    mov  bl,al       ; get the pair
2    lea  di,both_weights[bx]; start of weights + 1/2 offset
4    mov  dx,[di+bx]; move to the accumulator
--
8    cycles total time (i386)
```

The lea instruction forms the address of its memory operand and stores it into its first operand, which must be a register, in this case di. At this point, di contains the starting address of the table of weights added to the entry number of the entry we want to retrieve. The next line effectively adds the entry number again, which means that we have added bx to the starting address twice, rather than doubling it and using it once. Therefore, we have to clear bh only before we enter the loop, rather than before every execution.

Now that we have taken care of the possible odd pair of weights, we test whether that was the only pair (line 111). If so, we jump to the end of the loop, as we are finished. Otherwise, we start processing all the remaining pairs of weights.

This code is actually very similar to the code for the odd pair we just examined. The basic difference is that we use the lodsw instruction to get two pairs of weights (two bytes) at once, rather than the lodsb, which gets one pair of weights (one byte). Each of these pairs is processed exactly like the odd pair, except that the value retrieved from the both_weights table is added to the accumulator (dx) rather than being stored into it. At the end of the loop, the loop instruction jumps back to the beginning of the loop if we have not yet finished.

Once we fall off the end of the loop, the result is in dx. Of course, we have to move it into a C variable (prev_cum) for further use in our program.

Getting There Is Half the Fun

What have we achieved by this modification? It should be fairly significant, as we have eliminated quite a few instructions from the C compiler's version. First, we are executing the loop instruction only half as many times, which reduces the degradation associated with flushing the prefetch queue. Also, our inner loop uses only registers to save temporary values, rather than memory, which should also speed up operations. Finally, the lodsw instruction replaces two loads and two index register increments. Figure 4.21 shows the results.

This version is 40% faster than the previous one and 2.5 times the speed of the first one we profiled, saving over two and a half seconds for our sample file of a little less than 11 Kbytes. This is quite respectable for a few dozen lines of assembly language. Is this the best we can do?

There aren't any more obvious "hot spots" that can easily be improved by the use of a small amount of assembly language. However, we can increase the speed of our implementation by using a more efficient representation of the characters to be encoded,

Figure 4.21 *Assembly language enhancements: multiply/divide and accumulation*

```
Turbo Profiler   Version 1.1   Mon Aug 26 21:54:40 1991
Program: C:\OPT\COMPRESS\ENCODE2.EXE
Total time: 1.7134 sec

_encode_symbol    0.7161 sec   47%
_main             0.3856 sec   25%
_update_model     0.3569 sec   23%
_start_model      0.0411 sec    2%
```

so that the accumulation loop will be executed fewer times in total. While we cannot spare the space for self-organizing tables of character translations (see page 181), a fixed translation of characters according to some reasonable estimate of their likelihood in the text is certainly possible. Let's see how that would affect our performance.

A Bunch of Real Characters

After analyzing a number of (hopefully representative) text files, I used the results to produce a list of the characters in descending order of number of occurrences. This is the symbol_translation table (listing 4.5, lines 21–33), which is used during decoding to translate from the internal code into ASCII. The inverse transformation, used by the encoder, is supplied by the char_translation table, which is initialized in lines 68–69 of the same listing.

To use these new values for each character when encoding and decoding, we have to make some small changes in the encoding and decoding main programs. Specifically, in encode.c we have to add line 17 and change lines 33 and 39–42, to use the translated character rather than the ASCII code as read from the input file (listing 4.4). Corresponding changes have to be made to decode.c, resulting in listing 4.12; figure 4.22 shows the results.

Figure 4.22 *Profile of encode3.exe, final enhancements*

```
Turbo Profiler   Version 1.1   Mon Aug 26 21:58:10 1991
Program: C:\OPT\COMPRESS\ENCODE3.EXE
Total time: 1.5468 sec

_encode_symbol    0.4968 sec   37%
_main             0.4418 sec   33%
_update_model     0.3515 sec   26%
_start_model      0.0398 sec    2%
```

There's another 11% improvement in speed over the previous version; our final version is 2.85 times as fast as the original program. Even though the accumulation loop is coded in assembly language, reducing the number of executions pays off. This last improvement took a total of about an hour, mostly to write and debug the character counting program and run it on a number of sample files. That's considerably less than the time to do the assembly language enhancements, but the resulting improvement in speed is still significant. Possibly of equal importance is that this last modification is portable to other compilers and processors, whereas the assembly language ones aren't.[59]

However, unlike the assembly language modifications, this last change isn't helpful in all cases. It will speed up the handling of files that resemble those used to calculate the translation tables, but will have much less impact on those having a significantly different mix of data characters. In the worst case, it might even slow the program down noticeably; for example, a file containing many nulls, or 0 characters, might be compressed faster without translation, as encoding the most common character would then require no executions of the accumulation loop. This is an example of the general rule that knowing the makeup of the data is important in deciding how to optimize the program.

For the record, all of the above profiles were run on a 386/33 with a 28-msec disk drive, with software disk caching disabled.

1994: A Space Odyssey?

The above was originally written in 1992, for the first edition of this book. Upon revisiting this chapter for the second edition, I discovered an oversight in the discussion of the unrolling of the accumulation loop.[60] The problem is that I didn't provide the code or the performance figures before the loop unrolling, so there's no way to determine from the text what the effect of unrolling the loop actually was.

The case of the missing code is easy to solve: it is reproduced in listing 4.9, lines 99–113. However, the performance figures are another story, as I have purchased a new computer and sold the one on which those tests were run. The purchaser has kindly allowed me to run a few tests, which demonstrate the performance improvement from one version to another, although the setup required to allow running full profiles would have been too much of an imposition.

Figure 4.23 shows the stopwatch timings for a 44K text file on the original 386/33 machine, with disk caching turned off.[61]

---

59. If we hadn't used any assembly language enhancements, this improvement would have made a much greater difference in the speed, since the time saved by eliminating each loop execution would have been much greater.

60. This discussion starts on page 150.

61. The reason I didn't use the same 11K file as in the profiles is that the times with that file were too short to measure accurately with a stopwatch.

Figure 4.23 *Timing of encoding programs*

ENCODE.EXE	12.0	sec (no assembly language)
ENCODE1.EXE	8.0	sec (multiply/divide in assembly)
ENCODE15.EXE	5.5	sec (accumulation loop in assembly)
ENCODE2.EXE	5.0	sec (loop unrolling)
ENCODE3.EXE	3.5	sec (character translation)

According to the profiler results earlier in the chapter, `encode_symbol` accounted for slightly less than 50% of the run time in the ENCODE2.EXE program. Thus, the 10% improvement in overall run time between ENCODE15.EXE and ENCODE2.EXE implies that the loop unrolling produced approximately a 20% reduction in the time taken by that routine.

On the other hand, experiments on my current 486/66DX2 machine indicate that loop unrolling had a negligible effect on performance, whether the internal cache was enabled or disabled. This merely reinforces the point that performance improvements at this level are very sensitive to processor architecture.

Summary

In this chapter, we have seen an example of the use of assembly language to speed up a program containing a few areas of code that are executed with great frequency. In the next chapter, we will see how to implement high-performance special-purpose interpreters in i386 assembly language, to make the best use of fast CPUs with slow memory access.

Problems

1. How could arithmetic coding be used where each of a number of blocks of text must be decompressed without reference to the other blocks?

2. If we knew that the data to be compressed consisted entirely of characters with ASCII codes 0 through 127, could we reduce the memory requirements of this algorithm further? If so, how much and how?

3. How could assembly language enhancements be applied to the Megasort routine from Chapter 3?

(You can find suggested approaches to problems in Chapter 8).

Listing 4.1 *arith.h: arithmentic coding constants*

```
1
2    /****keyword-flag*** "%v %f %n" */
3    /* "5 13-Sep-91,7:20:08 ARITH.H" */
4
5
6    #define CODE_VALUE_BITS 16
7    typedef long code_value;
8
9
10   #define TOP_VALUE        (((long)1<<CODE_VALUE_BITS)-1)
11
12   #define FIRST_QTR        (TOP_VALUE/4+1)
13   #define HALF             (2*FIRST_QTR)
14   #define THIRD_QTR        (3*FIRST_QTR)
15
```

Figure 4.2 *model.h translation table coding constants and variables*

```
 1
 2    /****keyword-flag*** "%v %f %n" */
 3    /* "9 12-May-92,17:46:24 MODEL.H" */
 4
 5
 6    #define NO_OF_CHARS 256
 7    #define EOF_SYMBOL (NO_OF_CHARS+1)
 8
 9    #define NO_OF_SYMBOLS (NO_OF_CHARS+1)
10
11    #define MAX_FREQUENCY 16383
12
13    typedef struct
14    {
15      unsigned total_freq;
16      unsigned char freq[(NO_OF_SYMBOLS+1+1)/2];
17    } FrequencyInfo;
18
19    extern FrequencyInfo frequency_info_data[NO_OF_CHARS];
20    extern FrequencyInfo *frequency_info[NO_OF_CHARS];
21
22    extern unsigned translate[16];
23
24    extern unsigned both_weights[256];
25
26    extern unsigned symbol_translation[NO_OF_CHARS];
27
28    extern unsigned char_translation[NO_OF_CHARS];
29
30    #define HIGH_MASK 240 /* the high four bits */
31    #define LOW_MASK 15   /* the low four bits */
32
33    #define HIGH_INCREMENT 16 /* the difference between two high values */
34    #define LOW_INCREMENT 1 /* the difference between two low values */
35
36    #define HIGH_SHIFT 4 /* how much to shift a high nibble */
37    #define LOW_SHIFT 0 /* how much to shift a low nibble */
38
39    #define UPPER_INDEX 15 /* how high is the last table index */
40
41    #define TRANSLATE_SIZE 16
42
43    #define TRANSLATE_TABLE \
44    {1,16,22,30,42,58,79,109,150,207,285,392,540,744,1024,16000}
45
46    int start_inputing_bits(void);
47    int start_model(void);
48    int update_model(int symbol,unsigned char oldch);
49    int start_decoding(void);
50    unsigned decode_symbol(unsigned oldch);
51    int input_bit(void);
```

Listing 4.2 *model.h translation table coding constants and variables (continued)*

```
52    int output_0(void);
53    int output_1(void);
54    int done_outputing_bits(void);
55    int start_outputing_bits(void);
56    int done_encoding(void);
57    int start_encoding(void);
58    int encode_symbol(unsigned symbol, unsigned oldch);
```

Listing 4.3 *encode.c: encoding main module*

```
1
2    /****keyword-flag*** "%v %f %n" */
3    /* "8.2 12-May-92,18:01:10 ENCODE.C" */
4
5
6    #include <stdio.h>
7    #include <stdlib.h>
8    #include "model.h"
9
10   FILE *infile;
11   FILE *outfile;
12
13   main(int argc, char *argv[])
14   {
15     unsigned oldch;
16     unsigned ch;
17
18     if (argc < 3)
19         {
20         printf("Usage: encode original compressed.\n");
21         exit(1);
22         }
23
24     infile = fopen(argv[1],"rb");
25     outfile = fopen(argv[2],"wb");
26     setvbuf(infile,NULL,_IOFBF,8000);
27     setvbuf(outfile,NULL,_IOFBF,8000);
28
29     start_model();
30     start_outputing_bits();
31     start_encoding();
32     oldch = 0;
33     for (;;)
34         {
35         ch = fgetc(infile);
36         if (ch == (unsigned)EOF)
37             break;
38         encode_symbol(ch,oldch);
39         update_model(ch,oldch);
40         oldch = ch;
41         }
42     encode_symbol(EOF_SYMBOL,oldch);
43     done_encoding();
44     done_outputing_bits();
45     fclose(infile);
46     fclose(outfile);
47     return(0);
48   }
```

Listing 4.4 *encode1.c: encoding main module*

```
1
2    /****keyword-flag*** "%v %f %n" */
3    /* "11 12-May-92,18:01:10 ENCODE1.C" */
4
5
6    #include <stdio.h>
7    #include <stdlib.h>
8    #include "model.h"
9
10   FILE *infile;
11   FILE *outfile;
12
13   main(int argc, char *argv[])
14   {
15      unsigned oldch;
16      unsigned ch;
17      unsigned symbol;
18
19      if (argc < 3)
20          {
21          printf("Usage: encode original compressed.\n");
22          exit(1);
23          }
24
25      infile = fopen(argv[1],"rb");
26      outfile = fopen(argv[2],"wb");
27      setvbuf(infile,NULL,_IOFBF,12000);
28      setvbuf(outfile,NULL,_IOFBF,12000);
29
30      start_model();
31      start_outputing_bits();
32      start_encoding();
33      oldch = char_translation[0];
34      for (;;)
35          {
36          ch = fgetc(infile);
37          if (ch == (unsigned)EOF)
38              break;
39          symbol = char_translation[ch];
40          encode_symbol(symbol,oldch);
41          update_model(symbol,oldch);
42          oldch = symbol;
43          }
44      encode_symbol(EOF_SYMBOL,oldch);
45      done_encoding();
46      done_outputing_bits();
47      return(0);
48   }
```

Listing 4.5 *adapt.c: adaptive modeling routines*

```
 1
 2   /****keyword-flag*** "%v %f %n" */
 3   /* "15 12-May-92,18:01:06 ADAPT.C" */
 4
 5
 6   #include <alloc.h>
 7   #include "model.h"
 8
 9   #define INIT_INDEX 7 /* where a new character starts out the first time */
10
11   #define BOTH_WEIGHTS_ZERO 2 /* this must be the total of two "unused" weights */
12   /* and must be the same for both (or all) translate tables */
13
14   unsigned translate[TRANSLATE_SIZE] = TRANSLATE_TABLE;
15
16   unsigned char upgrade_threshold[TRANSLATE_SIZE];
17
18   /* all possible combinations of 2 low weights */
19    unsigned both_weights[TRANSLATE_SIZE*TRANSLATE_SIZE];
20
21 unsigned symbol_translation[NO_OF_CHARS] = {32,101,116,111,97,105,110,114,115,
22 104,108,100,13,10,99,117,109,112,103,121,102,46,98,119,44,94,118,107,78,84,
23 69,39,65,83,41,40,120,66,45,73,34,77,58,80,85,67,49,82,48,87,79,47,88,72,
24 70,68,89,57,71,113,76,50,86,122,106,59,63,54,55,74,61,42,37,12,53,64,56,75,
25 33,52,51,90,62,38,81,35,26,255,254,253,252,251,250,249,248,247,246,245,244,
26 243,242,241,240,239,238,237,236,235,234,233,232,231,230,229,228,227,226,225,
27 224,223,222,221,220,219,218,217,216,215,214,213,212,211,210,209,208,207,206,
28 205,204,203,202,201,200,199,198,197,196,195,194,193,192,191,190,189,188,187,
29 186,185,184,183,182,181,180,179,178,177,176,175,174,173,172,171,170,169,168,
30 167,166,165,164,163,162,161,160,159,158,157,156,155,154,153,152,151,150,149,
31 148,147,146,145,144,143,142,141,140,139,138,137,136,135,134,133,132,131,130,
32 129,128,127,126,125,124,123,96,95,93,92,91,60,43,36,31,30,29,28,27,25,24,23,
33 22,21,20,19,18,17,16,15,14,11,9,8,7,6,5,4,3,2,1,0};
34
35   unsigned char_translation[NO_OF_CHARS];
36
37   FrequencyInfo frequency_info_data[NO_OF_CHARS];
38   FrequencyInfo *frequency_info[NO_OF_CHARS];
39
40   unsigned char char_total;
41
42   start_model()
43   {
44     int i;
45     int j;
46
47     for (i = 0; i < TRANSLATE_SIZE - 1; i ++)
48         {
49         upgrade_threshold[i] =
50         256*(1-(double)translate[i]/(double)translate[i+1]);
51         }
```

Listing 4.5 *adapt.c: adaptive modeling routines (continued)*

```
52
53      upgrade_threshold[TRANSLATE_SIZE-1] = 255;
54      char_total = 0;
55
56      for (i = 0; i < TRANSLATE_SIZE; i ++)
57           for (j = 0; j < TRANSLATE_SIZE; j ++)
58                both_weights[TRANSLATE_SIZE*i+j] = translate[i] + translate[j];
59
60      for (i = 0; i < NO_OF_CHARS; i ++)
61           {
62           frequency_info[i] = &frequency_info_data[i];
63           for (j = 0; j < (NO_OF_SYMBOLS+1+1)/2; j ++)
64                frequency_info[i]->freq[j] = 0;
65           frequency_info[i]->total_freq = translate[0] * (NO_OF_SYMBOLS + 1);
66           }
67
68      for (i = 0; i < NO_OF_CHARS; i ++)
69           char_translation[symbol_translation[i]] = i;
70
71      return(0);
72  }
73
74  update_model(int symbol,unsigned char oldch)
75  {
76      int i;
77      int index;
78      unsigned char *freq_ptr;
79      unsigned char freq;
80      int old_weight_code;
81      unsigned weight_gain;
82      unsigned char temp_freq;
83      long temp_total_freq;
84      FrequencyInfo *temp_freq_info;
85
86      char_total += (symbol_translation[symbol] & 255);
87
88      old_weight_code = -1;
89      temp_freq_info = frequency_info[oldch];
90      freq_ptr = temp_freq_info->freq;
91      index = symbol/2;
92      if (symbol % 2 == 0) /* if a high symbol */
93           {
94           temp_freq = (freq_ptr[index] & HIGH_MASK) >> HIGH_SHIFT;
95           if (temp_freq == 0)
96                {
97                freq_ptr[index] += INIT_INDEX << HIGH_SHIFT;
98                temp_freq_info->total_freq +=
99                translate[INIT_INDEX] - translate[0];
100               }
101          else if (char_total > upgrade_threshold[temp_freq])
102               {
```

Listing 4.5 *adapt.c: adaptive modeling routines (continued)*

```
103                        old_weight_code = temp_freq;
104                        freq_ptr[index] += HIGH_INCREMENT; /* bump it */
105                        }
106                }
107        else /* if a low one */
108                {
109                temp_freq = (freq_ptr[index] & LOW_MASK) >> LOW_SHIFT;
110                if (temp_freq == 0)
111                        {
112                        freq_ptr[index] += INIT_INDEX << LOW_SHIFT;
113                        temp_freq_info->total_freq +=
114                        translate[INIT_INDEX] - translate[0];
115                        }
116                else if (char_total > upgrade_threshold[temp_freq])
117                        {
118                        old_weight_code = temp_freq;
119                        freq_ptr[index] += LOW_INCREMENT; /* bump it */
120                        }
121                }
122
123        if (old_weight_code != -1) /* if there was an adjustment of weight */
124                {
125                weight_gain = translate[old_weight_code+1] - translate[old_weight_code];
126                temp_freq_info->total_freq += weight_gain;
127                }
128
129        temp_total_freq = temp_freq_info->total_freq;
130        while (temp_total_freq > MAX_FREQUENCY)
131                {
132                temp_total_freq = 0;
133                freq_ptr = temp_freq_info->freq;
134                for (i = 0; i < (NO_OF_SYMBOLS+1)/2; i ++)
135                        {
136                        if (*freq_ptr == 0) /* if this is at the bottom, forget it */
137                                temp_total_freq += BOTH_WEIGHTS_ZERO;
138                        else /* if it needs to be updated */
139                                {
140                                freq = *freq_ptr;
141                                if ((freq & HIGH_MASK) != 0)
142                                        {
143                                        /* if the top is not at the lowest value*/
144                                        *freq_ptr -= HIGH_INCREMENT; /* decrement it */
145                                        }
146                                if ((freq & LOW_MASK) != 0)
147                                        {
148                                        /* if the low is not at the lowest value*/
149                                        *freq_ptr -= LOW_INCREMENT; /* decrement it */
150                                        }
151                                temp_total_freq += both_weights[*freq_ptr];
152                                }
153                        freq_ptr ++;
```

Listing 4.5 *adapt.c: adaptive modeling routines (continued)*

```
154                 }
155             }
156     temp_freq_info->total_freq = (unsigned)temp_total_freq;
157     return(0);
158 }
159
```

Listing 4.6 *arenc.c: arithmetic encoding routines, no assembly*

```
1
2    /****keyword-flag*** "%v %f %n" */
3    /* "12 12-May-92,18:01:12 ARENC.C" */
4
5
6    #include "arith.h"
7    #include "model.h"
8    #include <stdio.h>
9
10   extern FILE *outfile;
11   int buffer;
12   int bits_to_go;
13   unsigned low,high;
14   unsigned bits_to_follow;
15
16   #define bit_plus_follow_0 \
17   { \
18     output_0(); \
19     while (bits_to_follow > 0) \
20           { \
21           output_1(); \
22           bits_to_follow -; \
23           } \
24   }
25
26   #define bit_plus_follow_1 \
27   { \
28     output_1(); \
29     while (bits_to_follow > 0) \
30           { \
31           output_0(); \
32           bits_to_follow -; \
33           } \
34   }
35
36
37   int start_encoding()
38   {
39     low = 0;
40     high = (unsigned)TOP_VALUE;
41     bits_to_follow = 0;
42     return(0);
43   }
44
45   int encode_symbol(unsigned symbol, unsigned oldch)
46   {
47     long range;
48     int i;
49     unsigned cum;
50     unsigned prev_cum;
51     unsigned char *freq_ptr;
```

Listing 4.6 *arenc.c: arithmetic encoding routines, no assembly (continued)*

```
52       int current_pair;
53       unsigned char high_half;
54       unsigned high_half_weight;
55       unsigned total_pair_weight;
56       unsigned total_freq;
57       FrequencyInfo *temp_freq_info;
58
59       temp_freq_info = frequency_info[oldch];
60       freq_ptr = temp_freq_info->freq;
61       total_freq = temp_freq_info->total_freq;
62       prev_cum = 0;
63       for (i = 0; i < symbol/2; i ++)
64            {
65            current_pair = *(freq_ptr++);
66            total_pair_weight = both_weights[current_pair];
67            prev_cum += total_pair_weight;
68            }
69       if (symbol % 2 == 0)   /* if even, prev cum is ok, update cum */
70            {
71            current_pair = *freq_ptr;
72            high_half = (current_pair & HIGH_MASK) >> HIGH_SHIFT;
73            high_half_weight = translate[high_half];
74            cum = prev_cum + high_half_weight;
75            }
76       else /* if odd, update both */
77            {
78            current_pair = *freq_ptr;
79            total_pair_weight = both_weights[current_pair];
80            cum = prev_cum + total_pair_weight;
81            high_half = (current_pair & HIGH_MASK) >> HIGH_SHIFT;
82            high_half_weight = translate[high_half];
83            prev_cum += high_half_weight;
84             }
85
86       range = (long)(high-low)+1;
87       high = low + (unsigned)((range * cum)/total_freq-1);
88       low = low + (unsigned)((range * prev_cum)/total_freq);
89
90       for (;;)
91            {
92            if (high < HALF)
93                 bit_plus_follow_0
94            else if (low >= HALF)
95                 {
96                 bit_plus_follow_1
97                 low -= (unsigned)HALF;
98                 high -= (unsigned)HALF;
99                 }
100           else if (low >= FIRST_QTR && high < THIRD_QTR)
101                {
102                bits_to_follow ++;
```

Listing 4.6 *arenc.c: arithmetic encoding routines, no assembly (continued)*

```
103                low -= (unsigned)FIRST_QTR;
104                high -= (unsigned)FIRST_QTR;
105                }
106          else
107                break;
108
109          low <<= 1;
110          high <<= 1;
111          high ++;
112          }
113    return(0);
114  }
115
116  int done_encoding()
117  {
118    bits_to_follow ++;
119    if (low < FIRST_QTR)
120          bit_plus_follow_0
121    else
122          bit_plus_follow_1
123    return(0);
124  }
125
126
127  int start_outputing_bits()
128  {
129    buffer = 0;
130    bits_to_go = 8;
131    return(0);
132  }
133
134
135  int output_0()
136  {
137    buffer >>= 1;
138
139    bits_to_go —;
140    if (bits_to_go == 0)
141          {
142          fputc(buffer,outfile);
143          bits_to_go = 8;
144          }
145    return(0);
146  }
147
148
149  int output_1()
150  {
151    buffer >>= 1;
152    buffer |= 0x80;
153
```

Listing 4.6 *arenc.c: arithmetic encoding routines, no assembly (continued)*

```
154     bits_to_go --;
155     if (bits_to_go == 0)
156         {
157             fputc(buffer,outfile);
158             bits_to_go = 8;
159         }
160     return(0);
161   }
162
163
164   int done_outputing_bits()
165   {
166     fputc(buffer>>bits_to_go,outfile);
167     return(0);
168   }
169
```

Listing 4.7 *longasm.c: comparison of C and assembly in long arithmetic*

```
1
2
3    #include <stdio.h>
4    #include <stdlib.h>
5    #include <time.h>
6    #include <dos.h>
7
8    main()
9    {
10     unsigned a;
11     unsigned b;
12     unsigned c;
13     unsigned d;
14     long i;
15     struct  time t;
16
17     a = 16384;
18     b = 4;
19     d = 37;
20
21     gettime(&t);
22     printf("Starting C at %2d:%02d:%02d.%02d\n",
23     t.ti_hour, t.ti_min, t.ti_sec, t.ti_hund);
24
25     for (i = 0; i < 100000; i ++)
26         {
27         c = (long)a * b / d;
28         c = (long)a * b / d;
29         c = (long)a * b / d;
30         c = (long)a * b / d;
31         c = (long)a * b / d;
32         c = (long)a * b / d;
33         c = (long)a * b / d;
34         c = (long)a * b / d;
35         c = (long)a * b / d;
36         c = (long)a * b / d;
37         }
38
39     gettime(&t);
40     printf("Starting asm at %2d:%02d:%02d.%02d\n",
41     t.ti_hour, t.ti_min, t.ti_sec, t.ti_hund);
42
43     for (i = 0; i < 100000; i ++)
44         {
45         asm  mov  ax,a;
46         asm  mul  word ptr b;
47         asm  div  word ptr d;
48         asm  mov  c,ax;
49
50         asm  mov  ax,a;
51         asm  mul  word ptr b;
```

Listing 4.7 *longasm.c: comparison of C and assembly in long arithmetic (continued)*

```
52          asm  div  word ptr d;
53          asm  mov  c,ax;
54
55          asm  mov  ax,a;
56          asm  mul  word ptr b;
57          asm  div  word ptr d;
58          asm  mov  c,ax;
59
60          asm  mov  ax,a;
61          asm  mul  word ptr b;
62          asm  div  word ptr d;
63          asm  mov  c,ax;
64
65          asm  mov  ax,a;
66          asm  mul  word ptr b;
67          asm  div  word ptr d;
68          asm  mov  c,ax;
69
70          asm  mov  ax,a;
71          asm  mul  word ptr b;
72          asm  div  word ptr d;
73          asm  mov  c,ax;
74
75          asm  mov  ax,a;
76          asm  mul  word ptr b;
77          asm  div  word ptr d;
78          asm  mov  c,ax;
79
80          asm  mov  ax,a;
81          asm  mul  word ptr b;
82          asm  div  word ptr d;
83          asm  mov  c,ax;
84
85          asm  mov  ax,a;
86          asm  mul  word ptr b;
87          asm  div  word ptr d;
88          asm  mov  c,ax;
89
90          asm  mov  ax,a;
91          asm  mul  word ptr b;
92          asm  div  word ptr d;
93          asm  mov  c,ax;
94          }
95
96      gettime(&t);
97      printf("Ending asm at %2d:%02d:%02d.%02d\n",
98      t.ti_hour, t.ti_min, t.ti_sec, t.ti_hund);
99      }
```

Figure 4.8 *arenc1.c: arithmetic encoding routines, assembly multiply/divide*

```
1
2     /****keyword-flag*** "%v %f %n" */
3     /* "2.15 13-Sep-91,7:05:04 ARENC1.C" */
4
5
6     #include "arith.h"
7     #include "model.h"
8     #include <stdio.h>
9
10    extern FILE *outfile;
11    int buffer;
12    int bits_to_go;
13    unsigned low,high;
14    unsigned bits_to_follow;
15
16
17    #define output_0\
18    {\
19      buffer >>= 1;\
20      bits_to_go --;\
21      if (bits_to_go == 0)\
22            {\
23            fputc(buffer,outfile);\
24            bits_to_go = 8;\
25            }\
26    }
27
28
29    #define output_1\
30    {\
31      buffer >>= 1;\
32      buffer |= 0x80;\
33      bits_to_go --;\
34      if (bits_to_go == 0)\
35            {\
36            fputc(buffer,outfile);\
37            bits_to_go = 8;\
38            }\
39    }
40
41
42    #define bit_plus_follow_0 \
43    { \
44      output_0\
45      while (bits_to_follow > 0) \
46            { \
47            output_1\
48            bits_to_follow --; \
49            } \
50    }
51
```

Listing 4.8 *arenc1.c: arithmetic encoding routines, assembly multiply/divide (continued)*

```
52    #define bit_plus_follow_1 \
53    { \
54      output_1\
55      while (bits_to_follow > 0) \
56            { \
57            output_0\
58            bits_to_follow —; \
59            } \
60    }
61
62
63    start_encoding()
64    {
65      low = 0;
66      high = TOP_VALUE;
67      bits_to_follow = 0;
68      return(0);
69    }
70
71
72    encode_symbol(unsigned symbol, unsigned oldch)
73    {
74      long range;
75      int i;
76      unsigned cum;
77      unsigned prev_cum;
78      unsigned char *freq_ptr;
79      int current_pair;
80      unsigned char high_half;
81      unsigned high_half_weight;
82      unsigned total_pair_weight;
83      unsigned total_freq;
84      FrequencyInfo *temp_freq_info;
85
86      range = (long)(high-low)+1;
87      temp_freq_info = frequency_info[oldch];
88      freq_ptr = temp_freq_info->freq;
89      total_freq = temp_freq_info->total_freq;
90      prev_cum = 0;
91      for (i = 0; i < symbol/2; i ++)
92            {
93            current_pair = *(freq_ptr++);
94            total_pair_weight = both_weights[current_pair];
95            prev_cum += total_pair_weight;
96            }
97      if (symbol % 2 == 0)  /* if even, prev cum is ok, update cum */
98            {
99            current_pair = *freq_ptr;
100           high_half = (current_pair & HIGH_MASK) >> HIGH_SHIFT;
101           high_half_weight = translate[high_half];
102           cum = prev_cum + high_half_weight;
```

Listing 4.8 *arenc1.c: arithmetic encoding routines, assembly multiply/divide (continued)*

```
103              }
104     else /* if odd, update both */
105              {
106              current_pair = *freq_ptr;
107              total_pair_weight = both_weights[current_pair];
108              cum = prev_cum + total_pair_weight;
109              high_half = (current_pair & HIGH_MASK) >> HIGH_SHIFT;
110              high_half_weight = translate[high_half];
111              prev_cum += high_half_weight;
112              }
113
114     if (range == 65536L)
115              {
116              high = low + (range * cum)/total_freq-1;
117              low = low + (range * prev_cum)/total_freq;
118              }
119     else
120              {
121              asm mov bx, word ptr range; /* get the range */
122              asm mov cx,total_freq; /* get the total freq for two uses */
123              asm mov si,low;             /* same for low value */
124              asm mov ax,bx;         /* copy range for multiply */
125              asm mul word ptr cum;     /* dx:ax = range * cum */
126              asm div cx;                 /* ax = (range * cum) / total_freq */
127              asm dec ax;                 /* ax = (range * cum) / total_freq - 1*/
128              asm add ax,si;        /* ax = low + (range * cum) / total_freq - 1 */
129              asm mov high,ax;            /* save the result in high */
130              asm mov ax,bx;        /* get the range again */
131              asm mul word ptr prev_cum; /* dx:ax = range * prev_cum */
132              asm div cx;                 /* ax = (range * prev_cum) / total_freq */
133              asm add ax,si;        /* ax = low + (range * prev_cum) / total_freq */
134              asm mov low,ax;             /* save the result in low */
135              }
136
137     for (;;)
138              {
139              if (high < HALF)
140                      bit_plus_follow_0
141              else if (low >= HALF)
142                      {
143                      bit_plus_follow_1
144                      low -= HALF;
145                      high -= HALF;
146                      }
147              else if (low >= FIRST_QTR && high < THIRD_QTR)
148                      {
149                      bits_to_follow ++;
150                      low -= FIRST_QTR;
151                      high -= FIRST_QTR;
152                      }
153              else break;
```

Listing 4.8 *arenc l.c: arithmetic encoding routines, assembly multiply/divide (continued)*

```
154
155              low <<= 1;
156              high <<= 1;
157              high ++;
158              }
159         return(0);
160    }
161
162
163    done_encoding()
164    {
165      bits_to_follow ++;
166      if (low < FIRST_QTR)
167             bit_plus_follow_0
168      else
169             bit_plus_follow_1
170      return(0);
171    }
172
173
174    start_outputing_bits()
175    {
176      buffer = 0;
177      bits_to_go = 8;
178      return(0);
179    }
180
181
182    done_outputing_bits()
183    {
184      fputc(buffer>>bits_to_go,outfile);
185      return(0);
186    }
187
```

Listing 4.9 *arenc15.c: arithmetic encoding routines, assembly mul/div & accumulation*

```
1
2     /****keyword-flag*** "%v %f %n" */
3     /* "2.16 13-Sep-91,7:05:04 ARENC15.C" */
4
5
6     #include "arith.h"
7     #include "model.h"
8     #include <stdio.h>
9
10    extern FILE *outfile;
11    int buffer;
12    int bits_to_go;
13    unsigned low,high;
14    unsigned bits_to_follow;
15
16
17    #define output_0\
18    {\
19      buffer >>= 1;\
20      bits_to_go —;\
21      if (bits_to_go == 0)\
22            {\
23            fputc(buffer,outfile);\
24            bits_to_go = 8;\
25            }\
26    }
27
28
29    #define output_1\
30    {\
31      buffer >>= 1;\
32      buffer |= 0x80;\
33      bits_to_go —;\
34      if (bits_to_go == 0)\
35            {\
36            fputc(buffer,outfile);\
37            bits_to_go = 8;\
38            }\
39    }
40
41
42    #define bit_plus_follow_0 \
43    { \
44      output_0\
45      while (bits_to_follow > 0) \
46            { \
47            output_1\
48            bits_to_follow —; \
49            } \
50    }
51
```

Listing 4.9 *arenc15.c: arithmetic encoding routines, assembly mul/div & accumulation (continued)*

```
52   #define bit_plus_follow_1 \
53   { \
54     output_1\
55     while (bits_to_follow > 0) \
56           { \
57           output_0\
58           bits_to_follow —; \
59           } \
60   }
61
62
63   start_encoding()
64   {
65     low = 0;
66     high = TOP_VALUE;
67     bits_to_follow = 0;
68     return(0);
69   }
70
71
72   encode_symbol(unsigned symbol, unsigned oldch)
73   {
74     long range;
75     int i;
76     unsigned cum;
77     unsigned prev_cum;
78     unsigned char *freq_ptr;
79     int current_pair;
80     unsigned char high_half;
81     unsigned high_half_weight;
82     unsigned total_pair_weight;
83     unsigned total_freq;
84     FrequencyInfo *temp_freq_info;
85
86     range = (long)(high-low)+1;
87     temp_freq_info = frequency_info[oldch];
88     freq_ptr = temp_freq_info->freq;
89     total_freq = temp_freq_info->total_freq;
90     prev_cum = 0;
91   #if 0
92     for (i = 0; i < symbol/2; i ++)
93           {
94           current_pair = *(freq_ptr++);
95           total_pair_weight = both_weights[current_pair];
96           prev_cum += total_pair_weight;
97           }
98   #else
99     asm   mov   cx,symbol;      /* number of entries to search*/
100    asm   shr   cx,1;           /* at two per byte */
101    asm   mov   di, word ptr freq_ptr; /* get the starting frequency pointer */
102    asm   mov   si,offset both_weights;/* get the weights pointer */
103    asm   xor   dx,dx;          /* clear the total weight accumulator */
```

Listing 4.9 *arenc15.c: arithmetic encoding routines, assembly mul/div & accumulation (continued)*

```
104     asm  jcxz symbol_loop_end; /* if symbol == 0, skip the whole thing */
105   symbol_loop:
106     asm  xor  bx,bx;        /* clear the index value */
107     asm  mov  bl,[di];      /* get a pair of weight indices */
108     asm  shl  bx,1;         /* compute their address in the table */
109     asm  inc  di;           /* and point to the next pair */
110     asm  add  dx,[si+bx];   /* update the total weights */
111     asm  loop symbol_loop;  /* do it again */
112   symbol_loop_end:
113     asm  mov  prev_cum,dx;  /* get the results back */
114     freq_ptr += symbol/2;
115   #endif
116     if (symbol % 2 == 0)  /* if even, prev cum is ok, update cum */
117         {
118         current_pair = *freq_ptr;
119         high_half = (current_pair & HIGH_MASK) >> HIGH_SHIFT;
120         high_half_weight = translate[high_half];
121         cum = prev_cum + high_half_weight;
122         }
123     else /* if odd, update both */
124         {
125         current_pair = *freq_ptr;
126         total_pair_weight = both_weights[current_pair];
127         cum = prev_cum + total_pair_weight;
128         high_half = (current_pair & HIGH_MASK) >> HIGH_SHIFT;
129         high_half_weight = translate[high_half];
130         prev_cum += high_half_weight;
131         }
132
133     if (range == 65536L)
134         {
135         high = low + (range * cum)/total_freq-1;
136         low = low + (range * prev_cum)/total_freq;
137         }
138     else
139         {
140         asm mov bx,range;          /* get the range */
141         asm mov cx,total_freq; /* get the total freq for two uses */
142         asm mov si,low;            /* same for low value */
143         asm mov ax,bx;         /* copy range for multiply */
144         asm mul word ptr cum;      /* dx:ax = range * cum */
145         asm div cx;                /* ax = (range * cum) / total_freq */
146         asm dec ax;                /* ax = (range * cum) / total_freq - 1*/
147         asm add ax,si;         /* ax = low + (range * cum) / total_freq - 1 */
148         asm mov high,ax;           /* save the result in high */
149         asm mov ax,bx;         /* get the range again */
150         asm mul word ptr prev_cum; /* dx:ax = range * prev_cum */
151         asm div cx;                /* ax = (range * prev_cum) / total_freq */
152         asm add ax,si;         /* ax = low + (range * prev_cum) / total_freq */
153         asm mov low,ax;            /* save the result in low */
154         }
155
```

Listing 4.9 *arenc15.c: arithmetic encoding routines, assembly mul/div & accumulation (continued)*

```
156    for (;;)
157        {
158        if (high < HALF)
159            bit_plus_follow_0
160        else if (low >= HALF)
161            {
162            bit_plus_follow_1
163            low -= HALF;
164            high -= HALF;
165            }
166        else if (low >= FIRST_QTR && high < THIRD_QTR)
167            {
168            bits_to_follow ++;
169            low -= FIRST_QTR;
170            high -= FIRST_QTR;
171            }
172        else break;
173
174        low <<= 1;
175        high <<= 1;
176        high ++;
177        }
178    return(0);
179    }
180
181
182    done_encoding()
183    {
184      bits_to_follow ++;
185      if (low < FIRST_QTR)
186            bit_plus_follow_0
187      else
188            bit_plus_follow_1
189      return(0);
190    }
191
192
193    start_outputing_bits()
194    {
195      buffer = 0;
196      bits_to_go = 8;
197      return(0);
198    }
199
200
201    done_outputing_bits()
202    {
203      fputc(buffer>>bits_to_go,outfile);
204      return(0);
205    }
206
```

Listing 4.10 *arenc2.c: arithmetic encoding routines, assembly mul/div & unrolled accumulation*

```
1
2    /****keyword-flag*** "%v %f %n" */
3    /* "2.16 13-Sep-91,7:05:04 ARENC2.C" */
4
5
6    #include "arith.h"
7    #include "model.h"
8    #include <stdio.h>
9
10   extern FILE *outfile;
11   int buffer;
12   int bits_to_go;
13   unsigned low,high;
14   unsigned bits_to_follow;
15
16
17   #define output_0\
18   {\
19     buffer >>= 1;\
20     bits_to_go -;\
21     if (bits_to_go == 0)\
22         {\
23         fputc(buffer,outfile);\
24         bits_to_go = 8;\
25         }\
26   }
27
28
29   #define output_1\
30   {\
31     buffer >>= 1;\
32     buffer |= 0x80;\
33     bits_to_go -;\
34     if (bits_to_go == 0)\
35         {\
36         fputc(buffer,outfile);\
37         bits_to_go = 8;\
38         }\
39   }
40
41
42   #define bit_plus_follow_0 \
43   { \
44     output_0\
45     while (bits_to_follow > 0) \
46         { \
47         output_1\
48         bits_to_follow -; \
49         } \
50   }
51
```

Listing 4.10 *arenc2.c: arithmetic encoding routines, assembly mul/div & unrolled accumulation (continued)*

```
52    #define bit_plus_follow_1 \
53    { \
54      output_1\
55      while (bits_to_follow > 0) \
56            { \
57            output_0\
58            bits_to_follow --; \
59            } \
60    }
61
62
63    start_encoding()
64    {
65      low = 0;
66      high = TOP_VALUE;
67      bits_to_follow = 0;
68      return(0);
69    }
70
71
72    encode_symbol(unsigned symbol, unsigned oldch)
73    {
74      long range;
75      int i;
76      unsigned cum;
77      unsigned prev_cum;
78      unsigned char *freq_ptr;
79      int current_pair;
80      unsigned char high_half;
81      unsigned high_half_weight;
82      unsigned total_pair_weight;
83      unsigned total_freq;
84      FrequencyInfo *temp_freq_info;
85
86      range = (long)(high-low)+1;
87      temp_freq_info = frequency_info[oldch];
88      freq_ptr = temp_freq_info->freq;
89      total_freq = temp_freq_info->total_freq;
90      prev_cum = 0;
91    #if 0
92      for (i = 0; i < symbol/2; i ++)
93            {
94            current_pair = *(freq_ptr++);
95            total_pair_weight = both_weights[current_pair];
96            prev_cum += total_pair_weight;
97            }
98    #else
99      asm   xor   bx,bx;           /* clear the index value */
100     asm   mov   cx,symbol;       /* number of entries to search*/
101     asm   shr   cx,1;            /* at two per byte */
102     asm   mov   si, word ptr freq_ptr; /* get the starting frequency pointer */
```

Listing 4.10 *arenc2.c: arithmetic encoding routines, assembly mul/div & unrolled accumulation (continued)*

```
103     asm   xor   dx,dx;             /* clear the total weight accumulator */
104     asm   jcxz  symbol_loop_end; /* if symbol == 0, skip the whole thing */
105     asm   shr   cx,1             /* and four per word */
106     asm   jnc   symbol_loop      /* if no carry, even already */
107     asm   lodsb                   /* get two weights */
108     asm   mov   bl,al;           /* get the pair */
109     asm   lea   di,both_weights[bx] /* start of weights + 1/2 offset */
110     asm   add   dx,[di+bx];      /* update the total weights */
111     asm   jcxz  symbol_loop_end; /* if symbol == 0, skip the whole thing */
112  symbol_loop:
113     asm   lodsw                   /* get four weights */
114     asm   mov   bl,al;           /* get the first pair */
115     asm   lea   di,both_weights[bx] /* start of weights + 1/2 offset */
116     asm   add   dx,[di+bx];      /* update the total weights */
117     asm   mov   bl,ah;           /* get the second pair */
118     asm   lea   di,both_weights[bx] /* start of weights + 1/2 offset */
119     asm   add   dx,[di+bx];      /* update the total weights */
120     asm   loop  symbol_loop;      /* do it again */
121  symbol_loop_end:
122     asm   mov   prev_cum,dx;      /* get the results back */
123     freq_ptr += symbol/2;
124  #endif
125     if (symbol % 2 == 0)   /* if even, prev cum is ok, update cum */
126          {
127          current_pair = *freq_ptr;
128          high_half = (current_pair & HIGH_MASK) >> HIGH_SHIFT;
129          high_half_weight = translate[high_half];
130          cum = prev_cum + high_half_weight;
131          }
132     else /* if odd, update both */
133          {
134          current_pair = *freq_ptr;
135          total_pair_weight = both_weights[current_pair];
136          cum = prev_cum + total_pair_weight;
137          high_half = (current_pair & HIGH_MASK) >> HIGH_SHIFT;
138          high_half_weight = translate[high_half];
139          prev_cum += high_half_weight;
140          }
141
142     if (range == 65536L)
143          {
144          high = low + (range * cum)/total_freq-1;
145          low = low + (range * prev_cum)/total_freq;
146          }
147     else
148          {
149          asm mov bx, word ptr range; /* get the range */
150          asm mov cx,total_freq; /* get the total freq for two uses */
151          asm mov si,low;          /* same for low value */
152          asm mov ax,bx;        /* copy range for multiply */
153          asm mul word ptr cum;     /* dx:ax = range * cum */
```

Listing 4.10 *arenc2.c: arithmetic encoding routines, assembly mul/div & unrolled accumulation (continued)*

```
154            asm div cx;                  /* ax = (range * cum) / total_freq */
155            asm dec ax;                  /* ax = (range * cum) / total_freq - 1*/
156            asm add ax,si;       /* ax = low + (range * cum) / total_freq - 1 */
157            asm mov high,ax;             /* save the result in high */
158            asm mov ax,bx;         /* get the range again */
159            asm mul word ptr prev_cum; /* dx:ax = range * prev_cum */
160            asm div cx;                  /* ax = (range * prev_cum) / total_freq */
161            asm add ax,si;       /* ax = low + (range * prev_cum) / total_freq */
162            asm mov low,ax;              /* save the result in low */
163            }
164
165      for (;;)
166            {
167            if (high < HALF)
168                  bit_plus_follow_0
169            else if (low >= HALF)
170                  {
171                  bit_plus_follow_1
172                  low -= HALF;
173                  high -= HALF;
174                  }
175            else if (low >= FIRST_QTR && high < THIRD_QTR)
176                  {
177                  bits_to_follow ++;
178                  low -= FIRST_QTR;
179                  high -= FIRST_QTR;
180                  }
181            else break;
182
183            low <<= 1;
184            high <<= 1;
185            high ++;
186            }
187      return(0);
188  }
189
190
191  done_encoding()
192  {
193    bits_to_follow ++;
194    if (low < FIRST_QTR)
195          bit_plus_follow_0
196    else
197          bit_plus_follow_1
198    return(0);
199  }
200
201
202  start_outputing_bits()
203  {
204    buffer = 0;
```

Listing 4.10 *arenc2.c: arithmetic encoding routines, assembly mul/div & unrolled accumulation (continued)*

```
205     bits_to_go = 8;
206     return(0);
207   }
208
209
210   done_outputing_bits()
211   {
212     fputc(buffer>>bits_to_go,outfile);
213     return(0);
214   }
215
```

Listing 4.11 *decode.c: decoding main module*

```
1
2    /****keyword-flag*** "%v %f %n" */
3    /* "6.2 12-May-92,18:01:10 DECODE.C" */
4
5
6    #include <stdio.h>
7    #include <stdlib.h>
8    #include "model.h"
9
10   FILE *infile;
11   FILE *outfile;
12
13   main(int argc, char *argv[])
14   {
15     unsigned oldch;
16     unsigned ch;
17
18     if (argc < 3)
19         {
20         printf("Usage: decode compressed original.\n");
21         exit(1);
22         }
23
24     infile = fopen(argv[1],"rb");
25     outfile = fopen(argv[2],"wb");
26     setvbuf(infile,NULL,_IOFBF,8000);
27     setvbuf(outfile,NULL,_IOFBF,8000);
28
29     start_model();
30     start_inputing_bits();
31     start_decoding();
32     oldch = 0;
33     for (;;)
34         {
35         ch = decode_symbol(oldch);
36         if (ch == EOF_SYMBOL)
37             break;
38         fputc(ch,outfile);
39         update_model(ch,oldch);
40         oldch = ch;
41         }
42
43     return(0);
44   }
```

Listing 4.12 *decode1.c: decoding main module*

```
1
2    /****keyword-flag*** "%v %f %n" */
3    /* "9 12-May-92,18:01:12 DECODE1.C" */
4
5
6    #include <stdio.h>
7    #include <stdlib.h>
8    #include "model.h"
9
10   FILE *infile;
11   FILE *outfile;
12
13   main(int argc, char *argv[])
14   {
15     unsigned oldch;
16     unsigned ch;
17     unsigned symbol;
18
19     if (argc < 3)
20         {
21         printf("Usage: decode compressed original.\n");
22         exit(1);
23         }
24
25     infile = fopen(argv[1],"rb");
26     outfile = fopen(argv[2],"wb");
27     setvbuf(infile,NULL,_IOFBF,8000);
28     setvbuf(outfile,NULL,_IOFBF,8000);
29
30     start_model();
31     start_inputing_bits();
32     start_decoding();
33     oldch = 0;
34     for (;;)
35         {
36         symbol = decode_symbol(oldch);
37         if (symbol == EOF_SYMBOL)
38             break;
39         ch = symbol_translation[symbol];
40         fputc(ch,outfile);
41         update_model(symbol,oldch);
42         oldch = ch;
43         }
44
45     return(0);
46   }
```

Listing 4.13 *ardec.c: arithmetic decoding routines*

```
1
2     /****keyword-flag*** "%v %f %n" */
3     /* "8 12-May-92,18:01:08 ARDEC.C" */
4
5
6     #include "arith.h"
7     #include "model.h"
8
9     unsigned value;
10    unsigned low,high;
11
12    int start_decoding()
13    {
14      int i;
15
16      value = 0;
17      for (i = 0; i < CODE_VALUE_BITS; i ++)
18            value = 2 * value + input_bit();
19      low = 0;
20      high = (unsigned)TOP_VALUE;
21      return(0);
22    }
23
24    unsigned decode_symbol(unsigned oldch)
25    {
26      long range;
27      unsigned cum_freq;
28      unsigned symbol;
29      unsigned cum;
30      unsigned prev_cum;
31      unsigned char *freq_ptr;
32      unsigned current_pair;
33      unsigned char low_half;
34      unsigned low_half_weight;
35      unsigned char high_half;
36      unsigned high_half_weight;
37      unsigned total_pair_weight;
38      unsigned total_freq;
39      unsigned test_cum_freq;
40      FrequencyInfo *temp_freq_info;
41
42      range = (long)(high-low)+1;
43      temp_freq_info = frequency_info[oldch];
44      freq_ptr = temp_freq_info->freq;
45      total_freq = temp_freq_info->total_freq;
46      cum = (unsigned)((((long)(value-low)+1)*total_freq-1)/range);
47
48      cum_freq = 0;
49      for (symbol = 0; cum_freq <= cum; symbol ++)
50            {
51            current_pair = *(freq_ptr++);
```

Listing 4.13 *ardec.c: arithmetic decoding routines (continued)*

```
 52                total_pair_weight = both_weights[current_pair];
 53                cum_freq += total_pair_weight;
 54                }
 55
 56        symbol += symbol;
 57
 58        low_half = (current_pair & LOW_MASK) >> LOW_SHIFT;
 59        low_half_weight = translate[low_half];
 60        test_cum_freq = cum_freq - low_half_weight;
 61
 62        if (test_cum_freq > cum) /* if we went past it by one */
 63                {
 64                high_half = (current_pair & HIGH_MASK) >> HIGH_SHIFT;
 65                high_half_weight = translate[high_half];
 66                cum_freq = test_cum_freq;
 67                prev_cum = cum_freq - high_half_weight;
 68                symbol --;
 69                }
 70        else /* if the low is correct */
 71                prev_cum = test_cum_freq;
 72
 73        if (symbol == EOF_SYMBOL)
 74                return(symbol);
 75        else
 76                symbol --;
 77
 78        high = low + (unsigned)((range*cum_freq)/total_freq-1);
 79        low = low + (unsigned)((range*prev_cum)/total_freq);
 80
 81        for (;;)
 82                {
 83                if (high < HALF)
 84                        {
 85                        }
 86                else if (low >= HALF)
 87                        {
 88                        value -= (unsigned)HALF;
 89                        low -= (unsigned)HALF;
 90                        high -= (unsigned)HALF;
 91                        }
 92                else if (low >= FIRST_QTR && high <THIRD_QTR)
 93                        {
 94                        value -= (unsigned)FIRST_QTR;
 95                        low -= (unsigned)FIRST_QTR;
 96                        high -= (unsigned)FIRST_QTR;
 97                        }
 98                else
 99                        break;
100
101                low = 2 * low;
102                high = 2 * high + 1;
```

Listing 4.13 *ardec.c: arithmetic decoding routines (continued)*

```
103             value = 2 * value + input_bit();
104             }
105
106     return(symbol);
107     }
```

5

Do You Need an Interpreter?

Introduction

In the mid-1970's, when microcomputers were a novelty, I walked into one of the first computer stores to see the 8080-based Altair computer. Upon learning that the only available language was assembly, I offered to write a BASIC interpreter for their machine. My proposal was that I would work for the minimum wage so I could survive while writing it, and receive a royalty on copies of the software that they sold. Such BASIC interpreters made a significant contribution to the usability of those early machines, and their descendants are still with us today; unfortunately, the visionaries in that company turned me down, and someone else became "Mr. BASIC". The rest is history.

Since the advent of compiled languages for microcomputers, though, interpreters have mostly fallen into disuse among professional programmers, due to their reputation for inferior performance. That's too bad, because interpreters have many advantages over compilers in the software development arena; as you may know, there are C interpreters available today which have been developed for the express purpose of making it easier to write and debug code before compiling it for production use. The interactive nature of development with interpreters provides very rapid feedback on whether you're headed in the right direction, in contrast to compilers, which have to translate the entire program and link it with libraries before you can try it out. Interpreted programs are also easier to debug than compiled ones, as stepping through the program to watch its execution is a natural operation when running an interpreter; by contrast, compiled languages require a great deal of extra baggage in order to make this possible, and even then, source-level debuggers are not legendary for their reliability. If only interpreters could provide the performance of compiled code, we might be able to dispense with the complexity of compilers and write and modify programs in a more "natural" way. Is there any way to get around the performance penalty of interpretation?

Lost in Translation

Before we can answer this question, we should take a look at how both kinds of language translators, i.e., compilers and interpreters, actually work. Compilers are simpler in concept, although much more complicated in practice: as you know, they translate source code into machine language, which is then bound together with already compiled library functions to produce an executable file. This executable file can be run directly by the CPU it is intended for.

By contrast, interpreters do not translate source code into machine language that can be executed by an actual CPU. How, then, does an interpreted program control the operation of the computer?

It's easier to start with the simplest possible model of interpretation, which might be called "direct interpretation". In this approach, the source code is read line by line and used to control the operation of the interpreter. For example, consider the BASIC program in figure 5.1.

When the RUN command is given to start execution, a direct interpreter starts at the first line, scanning the text of the program until it finds the string "DIM", which it looks up in a hash table to get the address of the data allocation routine in the interpreter. The needed arguments to this routine are then collected either by the interpreter or by the "DIM" routine itself; the final result in either case is that the "DIM" routine sets storage aside for an integer variable named i. Then the interpreter reads and decodes the next line, which starts a loop; this line causes i to be assigned the value 1 and an anonymous loop control variable to receive the value 10, for use in testing the end-of-loop condition. Next, the interpreter reads and decodes the line that requests the printing of the current value of i and displays that value in a human-readable format. The next line is then decoded to indicate that the loop index i should be incremented and the loop reexecuted from the top with the new value. At this point, such an interpreter searches for the beginning of the loop and starts the interpretation over again at that point.

This is obviously a very inefficient way to proceed, since the decoding and interpretation have to be done every time through the loop, even though the statements

Figure 5.1 *BASIC program to be interpreted*

```
DIM i AS INTEGER
FOR i = 1 TO 10
PRINT i
NEXT i
```

Figure 5.2 *BASIC program, preinterpreted*

```
{DIM} i {AS} {INTEGER}
{FOR} i {=} 1 {TO} 10
{PRINT} i
{NEXT} i
```

have not changed. Of course, even the simplest actual interpreters are cleverer than this. A more realistic description of how a BASIC interpreter works is that when you type in a line (or it is read in from a source code file), it is compiled into **p-code**, an abbreviation for "pseudocode".[62] This consists of tokens representing the operations that the BASIC interpreter knows how to perform, interspersed with literal values such as strings. In our example, the encoding of the "object program" might be something like figure 5.2, where the items in {} are each represented by a one-byte operation code.

This may be a bit confusing; if interpreters and compilers both translate the source code into an internal form, what differentiates them? Before we can answer this question, we should take a look at an interpretive language that uses a different method of controlling the execution of the CPU.

Go FORTH and Multiply

In the 1960's, Charles Moore invented the interpretive language FORTH, which uses a mechanism called "address-threaded interpretation". In such a language, the compilation phase converts a routine expressed in reverse Polish notation into p-code consisting of a list of addresses of subroutines to be executed, interspersed with binary forms of literal data needed by those routines, such as numbers and character strings. Reverse Polish notation, or **RPN**, is the native mode of HP calculators; operands are placed on the stack as they are encountered, and operations pop them off the stack and push their results, if any, on the stack. This process is much easier to interpret than parenthesized expressions with precedence rules, and in fact is often used as an intermediate language during the execution of language compilers, for that reason.[63]

The interpreter can execute a p-code program by picking up each routine address and jumping to that routine, incrementing its "interpreter pointer", or IP, after

---

62. The reason for this disrespectful term is that interpreted programs are not composed of the machine language of the physical CPU on which they are to be run.

63. A historical note, courtesy of Mike Mohle: Polish notation was invented by Jan Lukasiewicz in the 1930s to ease reducing complex logical equations by replacing nested parentheses with positions based on the priority and sequence of operators. Prefix or forward Polish prefixes operands with operators, while postfix or reverse Polish suffixes operands with operators. Reverse Polish notation is the basis of the design of many stack machines.

Figure 5.3 *Addresses for RPN code example*

Routine Name	Address
push a	3000[64]
push b	3010
push c	3020
multiply	2000
add	2020
sqrt	2040

Variable	Value
a	5
b	10
c	31

retrieving each address; the **IP** is analogous to the program counter in a physical CPU. To see how this works, let's take a look at a possible translation of a fairly simple arithmetic expression.

In order to make the example more concrete, we'll make the assumptions shown in figure 5.3.

Given those assumptions, the expression

```
sqrt(a * b + c)
```

would be written as follows in RPN code:

```
a b * c + sqrt
```

and the p-code might look like figure 5.4.

Before execution of this routine starts, the IP is set to 998, as it will be preincremented as part of the operation of the interpreter. To start execution, the interpreter increments the IP to 1000 and jumps to the address found there, which is 3000, the address of **a**. The routine **a** pushes the value of the variable **a** (5) onto the stack, and decrements the stack pointer by 2, after which it jumps back to the interpreter to continue execution. The interpreter increments the IP by 2 (to 1002), and jumps to address 3010 to execute routine **b**, because that is the function whose address is stored in location 1002. This routine pushes the value of **b** (10) onto the stack; then it jumps back to the interpreter. After incrementing the IP again, it's now 1004, so the inter-

---

64. You may wonder why we need separate routines to push the value of each variable. The reason is that variables in FORTH and similar languages are implemented as routines that refer to the addresses of their values. Actually, I'm simplifying for clarity; the normal implementation of variables in FORTH returns the address of the variable; another operation is needed to retrieve the value. The address is returned so that the variable can be stored into rather than merely retrieved.

Figure 5.4 *Compiled address-threaded code*

Interpreter pointer (IP)	Source code	P-code
1000	a	3000
1002	b	3010
1004	*	2000
1006	c	3020
1008	+	2020
1010	sqrt	2040

preter jumps to address 2000, the address of `multiply`; this routine multiplies the two elements on the stack, producing the result 50, which it pushes back onto the stack in place of its input arguments, and jumps to the interpreter. Now we execute `c`, which pushes 31 on the stack and jumps back to the interpreter. Next, `add` adds the top two elements, which are 31 and 50, producing the value 81, which it leaves on the stack in place of its input arguments, and jumps back to the interpreter main routine. Finally, the `sqrt` routine is executed, leaving 9 on the stack in place of its input argument, 81.

This is pretty similar to what a CPU does when executing a machine-language program, except that the FORTH interpreter is emulating a stack-based machine rather than executing native instructions of the CPU.

What's in a Name?

The answer to our question about the difference between compilation and interpretation, then, is that if the internal form is the machine language of a physical CPU that is going to execute the program directly, then the language translator is a compiler; if the internal form is p-code, the translator is an interpreter.[65] However, this seems like a lot of extra work compared to running a compiled program. What does this method of program execution buy us?

To answer this question, let's revisit our example of the arithmetic expression evaluation. In C, the expression

```
sqrt(a * b + c)
```

---

65. This is actually not a hard-and-fast rule, as at least one CPU was designed with FORTH as its machine language. For that matter, what about "microcoded" CPUs, including all of the most popular CISC machines? Their "machine language" instructions are actually interpreted by a lower level program; according to our definition, **all** programs on such machines are run via interpretation!

Figure 5.5 *Compiled C expression*

```
8B46FC        mov     ax,[bp-04]        ;ax = a
F76EFA        imul    word ptr [bp-06]  ;ax = ax * b
0346F8        add     ax,[bp-08]        ;ax = ax + c
8946F6        mov     [bp-0A],ax        ;store in temp
CD3B46F6      fild    word ptr[bp-0A]   ;load FPU from integer temp
83EC08        sub     sp,0008           ;make room for argument to sqrt
CD395EEE      fstp    qword ptr[bp-12]  ;store FPU to float temp
CD3D          fwait                     ;wait for completion
E8980B        call    _sqrt             ;call sqrt routine 83C408    add    sp,0008
                                        ;clean up stack from temp
```

would compile to something like the code in figure 5.5 (assuming a, b, and c are all ints).

A major difference between this version and the interpreted one is that p-code is significantly smaller than machine language; the reason is that each operation, no matter how complicated, is represented by one address, rather than by several instructions as in the case of subroutine calls (e.g., the call to _sqrt in the preceding code). Although this is nice, memory is fairly cheap these days, so why should we worry about the size of our code?

The Impossible Dream

In 1992, *Dr. Dobb's Journal* ran a series of articles on "Personal Supercomputing". In the first article of this very interesting series, the author took the position that the way to get the best performance out of RISC machines for FORTRAN applications was to treat their native instruction set as microcode, out of which one could build a tailored CISC machine designed to execute FORTRAN statements.[66] The reason for this approach is that performance on such machines is limited by the need to fit frequently executed code into the limited on-chip cache; the microcoding approach results in much smaller code than is output by native compilers, so the cache is utilized much better.

At first, I saw no way to apply this insight personally, having neither a RISC machine nor any FORTRAN applications to run. However, in browsing through the i486 instruction set manual recently, I noticed that many of the instruction timings were indicated as 1 cycle, that is, as long as the instruction in question is already decoded and available for execution. I already knew that on the clock-doubled 486/DX2 processors any reference to data or instructions that aren't contained in the

---

66. Hirschsohn, I. "Personal Supercomputing". *Dr. Dobb's Journal*, 17(6) 16–27 (June 1992).

i486 on-chip cache caused the clock speed to be halved, as well as incurring a wait for the external cache memory to respond.[67] As a result, a program that fits into the internal cache can execute up to twice as many CPU cycles per second as one that makes many references to main memory.

This is a perfect opportunity to use "token-threaded" interpretation. Whereas the p-code of an address-threaded program consists of a list of addresses of routines to be executed, the p-code of a compiled token-threaded program consists of indexes into a jump table of addresses of the machine-language code to execute each of these primitive operations, rather than the addresses themselves. In many applications, including our example here, these indexes can be represented by one byte, resulting in extremely compact p-code.[68]

The efficiency of the interpreter's dispatching mechanism is of the utmost importance to performance of such languages. Of course, as in any case where performance is critical, the interpreter must be written in assembly language.[69] However, even with the fastest possible lookup and dispatch of operations, this approach has a lot more overhead than does a compiled program that is executed directly by the CPU. Could the ability to execute from the internal cache offset the inherent performance disadvantage of interpretation?

Rather than continue to wonder, I decided to find out. In order to make a meaningful comparison between compiled machine language and token-threaded p-code, I had to come up with a realistic application that would demonstrate the relative performance of these two approaches to program execution. I chose to implement the typical operations needed to recalculate a simple spreadsheet and use these operations to calculate an amortization schedule for a 30-year mortgage, with interest rates and payments that could vary each month; since there aren't too many different operations needed, the programming task was reasonable.[70] However, the results should be fairly representative of a basic class of applications; typical spreadsheet recalculations consist primarily of add, subtract, multiply, divide, and totaling operations. I also needed to provide a way to get data into and out of the spreadsheet, so I added

---

67. Of course, the wait is much longer if even the external cache doesn't contain the data item or instruction in question, requiring it to be loaded from system RAM.

68. In addition to the advantage of small size, token-threading also makes it possible to move routines around in memory during the execution of the program, a feature unavailable in an address-threaded interpreter.

69. For some reason which eludes me, the seemingly obvious fact that machine language produced by a good assembly language programmer can always outperform machine language produced by a compiler is a source of controversy in some circles. Clearly, the assembly language programmer has an irrefutable advantage over the compiler writer: the former knows the application problem he is trying to solve, whereas the latter is writing a program to generate code for classes of problems. Given the same level of skill in both cases, the assembly programmer will always win.

70. The sample spreadsheet doesn't in fact have any changes in interest rates or payments, but no changes to the interpreter would be needed to handle such an example.

assignment and display functions. A few miscellaneous functions brought the total up to 11 in all, most of which translated into three or four CPU instructions each; as you can see by looking at listing 5.1, the listing of the token-threaded interpreter, complete with all implemented spreadsheet functions, a few hundred lines of assembly language does the job. Of course, a major reason for this economy is that all i486 DX and DX2 chips contain an integral floating-point unit, or FPU; therefore, I could dispense with floating-point emulation and code the actual FPU instructions directly. In addition, the floating point stack management is made much simpler by the fact that the 80x87 is addressable as a stack machine; see the comments in the code for explanations of the specific instructions used in the interpreter.[71]

Floating Alone

Let's get down to some specifics. As already noted, each operation is represented in the p-code as a one-byte operation code (or **op-code**), followed by any required data. For example, the following line multiplies the two spreadsheet cells B1 and A1 and subtracts the contents of A2, storing the result in B2:[72]

```
B1 A1 * A2 - -> B2
```

Its translation is shown in figure 5.6.

Of course, this p-code cannot be executed by the processor directly, but needs to be executed by an interpreter. Figure 5.7 was my first working version of the interpreter, which is the heart of any threaded interpretive language. As you can see, it's not very long, totalling only five instructions. What do they do?

To save time, the IP is always kept in an index register, in this case si; this allows the op-code to be obtained by the single instruction mov bl,[si], after which we increment the IP by inc si. In order to translate the op-code to an address, it has to be looked up in the table of such addresses; the table for this program is displayed in figure 5.8. Each entry in this table corresponds to one op-code, starting at 0; since the addresses are two bytes each in a small model program such as this one, the op-code has to be multiplied by two to convert it into an offset into the table. This is accomplished by the add bx,bx instruction; however, it is first necessary to clear the high part of the bx register via xor bh, bh, since loading bl doesn't have any effect on the high half of the register. If the high half of bx

---

71. For more details on these and other FPU instructions, see Borland's Turbo Assembler 3.0 Quick Reference Guide, or the appropriate Intel numeric processor reference manual.

72. The natural representation for these operations is RPN, as we have already seen. In order to simplify the compiler, I translate a "read" reference to variable A1, for example, into the index of the push operation, namely IQPUSH, followed by the address of the variable, rather than creating a new routine to push the value of each variable onto the stack. Similarly, a "write" reference to B2 translates to the index of the pop operation, namely IQPOP, followed by the address of the variable.

Figure 5.6 *Compiled token-threaded code*

```
db    IQPUSH      ;push
dw    3200        ;B1
db    IQPUSH      ;push
dw    0           ;A1
db    IQMUL       ;multiply
db    IQPUSH      ;push
dw    8           ;A2
db    IQSUB       ;subtract
db    IQPOP       ;pop
dw    3208        ;into B2
```

Figure 5.7 *A token-threaded interpreter*

```
next PROC NEAR ;begin   interpreter
        xor    bh,bh       ;clear high part of offset for calculation
        mov    bl,[si]     ;get next op-code byte
        inc    si          ;bump IP
        add    bx,bx       ;calculate offset into table
        jmp    address_table[bx];jump through table entry
next ENDP
```

Figure 5.8 *Table of routine addresses*

```
address_table  dw    qpush,qadd,qstop,qpushl,qpop,qdisplay
               dw    qmul,qdiv,qsub,qdiscard,qsumc
```

happened to be nonzero, our table lookup wouldn't produce the correct result. Finally, we dispatch execution to the address we have just retrieved, by means of the `jmp address_table[bx]` instruction.

A number of questions may have occurred to you. First, why aren't the instructions in figure 5.7 executed in the order I just described them? The original reason was that I happened to think of them in the order you see in the figure; however, when I started to explain what they did, I realized that it would seem more logical to execute them in the order described in the text above. Therefore, I reordered them in my test program and reran the profiler just to be sure I hadn't messed anything up. To my surprise, the program's execution time was lengthened by about 4%! Apparently, the order of execution is significant; the difference amounts to approximately one CPU cycle per execution of the interpreter, not an insignificant difference when that routine accounts for a large fraction of all the CPU time required to execute the program. Unfortunately, I don't know why this is the case; however, experiment is more conclusive than theory, so I decided to leave it as it was in the code.

Second, why can we use a `jmp` rather than a `call` instruction to start execution of the selected routine? This is possible because the next op-code to be executed is always pointed to by the `si` register; therefore, simply jumping back to the interpreter allows us to continue execution with the next op-code. Of course, without any facility for subroutines, we are limited to straight-line code; however, a subroutine facility could be added at a higher level if needed to handle more complex interpreted programs.

If you look at figure 5.9, you will notice that in the first row, with both the internal and external caches enabled, our first attempt at interpretation, labeled "Interpreted naive NEXT", produces about 78% of the performance of the equivalent compiled program written in C. However, with the external cache disabled, we have already reached our goal of parity and indeed are running 8% faster than the equivalent C program! The reason should be fairly obvious; since the C executable is much larger than the interpreter code, it spends a lot more of its time outside the 8K internal cache. Without the 64K external cache to reduce the penalty of internal cache misses, the interpreter's better locality of reference wins the day.

However, I wasn't satisfied that this was the best I could do. Surely there must be a way to improve the performance of the NEXT procedure, which I estimated accounted for about 40% of the entire CPU time needed to execute the spreadsheet calculations. But with only five instructions in the entire procedure, it would take a new approach to find a noticeable improvement.

386 Quick Avenue

The basic function of the NEXT procedure is to use the op-code pointed to by `si` as an index to look up the address of the function to be executed. The op-code is a one-

Figure 5.9 *Compilation vs. interpretation, times in seconds for 1000 iterations and performance relative to compiled C code*

	Compiled C code	Interpreted naive NEXT	Interpreted i386 NEXT	Interpreted macro NEXT
both caches	0.571	0.733	0.651	0.556
	100%	78%	88%	103%
internal only	0.846	0.782	0.700	0.614
	100%	108%	121%	138%
external only	2.04	4.72	4.37	3.99
	100%	43%	47%	51%
neither	3.14	12.3	10.5	8.63
	100%	26%	30%	36%

byte value, and it must be used as an index into a two-byte table. Luckily, there is an i386 addressing mode that is designed for that exact operation: the **scaled indexed** mode. This allows the specification of a scale factor of 2, 4, or 8, to be used to modify the index value used to access an array of elements of 2, 4, or 8 bytes, respectively. Therefore, rather than having to multiply bx by two explicitly, using up two instructions to do so (xor bh, bh to clear the high byte, and add bx,bx to scale the low byte by a factor of two), I could use the scaled indexed address mode to do the scaling in the jmp instruction itself. As you can see in figure 5.10, this reduced the five instructions to three.

However, it also meant dedicating the ebx register to this use; as the high three bytes of that register aren't affected by the scaled indexed addressing, they don't have to be cleared every time through NEXT. Instead, the ebx register is cleared once at initialization, at the same time that the si register is set up to point to the first byte to be decoded, and left that way throughout the entire program. Routines that need to use ebx (or bx, for that matter) must save and restore it; this is a small price to pay for knocking an additional instruction off the NEXT procedure.

This was not as simple a change as I have indicated so far. In fact, it took a lot of swearing and experimentation before I managed to get the program to assemble again; apparently, if you use even one 32-bit instruction, the assembler has to be told what kind of segments you're using.

We should probably take a closer look at how these few instructions allow us to transfer control between interpreter routines. For example, take the expression

```
B1 A1 *
```

Its translation is shown in figure 5.11.

Figure 5.10 *An improved token-threaded interpreter*

```
next PROC NEAR ;begin      interpreter
          mov    bl,[si]    ;get next op-code byte
          inc    si         ;and bump IP
          jmp    address_table[ebx*2];jump through table entry
next ENDP
```

Figure 5.11 *Short token-threaded code example*

```
db     IQPUSH     ;push
dw     3200       ;B1
db     IQPUSH     ;push
dw     0          ;A1
db     IQMUL      ;multiply
```

Let's assume that this code begins at address 1000, and IQPUSH and IQMUL are the indexes into the address table for "push a cell value on the stack" and "multiply the top two entries on the stack", respectively (see figure 5.12).

We start out with the si register pointing to the first byte of our code, namely IQPUSH. The first instruction of the interpreter, mov bl,[si], fetches the value IQPUSH (which happens to be 0) from the p-code. Next, si is incremented to point to the next byte of the p-code, which is the beginning of the integer value "3200"; that value is the address of cell B1 of our spreadsheet. Now we are ready to execute the jmp address_table[ebx*2] instruction. This fetches the 0th word from the address table, which in our example is 2000, and jumps to that address, where the qpush ("push cell value") routine is located (figure 5.13). That routine uses the si register to retrieve the address of the cell whose value is to be pushed from the next two bytes in the p-code, increments the si register by two past the data address, and uses the fld instruction to push the data onto the FPU stack. Finally, qpush jumps to the next routine.

This may be a bit mysterious: how do we get back to the next operation in our p-code? The answer is that the next routine does exactly what it did before, except that si is pointing to the second IQPUSH, rather than the first one. Therefore, we execute mov bl,[si] to fetch that op-code, increment si to point to the next p-code byte, and execute the jmp address_table[ebx*2] instruction to jump to the qpush routine again; this time, qpush pushes the value of cell A1 onto the FPU stack and jumps to next, with si pointing to the op-code IQMUL.

This time, next fetches the value IQMUL, which is 6. Therefore, the jmp instruction indexes 6 words into the address table, retrieving the value 2104, and jumps to the routine at that address, which is the multiplication routine, qmul (figure 5.14). That routine multiplies the top two entries on the stack, replacing them with the result. Then it jumps to next to continue execution.

I hope this example has clarified the operation of the interpreter. Now let's look at the results of using the "scaled indexed" addressing mode to eliminate two instructions; these results are shown in figure 5.9 under the heading "Interpreted i386 NEXT". The performance penalty with respect to the compiled version is now down to 12% even with both caches enabled, and our advantage with only an internal

Figure 5.12 *Sample table of routine addresses*

Literal index	Name of operation	Address table entry
0	IQPUSH	2000
1	IQADD	2012
2	IQSTOP	2032
3	IQPUSHL	2056
4	IQPOP	2072
5	IQDISPLAY	2080
6	IQMUL	2104

Figure 5.13 *qpush routine*

```
qpush       proc near ;push spreadsheet entry onto TOS
            mov  di,[si]    ;get data offset
            add  si,2       ;and bump IP
            fld  data_table[di]; move data to FPU
            jmp  next
qpush       endp
```

Figure 5.14 *qmul routine*

```
qmul        proc near        ;multiply two values on TOS
            fmulp st(1),st ;and pop
            jmp  next
qmul        endp
```

cache is up to 21%. Interestingly enough, I originally found that without the internal cache enabled, this version of the interpreter was actually SLOWER than the 8086 version! I was somewhat surprised when I saw these results and thought that I had made a methodological error. However, repeated testing convinced me that it was a real effect, not an artifact. After considerable experimentation, I discovered that this effect was caused by the misalignment of the NEXT procedure which resulted from the additional initialization needed to set up the i386 version of the interpreter. Apparently, when the code is cached, this misalignment has no significant effect on performance; however, when the cache isn't activated, the extra memory accesses caused by the jump to a misaligned address are very expensive.

In any event, I was temporarily at a loss as to how to improve performance further; three instructions aren't very much to work with.[73] However, I finally realized that there were actually four instructions required to chain between routines: the three in the NEXT procedure and the `jmp NEXT` that is used at the end of every routine to get back to the beginning of NEXT. Worse still, although the three instructions that

---

73. By the way, with this CPU architecture, there's almost no performance disadvantage for token-threaded interpreters vs. address-threaded ones such as most FORTH implementations. A FORTH interpreter could be at most one instruction shorter, as it still would have to increment the IP and jump. The only difference is that the jump could be executed indirectly through the IP without having to fetch the index first. This would save one cycle; however, incrementing the IP would have to be performed at the beginning of the target routine rather than in the NEXT routine, which would consist of exactly one instruction, if the IP is always pointing to the address of the next routine to be executed. Of course, if the IP were to be preincremented rather than postincremented, this problem could be avoided, but we would still require two instructions in either case, as opposed to three for our token-threaded interpreter. Preincrementing the IP might also impose a performance penalty on the i486 and higher Intel processors, because modifying a register and then using it immediately to address memory can cause an "address generation interlock", which stalls execution for one cycle.

make up the code listed under NEXT take one, one, and five cycles to execute, respectively, the `jmp NEXT` took another three cycles. A logical way to improve performance is to replace the NEXT routine with a macro expanded inline at the end of each routine; this eliminates the `jmp NEXT` instruction, reducing the cycle count from ten to seven cycles. As you can see from the "Interpreted macro NEXT" column in figure 5.9, our interpreter is now 3% faster than the compiled code with both caches enabled and approximately 38% faster with only the internal cache enabled. Figure 5.15 shows that the interpreter is unchanged from the previous version, except for being a macro rather than a normal routine.

Caveat Programmer

While we're discussing timing, I should warn you about performance penalties caused by executing several FPU instructions in quick succession; rearranging the order of the source code in the spreadsheet calculation from

B1 A1 * A2 - -> B2

to

B1 A1 A2 * - -> B2

slowed down processing by about 3%. The only explanation I can come up with for this phenomenon is that in the former case, the push of **A2** onto the FPU stack can be executed in parallel with the multiplication; in the latter case, of course, this is impossible. I also tried a combined *- operation to replace the individual * and - functions, in order to eliminate one execution of **next** per line; however, that was about 7% slower than the original. The necessity to add a `fxch` instruction to rearrange the stack elements before the multiply is part of the reason, and the rest is accounted for by the loss of overlapped execution between * and a following `qpush`. The moral is to try to interleave FPU instructions and CPU instructions as much as possible.

Timing Is Everything

You may be wondering about the the relevance of timings with one or both caches disabled. Although most real i486 systems have external caches, some systems based

Figure 5.15 *The ultimate(?) token-threaded interpreter*

```
NEXT MACRO
     mov  bl,[si]    ;get next op-code byte
     inc  si         ;and bump IP
     jmp  address_table[ebx*2];jump through table entry
     ENDM
```

on 486 clones, such as the 486DLC from Cyrix, don't. That chip has only a 1K internal cache, so high code density should be even more important than it is with the 8K cache found in the i486; therefore, this analysis should be of interest to those who use such systems. What is more germane in the long run, however, is that the future seems certain to bring even greater discrepancies between the internal clock speeds and access times to main memory and external caches, in the vein of Intel's DX4 "clock triplers". I fully expect that running a similar test on a DX4 machine, accounting for the larger cache size on such machines, would show that the interpretive solution will significantly surpass the compiled code even with both caches enabled; the advantage of referencing cached data and instructions will grow markedly with the higher clock-speed ratios.

Is this example representative of the performance you can expect from a token-threaded interpreter? Actually, for more complex operations which would have to be done in C via a subroutine call, the token-threaded alternative can be much faster, so long as you avoid clustering floating-point operations.

Of course, there's no reason to limit token threading to floating-point intensive applications. It is especially appropriate for any project where extremely compact code is desirable, such as adding programmability to application programs; however, as we have seen here, its performance can be quite competitive with compiled code even when memory use is not an issue.

Summary

In this chapter, we have seen a token-threaded interpreter whose code can run faster than equivalent compiled C code, due to its greater code density. In the next chapter, we will see how quantum files allow us to gain efficient random access to a large volume of variable-length textual data.

Auxiliary Programs

There are several programs and other files included on the source-code disk that are not reproduced here as they are not of much instructional value. However, you will need them in order to reproduce the results here or to run the interpreter for your own uses. Here are their names and functions:

compilex.c	C version of mortgage amortization spreadsheet calculation program
genint.c	Compiler that translates RPN into assembly language

interp.gen	RPN source for interpreter version of mortgage amortization spreadsheet calculation program
interp.cod	Output of RPN compiler for mortgage amortization spreadsheet
interpx.asm	Initial version of interpreter
interpy.asm	Initial i386 version of interpreter
makecomp.bat	Batch file to compile "compilex.c"
makegen.bat	Batch file to compile "genint.c"
makeint.bat	Batch file to assemble and link "interp.asm"
makeintx.bat	Batch file to assemble and link "interpx.asm"
makeinty.bat	Batch file to assemble and link "interpy.asm"
runint.bat	Batch file to compile "genint.c", run it to compile "interp.gen" into "interp.cod", assemble and link "interp.asm", and finally execute "interp.exe" to do the mortgage calculation
runintx.bat	Same as "runint.bat", except that it doesn't compile "genint.c" and it executes "interpx.exe" rather than "interp.exe"
runinty.bat	Same as "runint.bat", except that it doesn't compile "genint.c" and it executes "interpy.exe" rather than "interp.exe"

Problems

1. Given a token-threaded interpreter:

   a. How could the number of op-codes be extended beyond 256?

   b. How could a subroutine capability be added?

   c. How could new data types be added?

   d. What are some applications for the ability to move code around in memory during execution?

   (You can find suggested approaches to problems in Chapter 8).

Listing 5.1 *interp.asm: a token-threaded interpreter for the i386 and above*

```
 1    ;****keyword-flag*** "%v %f %n"
 2    ; "13 19-May-94,21:16:16 INTERP.ASM"
 3
 4    ;****revision-history****/
 5    ;*1 INTERP.ASM 8-Feb-93,18:41:56 Token-threaded interpreter for      */
 6    ;*       spreadsheet calculation.                                    */
 7    ;*2 INTERP.ASM 8-Feb-93,22:25:20 Working version including output.   */
 8    ;*3 INTERP.ASM 10-Feb-93,7:37:56 Changed program to use variables rather */
 9    ;*       than constants, for compactness.                           */
10    ;*4 INTERP.ASM 10-Feb-93,21:38:32 Handles negative values in display */
11    ;*       routine.                                                    */
12    ;*       Uses include of interp.cod to get data for interpretation.  */
13    ;*5 INTERP.ASM 14-Feb-93,8:12:42 Now using shifts rather than multiplies */
14    ;*       for index calculations.                                    */
15    ;*       Added code for column sum.                                 */
16    ;*       Changed number of rows to int from byte so that we could    */
17    ;*          theoretically do a thirty-year amortization schedule.    */
18    ;*6 INTERP.ASM 14-Feb-93,12:32:16 Now using offsets computed by genint */
19    ;*       program rather than computing them every time.             */
20    ;*7 INTERP.ASM 15-Feb-93,23:43:48 Using 386 instructions to speed up "next". */
21    ;*       We're now within 8% of parity with no external cache!      */
22    ;*8 INTERP.ASM 16-Feb-93,6:12:20 Changed NEXT to a macro: when the external */
23    ;*       cache is turned off, we're FASTER than the C code!         */
24    ;*9 INTERP.ASM 2-Mar-93,19:21:06 Now using dec cx, jne rather than loop, */
25    ;*       which is slower for some reason.                           */
26    ;*10 INTERP.ASM 14-Mar-93,17:54:38 Fixed headers, added history.     */
27    ;*       Removed unnecessary call.                                  */
28    ;*11 INTERP.ASM 14-Mar-93,18:52:34 Added alignment to speed up access */
29    ;*       Got rid of revision history, as the assembler doesn't like it */
30    ;*          in its C style, and I don't have the patience to fool around */
31    ;*       with it.                                                    */
32    ;*12 INTERP.ASM 15-May-94,21:16:00 Added title and tags for listing. */
33    ;*13 INTERP.ASM 19-May-94,21:16:16 Added revision log comments.      */
34    ;****revision-history****/
35
36    ;NOTE: This version of the interpreter executes the p-code 1000 times, to
37    ;give the profiler something to work with.  To run a program once, you can
38    ;get rid of the timing loop by changing the "outer_count" value to 1.
39    .386
40    model small
41
42    next            macro
43          mov     bl,[si] ;get next opcode byte
44          inc     si                 ;and bump IP
45          jmp     address_table[ebx*2];jump through table entry
46           endm
47
48    Code_Seg        segment use16
49
50            assume  CS:Code_Seg
51            assume  DS:Data_Seg
```

Listing 5.1 *interp.asm: a token-threaded interpreter for the i386 and above (continued)*

```
52
53   Start    proc near
54            mov      ax,Data_Seg
55            mov      ds,ax
56
57            mov      outer_count, 1000 ;change this to 1 to run once
58
59   TimingLoop        equ      $
60
61            lea      si,interp_code
62            xor      ebx,ebx          ;clear high part of offset
63            call     StartRun
64            dec      outer_count
65            jne      TimingLoop
66
67            mov      ah,4ch
68            int      21h
69            ret
70   Start    endp
71
72   StartRun          proc     near
73            next
74   StartRun          endp
75
76   align    4
77   qsumc    proc     near              ;sum a column or portion thereof
78            mov      di,[si] ;get starting offset
79            add      si,2             ;and bump IP
80
81            mov      cx,[si] ;get element count
82            add      si,2             ;and bump IP
83
84            fldz                       ;clear TOS value
85            jcxz     qsumc_lpe         ;if no elements, skip loop
86
87   qsumc_lp          equ      $                  ;loop to calculate sum
88            fadd     data_table[di]
89            add      di,data_size
90            dec      cx               ;count down
91            jne      qsumc_lp         ;and continue if not done
92   qsumc_lpe         equ      $
93            next
94   qsumc    endp
95
96   align    4
97   qpush    proc near         ;push spreadsheet entry onto TOS
98            mov      di,[si] ;get data offset
99            add      si,2             ;and bump IP
100           fld      data_table[di]; move data to FPU
101           next
102  qpush    endp
```

Listing 5.1 *interp.asm: a token-threaded interpreter for the i386 and above (continued)*

```
103
104    align    4
105    qadd             proc    near              ;add TOS and 2nd
106          faddp st(1),st ;replacing them with the result
107          next
108    qadd             endp
109
110    align    4
111    qmul             proc    near              ;multiply TOS and 2nd
112          fmulp st(1),st  ;replacing them with the result
113          next
114    qmul             endp
115
116    align    4
117    qdiv             proc    near              ;divide 2nd by TOS
118          fdivp st(1),st  ;replacing them with the result
119          next
120    qdiv             endp
121
122    align    4
123    qsub             proc    near              ;subtract TOS from 2nd
124          fsubp st(1),st  ;replacing them with the result
125          next
126    qsub             endp
127
128    align    4
129    qpushl  proc near                ;push literal value on TOS
130          fld     qword ptr [si]         ;load double
131          add     si,data_size;increment IP
132          next
133    qpushl  endp
134
135    align    4
136    qpop    proc    near    ;pop entry from TOS into spreadsheet
137          mov     di,[si] ;get data offset
138          add     si,2              ;and bump IP
139          fstp    data_table[di]; move data from FPU
140          next
141    qpop             endp
142
143    align    4
144    qdisplay         proc near                ;display result on screen
145          push    ebx
146          fmul    decimal_correction;
147          fbstp   display_value;
148          lea     di,display_value+bcd_size;get address of value
149          cmp     byte ptr -1[di], 80h     ;negative?
150          jne     qdis_sign_ok;if not, skip
151          mov     ah,02h
152          mov     dl,'-'
153          int     21h
```

Listing 5.1 *interp.asm: a token-threaded interpreter for the i386 and above (continued)*

```
154    qdis_sign_ok    equ    $
155            mov     bx,bcd_size-1   ;number of bytes to display
156            dec     di              ;skip sign byte
157            xor     dh,dh   ;keep track of leading zero suppression
158    qdis_lp equ     $
159            dec     di              ;point to next byte
160            mov     dl,[di] ;get packed decimal byte
161            mov     cl,4
162            shr     dl,cl
163            or      dh,dl   ;see if any non-zero bytes yet
164            je      qdis_1  ;if leading zeroes, skip
165            add     dl,'0'
166            mov     ah,02h  ;DOS interrupt code
167            int     21h             ;send it out
168    qdis_1  equ     $
169            mov     dl,[di] ;get packed decimal byte
170            and     dl,0fh  ;low digit only
171            or      dh,dl   ;see if any non-zero bytes yet
172            je      qdis_2  ;if leading zeroes, skip
173            add     dl,'0'
174            mov     ah,02h  ;DOS interrupt code
175            int     21h             ;send it out
176    qdis_2  equ     $
177            cmp     bx,2            ;ready for decimal point?
178            jne     qdis_3  ;if not, forget it
179            mov     ah,02h
180            mov     dl,'.'
181            int     21h
182    qdis_3  equ     $
183            dec     bx
184            jne     qdis_lp
185            mov     ah,02h
186            mov     dl,0dh
187            int     21h
188            mov     ah,02h
189            mov     dl,0ah
190            int     21h
191            pop     ebx
192            next
193    qdisplay        endp
194
195    align   4
196    qdiscard        proc near
197            ffree   st      ;pop
198            next
199    qdiscard        endp
200
201    align   4
202    qstop   proc near
203            mov     al,0            ;return good status
204            ret
```

Listing 5.1 *interp.asm: a token-threaded interpreter for the i386 and above (continued)*

```
205    qstop      endp
206    Code_Seg          ends
207
208
209    stack 200h      ;reserve stack space as needed for application
210
211    Data_Seg segment use16
212
213    ;Here is a list of the register assignments for the 80x86 interpreter:
214    ;AX:       scratch
215    ;BL:       scratch
216    ;EBX (except bl): 0
217    ;CX:       scratch
218    ;DX:       scratch
219    ;SI:       IP
220    ;DI:       scratch
221    ;SP:       return stack
222
223    iqpush     equ     0         ;push spreadsheet entry onto TOS
224    iqadd      equ     1         ;add two top entries on stack
225    iqstop     equ     2         ;stop the interpreter
226    iqpushl    equ     3         ;push literal value onto TOS
227    iqpop      equ     4         ;pop TOS into spreadsheet entry
228    iqdisplay          equ     5         ;display TOS on screen
229    iqmul      equ     6         ;multiply
230    iqdiv      equ     7         ;divide
231    iqsub      equ     8         ;subtract
232    iqdiscard          equ     9         ;discard value from TOS
233    iqsumc     equ     10        ;sum a column or portion thereof
234    iqlast     equ     iqsumc;highest value
235
236    col_count          equ     10        ;columns are headed by every letter A through J
237    row_count          equ     400       ;can handle thirty-year mortgage calc by months
238
239    bcd_size           equ     10        ;number of bytes in BCD value
240
241    outer_count        dw      0
242
243    data_size          dw      8
244    data_shift         equ     3
245
246    row_count_word  dw       row_count
247    display_value   dt       0
248    decimal_correction dq    100.00
249    data_table      dq       col_count dup (row_count dup (0.0))
250    address_table   dw       qpush,qadd,qstop,qpushl,qpop,qdisplay
251              dw       qmul,qdiv,qsub,qdiscard,qsumc
252              dw       (255-iqlast) dup (0)
253
254    interp_code        equ     $
255
```

Listing 5.1 *interp.asm: a token-threaded interpreter for the i386 and above (continued)*

```
256     include interp.cod
257
258         db      iqstop          ;stop the action
259
260     Data_Seg        ends
261
262     end             Start
```

Free at Last

A Customer Database Program with Variable-Length Records

ALGORITHM DISCUSSED
Quantum File Access Method

Introduction

In this chapter we will develop a program which uses the quantum file access method to handle a customer database containing a large number of records that can vary dynamically in size. In order to appreciate the power of this access method, we will start by considering the much simpler problem of access to fixed-length records.

A Harmless Fixation

Let us suppose that we want to access a number of fixed-length customer records by their record numbers.[74] Given the record number, we can locate that customer's record by multiplying the record number by the length of each record, which gives us

---

74. Obviously, this is a simplification: normally, we would want to be able to find a customer's record by his name or other salient characteristic. However, that part of the problem can be handled by, for example, a hash coded lookup from the name into a record number. Here we are concerned with what happens after we know the record number.

the offset into the file where that record will be found. We can then read or write that record as needed.

Of course, a real application needs to reuse records of customers who have become inactive, to prevent the customer file from growing indefinitely. We could set a limit on the file size and, when it is reached, start reusing records that haven't been referenced for a long time, making sure to correct or delete any records in other files that refer to the deleted customer.

This fixed-length record system is not very difficult to implement, but it has significant drawbacks; address fields, for example, tend to vary greatly in length, with some records needing 25 or 30 characters for a city name or street address and others needing only 10. If we allocate enough storage for the extreme case, the records become much longer than if we had to handle only the average case. However, allocating enough for only the average case will leave those with longer fields quite unhappy, as I know from personal experience! The solution is to allow the fields (and therefore the records) to vary in length as necessary.

Checking out of the Hotel Procrustes

Unfortunately, variable-length records are much more difficult to deal with than fixed-length ones. The most obvious reason, as discussed above, is that determining where fixed-length records are stored requires only a simple calculation; this is not true of variable-length records. However, we could remedy this fairly easily by maintaining a **record index** consisting of an array of structures containing the starting location and length of each record, as depicted in figure 6.1.

Figure 6.1 *A sample record index array and data for variable-length records*

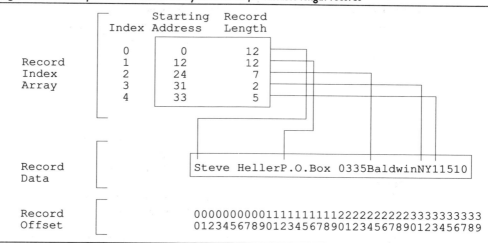

We encounter a more serious difficulty when we want to delete a record and reuse the space it occupied.[75] In some situations we can sidestep the problem by adding the new version of the record to the end of the file and changing the record pointer; however, in the case of an actively updated file such an approach would cause the file to grow rapidly.

But how can we reuse the space vacated by a deleted record of some arbitrary size? The chances of a new record being exactly the same size as any specific deleted one are relatively small, especially if the records average several hundred bytes each, as is common in customer file applications. A possible solution is to keep a separate free list for each record size and reuse a record of the correct size. However, there is a very serious problem with this approach: a new record may need 257 bytes, for example, and there may be no available record of exactly that size. Even though half of the records in the file might be deleted, none of them could be reused, and we would still be forced to extend the file. The attempt to solve this difficulty by using a record that is somewhat larger than necessary leads to many unusably small areas being left in the file (a situation known as fragmentation).

However, there is a way to make variable-length records more tractable, known as the quantum file access method.[76] The key is to combine them into groups of fixed length, which can then be allocated and deallocated in an efficient manner.

The Quantum File Access Method

In this algorithm, our file is divided into blocks[77] known as **quanta** (plural of **quantum**), generally divided into a number of addressable units called **items**.[78] When adding a record to the file, we search a free space list, looking for a quantum with enough free space for the new record. When we find one, we add the record to that quantum and store the record's location in the **item reference array**, or IRA, which replaces the record index; this array consists of entries of the form "quantum number,

---

75. The problem of changing the length of an existing record can be handled by deleting the old version of the record and adding a new version having a different length.

76. I am indebted for this extremely valuable algorithm to its inventor, Henry Beitz, who generously shared it with me in the mid-1970's.

77. In the current implementation, the block size is 2048 bytes. However, it would not be difficult to increase that size in order to be able to handle larger individual items, as discussed in Chapter 7, where we reimplement this algorithm in C++.

78. Some quanta used to store internal tables such as the free space list are not divided into items.

item number".[79] The **item number** refers to an entry in the **quantum index** stored at the beginning of the quantum; the items are stored in the quantum in order of their quantum index entries, which allows the size of an item to be calculated rather than having to be stored.

For example, if we were to create an array of variable-length strings, some of its item references might look like those in figure 6.2.

When we delete an item from a quantum, we have to update the free space list entry for that quantum to reflect the amount freed, so the space can be reused the next time an item is to be added to the file.[80] We also have to slide the remaining

Figure 6.2 *Sample item reference array (IRA), quantum index, and data, before deletions*

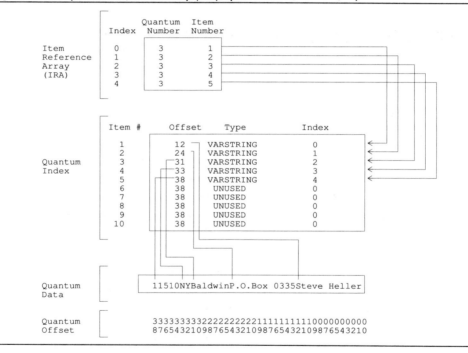

---

79. For simplicity, in our sample application each user record is stored in one item; however, since any one item must fit within a quantum, applications dealing with records that might exceed the size of a quantum should store each potentially lengthy field as a separate item. We also use some items to store internal bookkeeping data.

80. As you will see, we will be able to handle multiple IRAs in the actual implementation. In order to facilitate reconstruction of the file if part of the IRA is lost, we won't use the same quantum for items from two different IRAs; as a result, the space freed by deleting an item will only be reused when an item is to be added to the same IRA.

items in the quantum together so that the free space is in one contiguous block, rather than in slivers scattered throughout the quantum. With a record index like the one in figure 6.1, we would have to change the record index entries for all the records that were moved. Since the records that were moved might be anywhere in the record index, this could impose unacceptable overhead on deletions; to avoid this problem, we will leave the quantum index entry for a deleted item empty rather than sliding the other entries down in the quantum, so that the IRA is unaffected by changes in the position of records within a quantum. If we delete element 1 from the array, the quantum looks like figure 6.3.

Note that we set the offset value of the deleted item equal to the offset of the item before it so that its length can be calculated as zero. Now let us add a new street

Figure 6.3 *Sample item reference array (IRA), quantum index, and data*

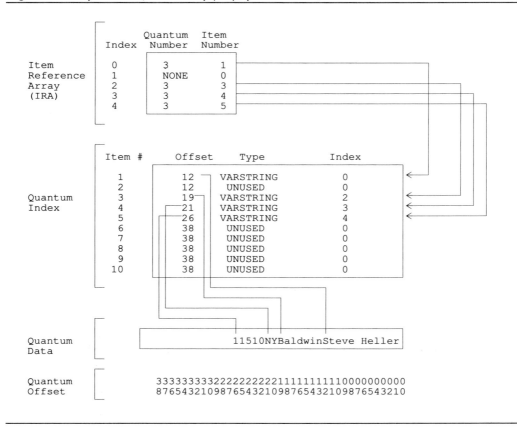

address of "123 Main Street". After this change, our data structures look like those in figure 6.4.

This is the actual mechanism used to change the value of an item: we delete the old item and add the new one. Of course, an item that increases in size may no longer fit in the same quantum, in which case we have to move it to a different quantum. Keeping track of such changes is not difficult as long as we always use the standard method of finding the address of an item: look it up in the IRA to get its quantum number and item number, then use its quantum number and item number to look it up in the quantum index. This allows us to move the item to a new quantum and change only its entries in the IRA and affected quantum indexes.

For example, if an item was originally in quantum 3 but now no longer fits there, we might move it to quantum 6. In order to do this, we first delete it from quantum 3 and then add it to quantum 6. As before, all the other IRA entries for items in quantum 3 still refer to the same data items as before, after we have adjusted the quantum index to account for the removed data.

Figure 6.4 *Sample IRA, quantum index, and data, after field change*

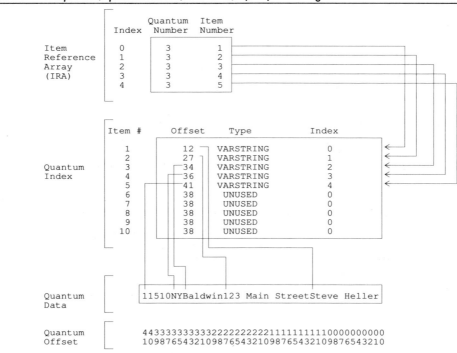

Of course, the deleted item still takes up a slot in the quantum index of the old quantum; in our implementation this requires four bytes of storage.[81] We need a method of reclaiming that space, so that we do not gradually fill our quanta with indexes pointing to nothing. We have already seen part of the solution to this problem: whenever we are adding an item to a quantum, we search for an unused quantum index entry rather than simply adding a new entry at the end.

This mechanism alone would only slow the growth of the quantum indexes; actually reducing the size of an index requires us to check for empty entries at the end of the quantum index after deleting an item. If such excess entries exist, we reclaim the space they occupy by reducing the entry count in the quantum index header to the number actually in use. This reduces wasted space in the quantum index without affecting entries in the IRA. Since we remove unused quantum index entries only when they are at the end of the index, no IRA entries can refer to items later in the same quantum.

A Large Array

Our customer records are stored in the quanta pointed to by our IRA. The IRA will be stored in its own quanta, which allows us to make it as large as needed. However, this means that we can't allocate the IRA in one piece; since a quantum has a fixed size, we will have to break up our IRA into segments that will fit in a quantum. We'll also need some way to find the segment that we need for a particular element in the IRA. These needs are served by the **big pointer array**.

Figure 6.5 shows the relationship between the big pointer array and the IRA segments. Each IRA segment in the real program, of course, holds more than five entries: with a 2-Kbyte quantum, about 650 entries will fit in one quantum. However, the segmentation of the IRA works in the same way as this example. The segment number can be determined by dividing the element number by the number of elements in each IRA segment; the index into the IRA segment is the remainder of that division.

The big pointer array sets a limit on the number of elements referenced by an IRA, since that array has to fit in one quantum. However, this is not a very restrictive limit, since one big pointer array can contain about 1000 elements, using a 2-Kbyte quantum. Each of these elements points to a little pointer array, which contains pointers to about 650 entries, as mentioned above. Therefore, we could theoretically create an array with about 650,000 items in it. However, for purposes of space efficiency, our `ArrayIndex` type is defined as an `unsigned short`, which is usually 2

---

81. Two of these bytes are used to hold the index in the IRA to which this item corresponds; this information would be very helpful in reconstructing as much as possible of the file if it should become corrupted.

Figure 6.5 *From the big pointer array to the IRA*

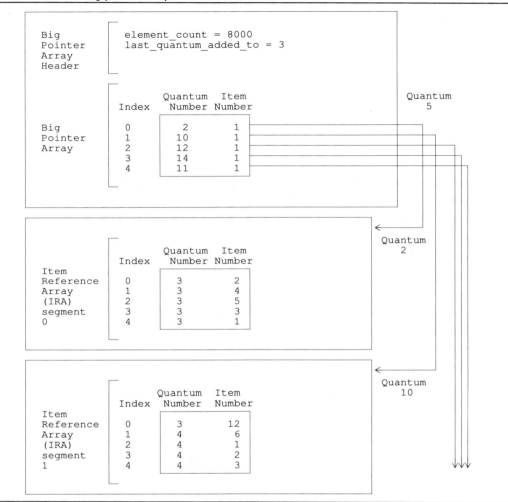

bytes, allowing us to store 64K elements in an array. For applications in which this is too confining, we could easily change the **ArrayIndex** type to an **unsigned long**.[82]

Thus, we have effectively removed the limitation on the number of elements in an array. However, there is one more generalization needed to make the quantum file access method useful in many applications; being able to create more than one array of variable-length items.

---

82. In the dynamic hashing algorithm in Chapter 7, we pack several logical records into one item, which is another method of getting around this 64K limit on array indexing.

Many Large Arrays

The mechanism by which we will be able to access a number of arrays is called the "main object index",[83] which contains the quantum number of the big pointer array for each object. The number of an object is set by the program that requests its creation by calling `qf_create_main_object`; any other operations on that object require its object number.[84] For example, to find an element in a main object, we index into the main object index by the object's number, retrieving the big pointer array quantum number for that object. Then we calculate the IRA segment and the index into that segment and retrieve the quantum number and item number for the element we want. The last step is to index into the quantum index to find the exact location of the element.

Of course, we need a place to store the main object index. A normal application might have five or ten main objects; therefore, our default allocation of 1024 entries in the main object index (one quantum's worth) is extremely generous.[85] Since the main object index is referenced during the lookup of every element, it is reasonable to load it from a specific location in the quantum file into a dedicated block of memory during `qf_open_quantum_file`; this avoids the overhead of calling `get_quantum` to locate the main object index during every object lookup. However, any changes to the index are written to the disk immediately, so that the disk copy of the index will be up to date. The header in the quantum file specifies the number of elements in the main object index and where it starts in the quantum file, so we can easily handle quantum files that differ in the number of main objects they can contain.

Figure 6.6 shows the path from the main object index through the big pointer array, the IRA segment, and the quantum index, to finally arrive at the data.

The Light at the End of the Tunnel

There are two more topics we have to cover before we start to look at the code. First, a note on function names: function names that start with `qf_` are the routines that are intended to be called from user programs; the other functions are intended only for internal use in the quantum file access routines. This is enforced by prototyping the internal functions as **static** in "quantum.c"; the private

---

83. Why not call it the "main array index"? When I first implemented this algorithm, over ten years ago, I chose the term "object" rather than "array" in order to be more general; there is no requirement that all of the elements in an object be of the same structure, as might be implied by the term "array".

84. In the C++ implementation of this algorithm in Chapter 7, we will implement a primitive directory system, so that objects can be looked up by name.

85. The C++ implementation reduces this to 256 so that an object number can fit into one byte; this facilitates changes to the free space list.

Figure 6.6 *From the main object index to the data*

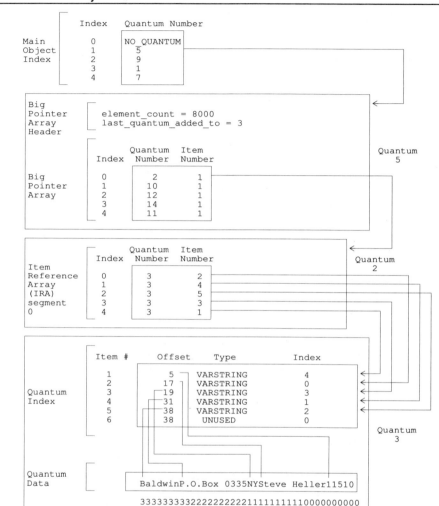

structures and **#define**'d constants used to control the quantum file are defined only in "quantum.c" for the same reason.[86]

---

86. This illustrates that encapsulating the details of an algorithm, one of the benefits of object-oriented programming,is not terribly difficult in C. As we will see in Chapter 7, the real advantage of a C++ implementation to the user of this algorithm is in making the use of quantum files transparent to the user; a set of quantum file handling classes can provide virtual-memory variable-length arrays as a seamlessly integrated data type.

Second, we should take a look at the quantum header; this structure contains information needed to access a particular quantum file, as we may have more than one open simultaneously. The `qf_open_quantum_file` routine will return a pointer to this header, cast as a `FILE *` to hide the internal structure from the calling program.[87] Let's take a look at the information in the header (listing 6.5, lines 92–111).

The Quantum File Header Record

We begin by examining the `typedef`'s used in this structure to make the usage of its elements clearer; they are also used in the prototypes for functions using the structure elements. The `ArrayIndex` type is defined as `unsigned short` in "quantum.h" (listing 6.4); the remainder are defined in "quantum.c", as they are intended for internal use only. The `QuantumNumber` type is defined as `unsigned short`; the `Quantum` type is a `char *`; and a `FreeSpaceEntry` is another `unsigned short`.

Now to the `QuantumFile` structure. The `quantum_version_info` element is used to keep track of the version of the program that was used to create the quantum file.[88] The current program simply tests whether the version of the program that created the file is different from the one reading it and aborts if they are different. A production program would use this information to determine whether the versions were compatible, so that if we changed the program in a way that makes old files unusable, we could warn the user that the file is of an old type and should be converted. Alternatively, we might automatically convert it to a new format; in either case, it is essential that we know what version of our program created the file.

The `dos_file_ptr` element is used to keep track of the DOS file pointer returned by `fopen`, so that the physical layer routines can read, write, and close the quantum file.

The `file_name` element points to the name of the quantum file, so that it could be used in error messages, for example.[89]

---

87. While this "information hiding" is one of the primary benefits of an object-oriented approach, I have encountered some objections to it; don't I trust the application programmer? Well, since I am often the only one to be protected, obviously I don't do it out of a sense of superiority. I do it to reduce the amount of information that the application programmer has to keep in mind when writing an application program, and to enable the systems programmer to make changes to the internal implementation without breaking the application programs. This is extremely valuable even when the systems programmer and the application programmer happen to be the same person.

88. This element is initialized from a variable called `program_version_info`, controlled by line 6. This line is a directive to TLIB, a version control system from Burton Systems, Inc., to update a string constant on the following line to include version number, time, date, and file name information. Such a program is absolutely essential if you want to keep track of which version of your program you are sending out; TLIB is an inexpensive program which has received good reviews, and I have found it easy to use.

89. The current implementation of `qf_open_quantum_file` just makes a copy of the pointer to the file name; therefore, this feature will be reliable only if the quantum file name is a string constant. A commercial version would have to save the file name itself.

The `main_object_index_count` element is used to control the number of main objects (arrays) that can be allocated. In this program, we initialize this variable to a manifest constant `MAIN_OBJECT_INDEX_COUNT` when creating a quantum file; however, it is read in from the quantum file at open time so that we can automatically handle files with different values for this variable.

The `free_space_list_count` element is used to control the `free_space_list` for this file; the `free_space_list` contains a `FreeSpaceEntry` code for each quantum that can be allocated. As with the `main_object_index_count`, the `free_space_list_count` is initialized to a manifest constant when creating a quantum file (`MAX_FILE_QUANTUM_COUNT` in this case), but is read in at open time to allow us to handle files with different maximum sizes automatically.

The `memory_resident_quantum_count` element keeps track of the current number of quantum buffers, each able to hold one quantum. The number of quantum buffers is set at open time in the current program and not changed thereafter; however, it could be changed at run time, if care were taken to flush the buffers before reducing their number. Generally, more buffers will improve performance by reducing the number of disk accesses, while consuming more memory. Some experimentation is usually needed to find the most appropriate number of buffers.

The `main_object_index` element is a pointer to an array of `main_object_index_count` elements, each of which is the `QuantumNumber` of the quantum containing the big pointer array for each main object (array) that can exist in the system.

The `memory_resident_quantum_list` element points to an array of `QuantumNumber`s, one entry for each quantum buffer, indicating which quantum, if any, is resident in that buffer. Since quantum numbers start at one, a zero entry indicates that the buffer has no quantum resident.

The `quantum_buffer` element points to an array of `Quantum` pointers, one for each memory resident quantum.

The `most_recently_used_list` element points to an array of `int`s, which is used to keep track of which quanta have been most recently used. When we have to discard a quantum from memory in order to make room for another, this list allows us to choose the one that hasn't been referenced for the longest time, on the theory that it's the least likely to be needed soon.

The `locked_list` element points to an array of `int`s, one for each quantum buffer, which is used to keep track of whether the quantum in that buffer is locked in memory; a locked quantum cannot be discarded to allow another quantum to use that buffer.

The `dirty_list` element points to an array of `int`s, one for each quantum buffer, which is used to keep track of whether the quantum in that buffer has been modified since it was read in from the disk. If so, it has to be written back to the disk when its buffer is to be reused. If the quantum hasn't been modified since being read from the disk, however, the buffer can be reused without rewriting the quantum to the disk, as the copy on the disk is the same as the one in memory.

The `free_space_list` element points to an array of `FreeSpaceEntrys`, one for each quantum that can exist in a quantum file. This is used to keep track of the amount of space available in each quantum, so that when we need to move an item from one quantum to another, we know which ones to consider as the recipient.

The `main_object_index_offset`, `free_space_list_offset`, and `starting_quantum_offset` hold the offsets in the quantum file of the `main_object_index`, `free_space_list`, and quantum number 1, respectively (as mentioned previously, there is no quantum number zero).

The Itinerary

The itinerary of our trip through the code will be somewhat different in this chapter. Since we have so much to cover and the nesting of function calls is so deep, our usual practice of following the execution of the program through each procedure in the order encountered would be very difficult to follow. Instead, we'll divide the code into two layers: the physical layer, which deals with reading, writing, and locating quanta on the disk and in memory; and the logical layer, which handles the contents of the quanta and relies on the physical layer for disk access. This approach will reduce the amount of information that we'll have to keep in mind when going through each layer of routines.

Let's Get Physical

The physical layer of functions consists primarily of `get_quantum` and its subsidiary functions. These functions perform the vital task of making sure that a particular quantum is in memory, which may involve removing another quantum from memory. Figure 6.7 is a list of the physical layer routines, in order of discussion.

Figure 6.7 *Physical layer routines*

- `get_quantum`
- `find_buffer`
- `read_quantum`
- `write_quantum`
- `position_quantum`
- `allocate_quantum_buffers`
- `deallocate_quantum_buffers`
- `qf_flush_buffers`

get_quantum

In get_quantum (listing 6.5, lines 763–811), as with all routines that are called with a FILE * pointer to the quantum file, the first operation is to cast that pointer to a QuantumFile *, so that we can access the fields of the quantum file header. Next, we call find_buffer, which gives us the address of the buffer that contains the quantum we are looking for, if it is in memory; if our quantum is not in memory, this is the buffer that should be used to hold the quantum when we read it into memory. The return value from find_buffer indicates which of these is the current situation: the value of status will be OKAY if the quantum is already in the buffer, and NOT_IN_LIST otherwise.

At this point (line 778), we may already have the quantum we want in the buffer whose index is buffer_number, or we may still have to read it into that buffer. If we do have it, we are almost ready to return its address to the calling routine. However, first we have to make sure that any modifications to the quantum's status that were requested by the calling routine are performed. The changes that can be requested are to set the DIRTY flag, to LOCK the quantum, or to UNLOCK it. What effects do these flags have?

THE STATUS SETTERS

The DIRTY flag indicates that the calling routine intends to modify the contents of the quantum; therefore, before we remove it from memory to make its buffer available for another quantum, we must write its contents back to the disk. Since we often want to read some data from a quantum without altering it, we can eliminate a significant number of disk accesses by not rewriting any quantum whose contents have not been changed; the next time we need its contents, we can get a fresh copy from the disk.[90]

The LOCK and UNLOCK status change requests determine whether the quantum in question may be removed from memory to free its buffer for another quantum. The qf_store_item routine, for example, calls get_quantum for a second time while it still needs access to the first quantum it retrieved. Since the first call to get_quantum has the LOCK flag set, we do not have to worry about the first quantum being removed from memory during the second call to get_quantum. In general, a routine should make sure to lock any quanta which it will need to access after operations that might cause other quanta to be loaded into memory (and therefore might displace currently loaded quanta). When the routine is finished using the quanta it has locked, it should unlock them by calls to get_quantum with UNLOCK set, so that their buffers can be reused for newly referenced quanta.[91]

---

90. One seeming oddity is that there is no provision for the calling routine to clear the DIRTY flag. This flag is cleared whenever the quantum's contents are written back to the disk by qf_flush_buffers, which writes all quanta that have the DIRTY bit set back to the disk. On the other hand, if the quantum is rewritten because its buffer is to be reused, the dirty_list entry refers to the new quantum rather than the old. Therefore, there is no need for the user program to concern itself with this function.

91. The need to lock and unlock quanta explicitly adds considerable complexity, which is an invitation to bugs in the program; as a result, one of the goals of the C++ implementation was to eliminate this operation.

If the quantum we want is already in memory, we return to the calling routine with the address of the buffer holding the quantum as our return value. However, let us assume that our quantum is not in memory, so that we have to continue in `get_quantum`. The next operation is to determine whether the old quantum in the buffer we are going to use is dirty, by checking the `dirty_list` entry for that buffer. If it is dirty, we have to call `write_quantum` to write it back to the disk before we load our new quantum into it.

Now the buffer is available, so we set the element in the `dirty_list` for this buffer if the quantum we are going to read is to be modified, as indicated by the value of the `mode` argument. Then we copy the quantum number for our new quantum into the `memory_resident_quantum_list`, as it is the new occupant of the buffer, and read the quantum into the buffer via `read_quantum`.

We're almost done with `get_quantum`. The last remaining tasks are to set or clear the LOCK bits in the `locked` list, if either of those operations was requested by the caller by setting the appropriate bit in the value of the `mode` argument, and return the address of the quantum's buffer to the calling routine.

find_buffer

Now we should take a look at `find_buffer` (listing 6.5, lines 874–970), which actually handles much of the complexity of `get_quantum`.

After our standard prologue of casting the `quantum_file` argument to its real type of a `QuantumFile *`, we make local copies of the variables we will need to use frequently in `find_buffer`. These are: `memory_resident_quantum_count`, the number of quantum buffers; `memory_resident_quantum_list`, an array of pointers to the quantum buffers; `most_recently_used_list`, used to keep track of which buffers have been used most recently, so that we can reuse those that haven't been used for a while; and `locked_list`, used to prevent discarding quanta that we need to keep in memory. Then we make a note that we haven't found the quantum yet, by setting `quantum_found` to `NOT_IN_LIST`.

CHECKING IT ONCE

Looking through the buffers to find the quantum we want is quite simple (lines 908–916); we search the `memory_resident_quantum_list`, which associates quantum numbers with buffer numbers, until we either find the quantum number we are looking for or get to the end of the list.

If we still haven't found our quantum, we have to locate a buffer to reuse. That is the job of the next loop, which finds the lowest-priority quantum that isn't locked; all locked quanta effectively have a priority high enough not to be reused, since that is the purpose of locking a quantum in memory. Therefore, the loop sets `lowest_unlocked_priority` to a value higher than any that will be encountered;

this ensures that the first time we find an unlocked quantum, we will reset that variable to the priority of that quantum, without needing to execute a conditional statement in the loop. The loop resets `lowest_unlocked_priority` every time it finds an unlocked quantum with a priority lower than the previous lowest value.

Then we check whether the highest priority is more than 32000, which means it is time for us to redo the priority list to make sure that none of its entries gets too large to be represented by an `unsigned short` value. If `highest_priority` exceeds the limit, we sort the list by priority number, rearranging both the list and a list of entry numbers according to the ranking of the priorities and then replacing the priority numbers by their location in the sorted list. This has the effect of reducing the possible priorities to the values between 0 and one less than the number of quantum buffers, which is logically equivalent to reorganizing the list every time we access any quantum, so that the numbers always stay in that range. However, these two approaches are not equivalent in terms of processing time; even though each execution of this method of recalculating the priorities is considerably more time-consuming than rearranging the priority list for each quantum access, it is done only every 32000 accesses, rather than at every access. Its contribution to the CPU time of the average access is therefore very small.

In either case, we now have an updated priority list, so our next job is to set the selected buffer's priority to the highest value, as it is the most recently referenced buffer. We also copy the buffer number into the output variable pointed to by `buffer_number_pointer`, for use by the calling program.

Finally, we return to `get_quantum`, the return value being `OKAY` if we have found the quantum and `NOT_IN_LIST` if we haven't.

Reading, Writing, and...

There are a few physical layer routines left to cover. One of them is `read_quantum` (lines 974–987). This is a very simple routine: all we have to do is to clear the quantum buffer, position the quantum file using `position_quantum_file`, and read the quantum into the buffer. The `write_quantum` routine (lines 991–1003) is almost identical, except of course for writing the buffer rather than reading it.

The `position_quantum_file` routine (lines 1007–1024) is just as simple: all it does is multiply the length of a quantum by one less than the quantum number (because the first quantum number is 1, not 0) and add the starting quantum offset (the position of quantum number 1 in the file). Then it uses `fseek` to position the file for the subsequent read or write operation.

The last three physical layer routines are responsible for managing the memory used to hold quanta in memory. In the first, `allocate_quantum_buffers` (lines 279–291) we allocate a block of memory containing enough storage for all of the quantum pointers requested in the call, and then call the memory allocation routine for each buffer requested.[92]   We then return the address of the block of pointers. In the second function, `deallocate_quantum_buffers` (lines 373–312), we free the memory allocated in `allocate_quantum_buffers`.

Finally, `qf_flush_buffers` (lines 814–871) makes sure that we write all "dirty" quanta back to the disk; these were the ones which were marked as being changeable when we called `get_quantum` to access them. This operation is a bit tricky: we look through the `dirty_list`, and whenever we find a nonzero entry, we collect the slot number and the address of the quantum number in that slot. Then we sort the slot numbers in order of the quantum numbers and write out each quantum in order by the sorted slot numbers; i.e., sorted by quantum number. Of course, we reset the dirty bits after we write all these quanta out, as they now have an identical representation on the disk.

You may be wondering why we don't just write the quanta in the order we find them in the `memory_resident_quantum_list`. The reason is that if the quanta are written in ascending order of address in the file, less head motion will be needed than if they are written out in another order; this is the equivalent of the "elevator sorting" algorithm used by some sophisticated disk controllers to speed up disk writes. We should benefit from this optimization if the file is not terribly fragmented (and if we are running on a system without such a disk controller); a production system should probably be optimized with a utility like the Norton Speed Disk program on a regular basis, for this reason.[93]

92. The `x_calloc` and `x_free` function names are references to replacements for the usual `calloc` and `free` routines in the C library; these routines keep track of memory that has been allocated and give an error message when we try to free memory that hasn't been allocated; `x_chkfree`, another routine in the same group, allows a check for unfreed memory at the end of the program. It is well known that memory allocation errors are the most common errors in C programming, and that such errors can be extremely elusive; therefore, routines such as these are essential in C programs that do any significant amount of dynamic memory allocation. The routines I used to develop this program are modifications of those presented in Randall Merilatt's article "C Dynamic Memory Use", in *Dr. Dobb's Journal of Software Tools*, 14(August 1989), 62–67, 125–127. However, since these routines are not really relevant to the topic at hand, I have omitted them from the listings: the first two are `#define`'d (in "xmemd.h", listing 6.3) to their standard C library equivalents, and the last one is `#define`'d to nothing.

Of course, commercial programs are now available that catch these errors at runtime without having to modify the code. Bounds Checker,™ from NuMega Technologies, Inc., is probably the best known; although it is not the most user-friendly program I've used, I recommend it highly.

93. The reason that I can't provide a quantitative estimate of the improvement due to this optimization is that my development system's disk controller provides hardware elevator sorting, which makes this optimization redundant.

A Logical Analysis

Now that we have gone over the lowest layer of routines, the ones that provide the physical storage management for the quantum file mechanism, we are ready to tackle the routines at the next higher layer, which provide the logical management of the data stored in the quanta. Figure 6.8 is a list of the routines in the logical layer.

qf_open_quantum_file

A good place to start is `qf_open_quantum_file` (listing 6.5, lines 171–275), since we can't do anything to a quantum file until we open it, as with any other file. First, we try to open the file for reading, to see whether it is already there. If it isn't, the `fopen` returns NULL, in which case we create the file, allocate storage for the `QuantumFile` header record, and initialize the header. Then we allocate storage for the `quantum_file_header` structure, set the `main_object_index_count` and `free_space_list_count` to their default values, and copy the current `program_version_info` into the `quantum_version_info` structure element.

The next operation is to initialize the offsets of the `main_object_index`, the `free_space_list`, and quantum number 1, so that these areas of the file can be located when we open the file again. Next, we allocate the `quantum_padding` structure and write both the header and the padding to the quantum file.[94]

Since we haven't created any main objects yet, our next task is to clear the main object index. We allocate storage for the in-memory copy of `main_object_index`, clearing it to zeros (which indicates available entries, as quantum number zero is not used), except for the entry for object number zero, which is set to `INVALID_QUANTUM_NUMBER`; we will not allow a main object number zero, for better error control. Then we write this initialized `main_object_index` to the file, so it will be available for our next use.

Figure 6.8 *Logical layer routines*

- o qf_open_quantum_file
- o qf_create_main_object
- o reserve_available_quantum
- o initialize_big_pointer_array
- o qf_store_item
- o qf_get_item
- o add_item_to_quantum
- o delete_item_in_quantum

---

94. The padding is used to clear the file to the next quantum size boundary, so that later versions of the program can extend the size of the header up to the size of a quantum while remaining downward-compatible with files having old headers.

The last operation in the new file initialization is to set up the `free_space_list` to indicate that all quanta have the maximum available free space, except of course for quantum zero, which is not used. The `free_space_list` is also written to disk, to make it permanent.

Of course, the process of opening an already existing quantum file starts differently (lines 221–246); we have to read in the quantum file header and check whether it was created by the same version of the program. Similarly, we have to read the `main_object_index` and the `free_space_list` that were created previously, rather than initializing them for an empty file. After this point, however, the code for opening either an old or a new file is common.

We are almost done with the initialization, but there are a few more data structures to deal with; these are the ones that are of significance only while the file is open, whereas up till now we have been concerned with those that are maintained during the lifetime of the quantum file.

First, we have to set `memory_resident_quantum_count` to the number of quanta that the calling routine has specified in `buffer_count`. Next, we allocate storage for the control arrays `memory_resident_quantum_list`, `locked_list`, `dirty_list`, and `most_recently_used_list`. Then we allocate the number of quantum buffers specified by the calling routine, via `allocate_quantum_buffers` (lines 279–291), which allocates an array of `Quantum *`s and allocates a buffer the size of a quantum to each entry in that array. Finally, we copy the `dos_file_ptr` and a pointer to the quantum file's `filename` to the `quantum_file_header`, set the I/O buffer to the size of one quantum, and return the `quantum_file_header`, cast as a `FILE *`, to the calling routine.

qf_create_main_object

Now we will examine `qf_create_main_object` (lines 376–404). A main object, as defined earlier, is something that has an entry in the `main_object_index`. Our example program has one main object: a customer database array, which we will specify as having main object number `CUSTOMER_ARRAY_OBJECT_NUMBER`, and allocate 8000 entries in its IRA (see figure 6.2 for a sample IRA).

First, we have to determine whether the object number passed to us is available for creating a new object. If there is a quantum number already specified in the `main_object_index` for this main object, then the object already exists. Therefore, trying to create it is an error, and we report it as such. In our sample program, our error handling is primitive; we report the error and terminate the program. A real production program, of course, would try to recover from the error.

Assuming that we've passed that first hurdle, we call `reserve_available_quantum` to reserve a quantum to contain the big pointer array, which holds pointers to the segments of the IRA for this main object. After that is a call to the `get_quantum` function, to get a pointer to the quantum we have just reserved.

Next, we store the quantum number of the big pointer array in the `main_object_index` entry for our new object and call `initialize_big_pointer_array`, which creates an array of pointers to the segments of the IRA for this main object.

The final operation in `qf_create_main_object` is to call `rewrite_object_index`, so that the information about our new main object is written to the disk. Then we return to the caller.

reserve_available_quantum

Now let's look at the logical layer functions called by `qf_create_main_object`. The first such routine is `reserve_available_quantum` (lines 408–430). The `reserve_available_quantum` routine is quite simple: we look through the `free_space_list` until we find a quantum that has the maximum available space in it, indicated by `AVAILABLE_QUANTUM`. Then we set that quantum's `free_space_list` entry to 0, indicating that it has no available space, so that it won't be selected again by the next call to `reserve_available_quantum`, and we return the quantum number.

You may be wondering why we insist on a quantum that has nothing in it, rather than taking the first one that has enough space in it. The reason is that we don't allow the sharing of a quantum among arrays, to make it easier to reconstruct an array if its control information has been corrupted. As we will see later, our implementation will store enough information to make this possible.

A related question is why we set the `free_space_list` entry for our selected quantum to 0. The reason for this is that `reserve_available_quantum` doesn't know how much space we want; the space available will be updated when we actually store the quantum later.

initialize_big_pointer_array

The next logical layer function called by `qf_create_main_object` is `initialize_big_pointer_array` (lines 452–515). This starts out by calculating the number of little pointer quanta (also known as IRA segments) needed to hold pointers to `item_count` items, as specified in the calling sequence, and allocating storage for an array of QuantumNumbers, one for each of those little pointer quanta. Now we are ready to call `initialize_quantum` (lines 434–448), which prepares a quantum for storing items, by clearing it to all zeros and setting three fields in its `quantum_header`: its `main_object_number` and its `quantum_type` to the corresponding values specified by the caller, and its `item_count` to 0, since it has no items stored in it yet.

Back in `initialize_big_pointer_array`, we call `reserve_available_quantum` for each little pointer quantum we need and store the resulting quantum numbers in `little_pointer_quantum_number_array`. Then we set the `element_count` and `last_quantum_added_to` fields in the `big_array_header` structure; the `element_count` field, as the name implies, indicates the number of elements allocated in the array, so that we can detect an attempt to store or retrieve an element that is past the end of the array. The last_quantum_added_to structure element is used to speed up the process of finding a place to put a new item during the initialization of an array.[95]

Since the header is filled in, we can now call add_item_to_quantum twice to add both the big_array_header and the little_pointer_quantum_number_array to the big pointer array quantum. Then we allocate memory for the little_pointer_array, which will contain ITEM_REFERENCE_PACKING_FACTOR elements, each of which is an ItemReference, defined in lines 39–43. The little_pointer_array is one segment of the IRA, which contains one entry of type ItemReference for each element in the array; in our case these array elements are customer database records.

Now we have to initialize the little_pointer_array to indicate that none of the item references in this array are pointing to anything. So we create a null_item_reference variable, set it to indicate that it has no associated data, and copy this variable into every element of the little_pointer_array.

We're almost done with initialize_big_pointer_array. For each little pointer quantum, we have to get its quantum into memory, initialize it to an empty state, and then add the empty little_pointer_array_quantum we just created to it, so that the little_pointer_array will be available for storing items. Then we free the storage used by our temporary variables and return to qf_create_main_object. The last function here is rewrite_object_index (lines 316–329), which does just that: it writes the main_object_index back to the disk to reflect our new main object.

qf_store_item and qf_get_item

The qf_store_item routine and its counterpart qf_get_item are the functions most used by the application program to obtain access to quantum file contents. Since we can hardly retrieve information before we store it, the logical place to start is with qf_store_item (lines 1026–1196). Its input arguments are: the quantum_file pointer, cast as a FILE *; the main_object_number for the array we are interested in; the element_index indicating which element we wish to store; item, which points to the data for the item; and item_size, which tells us the number of bytes to store.[96]

The first thing we do is to check that the item_size value is not greater than the maximum size of an individual item, MAX_ITEM_SIZE. The consequences of an error of this kind in the calling program would be very serious, so we make the check here, and exit with an error return if this condition exists. Next we cast the quantum_file argument to its real type, a QuantumFile *, and use it to retrieve pointers to the free_space_list and to the main_object_index; then we index into the main_object_index to find the quantum number that holds the big

---

95. We often will step through an array assigning values to each element in turn, for example when importing a data base from an ASCII file; since we are not modifying previously stored values, the quantum we used last is the most likely to have room to add another item.

96. Since the data can consist of anything, including null bytes, we can't use strlen to tell us the length of the data.

pointer array for our object. Now we can use `get_quantum` to return a pointer to that quantum; this gives us access to the big pointer array header and the big pointer array itself via `get_pointer_to_item`, which furnishes a pointer to an item whose position in the quantum index is known.[97] Notice that we set the `DIRTY` and `LOCK` flags when calling `get_quantum`, since we don't want the big pointer array quantum to be removed from memory while we have a pointer to it, and we may change the `last_quantum_added_to` element of the big pointer array header.

Now we can use the `big_array_header_pointer` to extract the `element_count` from the header for the big pointer array. This tells us how many elements we have allocated to this array, so we can check the index for validity. If the index is out of bounds, we exit with an error. Otherwise, we use `get_pointer_to_item` again, this time to get the address of the array of quantum numbers of the little pointer arrays (a.k.a. segments of the item reference array). The result goes in `little_quantum_number_array`. Notice that in this call we check the return value from `get_pointer_to_item` to ensure that we have indeed retrieved an item of `BIG_POINTER_ARRAY` type. If the type is wrong, we exit with an error, since the quantum file is corrupted. The error message tells the user to run QFIX, which would fix the file by retrieving the redundant information from the quanta, the main object table, and the big and little pointer blocks and sorting the whole thing out.[98]

Assuming that the type check is successful, we calculate which little pointer quantum needs to be loaded into memory. Then we make sure that the quantum number we need is within range in the big pointer array. If not, we have a corrupted file, with the same result as before. However, if it is okay, we get its quantum number and call `get_quantum` to load that quantum into memory. As in the case of the big pointer array, we set `DIRTY` and `LOCK` in the call to `get_quantum`; this time, we intend to change the element of the little pointer array that represents our item, and we don't want the little pointer array to be removed from memory while we are using it. Once we have a pointer to the little pointer array quantum, we call `get_pointer_to_item` to load `little_pointer_array` with a pointer to that array, check that it is the correct type, and calculate the index of the item we want in the little pointer array. If that index is past the end of the little pointer array, we have a corrupted file.

Assuming we pass all of these tests, we can get the `item_reference` for the item we want from the `little_pointer_array`. The `item_reference` we retrieve may be either a real reference to an item (in which case `real_reference` will return a nonzero number), or a reference to a null item (one that contains no data). In the former case, we use `get_quantum` to ensure that its quantum is in memory,

---

97. For items defined by the application program, we get this information from the item reference array, but the big pointer array header and the big pointer array items were stored in a specific order by us when we created the big pointer array. Therefore, we can use the constants `BIG_POINTER_HEADER_ITEM` and `BIG_POINTER_ARRAY_ITEM`, respectively, to retrieve them from their quantum.

98. Writing such a program is one of the problems at the end of this chapter.

call `delete_item_in_quantum` to remove the old item from its position in its quantum, and call `get_space_available` to inform us as to the new available space in that quantum. The results of that call are used to update the `free_space_list`, so that we will know how much space is left in that quantum the next time we are looking for a place to store new items belonging to this object. But what if this item reference is a null item?

SOME ADO ABOUT NOTHING

A null item is an optimization: we could treat items containing no data like all other items. However, special handling for this case is worthwhile, since it is very common. For example, a word processor might store each line of a file as a string, removing the trailing null from each string before storing it; strings consisting only of a trailing null would be stored as null items. The advantage of using null items is that, rather than occupying a quantum index slot indicating a length of zero, they are represented by item references that contain a special quantum number called `NO_QUANTUM` and a special item number called `NULL_ITEM_NUMBER`, neither of which can appear in a real item reference. This means that a null item does not occupy any space in a quantum index, and that we can avoid loading in a quantum to retrieve its value.

Now that we are ready to store the new item (line 1122), we see that if the size of the new item is zero, its item reference element is set to the values for a null item, rather than being stored in a quantum. Otherwise, we actually have to store the data. The first order of business is to find a quantum that has enough space to store this new item. Here is where we make use of another optimization: the `last_quantum_added_to` field in the structure pointed to by the `big_array_header_pointer`. The reason for checking this quantum's available space first is that we often want to fill up an array before we start updating previously existing records in that array. In this case, the most recently written-to quantum is half full on the average; this makes it a good place to look for some free space. In addition, it is very likely to be already in memory, so we won't have to do any disk accesses to get at it.

So we start by getting the amount of free space listed for this quantum in the `free_space_list`. If it indicates that there is enough space for our item, we get a pointer to the quantum by calling `get_quantum`, and then calculate the actual free space via `get_space_available`. If it is sufficient, we have found our target.[99]

On the other hand, there might not be enough space left in the last quantum we used. In that case, we have to search for another one with the amount of space we need. As we saw previously, we don't want to share a quantum among several objects, because our planning for error recovery makes use of the fact that all items in a quantum belong to the same object. So we will look through the little pointer array for the object we are involved with, checking all of the quanta listed in that array.

---

99. The reason for checking the actual free space rather than taking the information in the free space list at face value is that, in order to save memory, the free space list contains a one-byte code which represents an approximation of the amount of space available.

This is the task of lines 1144–1168. We start out by initializing a `little_pointer_array_pointer` to one entry before the beginning of the `little_pointer_array`. Then we check each element in the `little_pointer_array` to see whether it is a real reference. If so, we extract its quantum number and test it for available space as we did with the last added-to quantum above. We stop whenever we find a quantum in this list with enough space to hold our new item. If this search is successful, we call `get_quantum` to set the DIRTY flag for this quantum, as we are going to modify it.

However, if the search fails, we need to call `reserve_available_quantum` to extend the file by one quantum; then we load it into memory with `get_quantum`, setting the DIRTY flag as in the above case, and initialize it via `initialize_quantum`. In either case, now we can set the `last_quantum_added_to` field of the big array header, and the `quantum_number` and `relative_item_number` fields of the `item_reference` structure. The latter value is the result of calling `add_item_to_quantum`, which finds a free item slot in the quantum's item index and stores the item in the quantum.

We are nearly finished with `qf_store_item`. All we have left to do is to copy the `item_reference` structure to the `little_pointer_array` element representing the item being added, unlock the quanta containing the `little_pointer_array` and the `big_pointer_array`, and update the `free_space_list`. Then we return to the calling program.

The `qf_get_item` routine (lines 1200–1299) is quite similar to `qf_store_item`, but much simpler, as we do not need to change anything in the quantum file system. We start out by retrieving the big pointer array and the little pointer array and checking that the types of all the items retrieved during this process are correct. Then, at line 1273, we check whether the item reference for the item we are retrieving is real or a null item. If it is a null item, we allocate 1 byte (so that string operations will treat it as a null string), set the item size to zero, and return.

On the other hand, if it is a real item reference, we get its quantum via `get_quantum`, get a pointer to the item by calling `get_pointer_to_item`, set the item size and item address in the calling routine by means of the `item_size` and `item` arguments, and copy the item into the temporary storage allocated to the item. Then we return to the calling program.

add_item_to_quantum

One of the routines called by `qf_store_item` is `add_item_to_quantum` (lines 667–759). This routine is one of the critical routines of this algorithm; it is responsible for a large part of the maintenance of the quantum index, which is the table that allows the upper-level routines to ignore the actual position of the items in the array. The quantum index is made of structures of type `ItemIndex` (lines 45–50). The elements of this structure are `offset`, which indicates how far from the end of the quantum this item starts; `type`, which indicates the type of the data stored in this item; and index, which indicates the `index` of this item in the main object.

The possible values of `type` are defined in the `ObjectType` enum structure, which is located at lines 35–36. These values are used primarily to check that the item being referenced is of a type appropriate to its use. The calling program knows the type it is looking for, or possibly a set of types that would be acceptable.[100] Another possible use is to implement variant arrays, in which the structure of the array is variable. In that case, we might use the type to determine whether we have the item we want or a pointer to the item, requiring further dereferencing.

The `index` value is used primarily for error handling; if the `big_pointer_array` or `little_pointer_array` controlling this main object were to become corrupted, it would still be possible to reconstruct the data of the main object with the information stored in the quanta that make up the lowest level of that object. The code to do the reconstruction is not present in the current implementation, but all the data needed to provide it are available.[101]

After retrieving the number of items already in the quantum from the `quantum_header` structure, we get a pointer to the quantum index, which is kept in `quantum_index_pointer` during execution of the routine. Then we look through the quantum index for the first item that has a type of `UNUSED_ITEM`, meaning that it is available for use. If we find one, we break out of the loop, setting the `item_index` variable to that index.[102]

The next thing we have to do is to calculate how much free space is left in the quantum. We start out by subtracting the size of the `quantum_header` structure from the size of a quantum. Then, if there are already some items in the quantum, we subtract the number of items multiplied by the size of an `ItemIndex` record, to account for the size of the index, and the offset of the last item, to account for the data in the quantum. Finally, if we have to create a new index entry, rather than reusing one, we subtract the size of that additional `ItemIndex` record as well.

Next, we check whether the size of the item to be stored exceeds the amount of space we have left after our deductions. This should never happen, since the calling program is responsible for determining that the quantum being added to has enough space. However, such an error would result in corrupting the contents of this quantum and possibly whatever follows it in memory, so this additional check is warranted.

Now we are ready to set up the `ItemIndex` record and store the data in the appropriate place. The exact code required depends on whether we are reusing an `ItemIndex` record that already exists or adding a new one to the end of the index. Let's start with the case of reusing an item already in the index, which is the first branch of the `if` statement.

---

100. For example, during the lookup of an item, we check whether a big pointer array is of type `BIG_POINTER_ARRAY`.

101. In the current implementation, one piece of information would be lost if the `big_pointer_array` quantum were to become unreadable: the maximum number of elements in the object, which is stored only in that one place. However, as this is used only for error checking, its loss would not prevent reconstruction of the array; we could proceed on the assumption that the number of elements in the array is determined by the number of little pointer quanta. In any event, one generalization of the algorithm is to allow an object to expand when an element past its end is accessed, which would render the array size information dispensable. This facility has been implemented in the C++ version in Chapter 7.

102. As previously discussed on page 316, such reuse of item index records is needed to prevent them from eventually taking over the entire quantum.

SOMETHING OLD

In this case, we set the `type` and `element_index` fields of the temporary `item_to_use` structure to the values of the `item_type` and `element_index` arguments, described above. Then we copy the temporary structure to the appropriate element of the `quantum_index_pointer` array.

Now we have to calculate the parameters needed for calling `memmove` to shift the data that are already in the quantum so that we have room for our new item. The `offset` element of the `last_item` structure is equal to the distance in bytes from the beginning of the last item in the quantum to the byte after the end of the quantum. Therefore, the address of the beginning of the last item in the quantum, `data_from`, can be calculated as `quantum + QUANTUM_SIZE - last_item.offset`, as we do next. The byte at that address, and all those after it up to the starting address of the new item's data, must be moved down in memory by enough to leave room for the new data. Therefore, the new address of that byte, `data_to`, will be its old address minus `item_size`. We want to move all of the items that precede our new item in memory, which means those that have higher item numbers; therefore, the number of bytes we want to move, `data_length`, is equal to the distance from the beginning of the last item to the beginning of our new item. Now that we have these parameters calculated, we can call `memmove` to relocate the data to make room for the new item.

For example, suppose that we want to insert a new field with index number 6 to store the company name ("Chrysalis") in the following quantum, reusing the currently unused fourth item (see figure 6.9).

Figure 6.9 *Quantum index and data before item insertion*

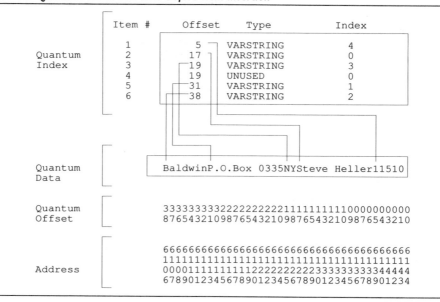

To do this, we have to move items 5 and 6 toward the beginning of the quantum by 9 characters, which is the length of the new item. Assuming that the address of the beginning of the buffer holding the quantum is 4096 and QUANTUM_SIZE is 2048, the address of the beginning of the last item is 4096+2048–38, or 6106, which is the value of data_from. The value of data_to is calculated from data_from by subtracting the length of the new item, or 9, resulting in 6097. The value of data_length is the amount of data to move; we have to move everything from the last item up to but not including the place where we are going to put the new data. We could add up the lengths of all of the items from the last item to the one before which we will insert our new data, but it is easier simply to subtract the offset of that item from the offset of the last item, which produces the same result: 38 – 19, or 19 bytes to be moved.

After the move, the quantum looks like figure 6.10.

Of course, all of the quantum index entries from the one we are inserting to the last one now have the wrong offset; we have to add the size of the new item to these offsets, to account for the move we just did, which we do in the loop at lines 730–731.

We're almost done with this insertion. All we have left to do is to calculate the actual position of the new item in the quantum as the quantum buffer's address + the size of a quantum – the offset of this item, (4096+2048–28, or 6116) and store the result in data_to. Then we can call memmove to copy the new item's data to that position, and finally set the relative item number (which is the return value from this

Figure 6.10 *Quantum index and data after move*

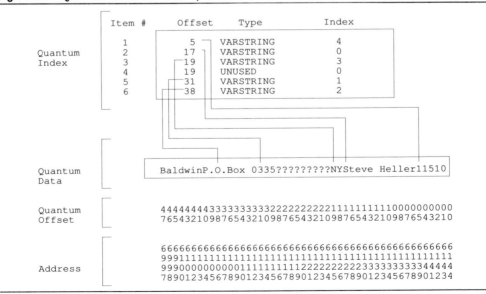

Figure 6.11 *Quantum index and data after item insertion*

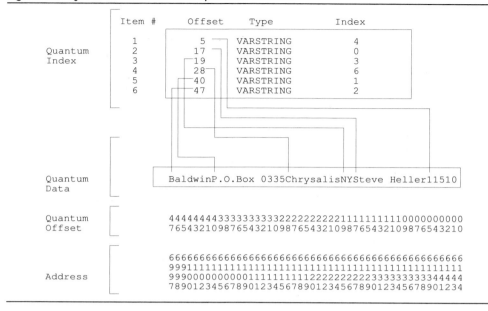

function) to `item_index + 1`, and return it. The final quantum contents look like figure 6.11.

The above scenario handles the case of reusing an item index slot. The code starting at line 738 deals with the case where we have to add a new item index record at the end of the index, which is somewhat simpler, as we don't have to move any pre-existing data: our new item is the last in the quantum.

SOMETHING NEW

Of course, the simplest case of all is the one where there aren't any items in the quantum as yet. In this case, the offset of the new item is equal to its size. However, if there are some items in the quantum already, then the offset of the new item is equal to the offset of the last item in the quantum added to the size of the new item. Once we have calculated the offset, we can move the new item's data to its position in the quantum. All we have left to do here is to set the type and index of the new item and store it in the last position of the `quantum_index_pointer` array, set the `relative_item_number` to one more than the number of items that were in the array before, increment the item count, and return the relative item number to the calling routine.

delete_item_in_quantum

Another routine called by `qf_store_item` is `delete_item_in_quantum` (lines 558–632); this routine shares responsibility for the maintenance of the quantum index with `add_item_to_quantum`. We start by checking for a `NULL_ITEM_NUMBER` in the `relative_item_number` argument, which is an error. Assuming the `relative_item_number` is legal, we cast `quantum` to a `QuantumHeader *`, so we can access the quantum header. If the `relative_item_number` argument is greater than `item_count` in the quantum header, this too is an error.

Once we pass this check, we set `quantum_index_pointer` to the address of the quantum index, by adding the size of the quantum header structure to the address of the beginning of the quantum. Then we copy the item reference corresponding to the `relative_item_number` argument from the appropriate entry in the quantum index; because the first entry has `relative_item_number` 1, not 0, the corresponding quantum index entry is `relative_item_number - 1`.

If the `item_count` is equal to the `relative_item_number`, then this is the last item in the quantum. Therefore, we don't have to move any data when we delete it. However, we do have to delete any unused items that are at the end of the quantum index (lines 590–600); this allows us to reduce the number of item index entries in the quantum. If we did not perform this cleanup, the number of entries in a quantum index could only increase with time; eventually, the entire quantum would consist of entries with no associated data.

On the other hand, if the item we're deleting isn't the last item, we have a considerably different set of operations to perform (lines 603–629). We have to get the `item_length` so that we can move the other items the proper distance toward the end of the quantum. For the first item, the `item_length` is equal to the `offset` field in the item, because the data for the first item in the quantum is stored at the end of the quantum, as illustrated in figure 6.2. For other items, the `item_length` is equal to the `offset` of the previous item subtracted from the `offset` of the current item. This may seem backward, as the figure shows that the second item is stored before the first, the third before the second, and so on. However, the `offset` of an item is defined as the distance in bytes from the start of the item to the first byte after the end of the quantum, which is always nonnegative.

We also have to set the `offset` of this item to the `offset` of the previous item (if there is a previous item), which will indicate that this item's length is zero. For the first item, we can just set the `offset` to zero, since there is no previous item to worry about.

Whether we are deleting the first item or another item, we are now ready to calculate the addresses for the movement of the items after the one we are deleting, starting at line 617. First, we get a copy of the offset of the last item in the index, as we will need to use it twice. Then we calculate the source address (`data_from`) as the address of the last item (`quantum+QUANTUM_SIZE-last_item_offset`), the destination address (`data_to`) as the source address added to the length of the item we are deleting (`data_from+item_length`), and the number of bytes to move (`data_length`) as the total length of all the items from the one we are deleting to the last item (`last_item_offset - this_item.offset`). Then we call `memmove` to do the actual data transfer.

To make this clearer, let's look at what happens if we delete the item holding the state name from the example in figure 6.12. Let's suppose the address of the quantum is 4096. The `offset` of the last item, marked by ""^"", is 41; substituting values in the expression for `data_from`, `quantum+QUANTUM_SIZE-last_item_offset` equals 4096+2048 – 41, or 6103. The `offset` of the item we're deleting, marked by the "*", is 19, and the `offset` of the previous item (marked by the "&") is 17, which makes the `item_length` 2; therefore, the `data_to` address is 6103+2, or 6105. This is where the last item will start after the move, since we are removing the 2 bytes of the item being deleted. Finally, `data_length` is the amount of data to be moved, which is the length of all the items after the one being deleted, in this case 41– 19, or 22. After we do the move, the result looks like figure 6.13.

The data are in the right place now, but the pointers are wrong. Specifically, the `offset` fields of the items that have higher item numbers than the one we have deleted are off by the length of the deleted field. That's what the loop starting at line 625 is for. It reduces the `offset` of every item after the deleted one by `item_length`, which is the length of the deleted item. Then we set the data type of the deleted item in the quantum index to `UNUSED_ITEM`. Now our quantum looks like figure 6.14.

Figure 6.12 *Sample IRA, etc., before deletion*

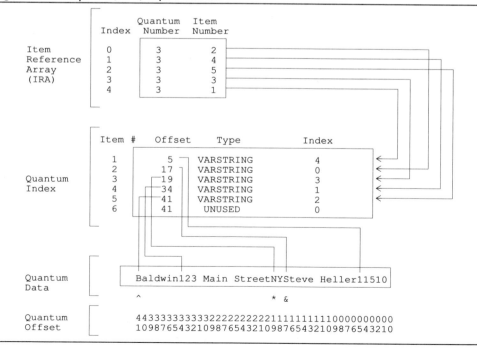

Figure 6.13 *Sample IRA, etc., during deletion*

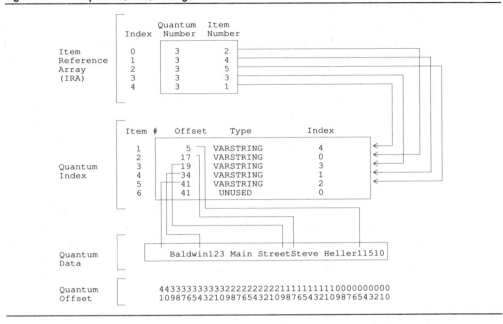

Figure 6.14 *Sample IRA, etc., after deletion*

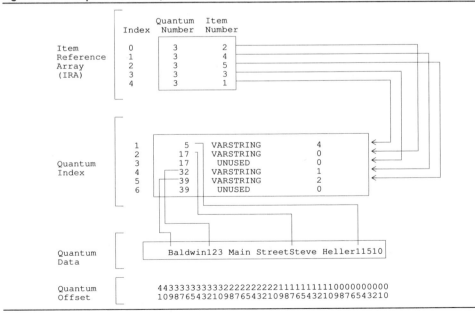

We finish up `delete_item_in_quantum` by returning the `item_count` to the calling program.

qf_close_quantum_file

Another logical layer routine is `qf_close_quantum_file` (lines 333–373). In this function, we perform a number of cleanup operations needed when closing a quantum file. First, we rewrite the `quantum_file_header`, so that any changes made to that structure will be preserved. The same is true for the `main_object_index` and the `free_space_list`, which must be carried over to the next use of the file. The call to `qf_flush_buffers` makes sure that any data that we have stored in the quantum file will be actually written to the disk.

get_pointer_to_item

A utility function used by `qf_get_item` and `qf_store_item` is `get_pointer_to_item` (lines 519–554). This function takes a quantum pointer and an item number and returns a pointer to the item and an indication of its size. This routine is much faster than `qf_get_item` because it does not make a copy of the item, as `qf_get_item` does. This routine is for our use only, within the quantum files implementation; it would be too dangerous for us to return a pointer to the interior of a quantum to the user program, since if that program accidentally stored data after the end of the item, the result would probably be fatal to the integrity of the system. The algorithm of `get_pointer_to_item` is fairly simple: it looks up the item in the item index at the beginning of the quantum and calculates the length of the item as the difference between its offset and the previous item's offset (the exception being for the first item, whose length is equal to its offset). Then it returns the address and the length of the item to the calling program.

The Grab Bag

A number of routines don't fit into our classification scheme, for one reason or another (see figure 6.15), so we'll go over them here.

The `quantum_error` function (lines 1302–1307) displays an error message and exits the program. The purpose of this function is to allow us to customize error handling as appropriate for our environment.

Figure 6.15 *Miscellaneous routines*

o   `quantum_error`

o   `real_reference`

o   `get_space_available`

The `real_reference` routine (lines 119–124) is actually a macro, for purposes of speed, since it is used inside a loop in `qf_store_item` when we are looking through a little pointer array to find a quantum that has enough space to store a new item. All it does is check whether an item reference has `NO_QUANTUM` and `NULL_ITEM_NUM-BER` as its component values. If both of its components meet this criterion, it is a null reference; if neither of them does, it is a real reference. However, if one of them has a valid value and the other doesn't, it is an error, which is reported as such.

The `get_space_available` routine (lines 635–663) calculates the amount of space available in the quantum whose address is passed to it. It does this by deducting the sizes of the `QuantumHeader`, the `ItemIndex`, and the offset of the last item from the size of a quantum. It also leaves a margin of `MARGIN` bytes (set to 10 in this implementation) to allow a new item index entry to be assigned when storing a new item, and to prevent the last item from running up against the item index; this latter provision eases debugging.

Taking It from the Top

Now that we have finished our examination of the quantum file access routines, we can proceed to the driver program, "custdata.c" (listing 6.2, lines 25–58). The main procedure allows us to initialize the file, edit customer records, or quit the program. Almost all of the activity in this function is performed by two subroutines: the first is `initialize_quantum_file`, and the second is `edit_customer_records`. Of course, quitting the program requires only calling `x_chkfree` to check on our storage allocation[103] and returning to DOS.

Our example uses an ASCII file of the same format as we used to initialize our mailing list file in Chapter 3. The format of each record in the file is defined by two arrays: `ascii_field_length` and `quoted_field` (lines 74–77). The `ascii_field_length` array defines the length of each field in the ASCII customer record, using definitions from the "custdata.h" file (listing 6.1). As indicated in the `quoted_field` array, all of the fields are quoted except for the last, which is the year-to-date spent by the customer, in cents. In Chapter 3, we were concentrating on the retrieval process; therefore, we didn't examine the initialization, which was done by a separate program. In this case, however, initialization is just as significant as lookup, so we will go through the process from the beginning.

initialize_quantum_file
The function `initialize_quantum_file` (listing 6.2, lines 62–185) asks for the name of the customer file. Then it makes sure any previous version of the quantum file is removed and opens the quantum file via `qf_open_quantum_file`.

103. The call to `x_chkfree` actually has no effect in our implementation, as that routine is not present. See the discussion in footnote 92 on page 338.

Once the quantum file is opened (which includes creating it if necessary), we call `qf_create_main_object` to create our array of customer records. Then we open the input data file and set up a buffer to speed up reading records from it. Next, we clear a temporary customer record and set its field types according to the `field_type` array.

Now we are ready to read records from the input file, translate them into an appropriate format, and write them to the quantum file. For each record, text fields are concatenated and stored as one long string, using their stored lengths to break up the string when we unpack the record during retrieval; date fields are converted to integers, and cents fields to longs, in `memory_record_to_disk` (listing 6.2, lines 406–39). We calculate the total length of all the strings and add that to the length of the rest of the record. The concatenated strings are stored at the end of the record. Then we call `qf_store_item` to store the record at the current position in the array and free the temporary storage.

When we have handled all the records in the input file, we store the number of records read as another item in the quantum file, call `qf_close_quantum_file` to close it and the input file, and we are done with `initialize_quantum_file`.

`edit_customer_records`

Once we have initialized the quantum file, we can read and change some of the records, which is the purpose of `edit_customer_records` (listing 6.2, lines 188–221). We start, logically enough, by opening the quantum file, via `qf_open_quantum_file`. Then we retrieve the number of items in the file (which we stored when we initialized the file). Then we ask the user for the customer number of the record to be edited. If he just hits the ENTER key, the customer number will be zero, so we will stop. Otherwise, we check whether he has entered a valid number. If not, we skip to the end of the loop, go back, and ask again.

Assuming the user has entered a valid number, we set up the record that we will use to read the information from the file, using the field information from the `field_type` array.[104] Now we get the record he has requested via `qf_get_item` and convert it to memory format with `disk_record_to_memory` (lines 434–462), which retrieves pointers to the data packed by `memory_record_to_disk`. Then we allocate storage for string versions of all its data and format the data into the newly created strings. Date conversions use `days_to_date_string`, which changes a number of days since 1/1/1980 into a MM/DD/YYYY format.

After displaying the data for this record, we enter a `while` loop in which we ask the user which field he wants to change, accept a new value for that field, and replace the old string with the new one. When he says he is done editing fields (by hitting only ENTER), we convert the data back to internal format and use `qf_store_item` to put the record back into the quantum file. Then we ask if the user wants to edit another record.

---

104. Of course, we could increase the flexibility of this program by storing the field information in the quantum file as well, but our example is complicated enough already.

When he hits only ENTER rather than the record number to be edited, we close the quantum file by calling `qf_close_quantum_file`, and we are done.

Summary

In this chapter, we have seen how quantum files allow us to gain efficient random access to a large volume of variable-length textual data. In the next chapter, we will reimplement the quantum file access method in an object-oriented manner and use this algorithm as a building block to provide random access by key to large quantities of variable-length data.

Problems

1. What would be required to allow arrays to be extended automatically when the user references an element past the end of the array?

2. How would the QFIX program mentioned on page 232 operate?

(You can find suggested approaches to problems in Chapter 8).

Listing 6.1 *custdata.h: customer data base include file*

```
1
2    /****keyword-flag*** "%v %f %n" */
3    /* "5 16-May-92,8:06:18 CUSTDATA.H" */
4
5
6    #define FIELD_COUNT 9
7    #define BATCH_SIZE 100
8    #define ZIP_BLOCK_COUNT 150
9    #define ZIP_BLOCK_ENTRIES 100
10
11   #define MAX_ASCII_FIELD_LENGTH 15
12
13   #define LAST_NAME_LENGTH 15
14   #define FIRST_NAME_LENGTH 9
15   #define ADDRESS1_LENGTH 15
16   #define ADDRESS2_LENGTH 15
17   #define CITY_LENGTH 12
18   #define STATE_LENGTH 2
19   #define ZIP_LENGTH 9
20
21   #define ASCII_DATE_LENGTH 10
22   #define ASCII_CENTS_LENGTH 10
23
24   #define BINARY_DATE_LENGTH 2
25   #define BINARY_DOLLARS_LENGTH 2
26
27   enum fieldtype {TEXT,DATE,CENTS};
28   typedef enum fieldtype FieldType;
29
30   typedef union
31   {
32     char *char_pointer;
33     int  int_value;
34     long long_value;
35   } FieldValue;
36
37   typedef struct
38   {
39     FieldType field_type;
40     char field_length;
41     FieldValue field_value;
42   } FieldDefinition;
43
44   typedef struct
45   {
46     FieldDefinition field[FIELD_COUNT];
47   } CustomerRecord;
48
49   typedef struct
50   {
51     long disk_field[FIELD_COUNT];
```

Listing 6.1 *custdata.h: customer data base include file (continued)*

```
52    } DiskCustomerRecord;
53
54    #define CUSTOMER_ARRAY_OBJECT_NUMBER 1
55
56    void blank_trim(char *string);
57
58    void memory_record_to_disk(DiskCustomerRecord *disk_customer,
59    CustomerRecord *memory_customer);
60
61    void disk_record_to_memory(CustomerRecord *memory_customer,
62    DiskCustomerRecord *disk_customer);
63
64    extern int field_type[FIELD_COUNT];
65    extern char *field_name[FIELD_COUNT];
66
67    void initialize_quantum_file(void);
68
69    void edit_customer_records(void);
70
```

Listing 6.2 *custdata.c: customer database program*

```
1
2    /****keyword-flag*** "%v %f %n" */
3    /* "15 2-Sep-92,19:56:02 CUSTDATA.C" */
4
5
6    #include <stdio.h>
7    #include <stdlib.h>
8    #include <conio.h>
9    #include <alloc.h>
10   #include <xmemd.h>
11   #include <string.h>
12   #include <date.h>
13   #include <quantum.h>
14   #include <custdata.h>
15
16   extern unsigned _stklen = 32000;
17
18   #define LINE_LENGTH 200
19
20   int field_type[FIELD_COUNT] = {TEXT, TEXT, TEXT, TEXT, TEXT, TEXT, TEXT,
21   DATE, CENTS};
22   char *field_name[FIELD_COUNT] = {"Last Name","First Name","Address 1",
23   "Address 2","City","State","Zip","Date Last Here","Year-to-date Total"};
24
25   int main()
26   {
27     int response;
28     char string[80];
29
30     response = 0;
31     while (response < 3)
32         {
33         clrscr();
34         printf("Please make one of the following selections.\n\n");
35         printf("1.  Initialize quantum file.\n");
36         printf("2.  Edit customer records.\n");
37         printf("3.  Quit program.\n");
38         gets(string);
39         response = atoi(string);
40         if (response > 3 || response < 1)
41             {
42             printf("Available selections are 1,2 and 3.");
43             printf(" Hit ENTER to continue.\n");
44             gets(string);
45             response = 0;
46             continue;
47             }
48         if (response == 1)
49             initialize_quantum_file();
50         else if (response == 2)
51             edit_customer_records();
```

Listing 6.2 *custdata.c: customer database program* *(continued)*

```
 52          }
 53
 54
 55      x_chkfree();
 56
 57      return(0);
 58   }
 59
 60
 61
 62   void initialize_quantum_file()
 63   {
 64
 65      FILE *quantum_file;
 66      FILE *infile;
 67      ArrayIndex i;
 68      char infilename[100];
 69      int buffer_count;
 70      ArrayIndex j;
 71      char line_in[LINE_LENGTH];
 72      char *status;
 73      char *here;
 74      int ascii_field_length[FIELD_COUNT] = {LAST_NAME_LENGTH,FIRST_NAME_LENGTH,
 75      ADDRESS1_LENGTH,ADDRESS2_LENGTH,CITY_LENGTH,STATE_LENGTH,ZIP_LENGTH,
 76      ASCII_DATE_LENGTH,ASCII_CENTS_LENGTH};
 77      int quoted_field[FIELD_COUNT] = {1,1,1,1,1,1,1,1,0};
 78      char field[FIELD_COUNT][MAX_ASCII_FIELD_LENGTH+1];
 79      int temp_int;
 80      CustomerRecord customer_record;
 81      DiskCustomerRecord disk_customer_record;
 82      FieldDefinition *current_field_pointer;
 83      int total_text_length;
 84      unsigned short item_size;
 85      char *item_storage;
 86      char *string_position;
 87      long temp_long;
 88
 89      buffer_count = 50;
 90
 91      clrscr();
 92      printf("File initialization.\n\n");
 93      printf("Please enter name of customer file: ");
 94      gets(infilename);
 95
 96      remove("TEST.QNT");
 97
 98      quantum_file = qf_open_quantum_file("TEST.QNT",buffer_count);
 99
100      qf_create_main_object(quantum_file,CUSTOMER_ARRAY_OBJECT_NUMBER,8000);
101      infile = fopen(infilename,"rb");
102      setvbuf(infile,NULL,_IOFBF,16384);
```

Listing 6.2 *custdata.c: customer database program (continued)*

```
103
104    memset((char *)&customer_record,0,sizeof(CustomerRecord));
105    for (i = 0; i < FIELD_COUNT; i ++)
106        customer_record.field[i].field_type = field_type[i];
107
108    for (i = 1; ; i ++)
109        {
110        status = fgets(line_in, LINE_LENGTH, infile);
111        if (status == NULL)
112            break;
113        here = line_in;
114
115        for (j = 0; j < FIELD_COUNT; j ++)
116            {
117            if (quoted_field[j])
118                here ++; /* leading quote */
119            memset(field[j],0,MAX_ASCII_FIELD_LENGTH+1);
120            memcpy(field[j],here,ascii_field_length[j]);
121            here += ascii_field_length[j];
122            if (quoted_field[j])
123                here ++; /* trailing quote */
124            here ++; /* comma */
125            }
126
127        total_text_length = 0;
128        for (j = 0; j < FIELD_COUNT; j ++)
129            {
130            current_field_pointer = &customer_record.field[j];
131            switch (current_field_pointer->field_type)
132                {
133                case TEXT:
134                    blank_trim(field[j]);
135                    current_field_pointer->field_length = strlen(field[j]);
136                    total_text_length += current_field_pointer->field_length;
137                    break;
138                case DATE:
139                    temp_int = date_string_to_days(field[j]);
140                    current_field_pointer->field_length = sizeof(int);
141                    current_field_pointer->field_value.int_value = temp_int;
142                    break;
143                case CENTS:
144                    temp_long = atol(field[j]);
145                    current_field_pointer->field_length = sizeof(long);
146                    current_field_pointer->field_value.long_value = temp_long;
147                    break;
148                }
149            }
150
151        memory_record_to_disk(&disk_customer_record,&customer_record);
152
153        item_size = sizeof(DiskCustomerRecord)+total_text_length;
```

Listing 6.2 *custdata.c: customer database program (continued)*

```
154          item_storage = x_calloc(item_size,1);
155          memcpy(item_storage,(char *)&disk_customer_record,
156          sizeof(DiskCustomerRecord));
157          string_position = item_storage+sizeof(DiskCustomerRecord);
158
159          for (j = 0; j < FIELD_COUNT; j ++)
160              {
161              current_field_pointer = &customer_record.field[j];
162              switch (current_field_pointer->field_type)
163                  {
164                  case TEXT:
165                      memcpy(string_position,field[j],
166                      current_field_pointer->field_length);
167                      string_position += current_field_pointer->field_length;
168                      break;
169                  }
170              }
171
172          qf_store_item(quantum_file, CUSTOMER_ARRAY_OBJECT_NUMBER, i,
173          item_storage, item_size);
174
175          x_free(item_storage);
176          }
177
178      i --;
179      qf_store_item(quantum_file, CUSTOMER_ARRAY_OBJECT_NUMBER, 0, (char *)&i,
180      sizeof(int));
181
182      qf_close_quantum_file(quantum_file);
183
184      fclose(infile);
185  }
186
187
188  void edit_customer_records()
189  {
190      FILE *quantum_file;
191      ArrayIndex i;
192      int buffer_count;
193      ArrayIndex j;
194      ArrayIndex k;
195      int temp_int;
196      CustomerRecord customer_record;
197      DiskCustomerRecord disk_customer_record;
198      FieldDefinition *current_field_pointer;
199      int total_text_length;
200      ItemSize item_size;
201      char *item_storage;
202      char *string_position;
203      long temp_long;
204      int terminate;
```

Listing 6.2 *custdata.c: customer database program (continued)*

```
205     char string[80];
206     ArrayIndex customer_number;
207     ArrayIndex customer_count;
208     int field_number;
209     char *current_string;
210     ArrayIndex current_length;
211
212
213     buffer_count = 50;
214     terminate = 0;
215
216     quantum_file = qf_open_quantum_file("TEST.QNT",buffer_count);
217
218     qf_get_item(quantum_file, CUSTOMER_ARRAY_OBJECT_NUMBER, 0,
219     &item_storage, &item_size);
220
221     customer_count = *(ArrayIndex *)item_storage;
222     x_free(item_storage);
223
224     while (terminate == 0)
225         {
226         clrscr();
227         printf("Customer record editing.\n\n");
228
229         printf("Please enter customer number or ENTER to exit: ");
230         gets(string);
231         customer_number = atoi(string);
232         if (customer_number == 0)
233             {
234             terminate = 1;
235             break;
236             }
237         else if (customer_number > customer_count)
238             {
239             printf("Highest customer number is %d.  Hit ENTER to continue.\n",
240             customer_count);
241             gets(string);
242             continue;
243             }
244
245         memset((char *)&customer_record,0,sizeof(CustomerRecord));
246         for (i = 0; i < FIELD_COUNT; i ++)
247             customer_record.field[i].field_type = field_type[i];
248
249         qf_get_item(quantum_file, CUSTOMER_ARRAY_OBJECT_NUMBER,
250         customer_number, &item_storage, &item_size);
251
252         memcpy((char *)&disk_customer_record,item_storage,
253         sizeof(DiskCustomerRecord));
254
255         disk_record_to_memory(&customer_record,&disk_customer_record);
```

Listing 6.2 *custdata.c: customer database program (continued)*

```
256
257        string_position = item_storage+sizeof(DiskCustomerRecord);
258
259        for (j = 0; j < FIELD_COUNT; j ++)
260            {
261            current_field_pointer = &customer_record.field[j];
262            switch (current_field_pointer->field_type)
263                {
264                case TEXT:
265                    current_field_pointer->field_value.char_pointer =
266                    x_calloc(current_field_pointer->field_length+1,1);
267                    memcpy(current_field_pointer->field_value.char_pointer,
268                    string_position,current_field_pointer->field_length);
269                    string_position += current_field_pointer->field_length;
270                    break;
271                case DATE:
272                    days_to_date_string(string,
273                    current_field_pointer->field_value.int_value);
274                    current_field_pointer->field_value.char_pointer =
275                    x_calloc(strlen(string)+1,1);
276                    strcpy(current_field_pointer->field_value.char_pointer,string);
277                    break;
278                case CENTS:
279                    temp_long = current_field_pointer->field_value.long_value;
280                    sprintf(string,"%ld.%02d",temp_long/100,temp_long%100);
281                    current_field_pointer->field_value.char_pointer =
282                    x_calloc(strlen(string)+1,1);
283                    strcpy(current_field_pointer->field_value.char_pointer,string);
284                    break;
285                }
286            }
287
288        field_number = -1;
289        while(field_number != 0)
290            {
291            clrscr();
292            printf("Field editing\n\n");
293            for (j = 0; j < FIELD_COUNT; j ++)
294                {
295                current_field_pointer = &customer_record.field[j];
296                printf("%d. %20s : %s\n",j+1,field_name[j],
297                current_field_pointer->field_value.char_pointer);
298                }
299
300            printf("\nPlease type field number to change, or ENTER if none: ");
301            gets(string);
302            field_number = atoi(string);
303            if (field_number == 0)
304                break;
305
306            current_field_pointer = &customer_record.field[field_number-1];
```

Listing 6.2 *custdata.c: customer database program (continued)*

```
307              printf("%d. %20s : ",field_number,field_name[field_number-1]);
308              gets(string);
309              x_free(current_field_pointer->field_value.char_pointer);
310              current_field_pointer->field_value.char_pointer =
311              x_calloc(strlen(string)+1,1);
312              strcpy(current_field_pointer->field_value.char_pointer,string);
313              printf("\nPlease hit ENTER to continue.\n");
314              gets(string);
315              }
316
317         x_free(item_storage);
318
319         total_text_length = 0;
320         for (j = 0; j < FIELD_COUNT; j ++)
321             {
322             current_field_pointer = &customer_record.field[j];
323             current_string =
324             current_field_pointer->field_value.char_pointer;
325             switch (current_field_pointer->field_type)
326                 {
327                 case TEXT:
328                     blank_trim(current_string);
329                     current_field_pointer->field_length = strlen(current_string);
330                     total_text_length += current_field_pointer->field_length;
331                     break;
332                 case DATE:
333                     temp_int = date_string_to_days(current_string);
334                     x_free(current_string);
335                     current_field_pointer->field_length = sizeof(int);
336                     current_field_pointer->field_value.int_value = temp_int;
337                     break;
338                 case CENTS:
339                     strcpy(string,"");
340                     current_length = strlen(current_string);
341                     for (k = 0; k < current_length; k ++)
342                         if (current_string[k] == '.')
343                             {
344                             strcpy(string,current_string+k+1);
345                             break;
346                             }
347                     temp_long = 100*atol(current_string)+atol(string);
348                     x_free(current_string);
349                     current_field_pointer->field_length = sizeof(long);
350                     current_field_pointer->field_value.long_value = temp_long;
351                     break;
352                 }
353             }
354
355         memory_record_to_disk(&disk_customer_record,&customer_record);
356
357         item_size = sizeof(DiskCustomerRecord)+total_text_length;
```

Listing 6.2 *custdata.c: customer database program (continued)*

```
358            item_storage = x_calloc(item_size,1);
359            memcpy(item_storage,(char *)&disk_customer_record,
360            sizeof(DiskCustomerRecord));
361            string_position = item_storage+sizeof(DiskCustomerRecord);
362
363            for (j = 0; j < FIELD_COUNT; j ++)
364                {
365                current_field_pointer = &customer_record.field[j];
366                current_string =
367                current_field_pointer->field_value.char_pointer;
368                switch (current_field_pointer->field_type)
369                    {
370                    case TEXT:
371                        memcpy(string_position,current_string,
372                        current_field_pointer->field_length);
373                        x_free(customer_record.field[j].field_value.char_pointer);
374                        string_position += current_field_pointer->field_length;
375                        break;
376                    }
377                }
378
379            qf_store_item(quantum_file, CUSTOMER_ARRAY_OBJECT_NUMBER,
380            customer_number,  item_storage, item_size);
381
382            x_free(item_storage);
383            }
384
385      qf_close_quantum_file(quantum_file);
386
387      x_chkfree();
388  }
389
390
391
392  void blank_trim(char *string)
393  {
394    char *where;
395
396    where = string + strlen(string)-1;
397    for (; where >= string; where-)
398        {
399        if (*where == ' ')
400            *where = 0;
401        else
402            break;
403        }
404  }
405
406  void memory_record_to_disk(DiskCustomerRecord *disk_customer,
407  CustomerRecord *memory_customer)
```

Listing 6.2 *custdata.c: customer database program (continued)*

```
408    {
409       int i;
410
411       memset(disk_customer,0,sizeof(DiskCustomerRecord));
412
413       for (i = 0;  i < FIELD_COUNT;  i ++)
414            {
415            switch (field_type[i])
416                 {
417                 case TEXT:
418                      disk_customer->disk_field[i] =
419                      memory_customer->field[i].field_length;
420                      break;
421                 case DATE:
422                      disk_customer->disk_field[i] =
423                      memory_customer->field[i].field_value.int_value;
424                      break;
425                 case CENTS:
426                      disk_customer->disk_field[i] =
427                      memory_customer->field[i].field_value.long_value;
428                      break;
429                 }
430            }
431    }
432
433
434    void disk_record_to_memory(CustomerRecord *memory_customer,
435    DiskCustomerRecord *disk_customer)
436    {
437       int i;
438
439       memset(memory_customer,0,sizeof(CustomerRecord));
440
441       for (i = 0;  i < FIELD_COUNT;  i ++)
442            {
443            switch (field_type[i])
444                 {
445                 case TEXT:
446                      memory_customer->field[i].field_type = TEXT;
447                      memory_customer->field[i].field_length =
448                      (int)disk_customer->disk_field[i];
449                      break;
450                 case DATE:
451                      memory_customer->field[i].field_type = DATE;
452                      memory_customer->field[i].field_value.int_value =
453                      (int)disk_customer->disk_field[i];
454                      break;
455                 case CENTS:
456                      memory_customer->field[i].field_type = CENTS;
457                      memory_customer->field[i].field_value.long_value =
```

Listing 6.2 *custdata.c: customer database program* *(continued)*

```
458                        disk_customer->disk_field[i];
459                        break;
460                }
461            }
462    }
```

Listing 6.3 *xmemd.h include file to provide dummy error-checking memory allocation routines*

```
 1
 2    /****keyword-flag*** "%v %f %n" */
 3    /* "1 25-Aug-91,9:33:42 XMEMD.H" */
 4
 5
 6    /* ******************** GLOBAL FUNCTIONS ******************** */
 7
 8    #define x_malloc(n) malloc(n)
 9    #define x_calloc(n,m) calloc(n,m)
10    #define x_free(p) free(p)
11    #define x_chkfree()
```

Listing 6.4 *quantum.h: quantum file header*

```
 1
 2
 3
 4    /****keyword-flag*** "%v %f %n" */
 5    /* "8 2-Sep-92,19:56:00 QUANTUM.H" */
 6
 7
 8    typedef unsigned short ObjectNumber;
 9    typedef unsigned short ArrayIndex;
10    typedef unsigned short ItemSize;
11
12    enum statustype {OKAY,ERROR};
13    typedef enum statustype StatusType;
14
15
16    FILE *qf_open_quantum_file(char *filename, int buffer_count);
17
18    StatusType qf_create_main_object(FILE *quantum_file, ObjectNumber object_number,
19    ArrayIndex item_count);
20
21    StatusType qf_store_item(FILE *quantum_file, ObjectNumber main_object_number,
22    ArrayIndex element_index, char *item, ItemSize item_size);
23
24    StatusType qf_get_item(FILE *quantum_file, ObjectNumber main_object_number,
25    ArrayIndex element_index, char **item, ItemSize *item_size);
26
27    void qf_flush_buffers(FILE *quantum_file);
28
29    StatusType qf_close_quantum_file(FILE *quantum_file);
30
31    void Megasort(unsigned char **PtrArray, unsigned short *RecNums, int KeyLength,
32    char KeyType, unsigned ArraySize);
33
```

Listing 6.5 *quantum.c: quantum file functions*

```
 1
 2    /****keyword-flag*** "%v %f %n" */
 3    /* "22 1-Mar-94,20:03:12 QUANTUM.C" */
 4
 5
 6    /****keyword-flag*** "%v %f %n" */
 7    char program_version_info[] = "22 1-Mar-94,20:03:12 QUANTUM.C";
 8
 9
10    #include <stdio.h>
11    #include <stdlib.h>
12    #include <alloc.h>
13    #include <xmemd.h>
14    #include <string.h>
15    #include <quantum.h>
16
17    typedef unsigned short QuantumIndex;
18    typedef unsigned short QuantumNumber;
19    typedef unsigned short RelativeItemNumber;
20    typedef unsigned short SlotNumber;
21    typedef unsigned char FreeSpaceEntry;
22    typedef char Quantum;
23    typedef long FileOffset;
24
25    #define QUANTUM_SIZE 2048
26    #define MARGIN 10
27
28    #define FREE_SPACE_SHIFT 3 /* from pages of 256 to actual bytes avail. */
29    #define AVAILABLE_QUANTUM ((QUANTUM_SIZE-1) >> FREE_SPACE_SHIFT)
30
31    #define MAIN_OBJECT_INDEX_COUNT 1024
32    #define MAX_FILE_QUANTUM_COUNT 16384
33    #define MEMORY_RESIDENT_QUANTUM_COUNT 50
34
35    enum objecttype {UNUSED_ITEM=1,VARIABLE_LENGTH_STRING,LITTLE_POINTER_ARRAY,
36    BIG_POINTER_ARRAY,LEAF_NODE,BIG_ARRAY_HEADER};
37    typedef enum objecttype ObjectType;
38
39    typedef struct
40    {
41      unsigned quantum_number:14;
42      unsigned relative_item_number:10;
43    } ItemReference;
44
45    typedef struct
46    {
47      unsigned offset:11;
48      unsigned type:5;
49      ArrayIndex index;
50    } ItemIndex;
51
```

Listing 6.5 *quantum.c: quantum file functions (continued)*

```
52   typedef struct
53   {
54     ObjectType quantum_type;
55     ObjectNumber main_object_number;
56     ArrayIndex item_count;
57   } QuantumHeader;
58
59   typedef struct
60   {
61     ArrayIndex element_count;
62     QuantumNumber last_quantum_added_to;
63   } BigArrayHeader;
64
65   #define MAX_ITEM_SIZE (QUANTUM_SIZE-(sizeof(QuantumHeader)+MARGIN))
66
67   enum quantumstatus {NO_STATUS_CHANGE=0,DIRTY=1,LOCK=2,UNLOCK=4};
68   typedef enum quantumstatus QuantumStatus;
69
70   #define BIG_POINTER_HEADER_ITEM 1
71   #define BIG_POINTER_ARRAY_ITEM 2
72
73   #define ITEM_REFERENCE_PACKING_FACTOR \
74   ((QUANTUM_SIZE - (sizeof(QuantumHeader) + \
75   sizeof(BigArrayHeader)+16)) / sizeof(ItemReference))
76
77   #define NO_QUANTUM 0
78   #define NULL_ITEM_NUMBER 1023
79   #define NOT_IN_LIST (-1)
80
81   #define INVALID_QUANTUM_NUMBER ((QuantumNumber)-1)
82
83   #define MAIN_OBJECT_INDEX_OFFSET  QUANTUM_SIZE
84
85   #define FREE_SPACE_LIST_OFFSET  (MAIN_OBJECT_INDEX_OFFSET \
86   + MAIN_OBJECT_INDEX_COUNT * sizeof(QuantumNumber))
87
88   #define STARTING_QUANTUM_OFFSET (FREE_SPACE_LIST_OFFSET \
89   + MAX_FILE_QUANTUM_COUNT * sizeof(FreeSpaceEntry))
90
91
92   typedef struct
93   {
94     char quantum_version_info[64];
95     FILE *dos_file_ptr;
96     char *file_name;
97     ArrayIndex main_object_index_count;
98     ArrayIndex free_space_list_count;
99     ArrayIndex memory_resident_quantum_count;
100    int highest_priority;
101    QuantumNumber *main_object_index;
102    QuantumNumber *memory_resident_quantum_list;
```

Listing 6.5 *quantum.c: quantum file functions (continued)*

```
103     Quantum **quantum_buffer;
104     int *most_recently_used_list;
105     int *locked_list;
106     int *dirty_list;
107     FreeSpaceEntry *free_space_list;
108     FileOffset main_object_index_offset;
109     FileOffset free_space_list_offset;
110     FileOffset starting_quantum_offset;
111  } QuantumFile;
112
113
114  typedef struct
115  {
116    char padding[QUANTUM_SIZE-sizeof(QuantumFile)];
117  } QuantumPadding;
118
119  #define real_reference(item_reference) \
120    ((item_reference.quantum_number == NO_QUANTUM && \
121    item_reference.relative_item_number == NULL_ITEM_NUMBER) \
122        ? 0 : ((item_reference.quantum_number != NO_QUANTUM && \
123    item_reference.relative_item_number != NULL_ITEM_NUMBER) \
124        ? 1 : (quantum_error("Invalid item reference. Run QFIX."),1)))
125
126
127  static Quantum *get_quantum(FILE *quantum_file, QuantumNumber quantum_number,
128  QuantumStatus mode);
129
130  static StatusType find_buffer(FILE *quantum_file,
131  QuantumNumber quantum_number, int *buffer_number_ptr);
132
133  static initialize_big_pointer_array(FILE *quantum_file,
134  ObjectNumber main_object_number, Quantum *big_pointer_array_quantum,
135  ArrayIndex item_count);
136
137  static StatusType read_quantum(FILE *quantum_file,
138  QuantumNumber quantum_number, Quantum *quantum_buffer);
139
140  static StatusType write_quantum(FILE *quantum_file,
141  QuantumNumber quantum_number, Quantum *quantum_buffer);
142
143  static QuantumNumber reserve_available_quantum(FILE *quantum_file);
144
145  static RelativeItemNumber add_item_to_quantum(Quantum *quantum,
146  ObjectType item_type, ArrayIndex element_index, char *item,
147  ItemSize item_size);
148
149  static StatusType delete_item_in_quantum(Quantum *quantum,
150  RelativeItemNumber relative_item_number);
151
152  static ObjectType get_pointer_to_item(Quantum *quantum,
153  ArrayIndex item_number, char **item, ItemSize *item_size);
```

Listing 6.5 *quantum.c: quantum file functions (continued)*

```
154
155    static StatusType initialize_quantum(Quantum *quantum,
156    ObjectNumber main_object_number, ObjectType quantum_type);
157
158    static StatusType position_quantum_file(FILE *quantum_file,
159    QuantumNumber quantum_number);
160
161    static Quantum **allocate_quantum_buffers(
162    ArrayIndex memory_resident_quantum_count);
163
164    static StatusType quantum_error(char *message);
165
166    static StatusType deallocate_quantum_buffers(FILE *quantum_file);
167
168    static StatusType rewrite_object_index(FILE *quantum_file);
169
170
171    FILE *qf_open_quantum_file(char *filename, int buffer_count)
172    {
173      FILE *dos_file_ptr;
174      QuantumFile *quantum_file_header;
175      QuantumPadding *quantum_padding;
176      ArrayIndex memory_resident_quantum_count;
177      int version_diff;
178
179      dos_file_ptr = fopen(filename,"r+b");
180      if (dos_file_ptr == NULL) /* file does not exist */
181          {
182          dos_file_ptr = fopen(filename,"w+b"); /* create it */
183
184          /* clear the header and pad it to a quantum boundary */
185          quantum_file_header = (QuantumFile *)x_calloc(sizeof(QuantumFile),1);
186          quantum_file_header->main_object_index_count = MAIN_OBJECT_INDEX_COUNT;
187          quantum_file_header->free_space_list_count = MAX_FILE_QUANTUM_COUNT;
188          strcpy(quantum_file_header->quantum_version_info,program_version_info);
189          quantum_file_header->main_object_index_offset = MAIN_OBJECT_INDEX_OFFSET;
190          quantum_file_header->free_space_list_offset = FREE_SPACE_LIST_OFFSET;
191          quantum_file_header->starting_quantum_offset = STARTING_QUANTUM_OFFSET;
192          quantum_padding = (QuantumPadding *)x_calloc(sizeof(QuantumPadding),1);
193          fwrite(quantum_file_header,1,sizeof(QuantumFile), dos_file_ptr);
194          fwrite(quantum_padding,1,sizeof(QuantumPadding), dos_file_ptr);
195          x_free(quantum_padding);
196
197          /* clear the main object index */
198          quantum_file_header->main_object_index = (QuantumNumber *)
199          x_calloc(quantum_file_header->main_object_index_count,
200          sizeof(QuantumNumber));
201          quantum_file_header->main_object_index[0] = INVALID_QUANTUM_NUMBER;
202          fseek(dos_file_ptr,quantum_file_header->main_object_index_offset,
203          SEEK_SET);
204          fwrite(quantum_file_header->main_object_index,sizeof(QuantumNumber),
```

Listing 6.5 *quantum.c: quantum file functions (continued)*

```
205                quantum_file_header->main_object_index_count,dos_file_ptr);
206
207            /* clear the free space list */
208            quantum_file_header->free_space_list = (FreeSpaceEntry *)
209            x_calloc(quantum_file_header->free_space_list_count,
210            sizeof(FreeSpaceEntry));
211
212            memset(quantum_file_header->free_space_list,AVAILABLE_QUANTUM,
213            quantum_file_header->free_space_list_count*sizeof(FreeSpaceEntry));
214            quantum_file_header->free_space_list[0] = 0; /* Q #0 unavailable */
215            fseek(dos_file_ptr,quantum_file_header->free_space_list_offset,SEEK_SET);
216            fwrite(quantum_file_header->free_space_list,sizeof(FreeSpaceEntry),
217            quantum_file_header->free_space_list_count,dos_file_ptr);
218            }
219        else
220            {
221            /* read the header */
222            quantum_file_header = (QuantumFile *)x_calloc(sizeof(QuantumFile),1);
223            fread(quantum_file_header,1,sizeof(QuantumFile),dos_file_ptr);
224
225            version_diff = strcmp(quantum_file_header->quantum_version_info,
226            program_version_info);
227            if (version_diff != 0)
228                quantum_error("Version of program differs from that of file");
229
230            /* read the main object index */
231            quantum_file_header->main_object_index = (QuantumNumber *)
232            x_calloc(quantum_file_header->main_object_index_count,
233            sizeof(QuantumNumber));
234            fseek(dos_file_ptr,quantum_file_header->main_object_index_offset,
235            SEEK_SET);
236            fread(quantum_file_header->main_object_index, sizeof(QuantumNumber),
237            quantum_file_header->main_object_index_count,dos_file_ptr);
238
239            /* read the free space list */
240            quantum_file_header->free_space_list = (FreeSpaceEntry *)
241            x_calloc(quantum_file_header->free_space_list_count,
242            sizeof(FreeSpaceEntry));
243            fseek(dos_file_ptr,quantum_file_header->free_space_list_offset,SEEK_SET);
244            fread(quantum_file_header->free_space_list,sizeof(FreeSpaceEntry),
245            quantum_file_header->free_space_list_count,dos_file_ptr);
246            }
247
248        quantum_file_header->memory_resident_quantum_count = buffer_count;
249        memory_resident_quantum_count = buffer_count;
250
251        /* clear the memory resident quantum list */
252        quantum_file_header->memory_resident_quantum_list = (QuantumNumber *)
253        x_calloc(memory_resident_quantum_count,sizeof(QuantumNumber));
254
255        /* clear the locked list */
```

Listing 6.5 *quantum.c: quantum file functions (continued)*

```
256      quantum_file_header->locked_list = (int *)
257      x_calloc(memory_resident_quantum_count,sizeof(int));
258
259      /* clear the dirty list */
260      quantum_file_header->dirty_list = (int *)
261      x_calloc(memory_resident_quantum_count,sizeof(int));
262
263      /* initialize the most recently used list */
264      quantum_file_header->most_recently_used_list = (int *)
265      x_calloc(memory_resident_quantum_count,sizeof(int));
266
267      /* allocate the quantum buffers and set storage type */
268      quantum_file_header->quantum_buffer =
269      allocate_quantum_buffers(memory_resident_quantum_count);
270
271      quantum_file_header->dos_file_ptr = dos_file_ptr;
272      quantum_file_header->file_name = filename;
273      setvbuf(dos_file_ptr,NULL,_IOFBF,QUANTUM_SIZE);
274      return((FILE *)quantum_file_header);
275   }
276
277
278
279   Quantum **allocate_quantum_buffers(ArrayIndex memory_resident_quantum_count)
280   {
281     Quantum **buffer_address;
282     ArrayIndex i;
283
284     buffer_address = (Quantum **)
285     x_calloc(memory_resident_quantum_count,sizeof(Quantum *));
286
287     for (i = 0; i < memory_resident_quantum_count; i ++)
288         buffer_address[i] = (Quantum *)x_calloc(QUANTUM_SIZE,1);
289
290     return(buffer_address);
291   }
292
293
294
295   StatusType deallocate_quantum_buffers(FILE *quantum_file)
296   {
297     QuantumFile *quantum_file_header;
298     ArrayIndex memory_resident_quantum_count;
299     ArrayIndex i;
300
301     quantum_file_header = (QuantumFile *)quantum_file;
302
303     memory_resident_quantum_count =
304     quantum_file_header->memory_resident_quantum_count;
305
306     for (i = 0; i < memory_resident_quantum_count; i ++)
```

Listing 6.5 *quantum.c: quantum file functions (continued)*

```
307            x_free(quantum_file_header->quantum_buffer[i]);
308
309     x_free(quantum_file_header->quantum_buffer);
310
311     return(OKAY);
312   }
313
314
315
316   StatusType rewrite_object_index(FILE *quantum_file)
317   {
318     FILE *dos_file_ptr;
319     QuantumFile *quantum_file_header;
320
321     quantum_file_header = (QuantumFile *)quantum_file;
322     dos_file_ptr = quantum_file_header->dos_file_ptr;
323
324     fseek(dos_file_ptr,quantum_file_header->main_object_index_offset,SEEK_SET);
325     fwrite(quantum_file_header->main_object_index,sizeof(QuantumNumber),
326     quantum_file_header->main_object_index_count,dos_file_ptr);
327
328     return(OKAY);
329   }
330
331
332
333   StatusType qf_close_quantum_file(FILE *quantum_file)
334   {
335     FILE *dos_file_ptr;
336     QuantumFile *quantum_file_header;
337     int i;
338
339     quantum_file_header = (QuantumFile *)quantum_file;
340     dos_file_ptr = quantum_file_header->dos_file_ptr;
341
342     fseek(dos_file_ptr,0,SEEK_SET);
343     fwrite(quantum_file_header,1,sizeof(QuantumFile),
344     dos_file_ptr);
345
346     rewrite_object_index(quantum_file);
347
348     fseek(dos_file_ptr,quantum_file_header->free_space_list_offset,SEEK_SET);
349     fwrite(quantum_file_header->free_space_list, sizeof(FreeSpaceEntry),
350     quantum_file_header->free_space_list_count,dos_file_ptr);
351
352     qf_flush_buffers(quantum_file);
353
354     deallocate_quantum_buffers(quantum_file);
355
356     for (i = 0; i < quantum_file_header->memory_resident_quantum_count; i ++)
357            {
```

Listing 6.5 *quantum.c: quantum file functions (continued)*

```
358          if (quantum_file_header->locked_list[i])
359              printf("Warning: Buffer %u, quantum # %u still locked at exit\n",
360              i,quantum_file_header->memory_resident_quantum_list[i]);
361          }
362      x_free(quantum_file_header->most_recently_used_list);
363      x_free(quantum_file_header->dirty_list);
364      x_free(quantum_file_header->locked_list);
365      x_free(quantum_file_header->memory_resident_quantum_list);
366      x_free(quantum_file_header->free_space_list);
367      x_free(quantum_file_header->main_object_index);
368      x_free(quantum_file_header);
369
370      fclose(dos_file_ptr);
371
372      return(OKAY);
373  }
374
375
376  StatusType qf_create_main_object(FILE *quantum_file,
377  ObjectNumber object_number, ArrayIndex item_count)
378  {
379    QuantumFile *quantum_file_header;
380    QuantumNumber *main_object_index;
381    QuantumNumber big_pointer_array_quantum_number;
382    Quantum *big_pointer_array_quantum;
383
384    quantum_file_header = (QuantumFile *)quantum_file;
385    main_object_index = quantum_file_header->main_object_index;
386
387    if (main_object_index[object_number] != NO_QUANTUM)
388        quantum_error("Object already exists.");
389
390    big_pointer_array_quantum_number =
391    reserve_available_quantum(quantum_file);
392
393    big_pointer_array_quantum =
394    get_quantum(quantum_file,big_pointer_array_quantum_number,DIRTY);
395
396    main_object_index[object_number] = big_pointer_array_quantum_number;
397
398    initialize_big_pointer_array(quantum_file, object_number,
399    big_pointer_array_quantum, item_count);
400
401    rewrite_object_index(quantum_file);
402
403    return(OKAY);
404  }
405
406
407
408  QuantumNumber reserve_available_quantum(FILE *quantum_file)
```

Listing 6.5 *quantum.c: quantum file functions (continued)*

```
409    {
410      ArrayIndex i;
411      QuantumNumber quantum_number;
412      QuantumFile *quantum_file_header;
413      FreeSpaceEntry *free_space_list;
414
415      quantum_file_header = (QuantumFile *)quantum_file;
416      free_space_list = quantum_file_header->free_space_list;
417
418      for (i = 1; i < quantum_file_header->free_space_list_count; i ++)
419          {
420          if (free_space_list[i] == AVAILABLE_QUANTUM)
421              {
422              quantum_number = i;
423              break;
424              }
425          }
426
427      free_space_list[quantum_number] = 0; /* claimed by this object */
428
429      return(quantum_number);
430    }
431
432
433
434    StatusType initialize_quantum(Quantum *quantum, ObjectNumber main_object_number,
435    ObjectType quantum_type)
436    {
437      QuantumHeader *quantum_header;
438
439      quantum_header = (QuantumHeader *)quantum;
440
441      memset(quantum,0,QUANTUM_SIZE);
442
443      quantum_header->main_object_number = main_object_number;
444      quantum_header->item_count = 0;
445      quantum_header->quantum_type = quantum_type;
446
447      return(OKAY);
448    }
449
450
451
452    initialize_big_pointer_array(FILE *quantum_file,
453    ObjectNumber main_object_number, Quantum *big_pointer_array_quantum,
454    ArrayIndex item_count)
455    {
456      ItemSize little_pointer_quantum_count;
457      ItemSize little_pointer_quantum_info_size;
458      ArrayIndex i;
459      QuantumNumber *little_pointer_quantum_number_array;
```

Listing 6.5 *quantum.c: quantum file functions (continued)*

```
460        Quantum *little_pointer_array_quantum;
461        ItemReference *little_pointer_array;
462        ItemReference null_item_reference;
463        BigArrayHeader big_array_header;
464
465        little_pointer_quantum_count = 1 +
466        item_count / ITEM_REFERENCE_PACKING_FACTOR;
467
468        little_pointer_quantum_info_size =
469        little_pointer_quantum_count * sizeof(QuantumNumber);
470
471        little_pointer_quantum_number_array = (QuantumNumber *)
472        x_calloc(little_pointer_quantum_count, sizeof(QuantumNumber));
473
474        initialize_quantum(big_pointer_array_quantum, main_object_number,
475        BIG_POINTER_ARRAY);
476
477        for (i = 0; i < little_pointer_quantum_count; i ++)
478            little_pointer_quantum_number_array[i] =
479            reserve_available_quantum(quantum_file);
480
481        big_array_header.element_count = item_count;
482        big_array_header.last_quantum_added_to = NO_QUANTUM;
483
484        add_item_to_quantum(big_pointer_array_quantum, BIG_ARRAY_HEADER, 0,
485        (char *)&big_array_header,sizeof(BigArrayHeader));
486
487        add_item_to_quantum(big_pointer_array_quantum, BIG_POINTER_ARRAY, 1,
488        (char *)little_pointer_quantum_number_array,
489        little_pointer_quantum_info_size);
490
491        little_pointer_array = (ItemReference *)x_calloc(ITEM_REFERENCE_PACKING_FACTOR,
492        sizeof(ItemReference));
493
494        null_item_reference.quantum_number = NO_QUANTUM;
495        null_item_reference.relative_item_number = NULL_ITEM_NUMBER;
496
497        for (i = 0; i < ITEM_REFERENCE_PACKING_FACTOR; i ++)
498            little_pointer_array[i] = null_item_reference;
499
500        for (i = 0; i < little_pointer_quantum_count; i ++)
501            {
502            little_pointer_array_quantum = get_quantum(quantum_file,
503            little_pointer_quantum_number_array[i],DIRTY);
504            initialize_quantum(little_pointer_array_quantum, main_object_number,
505            LITTLE_POINTER_ARRAY);
506            add_item_to_quantum(little_pointer_array_quantum, LITTLE_POINTER_ARRAY,
507            1, (char *)little_pointer_array,
508            ITEM_REFERENCE_PACKING_FACTOR*sizeof(ItemReference));
509            }
510
```

Listing 6.5 *quantum.c: quantum file functions (continued)*

```
511    x_free(little_pointer_quantum_number_array);
512    x_free(little_pointer_array);
513
514    return(OKAY);
515  }
516
517
518
519  ObjectType get_pointer_to_item(Quantum *quantum, ArrayIndex item_number,
520  char **item, ItemSize *item_size)
521  {
522    ItemIndex *quantum_index_pointer;
523    ArrayIndex item_count;
524    ItemIndex this_item;
525    ItemIndex previous_item;
526    QuantumHeader *quantum_header;
527    ItemSize item_length;
528
529    quantum_header = (QuantumHeader *)quantum;
530
531    item_count = quantum_header->item_count;
532
533    quantum_index_pointer = (ItemIndex *)(quantum+sizeof(QuantumHeader));
534
535    /* the item number starts at 1 */
536    if (item_number == 0 || item_number > item_count)
537        quantum_error("Illegal item number");
538
539    this_item = quantum_index_pointer[item_number-1];
540    if (item_number == 1) /* the first entry goes to the end */
541        item_length = this_item.offset;
542    else
543        {
544        previous_item = quantum_index_pointer[item_number-2];
545        item_length = this_item.offset-previous_item.offset;
546        }
547
548    *item = quantum+QUANTUM_SIZE-this_item.offset;
549
550    if (item_size != NULL)
551        *item_size = item_length;
552
553    return(this_item.type);
554  }
555
556
557
558  StatusType delete_item_in_quantum(Quantum *quantum,
559  RelativeItemNumber relative_item_number)
560  {
561    ItemIndex *quantum_index_pointer;
```

Listing 6.5 *quantum.c: quantum file functions (continued)*

```
562        QuantumHeader *quantum_header;
563        ArrayIndex item_count;
564        ItemIndex this_item;
565        ItemIndex previous_item;
566        ItemSize last_item_offset;
567        ItemSize item_length;
568        char *data_from;
569        char *data_to;
570        ItemSize data_length;
571        ArrayIndex i;
572        int is;   // signed loop index
573
574        if (relative_item_number == NULL_ITEM_NUMBER)
575            quantum_error("Bad item reference: please run QFIX.");
576
577        quantum_header = (QuantumHeader *)quantum;
578
579        item_count = quantum_header->item_count;
580
581        if (relative_item_number > item_count)
582            quantum_error("Bad item reference: please run QFIX.");
583
584        quantum_index_pointer = (ItemIndex *)(quantum+sizeof(QuantumHeader));
585
586        this_item = quantum_index_pointer[relative_item_number-1];
587        if (relative_item_number == item_count) /* this is the last item */
588            {
589            quantum_index_pointer[item_count-1].type = UNUSED_ITEM;
590            for (is = item_count - 1; is >= 0; is --)
591                {
592                if (quantum_index_pointer[is].type == UNUSED_ITEM)
593                    {
594                    quantum_index_pointer[is].offset = 0;
595                    quantum_index_pointer[is].index = 0;
596                    quantum_header->item_count --;
597                    }
598                else
599                    break;
600                }
601            }
602        else
603            {
604            if (relative_item_number == 1) /* the first item? */
605                {
606                item_length = this_item.offset; /* yes */
607                quantum_index_pointer[relative_item_number-1].offset = 0;
608                }
609            else /* not the first item */
610                {
611                previous_item = quantum_index_pointer[relative_item_number-2];
612                item_length = this_item.offset-previous_item.offset;
```

Listing 6.5 *quantum.c: quantum file functions (continued)*

```
613                        quantum_index_pointer[relative_item_number-1].offset =
614                        previous_item.offset;
615                        }
616
617            last_item_offset = quantum_index_pointer[item_count-1].offset;
618
619            data_from = quantum+QUANTUM_SIZE-last_item_offset;
620            data_to = data_from + item_length;
621            data_length = last_item_offset-this_item.offset;
622
623            memmove(data_to,data_from,data_length);
624
625            for (i = relative_item_number; i < item_count; i ++)
626                    quantum_index_pointer[i].offset -= item_length;
627
628            quantum_index_pointer[relative_item_number-1].type = UNUSED_ITEM;
629            }
630
631        return(item_count);
632    }
633
634
635    int get_space_available(Quantum *quantum)
636    {
637        ItemIndex *quantum_index_pointer;
638        QuantumHeader *quantum_header;
639        ArrayIndex item_count;
640        ItemIndex last_item;
641        int free_space;
642
643        quantum_header = (QuantumHeader *)quantum;
644
645        item_count = quantum_header->item_count;
646
647        quantum_index_pointer = (ItemIndex *)(quantum+sizeof(QuantumHeader));
648
649        free_space = QUANTUM_SIZE - (MARGIN + sizeof(QuantumHeader));
650
651        if (item_count == 0)
652            return(QUANTUM_SIZE-1);
653
654        last_item = quantum_index_pointer[item_count-1];
655
656        free_space -= sizeof(ItemIndex) * item_count;
657        free_space -= last_item.offset;
658
659        if (free_space < 0)
660            free_space = 0;
661
662        return(free_space);
663    }
```

Listing 6.5 *quantum.c: quantum file functions (continued)*

```
664
665
666
667   RelativeItemNumber add_item_to_quantum(Quantum *quantum, ObjectType item_type,
668   ArrayIndex element_index, char *item, ItemSize item_size)
669   {
670     ItemIndex *quantum_index_pointer;
671     ArrayIndex item_count;
672     int item_index;
673     ItemIndex last_item;
674     ItemIndex new_item;
675     QuantumHeader *quantum_header;
676     ItemIndex item_to_use;
677     ArrayIndex i;
678     char *data_from;
679     char *data_to;
680     ItemSize data_length;
681     int relative_item_number;
682     ItemSize free_space;
683
684     quantum_header = (QuantumHeader *)quantum;
685
686     item_count = quantum_header->item_count;
687
688     quantum_index_pointer = (ItemIndex *)(quantum+sizeof(QuantumHeader));
689
690     item_index = -1;
691     for (i = 0; i < item_count; i ++)
692         {
693         item_to_use = quantum_index_pointer[i];
694         if (item_to_use.type == UNUSED_ITEM)
695             {
696             item_index = i;
697             break;
698             }
699         }
700
701     free_space = QUANTUM_SIZE - sizeof(QuantumHeader);
702
703     if (item_count > 0)
704         {
705         last_item = quantum_index_pointer[item_count-1];
706         free_space -= sizeof(ItemIndex) * item_count;
707         free_space -= last_item.offset;
708         }
709
710     if (item_index < 0)
711         free_space -= sizeof(ItemIndex);
712
713     if (free_space <= item_size)
714         quantum_error("Attempt to store oversized item.\n");
```

Listing 6.5 *quantum.c: quantum file functions (continued)*

```
715
716        if (item_index >= 0) /* a reusable item exists */
717            {
718            item_to_use.type = item_type;
719            item_to_use.index = element_index;
720            quantum_index_pointer[item_index] = item_to_use;
721
722            last_item = quantum_index_pointer[item_count-1];
723
724            data_from = quantum+QUANTUM_SIZE-last_item.offset;
725            data_to = data_from - item_size;
726            data_length = last_item.offset-item_to_use.offset;
727
728            memmove(data_to,data_from,data_length);
729
730            for (i = item_index; i < item_count; i ++)
731                quantum_index_pointer[i].offset += item_size;
732
733            data_to = quantum+QUANTUM_SIZE-quantum_index_pointer[item_index].offset;
734            memmove(data_to,item,item_size);
735
736            relative_item_number = item_index+1;
737            }
738        else /* must make a new one */
739            {
740            if (item_count == 0)
741                new_item.offset = item_size;
742            else
743                {
744                last_item = quantum_index_pointer[item_count-1];
745                new_item.offset = last_item.offset+item_size;
746                }
747
748            memmove(quantum+QUANTUM_SIZE-new_item.offset, item, item_size);
749
750            new_item.type = item_type;
751            new_item.index = element_index;
752            quantum_index_pointer[item_count] = new_item;
753
754            relative_item_number = item_count+1;
755            quantum_header->item_count ++; /* increment count before use */
756            }
757
758        return(relative_item_number);
759    }
760
761
762
763    Quantum *get_quantum(FILE *quantum_file, QuantumNumber quantum_number,
764    QuantumStatus mode)
765    {
```

Listing 6.5 *quantum.c: quantum file functions (continued)*

```
766     Quantum *quantum_buffer;
767     int buffer_number;
768     QuantumNumber old_quantum_number;
769     StatusType status;
770     QuantumFile *quantum_file_header;
771
772     quantum_file_header = (QuantumFile *)quantum_file;
773
774     status = find_buffer(quantum_file, quantum_number, &buffer_number);
775
776     quantum_buffer = quantum_file_header->quantum_buffer[buffer_number];
777
778     if (status == OKAY)
779         {
780         if (mode & DIRTY) /* if we want this to be rewritten later */
781             quantum_file_header->dirty_list[buffer_number] = 1;
782         if (mode & LOCK)
783             quantum_file_header->locked_list[buffer_number] = 1;
784         else if (mode & UNLOCK)
785             quantum_file_header->locked_list[buffer_number] = 0;
786         return(quantum_buffer);
787         }
788
789     old_quantum_number =
790     quantum_file_header->memory_resident_quantum_list[buffer_number];
791
792     if (quantum_file_header->dirty_list[buffer_number])
793         write_quantum(quantum_file, old_quantum_number, quantum_buffer);
794
795     if (mode & DIRTY) /* if the new one is going to be updated */
796         quantum_file_header->dirty_list[buffer_number] = 1;
797     else
798         quantum_file_header->dirty_list[buffer_number] = 0;
799
800     quantum_file_header->memory_resident_quantum_list[buffer_number] =
801     quantum_number; /* now using this buffer for our new quantum */
802
803     read_quantum(quantum_file, quantum_number, quantum_buffer);
804
805     if (mode & LOCK)
806         quantum_file_header->locked_list[buffer_number] = 1;
807     else if (mode & UNLOCK)
808         quantum_file_header->locked_list[buffer_number] = 0;
809
810     return(quantum_buffer);
811 }
812
813
814 void qf_flush_buffers(FILE *quantum_file)
815 {
816     QuantumNumber *memory_resident_quantum_list;
```

Listing 6.5 *quantum.c: quantum file functions (continued)*

```
817      QuantumFile *quantum_file_header;
818      ArrayIndex memory_resident_quantum_count;
819      QuantumNumber quantum_number;
820      Quantum *quantum_buffer;
821      QuantumNumber **quantum_number_pointer;
822      int *dirty_list;
823      ArrayIndex i;
824      ArrayIndex dirty_count;
825      SlotNumber *slot_number;
826
827      quantum_file_header = (QuantumFile *)quantum_file;
828
829      memory_resident_quantum_count =
830      quantum_file_header->memory_resident_quantum_count;
831
832      memory_resident_quantum_list =
833      quantum_file_header->memory_resident_quantum_list;
834
835      dirty_list = quantum_file_header->dirty_list;
836
837      slot_number = (SlotNumber *)x_calloc(memory_resident_quantum_count,
838      sizeof(SlotNumber));
839
840      quantum_number_pointer = (QuantumNumber **)
841      x_calloc(memory_resident_quantum_count,sizeof(QuantumNumber *));
842
843      dirty_count = 0;
844      for (i = 0; i < memory_resident_quantum_count; i ++)
845          {
846          if (dirty_list[i])
847              {
848              slot_number[dirty_count] = i;
849              quantum_number_pointer[dirty_count] =
850              &memory_resident_quantum_list[i];
851              dirty_count ++;
852              }
853          }
854
855      Megasort((unsigned char **)quantum_number_pointer,slot_number,sizeof(int),'I',
856      dirty_count);
857
858      for (i = 0; i < dirty_count; i ++)
859          {
860          quantum_number = memory_resident_quantum_list[slot_number[i]];
861          quantum_buffer = quantum_file_header->quantum_buffer[slot_number[i]];
862          write_quantum(quantum_file, quantum_number, quantum_buffer);
863          }
864
865      for (i = 0; i < memory_resident_quantum_count; i ++)
866          dirty_list[i] = 0;
867
```

Listing 6.5 *quantum.c: quantum file functions (continued)*

```
868        x_free(slot_number);
869        x_free(quantum_number_pointer);
870
871    }
872
873
874    StatusType find_buffer(FILE *quantum_file, QuantumNumber quantum_number,
875    int *buffer_number_ptr)
876    {
877      QuantumFile *quantum_file_header;
878      QuantumNumber *memory_resident_quantum_list;
879      ArrayIndex i;
880      int *most_recently_used_list;
881      int quantum_found;
882      int buffer_number;
883      int *locked_list;
884      int lowest_unlocked_priority;
885      ArrayIndex memory_resident_quantum_count;
886      SlotNumber *slot_number;
887      int **priority_pointer;
888      int highest_priority;
889
890
891      quantum_file_header = (QuantumFile *)quantum_file;
892
893      memory_resident_quantum_count =
894      quantum_file_header->memory_resident_quantum_count;
895
896      memory_resident_quantum_list =
897      quantum_file_header->memory_resident_quantum_list;
898
899      most_recently_used_list = quantum_file_header->most_recently_used_list;
900
901      locked_list = quantum_file_header->locked_list;
902
903      highest_priority = quantum_file_header->highest_priority;
904
905      quantum_found = NOT_IN_LIST;
906
907      buffer_number = -1;
908      for (i = 0; i < memory_resident_quantum_count; i ++)
909          {
910          if (memory_resident_quantum_list[i] == quantum_number)
911              {
912              quantum_found = i;
913              buffer_number = i;
914              break;
915              }
916          }
917
918      lowest_unlocked_priority = 0;
```

Listing 6.5 *quantum.c: quantum file functions (continued)*

```
919     /* if not, select a bootee */
920     if (quantum_found == NOT_IN_LIST)
921         {
922         lowest_unlocked_priority = highest_priority+1;
923         for (i = 0; i < memory_resident_quantum_count; i ++)
924             {
925             if (most_recently_used_list[i] < lowest_unlocked_priority &&
926             locked_list[i] == 0)
927                 {
928                 lowest_unlocked_priority = most_recently_used_list[i];
929                 buffer_number = i;
930                 }
931             }
932         }
933
934     if (buffer_number == -1)
935         {
936         qf_flush_buffers(quantum_file);
937         quantum_error("No unlocked buffers available: please increase buffer count.");
938         }
939
940     highest_priority ++;
941     if (highest_priority > 32000) /* must redo the list */
942         {
943         slot_number = (SlotNumber *)x_calloc(memory_resident_quantum_count,
944         sizeof(SlotNumber));
945         priority_pointer =
946         (int **)x_calloc(memory_resident_quantum_count,sizeof(int *));
947         for (i = 0; i < memory_resident_quantum_count; i ++)
948             {
949             slot_number[i] = i;
950             priority_pointer[i] = &most_recently_used_list[i];
951             }
952         Megasort((unsigned char **)priority_pointer,slot_number,sizeof(int),'I',
953         memory_resident_quantum_count);
954         for (i = 0; i < memory_resident_quantum_count; i ++)
955             most_recently_used_list[slot_number[i]] = i;
956         highest_priority = memory_resident_quantum_count;
957         x_free(slot_number);
958         x_free(priority_pointer);
959         }
960
961     quantum_file_header->highest_priority = highest_priority;
962
963     most_recently_used_list[buffer_number] = highest_priority;
964     *buffer_number_ptr = buffer_number;
965
966     if (quantum_found == NOT_IN_LIST)
967         return(NOT_IN_LIST);
968     else
969         return(OKAY);
```

Listing 6.5 *quantum.c: quantum file functions (continued)*

```
970   }
971
972
973
974   StatusType read_quantum(FILE *quantum_file, QuantumNumber quantum_number,
975   Quantum *quantum_buffer)
976   {
977     QuantumFile *quantum_file_header;
978
979     quantum_file_header = (QuantumFile *)quantum_file;
980
981     memset(quantum_buffer,0,QUANTUM_SIZE);
982
983     position_quantum_file(quantum_file,quantum_number);
984
985     fread(quantum_buffer,1,QUANTUM_SIZE,quantum_file_header->dos_file_ptr);
986
987     return(OKAY);
988   }
989
990
991   StatusType write_quantum(FILE *quantum_file, QuantumNumber quantum_number,
992   Quantum *quantum_buffer)
993   {
994     QuantumFile *quantum_file_header;
995
996     quantum_file_header = (QuantumFile *)quantum_file;
997
998     position_quantum_file(quantum_file,quantum_number);
999
1000    fwrite(quantum_buffer,1,QUANTUM_SIZE,quantum_file_header->dos_file_ptr);
1001
1002    return(OKAY);
1003  }
1004
1005
1006
1007  StatusType position_quantum_file(FILE *quantum_file,
1008  QuantumNumber quantum_number)
1009  {
1010    long desired_position;
1011    FILE *dos_file_ptr;
1012    QuantumFile *quantum_file_header;
1013
1014    quantum_file_header = (QuantumFile *)quantum_file;
1015
1016    dos_file_ptr = quantum_file_header->dos_file_ptr;
1017
1018    desired_position = quantum_file_header->starting_quantum_offset+
1019    (long)(quantum_number-1)*(long)QUANTUM_SIZE;
1020
```

Listing 6.5 *quantum.c: quantum file functions (continued)*

```
1021      fseek(dos_file_ptr,desired_position,SEEK_SET);
1022
1023      return(OKAY);
1024    }
1025
1026    StatusType qf_store_item(FILE *quantum_file, ObjectNumber main_object_number,
1027    ArrayIndex element_index, char *item, ItemSize item_size)
1028    {
1029      QuantumFile *quantum_file_header;
1030      QuantumNumber big_pointer_array_quantum_number;
1031      Quantum *big_pointer_array_quantum;
1032      Quantum *old_item_quantum;
1033      ArrayIndex which_little_pointer_quantum_number;
1034      QuantumNumber little_pointer_array_quantum_number;
1035      Quantum *little_pointer_array_quantum;
1036      QuantumNumber *little_quantum_number_array;
1037      ItemReference *little_pointer_array;
1038      ItemReference item_reference;
1039      ObjectType big_pointer_type;
1040      ItemSize big_pointer_size;
1041      ObjectType little_pointer_type;
1042      ItemSize little_pointer_size;
1043      ArrayIndex little_pointer_index;
1044      ItemSize big_pointer_count;
1045      ItemSize little_pointer_count;
1046      FreeSpaceEntry *free_space_list;
1047      ItemSize free_space;
1048      QuantumNumber possible_quantum_number;
1049      Quantum *possible_quantum;
1050      ItemSize actual_free_space;
1051      QuantumNumber found_one;
1052      ArrayIndex i;
1053      Quantum *quantum_to_use;
1054      ItemReference *little_pointer_array_pointer;
1055      BigArrayHeader *big_array_header_pointer;
1056
1057      if (item_size > MAX_ITEM_SIZE)
1058          return(ERROR);
1059
1060      quantum_file_header = (QuantumFile *)quantum_file;
1061
1062      free_space_list = quantum_file_header->free_space_list;
1063
1064      big_pointer_array_quantum_number =
1065      quantum_file_header->main_object_index[main_object_number];
1066
1067      big_pointer_array_quantum =
1068      get_quantum(quantum_file,big_pointer_array_quantum_number,DIRTY+LOCK);
1069
1070      get_pointer_to_item(big_pointer_array_quantum, BIG_POINTER_HEADER_ITEM,
1071      (char **)&big_array_header_pointer, NULL);
```

Listing 6.5 *quantum.c: quantum file functions (continued)*

```
1072
1073    if (element_index >= big_array_header_pointer->element_count)
1074        quantum_error("Element index out of bounds.");
1075
1076    big_pointer_type = get_pointer_to_item(big_pointer_array_quantum,
1077    BIG_POINTER_ARRAY_ITEM, (char **)&little_quantum_number_array,
1078    &big_pointer_size);
1079
1080    if (big_pointer_type != BIG_POINTER_ARRAY)
1081        quantum_error("Big pointer type error: please run QFIX.");
1082
1083    which_little_pointer_quantum_number =
1084    element_index / ITEM_REFERENCE_PACKING_FACTOR;
1085
1086    big_pointer_count = big_pointer_size / sizeof(QuantumNumber);
1087    if (which_little_pointer_quantum_number >= big_pointer_count)
1088        quantum_error("Big pointer size error: please run QFIX.");
1089
1090    little_pointer_array_quantum_number =
1091    little_quantum_number_array[which_little_pointer_quantum_number];
1092
1093    little_pointer_array_quantum =
1094    get_quantum(quantum_file,little_pointer_array_quantum_number,DIRTY+LOCK);
1095
1096    little_pointer_type = get_pointer_to_item(little_pointer_array_quantum,
1097    1, (char **)&little_pointer_array, &little_pointer_size);
1098
1099    if (little_pointer_type != LITTLE_POINTER_ARRAY)
1100        quantum_error("Little pointer type error: please run QFIX.");
1101
1102    little_pointer_index = element_index % ITEM_REFERENCE_PACKING_FACTOR;
1103
1104    little_pointer_count = little_pointer_size / sizeof(ItemReference);
1105    if (little_pointer_index >= little_pointer_count)
1106        quantum_error("Little pointer size error: please run QFIX.");
1107
1108    item_reference = little_pointer_array[little_pointer_index];
1109
1110    if (real_reference(item_reference))
1111        {
1112        old_item_quantum = get_quantum(quantum_file,
1113        (QuantumNumber)item_reference.quantum_number,DIRTY);
1114
1115        delete_item_in_quantum(old_item_quantum,
1116        (QuantumNumber)item_reference.relative_item_number);
1117
1118        free_space_list[item_reference.quantum_number] =
1119        get_space_available(old_item_quantum) >> FREE_SPACE_SHIFT;
1120        }
1121
1122    if (item_size == 0)
```

Listing 6.5 *quantum.c: quantum file functions (continued)*

```
1123              {
1124              item_reference.quantum_number = NO_QUANTUM;
1125              item_reference.relative_item_number = NULL_ITEM_NUMBER;
1126              }
1127      else
1128              {
1129              found_one = NO_QUANTUM;
1130              possible_quantum_number =
1131              big_array_header_pointer->last_quantum_added_to;
1132              free_space =
1133              free_space_list[possible_quantum_number] << FREE_SPACE_SHIFT;
1134              if (free_space >= item_size)
1135                  {
1136                  possible_quantum =
1137                  get_quantum(quantum_file,possible_quantum_number,NO_STATUS_CHANGE);
1138                  actual_free_space = get_space_available(possible_quantum);
1139                  if (actual_free_space > item_size)
1140                      found_one = possible_quantum_number;
1141                  }
1142              if (found_one == NO_QUANTUM)
1143                  {
1144                  little_pointer_array_pointer = little_pointer_array-1;
1145                  for (i = 0; i < little_pointer_count; i ++)
1146                      {
1147                      little_pointer_array_pointer ++;
1148                      if (real_reference((*little_pointer_array_pointer)))
1149                          {
1150                          possible_quantum_number =
1151                          little_pointer_array_pointer->quantum_number;
1152                          free_space =
1153                          free_space_list[possible_quantum_number] << FREE_SPACE_SHIFT;
1154                      if (free_space >= item_size)
1155                          {
1156                          possible_quantum =
1157                          get_quantum(quantum_file,possible_quantum_number,
1158                          NO_STATUS_CHANGE);
1159                          actual_free_space = get_space_available(possible_quantum);
1160                          if (actual_free_space > item_size)
1161                              {
1162                              found_one = possible_quantum_number;
1163                              break;
1164                              }
1165                          }
1166                      }
1167                  }
1168              }
1169
1170              if (found_one == NO_QUANTUM)
1171                  {
1172                  found_one = reserve_available_quantum(quantum_file);
1173                  quantum_to_use = get_quantum(quantum_file,found_one,DIRTY);
```

Listing 6.5 *quantum.c: quantum file functions (continued)*

```
1174                    initialize_quantum(quantum_to_use, main_object_number,
1175                    LEAF_NODE);
1176                    }
1177            else
1178                    quantum_to_use = get_quantum(quantum_file,found_one,DIRTY);
1179
1180            big_array_header_pointer->last_quantum_added_to = found_one;
1181            item_reference.quantum_number = found_one;
1182            item_reference.relative_item_number =
1183            add_item_to_quantum(quantum_to_use, VARIABLE_LENGTH_STRING,
1184            element_index, item, item_size);
1185            }
1186
1187        little_pointer_array[little_pointer_index] = item_reference;
1188
1189        get_quantum(quantum_file,little_pointer_array_quantum_number,UNLOCK);
1190        get_quantum(quantum_file,big_pointer_array_quantum_number,UNLOCK);
1191
1192        free_space_list[found_one] =
1193        get_space_available(quantum_to_use) >> FREE_SPACE_SHIFT;
1194
1195        return(OKAY);
1196    }
1197
1198
1199
1200    StatusType qf_get_item(FILE *quantum_file, ObjectNumber main_object_number,
1201    ArrayIndex element_index, char **item, ItemSize *item_size)
1202    {
1203        QuantumFile *quantum_file_header;
1204        QuantumNumber big_pointer_array_quantum_number;
1205        Quantum *big_pointer_array_quantum;
1206        ArrayIndex which_little_pointer_quantum_number;
1207        QuantumNumber little_pointer_array_quantum_number;
1208        Quantum *little_pointer_array_quantum;
1209        QuantumNumber *little_quantum_number_array;
1210        ItemReference *little_pointer_array;
1211        ItemReference item_reference;
1212        ObjectType big_pointer_type;
1213        ItemSize big_pointer_size;
1214        ObjectType little_pointer_type;
1215        ItemSize little_pointer_size;
1216        ArrayIndex little_pointer_index;
1217        ItemSize big_pointer_count;
1218        ItemSize little_pointer_count;
1219        Quantum *quantum_to_use;
1220        char *temp_item;
1221        ItemSize temp_item_size;
1222        BigArrayHeader *big_array_header_pointer;
1223
1224
```

Listing 6.5 *quantum.c: quantum file functions (continued)*

```
1225    quantum_file_header = (QuantumFile *)quantum_file;
1226
1227    big_pointer_array_quantum_number =
1228    quantum_file_header->main_object_index[main_object_number];
1229
1230    big_pointer_array_quantum =
1231    get_quantum(quantum_file,big_pointer_array_quantum_number,LOCK);
1232
1233    get_pointer_to_item(big_pointer_array_quantum, BIG_POINTER_HEADER_ITEM,
1234    (char **)&big_array_header_pointer, NULL);
1235
1236    if (element_index >= big_array_header_pointer->element_count)
1237        quantum_error("Element index out of bounds.");
1238
1239    big_pointer_type = get_pointer_to_item(big_pointer_array_quantum,
1240    BIG_POINTER_ARRAY_ITEM, (char **)&little_quantum_number_array,
1241    &big_pointer_size);
1242
1243    if (big_pointer_type != BIG_POINTER_ARRAY)
1244        quantum_error("Big pointer type error: please run QFIX.");
1245
1246    which_little_pointer_quantum_number =
1247    element_index / ITEM_REFERENCE_PACKING_FACTOR;
1248
1249    big_pointer_count = big_pointer_size / sizeof(QuantumNumber);
1250    if (which_little_pointer_quantum_number >= big_pointer_count)
1251        quantum_error("Big pointer size error: please run QFIX.");
1252
1253    little_pointer_array_quantum_number =
1254    little_quantum_number_array[which_little_pointer_quantum_number];
1255
1256    little_pointer_array_quantum =
1257    get_quantum(quantum_file,little_pointer_array_quantum_number,LOCK);
1258
1259    little_pointer_type = get_pointer_to_item(little_pointer_array_quantum,
1260    1, (char **)&little_pointer_array, &little_pointer_size);
1261
1262    if (little_pointer_type != LITTLE_POINTER_ARRAY)
1263        quantum_error("Little pointer type error: please run QFIX.");
1264
1265    little_pointer_index = element_index % ITEM_REFERENCE_PACKING_FACTOR;
1266
1267    little_pointer_count = little_pointer_size / sizeof(ItemReference);
1268    if (little_pointer_index >= little_pointer_count)
1269        quantum_error("Little pointer size error: please run QFIX.");
1270
1271    item_reference = little_pointer_array[little_pointer_index];
1272
1273    if (real_reference(item_reference) == 0) /* a zero-length item */
1274        {
1275        *item = (char *)x_calloc(0,1);
```

Listing 6.5 *quantum.c: quantum file functions (continued)*

```
1276          *item_size = 0;
1277          }
1278     else
1279          {
1280          quantum_to_use = get_quantum(quantum_file,
1281          (QuantumNumber)item_reference.quantum_number,NO_STATUS_CHANGE);
1282
1283          get_pointer_to_item(quantum_to_use,
1284          (QuantumNumber)item_reference.relative_item_number,
1285          &temp_item, &temp_item_size);
1286
1287          *item_size = temp_item_size;
1288          *item = (char *)x_calloc(temp_item_size,1);
1289          memmove(*item,temp_item,temp_item_size);
1290          }
1291
1292     little_pointer_array_quantum =
1293     get_quantum(quantum_file,little_pointer_array_quantum_number,UNLOCK);
1294
1295     big_pointer_array_quantum =
1296     get_quantum(quantum_file,big_pointer_array_quantum_number,UNLOCK);
1297
1298     return(OKAY);
1299  }
1300
1301
1302  StatusType quantum_error(char *message)
1303  {
1304    puts(message);
1305    exit(1);
1306    return(OKAY);
1307  }
1308
```

OO, What an Algorithm

Index and Key Access to Variable-Length Records

Introduction

While the quantum file access method described in the previous chapter is very powerful, its C implementation isn't terribly convenient in some respects.[105] For example, the user program has to pass pointers to size and storage address variables to `qf_get_item` and free the storage used by the data item when it's no longer needed; the interface would be much more intuitive if we could treat a quantum file "array" just like a normal array.

Unfortunately, this isn't possible in C; however, a major impetus behind the creation of C++ was to make it possible for class library designers to provide such facilities. Since the quantum file access method would benefit greatly from such an approach, I decided to rewrite it in C++.[106]

Rewriting History

Why am I using the word "rewrite", rather than "convert", "translate", or other euphemisms? Judging from the number of ads for "C/C++ programmers" I see in the

---

105. If you haven't yet read that chapter, you should do so before continuing, as the discussion here assumes detailed knowledge of the C implementation.

106. I'm afraid that in order to make sense out of this chapter, you're going to have to be reasonably proficient in C++. If you need a book teaching C++, you might want to start with Eric Nagler's *Learning C++: A Hands-On Approach* (West Publishing Company, St. Paul, MN, 1993).

newspapers, some employers have the notion that switching to C++ can be accomplished by changing source file extensions to ".cpp" and recompiling. After removing some syntax errors revealed by the stricter type checking of the C++ compiler, the program compiles and runs as it did before. What's so difficult about object-oriented programming?

If you are one of these employers, or you have tried the above experiment yourself and now believe that you are a "C++ programmer", let me break the news to you gently: all you have accomplished is to switch to the C subset of C++, which has nothing to do with object-oriented programming. As you will see from the tortuous (not to mention torturous) course that this project has followed, virtually none of the code or design from the original implementation has survived the transition to object orientation unscathed. This is despite the fact that, according to an expert on object-oriented design, my original C implementation was "object-oriented"!

However, my loss (if that's what it was) can be your gain: I am going to break a long-standing tradition of object-oriented design literature by disclosing not only the final design but also many of the missteps, errors, and difficulties that ensued from my original determination to tackle this rather complex project. So, with no further ado, let's begin with an often neglected concept which is at the core of the implementation of this project: operator overloading.

Warning: Overload!

One of the most powerful mechanisms for hiding the details of implementation from the class user in C++ is operator overloading, which means defining (or in some cases redefining) the semantics of one or more of the standard operators +, –, =, and so forth, as they apply to class objects. For better or worse, the semantics of these operators cannot be changed as they apply to "intrinsic" data types, so the calculation 2+2 is always going to result in 4; this restriction is probably necessary, as the potential confusion could be horrendous.[107]

A good example of the most common type of use for this facility is the implementation of +, –, etc., for manipulating **Complex** class objects, following the rules of complex arithmetic. The ability to provide this sort of intuitive operation to the number-

---

107. Another restriction in C++ operator overloading is that it's impossible to make up your own operators. According to Bjarne Stroustrup, this facility has been carefully considered by the standards committee and has failed of adoption due to difficulties with operator precedence and binding strength. Apparently, it was the exponentiation operator that was the deciding factor; it's the first operator that users from the numerical community usually want to define, but its mathematical properties don't match the precedence and binding rules of any of the "normal" C operators.

crunching user is starting to make C++ (with the proper class libraries, of course) a viable alternative to FORTRAN, long the dominant language for such users.

Hello, Operator?

As usual, it's probably best to start with a relatively simple example: in this case, we'll look at an example of overloading operator-.[108] Consider the program in figure 7.1.

Figure 7.1 *Overloading* operator-

```
#include <math.h>
#include <stdio.h>

class Point
{
protected:
double m_xValue;
double m_yValue;

public:
Point(double p_xValue=0, double p_yValue=0)
{
    m_xValue = p_xValue;
    m_yValue = p_yValue;
};

double operator-(const Point& p_Point)
{
    double xDiff;
    double yDiff;

    xDiff = m_xValue - p_Point.m_xValue;
    yDiff = m_yValue - p_Point.m_yValue;

    return sqrt(xDiff*xDiff + yDiff*yDiff);
};

};

main()
{

Point x(1,1);
Point y(4,5);

printf("%g\n",x-y);
}
```

---

108. I'm not claiming this is a good use for overloading; it's only for tutorial purposes.

As you can see, I've created a very simplified version of the dreaded `Point` class, used in innumerable textbooks to represent a point on the Euclidean plane. The result of running our sample program is 5, which is the distance between the `Point` `(1,1)` and the `Point` `(4,5)`, calculated by the normal Euclidean calculation

```
:Distance = sqrt(xdiff*xdiff + ydiff*ydiff)
```

where `xdiff` is the difference between the *x* coordinates of the two `Points`, and `ydiff` is the difference between their *y* coordinates; `sqrt`, of course, represents the square root function.

The "magic" is in the definition of `operator-`, which is the syntax for redefining an operator; in this case it's the subtraction operator. When the compiler sees the expression `x-y`, it looks for a definition of `operator-` that is specified for class `Point`, taking an argument which is also of class `Point`. Since there is such a definition, the compiler generates a call to the code specified in that definition. Had there not been such a definition, a syntax error would have resulted, since the compiler doesn't have any built-in knowledge of how to subtract two `Points`.

While this is undoubtedly interesting in an abstract way, you may be wondering what it has to do with the quantum file algorithm. Here's where we make that connection.

An Auto-loader

One of my cardinal goals in the design of the C++ quantum file implementation was to eliminate the need to lock blocks in memory to prevent them from being thrown out while their contents were being accessed. I also wanted to reduce the memory consumption caused by loading the entire free space list and main object list into memory; as long as we are implementing a virtual memory system, we ought to be able to use it for internal tables as well. In effect, I wanted the virtual memory system to be transparent even to the quantum file implementation itself. But how could this be achieved?

It turns out that overloading `operator->` is the key to eliminating these suboptimal features in the original C implementation, as well as adding new functionality. The reason is that by taking over `operator->`, we can ensure that every reference to a virtual memory data block is intercepted by our code, which loads the block into memory if needed, rather than having to reserve its memory in advance. In other words, the basic functionality of the virtual memory is implemented entirely inside `operator->`!

This immediately eliminates the need for locking and unlocking, since even if the block being referenced isn't resident when the `operator->` operation starts, it will be by the time it finishes. Similarly, the free space list and the main object list can use regular virtual memory blocks, which are managed by the same fundamental mechanism that is used for the quanta. This is the reason that the C++ version of this algorithm uses much less memory at run time than the C version does.

There's a trick to the overloading of `operator->`. When we overload other operators, such as our earlier example of `operator-`, our code takes over the implementation of the operator completely. That is, the result of calling our operator is whatever we say it is; in the `operator-` example, it's the `double` result of the Euclidean distance formula. However, this is not true with `operator->`; in that case alone, a different scheme is followed by the compiler. To explain the rules, let's suppose that we have a class called `BlockPtr`, which we're going to use to implement the virtual memory system needed for the quantum file algorithm. Figure 7.2 shows some code derived from an early version of the project; how does the compiler interpret it?[109]

The line `X->Get();` will be compiled as follows:

1. Since X is not a pointer to any type, its class definition is examined for a definition of operator->.
2. Since this definition is found, a call to that code is inserted in the function being compiled.
3. Then the return value of the operator-> code is examined. Since it is a pointer type (BlockPtr *, to be exact), the compiler continues by generating code to call BlockPtr->Get() with this equal to the result returned by operator->, which is the same BlockPtr that we started with. However, we can now be sure that the block to which it refers is memory resident, since that is the function of MakeBlockResident.

Type-Safety First

So far, this is doing exactly what we wanted it to do. However, there is one serious problem with this method of implementing `operator->`, which is illustrated by what happens when the line `Y->Get();` is compiled.

Unlike our previous example, Y *is* a pointer to a `BlockPtr`; therefore, the compiler doesn't look for a definition of `operator->`, but merely generates code to call `BlockPtr->Get()` with `this` equal to Y. As a result, our overloaded operator is never called, so that we cannot be sure that the block to which it refers to is memory resident.

Much the same problem will occur when the line `X.Get(1);` is compiled. The compiler is happy to generate a call to `BlockPtr.Get(1)` with `this` being equal to the address of X; again, though, our virtual memory code won't be executed.

Errors of this sort are exceedingly dangerous, for two reasons. First, the compiler is not going to help us catch them; and second, if we make such an error in only one place, it's quite likely that the correct block will happen to be in memory most of the time that we reference it. On the occasions when it's the wrong block, the file will be corrupted, but reproducing the error may be impossible.

---

109. Warning: do not compile and execute the program in figure 7.2. Although it will compile, it reads from random locations, which may cause a core dump on some systems.

Figure 7.2 *Dangerous* operator-> *overloading*

```
class BlockPtr {
protected:  char
*m_BlockData;
char *MakeBlockResident();

public:
BlockPtr();
BlockPtr *operator->();
char Get(int p_Index);
};

BlockPtr::BlockPtr()
{
    m_BlockData = 0;
}

BlockPtr *BlockPtr::operator->()
{
    m_BlockData = MakeBlockResident();
    return this;
}

char *BlockPtr::MakeBlockResident()
{
    return new char[1000];
}

char BlockPtr::Get(int p_Index)
{
    return m_BlockData[p_Index];
}

main()
{
    BlockPtr X;
    BlockPtr *Y;

    X->Get(1);
    Y->Get(1);
    X.Get(1);


}
```

The reason for this problem is that the compiler stops looking for operator->
overloading whenever an actual pointer is found. After all, if you already have a
pointer in a place where a pointer is needed, you must have what you want!
Obviously, we're going to have to come up with a type-safe solution, so we can't accidentally use the wrong syntax and end up with a nasty bug.[110]

110. By the way, this isn't just a theoretical problem: it happened to me.

The solution is to have not one, but two classes involved in the virtual memory mechanism, an "outer" one and an "inner" one. The outer class has two primary functions: the initializing of the inner class and the overloading of `operator->` to return a pointer to a member of the inner class, which actually does the work.[111] Figure 7.3 presents this solution.

One interesting thing about this program is that the main program refers to the Get function in exactly the same way as it did before: in fact, the only difference visible to the class user is that the compiler is now able to prevent him (and us) from compiling the illegal references as we did before.

However, there are some changes to the internals that deserve comment. First of all, in the class definition, the previous `BlockPtr` class has been renamed to `Block` and made a nested class of a new `BlockPtr`. The reason for the renaming is to prevent unnecessary changes to the user's code; that was successful, as noted above. Another design decision whose justification is not quite as obvious is the use of a nested class rather than a freestanding class. Why is this appropriate?

Hidden Virtues

Since the purpose of the nested `Block` class is solely to add type safety, rather than to provide any visible functionality, nesting it inside the `BlockPtr` class reduces "name space pollution"; that is, if the user needs a `Block` class for some other purpose, its name won't conflict with this one. Such potential conflicts are going to become more serious as the use of class libraries increases; we should do our part to "preserve the environment" when possible.[112]

The fact that the `Block` class is visible only to members of its enclosing class, `BlockPtr`, is responsible for the somewhat odd appearance of the member function declarations in figure 7.3. For example, what are we to make of the declaration "`char BlockPtr::Block::Get(int p_Index);`"?

Figure 7.3 *Type-safe* `operator->` *overloading*

```
class BlockPtr
{
class Block
{
friend BlockPtr;
protected:
```

(Continued on next page)

---

111. This is an example of the "handle/body" class paradigm, described in *Advanced C++; Programming Styles and Idioms*, by James O. Coplien (Addison-Wesley Publishing Company, Reading, Massachusetts, 1992). Warning: as its title indicates, this is *not* an easy book; however, it does reward careful study by those who already have a solid grasp of C++ fundamentals.

112. In order to solve this problem in a more general way, the ANSI standards committee for C++ has approved the addition of "namespaces", which allow the programmer to specify the library from which one or more functions are to be taken in order to prevent name conflicts.

Figure 7.3 *(continued)*

```
char *m_BlockData;
char *MakeBlockResident();
Block();

public:
char Get(int p_Index);
};

protected:
Block m_Block;

public:
Block *operator->();
BlockPtr();
};


BlockPtr::Block::Block()
{
    m_BlockData = 0;
}

BlockPtr::Block *BlockPtr::operator->()
{
    m_Block.m_BlockData = m_Block.MakeBlockResident();
    return &m_Block;
}

char *BlockPtr::Block::MakeBlockResident()
{
    return new char[1000];
}

char BlockPtr::Block::Get(int p_Index)
{
    return m_BlockData[p_Index];
}

main()
{
    BlockPtr X;
    BlockPtr *Y;
    BlockPtr::Block Z; // illegal; the constructor is protected
    X->Get(1); // okay; goes through operator-> to Block object
    Y->Get(1); // won't compile, since BlockPtr doesn't have Get
    X.Get(1);  // won't compile, for the same reason
}
```

Of course, we C++ programmers are used to "qualified" function names, such as `Block::Get`. But why do we need two qualifiers? Because the compiler knows the meaning of `Block` only in the context of `BlockPtr`; that's what prevents the global name pollution that would ensue if `Block` were declared outside of `BlockPtr`. This means that we could, for example, have another class called `Block` nested inside another enclosing class called `NewBlockPtr`. If that `Block` class had a `Get` member function, we could declare it as `"char NewBlockPtr::Block::Get(int p_Index);"`, and the compiler would have no problem telling which `Block::Get` we meant. Of course, `"Block::Get(int p_Index);"` would be yet another completely distinct function.

One more safety feature in this new arrangement is worthy of note: the constructor for `Block` is `protected`, so that the user can't accidentally create one and use it instead of referencing it through a `BlockPtr` object the way we intend. This isn't very likely anyway, since the user would have to specify `BlockPtr::Block` as the type, which isn't easy to do by accident; however, according to the principles of object-oriented programming, it is best to hide the internals of our classes whenever possible, so that class user code can't depend on those internals. That restriction makes it possible for us to improve the implementation of our classes without breaking user code.

Residence Permit

Now that we are able to overload `operator->` safely, how do we use this to make sure that any block we are referring to is memory resident? By calling the routine `MakeBlockResident` whenever a block is referenced. Figure 7.4 shows an early implementation of this routine.

This is a fairly straightforward implementation of a least recently used (LRU) priority algorithm, but there are a few wrinkles to reduce overhead. First, we use the reference parameter `p_OldBufferNumber` to retrieve the buffer number (if any) in which the searched-for block was located on our last attempt. If the number of the block held in that buffer matches the one we're looking for, we will be able to avoid the overhead of searching the entire buffer list. The reason that `p_OldBufferNumber` is a reference parameter is so that we can update the caller's copy when we locate the block in a different buffer; that way, the next time that `MakeBlockResident` is called to retrieve the same block's address, we can check that buffer number first.

In order to make this work, we can't implement the LRU priority list by moving the most recently used block to the front of the block list; the saved buffer number would be useless if the blocks moved around in the list every time a block other than the most recently used one was referenced. Instead, each slot has an attached time-stamp, updated by calling the `time` function every time the corresponding block is

Figure 7.4 *Early* `MakeBlockResident` *code*

```
BlockBuffer  *MRUBlockManager::MakeBlockResident(ArrayIndex
p_BlockNumber, ArrayIndex &p_OldBufferNumber)
{
    ArrayIndex i;
    ArrayIndex EarliestStamp;
    time_t TimeStamp;

    if (m_BlockNumber[p_OldBufferNumber] = = p_BlockNumber)
        {
        m_TimeStamp[p_OldBufferNumber] = time(NULL);
        return m_BlockBuffer[p_OldBufferNumber];
        }

    for (i = 0; i < m_BlockNumber.GetSize(); i ++)
        {
        if (m_BlockNumber[i] == p_BlockNumber)
            {
            m_TimeStamp[i] = time(NULL);
            return m_BlockBuffer[i];
            }
        }

    TimeStamp = WayInTheFuture;
    for (i = 0; i < m_TimeStamp.GetSize(); i ++)
        {
        if (m_TimeStamp[i] < TimeStamp) // find the earliest timestamp
            {
            TimeStamp = m_TimeStamp[i];
            EarliestStamp = i;
            }
        }

    if (m_BufferModified[EarliestStamp]) /* it needs to be written out */
        Write(EarliestStamp);

    m_BlockNumber[EarliestStamp] = p_BlockNumber; // set block number of new occupant
    m_BufferModified[EarliestStamp] = FALSE; // not modified yet
    m_TimeStamp[EarliestStamp] = time(NULL);
    Read(EarliestStamp);

    p_OldBufferNumber = EarliestStamp;

    return m_BlockBuffer[EarliestStamp];
}
```

referenced. When we need to free up a buffer, we select the one with the lowest (i.e., oldest) timestamp. If that buffer has the "modified" attribute set, then it has been updated in memory and needs to be written back to the disk before being reused, so we do that. Then we read the new block into the buffer, update the caller's p_OldBufferNumber for next time, and return the address of the buffer.

This seems simple enough, without much scope for vast improvements in efficiency; at least, it seemed that way to me, until I ran Turbo Profiler on it and discovered that it is horrendously inefficient. The profiler indicated that 73% of the CPU time of my test program was accounted for by calls to the time routine! To add insult to injury, the timing resolution of that routine is quite coarse (approximately 18 msec), with the result that most of the blocks would often get the same timestamp when running the program normally.[113]

Upon consideration, I realized that the best possible "timestamp" would be a simple count of the number of times that MakeBlockResident was called. This would entail almost no overhead and would be of exactly the correct resolution to decide which block was least recently used; this is the mechanism used in the current version.

Punching the Time Clock

One interesting consideration in the design of this new mechanism is what size of counter to use for the timestamp. At first, it seemed necessary (and sufficient) to use an unsigned long, which would allow 4 billion accesses before the counter would "turn over" to 0. However, is this really necessary?

After some thought, I decided that it wasn't. The question is: what happens when the counter turns over? To figure this out, let's do a thought experiment, using two-byte counters. Suppose that the priority list looks like figure 7.5, with the latest timestamp being 65535.

Let's suppose that the next reference is to block 9, with the counter turning over to 0. The list will now look like figure 7.6.

The next time that a new block has to be loaded, block 9 will be replaced, instead of block 23, which is actually the least recently used block. What effect will this have on performance? At first glance, it doesn't appear that the maximum possible effect could be very large; after all, each turnover would only cause each buffer to be replaced incorrectly once. If we have 100 buffers (a very large number), the worst case would be that the "wrong" buffer is replaced 100 times out of 64K, which is approximately 1.5% of the time; with fewer buffers, the effect is even smaller. There is no danger to the data, since the buffers will be written out if they have changed. I suspected that the cost of handling a unsigned long counter instead of an unsigned on every call to MakeBlockResident would probably be larger than the cost of this inefficient buffer use, but it didn't appear important either way.

---

113. Of course, while stepping through the program at human speeds in Turbo Debugger, the timestamps were nicely distributed; this is a demonstration of Heisenberg's Uncertainty Principle as it applies to debugging.

Figure 7.5 *Timestamps before turnover*

Block number	Timestamp
14	65533
22	65535
23	65000
9	65100

Figure 7.6 *Timestamps immediately after turnover*

Block number	Timestamp
14	65533
22	65535
23	65000
9	0

Getting Our Clocks Cleaned

Although the preceding analysis was good enough to convince me not to worry about the counter turning over, unfortunately it wasn't good enough to convince the machine. What actually happened was that after a large number of block references, the program started to run *very* slowly. I was right that the data wasn't in danger, but performance suffered greatly. Why?

Let's go back to our example. Which buffer would be replaced when the next block needed to be read in? The one currently holding block 9, since it has the "lowest" priority. If that block number happened to be 32, for example, that would leave us with the arrangement in figure 7.7.

The problem should now be obvious: the newest block still has the "lowest" priority! The reason that the program started to run very slowly after turnover was that the "fossil" timestamps on the old blocks were preventing them from being reused for more active blocks, so every block that had to be read in had to share buffers with the ones that had been read in after turnover. The solution was fairly simple; on turnover, I set all of the timestamps to 0 to give every buffer the same priority. This isn't really optimal, since it doesn't preserve the relative priority of the blocks already in memory; however, it has the virtue of simplicity, and does reduce the problem to the fairly insignificant level indicated by my first analysis of the turnover problem.

Speed Demon

Is this the end of our concern for the `MakeBlockResident` routine? Not at all; as befits its central role in the virtual memory mechanism, this routine has undergone quite a few transformations during the development process. One attempt to speed it

Figure 7.7 *Timestamps shortly after turnover*

Block number	Timestamp
14	65533
22	65535
23	65000
32	1

up took the form of creating a `FastResidenceCheck` routine that would have the sole purpose of checking whether the old buffer number saved from the previous call to load the same block number was still good; if so, it would return that buffer number after resetting the timestamp. The theoretical advantage of splitting this function off from the more general case was that such a routine might be simple enough to be inlined effectively, which would remove the overhead of one function call from the time needed to make sure that the block in question was memory resident. Unfortunately, this measure turned out to be ineffective; one reason was that the routines that called `MakeBlockResident` typically didn't reuse the object where the former buffer number was saved, but had to create another one every time they were called by their client routines. Therefore, the attempt to "remember" the previous buffer number wasn't successful in most cases.

While `FastResidenceCheck` was in use, it suffered from a bug caused by improperly initializing the old buffer number to 0, a valid buffer number. The result of this error was that when a block happened to get loaded into buffer number 0, `operator->` didn't initialize the pointer to the `ItemIndex` array, since the buffer number "matched" the old buffer number. This problem would have been solved anyway by the new versions of `operator->`, which always initialize any pointers that might need to be updated; after the attempt to avoid apparently redundant initializations of these pointers caused a couple of bugs, I decided that discretion was the better part of optimization.[114]

My eventual solution to the amount of time consumed by the `MakeBlockResident` function was to make the buffer search into a function called `FindBuffer` that could be implemented in assembly language. For some reason, such a function can't be inlined in the Borland C++ 3.1 compiler, so we still have to make a function call unless we physically copy the code into `MakeBlockResident`, which would impair portability. However, it's still much faster than the equivalent C code.

As a result of this change, we no longer have to inform the caller of the buffer number that this block contains, so the reference argument to `MakeBlockResident` for that purpose has been removed.

---

114. One such bug occurred when a new little pointer array was being constructed. Since the block was still in memory, and therefore didn't have to be loaded via `MakeBlockResident`, the `operator->` function didn't update the member variable `m_LittlePointerArray` after the new array was built; as a result, references to the array through the member variable were incorrect.

Virtual Perfection

The acid test of this virtual memory mechanism is to run the program with only one block buffer; unsurprisingly, this test revealed a nasty bug. It seems that I had neglected to initialize the value of the `EarliestStamp` variable, used to keep track of the buffer with the earliest timestamp. When running with only one buffer, it was possible under some circumstances for a block to be replaced before it was ever used; when this happened, the timestamp on the buffer it had occupied was left set to its initial value of `ULONG_MAX`. This initial value was significant because the search for the earliest timestamp also starts out by setting the `TimeStamp` variable to `ULONG_MAX`, which should be greater than any timestamp found in the search. If there were no blocks in the list with a "real" timestamp, the conditional statement that set the `EarliestStamp` value in the search loop was never executed. As a result, the `EarliestStamp` variable was left in an uninitialized state, which caused a wild access to a nonexistent block buffer. The fix was to initialize `EarliestStamp` to 0, so the first buffer will be selected under these circumstances; you can see this implemented in the current version of `MakeBlockResident` (listing 7.3, lines 26-68).

Open Season

`QuantumFile::Open` (see listing 7.3, lines 26–68) is another routine that deserves some attention. While it is quite similar in its general outline to its C counterpart, `qf_open_quantum_file`, `Open` has been the source of several interesting problems, including some bugs.

One consideration in the design of this routine was to be able to "bootstrap" from the C version into the C++ version of the program, by initially remaining compatible with the old file layout. The advantage of this approach was that the previously existing C programs could read (and more important, write) files in that format; therefore, the development of the new program could start with the easier task of reading preexisting data. If we created a brand-new file format, it would be impossible to read anything before the significantly more complex data-writing functions were working. It's also easier to find errors in the read logic of the new version when we can count on the files having been written correctly in the first place.

One new feature added in the C++ version is that when we're creating a new file, rather than opening an old one, we also create a "Directory" object. This persistent array of strings is used to hold the names of other objects, so that programs can use objects' names rather than hard- coded numbers. This facility is quite primitive at the moment; it stops looking for a name when it comes to a string of zero length, so deleting an object's name would cause other objects not to be found; obviously, a commercial implementation would need a more robust deletion mechanism!

A couple of bugs cropped up in the development of `QuantumFile::Open`. One particularly silly one was that I wasn't checking the return value from `fopen` to see whether the file existed before I called `setvbuf` to establish a buffer for the file.

The result was a wild write to low memory, which didn't have any obvious effects under DOS, but crashed the system when I compiled the same program as an EasyWin™ program; of course, the problem was caught by BoundsChecker instantly.[115] The silly part is that there's no reason to use `setvbuf` at all when we're always reading and writing large blocks explicitly!

Another bug came out to bite me when I made an apparently innocuous change.[116] The problem was that the calculation of the number of blocks occupied by the main object array was incorrect. It divided the number of main objects by the size of a block and threw away the remainder, which produces the correct answer if and only if the storage taken up by all the main objects entries happens to be a whole number of blocks. Before the change to one-byte main object numbers, this was true; however, after that change, the main object array took only one-half of a block, which was rounded down to 0 blocks, causing chaos. Of course, when I found this bug, I made the analogous change to the calculation of the free list block count as well.

The Crown of Creation

`CreateMainObject` (listing 7.5, lines 313–369) also has a number of interesting differences from the C version, `qf_create_main_object`. One of these is the addition of a new argument to specify the maximum size of the array. This argument was added to support the ability to increase the size of an array after its creation, which we will discuss shortly. Its default value is -1, which means "grow as required". The initial number of elements has a default value as well now (100), so it's not necessary to specify any size at all when creating a new object.

A related change involves another occurrence of our old friend "rounding error". To be precise, the calculation of the number of blocks needed to hold the little pointer arrays (`LittlePointerBlockCount`) produces correct results for all values of the element count that are greater than 0 but produces a nonsensical result when the element count is 0. This problem would not be likely to show up when arrays were

---

115. This wasn't the first time that NuMega's BoundsChecker saved my bacon, nor was it the last. If you develop DOS or MS-WINDOWS programs without using BoundsChecker, you're taking unnecessary risks. For those of you who don't know what this program does, a short explanation is that it checks memory accesses for validity at run time.

116. This is a demonstration of Mohle's Law; there is no such thing as an innocuous change to software.

fixed in size, since the ability to create an array with no elements isn't very useful if it can't grow. However, once arrays can grow in size, a zero- element array may be a reasonable thing to create; the simplest solution, and the one I adopted, was to treat a request to create a zero-element array as a request for a one-element array.

Free the Quantum 16K!

Another change in the quantum file implementation from the C version has to do with the free space list. In both the old and new implementations, we first check the last quantum to which we added an item; if that has enough space to add the new item, we use it.[117] In the old implementation, the free space list contained only a "free space code", indicating how much space was available in the quantum but not which object it belonged to. Therefore, when we wanted to find a quantum belonging to the current object that had enough space to store a new item, we couldn't use the free space list directly. As a substitute, we went through the current little pointer array, looking up each quantum referenced in that array in the free space list; if one of them had enough space, we used it. However, this is quite inefficient, since each quantum can hold dozens or hundreds of items, in which case this algorithm might require us to look at the same quantum that many times![118] Although this wasn't too important in the old implementation, where the free space list was held in memory, it could cause serious delays in the current one, if we used the standard virtual memory services to access the free space list. The free space list in the old program took up 16K, one byte for each quantum in the maximum quantum file size allowed. In the new implementation, using 2K blocks of virtual memory, that same free space list would occupy 8 blocks; therefore, accessing the free space list in the order in which quantum numbers appeared in the little pointer array could result in a number of extra disk accesses to load free space blocks that weren't resident. Even if the free space blocks were already resident, virtual memory accesses are considerably slower than "regular" accesses; it would be much faster to scan the free space list sequentially by quan-

---

117. In the C++ version, the "last quantum added to" variable is stored in the big pointer quantum. When first writing the code to update that variable, I had forgotten to update the "modified" flag for the big pointer quantum when the variable actually changed. As a result, every time the buffer used for the big pointer quantum was reused for a new block, that buffer was overwritten without being written out to the disk. When the big pointer quantum was reloaded, the "last quantum added to" variable was reset to an earlier, obsolete value, with the result that a new quantum was started unnecessarily. This error caused the file to grow very rapidly.

118. For the same reason, if we were adding an item to a large object with many little pointer arrays, each of which contained only a few distinct quantum number references, we wouldn't be gathering information about very much of the total storage taken up by the object; we might very well start a new quantum when there was plenty of space in another quantum owned by this object.

tum number than randomly according to the entries in the little pointer array. Of course, we could make a list of which quanta we had already examined and skip the check in those cases, but I decided to simplify matters by another method.

In the new implementation, the free space list contains not just the free space for each quantum but also which object it belongs to (if any).[119] This lets us write a `FindSpaceForItem` routine that finds a place to store a new item by scanning each block of the free list sequentially in memory, rather than using a virtual memory access to retrieve each free space entry; we stop when we find a quantum that belongs to the current object and has enough free space left to store the item (see listing 7.5, lines 144–186).[120] However, if there isn't such a quantum, then we have to start a new quantum; how do we decide which one to use?

One way is to keep track of the first free space block we find in our search and use it if we can't find a suitable block already belonging to our object. However, I want to bias the storage mechanism to use blocks as close as possible to the beginning of the file, which should reduce head motion, as well as making it possible to shrink the file's allocated size if the amount of data stored in it decreases. My solution is to take a free block whenever it appears; if that happens to be before a suitable block belonging to the current object, so be it. This appears to be a self-limiting problem, since the next time we want to add to the same object, the newly assigned block will be employed if it has enough free space.

This approach solves another problem as well, which is how we determine when to stop scanning the free space list in the first place. Of course, we could also maintain the block number of the last occupied block in the file and stop there. However, I felt this was unnecessary, since stopping at the first free block provides a natural shortcut, without contributing any obvious problems of its own. However, as with many design decisions, my analysis could be flawed: there's a possibility that using this algorithm with many additions and deletions could reduce the space efficiency of the file, although I haven't seen such an effect in my testing.

This mechanism did not mature without some growing pains. For example, the `ItemSizeCode`, the one-byte code used to indicate the approximate space available in a quantum, is calculated by dividing the size by 8 (in the case of 2K blocks) and discarding the remainder. As a result, the size code calculated for items of less than 8 bytes is 0. Since the original check for sufficient space in a quantum tested whether the space code for the quantum was greater than or equal to the space code for the new item, even blocks with no free space (i.e., those having a free space code of 0)

---

119. In order to reduce the size of the free space list entries, I've also reduced the number of objects in the main object list to 256, so that an object number will fit in one byte.

120. Another possible optimization would be of use when we are loading a large number of items into a quantum file; in that case, we could just start a new quantum whenever we run out of space in the "last added to" quantum. This would eliminate the search of the free space list entirely and might be quite effective in decreasing the time needed to do such a mass load. Of course, this solution would require some way for the class user to inform the quantum file system that a mass load is in progress, as well as when it is over, so that the default behavior could be reestablished.

were considered possible storage places for these very small items. Changing from ">=" to ">" in the test fixed this; of course, I could also have made the size calculation round up rather than down.

Another problem I encountered with the free space handling in the new algorithm is that blocks and quanta are no longer synonymous, as they were in the old program. That is, the virtual memory system deals not only with quanta (i.e., blocks containing user data) but also with free space blocks and the block(s) occupied by the main object list. At one point, some routines dealing with the free space list were using physical block numbers and others were using logical quantum numbers; however, since only quanta are controlled by the free space list, the correct solution was to use only logical quantum numbers in all such routines.

One Size Fits All

One of the advantages of writing code for textbooks is that if you run out of time in the implementation of a program, you can leave some of the functionality as an exercise for the reader; most employers don't appreciate that solution! In the original implementation of the quantum file method, I left the automatic resizing of arrays as such an exercise. However, the development of the dynamic hashing algorithm we will encounter later required such a facility, so I was forced to implement it myself. This required a number of changes to the `MainObjectArray` class which supplies the underpinnings of the persistent arrays used in the project, i.e., the variable-length string array type (accessed via the `FlexArray` class) and the `PersistArrayUlong` class that provides access to very large persistent arrays of unsigned longs.

One of these changes was to add a new function `GrowMainObject` (listing 7.5, lines 372–431), which expands the number of accessible elements in a main object. To simplify the accounting needed to keep track of the sizes of all of the little pointer arrays, I've decided always to allocate a little pointer array to the largest size that will fit into a quantum. However, setting the accessible size of an array to the actual number of elements allocated for its little pointer arrays has the drawback that the user wouldn't be able to find out when his program accessed an element that is within the allocated size but outside the number of elements he specified when he created the array. Therefore, I've crafted a compromise: when an array is created, I set the number of accessible elements to the number the user specifies[121]; however, if the array is increased in size, the new size is always equal to the total allocation for all little pointer arrays. This means that if an array is expanded by a reference to an element that was already allocated but was outside the specified array size, `GrowMainObject`

---

121. There's one exception to this rule, for reasons described above: if he specifies 0 elements, I change it to 1.

simply resets the size to the number of elements contained in all little pointer arrays already extant. Otherwise, a new little pointer array is allocated, and the big pointer array is updated to reflect the change.

I also added functions `GetMainObjectElementCount` and `GetMainObjectMaxElementCount` (listing 7.5, lines 572–581 and 583–592), which are used in the normal constructor and `operator[ ]` overloading function of `FlexArray`. When an attempt is made, via `FlexArray::operator[ ]` (listing 7.5, lines 624–631), to store an element past the current end of the array, `GrowMainObject` is called to increase the size as needed to accommodate the new element.[122]

Although this may seem simple enough, you may object that I've left out one important step in `FlexArray::operator[ ]`: what about that check to ensure that the element index doesn't exceed the maximum specified when the array was created? This brings us to the delicate topic of error handling.

Well-founded Assertions

The "right" way to handle an error such as trying to expand an array beyond its pre-programmed limit is to throw a C++ exception. Unfortunately, the design of an exception-handling mechanism for this program is outside the scope of this book, which is intended to introduce and explain algorithms, not design and implement industrial-grade software. In addition, compiler support for C++ exceptions isn't well developed yet; in particular, version 3.1 of Borland C++, the compiler I've used to develop the software in this chapter, doesn't have exception support.

In the absence of the "right" answer, what can we do? I've found the use of **asserts** helpful in the development of the C++ quantum file code; for an example of how to implement this error-trapping mechanism, see listing 7.5, lines 9–15. Asserts are used to specify conditions that should always be true at certain places in the code; when the program is compiled in "debug mode", a certain symbol such as DEBUG is `#defined`, which causes the assert macro to generate a statement that checks the condition that should hold and call an error-reporting routine if it doesn't hold.

An example of an assert is the statement `qfassert(p_ElementIndex < m_MaxElementCount);` (listing 7.5, line 626). As described above, if DEBUG is `#defined`, this statement is a macro call that effectively does nothing if the expression in the parentheses is "true" (i.e., nonzero). Otherwise, it executes a function call to an error-reporting function, here `QFAssertFail` (listing 7.13, lines 8–14). The error-reporting function then displays an error message based on the line number and filename where the `qfassert` macro call occurred and takes some action to handle the error; in this case, it generates an `int 3` instruction to enter the debugger.

This is useful behavior if we're running the program under a debugger. However, what if we're ready to send the program out to be used? In that case, we compile the

---

122. The method of operation of `operator[ ]` code and its auxiliary functions is anything but intuitively obvious. I explain how this all works starting on page 323.

program in "production mode" (also known as "release mode"), in which DEBUG isn't defined, so that the assert macro generates nothing at all. Of course, this means that if the error occurs in a "production" version of the program, it will not be trapped. Is this the best we can do?

The arguments in favor of this approach are basically four: first, testing should be exhaustive enough that this won't ever happen; second, there's nothing reasonable for the program to do if it ever does happen; third, it's better for the program to keep executing than to report an error and stop; and, fourth, executing the check takes time, thus slowing down the program.

The argument in favor of doing the check anyway is that it's better to have the program fail at a known place than to have the error propagate until it fails somewhere else where the error is harder to trace. However, in the case of a program that has to keep running no matter what, the only answer is to make sure that it won't fail completely even if such a problem erupts; of course, this is a lot easier to say than it is to do.

The best approach is quite dependent on the exact circumstances. Asserts aren't intended to handle conditions that could ever occur in a working program, but to trap program errors. As such, you have to make the decision whether the additional error checking of an assert is needed (and useful) at run time or can be dispensed with after thorough testing.

Running on Empty

After this short dissertation on error handling, let's get back to some code. Both CreateMainObject (discussed above) and GrowMainObject use a utility function called FindEmptyBlock (lines 115–141), which uses the member variable m_CurrentLowestFreeBlock to reduce the amount of time needed to find a free block as the file fills up. Each time that a free block with a block number less than the current value is created or located, m_CurrentLowestFreeBlock is updated to point to that block, and FindEmptyBlock starts at that location when looking for an empty block. FindEmptyBlock has an understandable resemblance to FindSpaceForItem, since both of them search the free space list looking for a quantum with a certain amount of space available; however, this resemblance misled me into introducing a bug in FindEmptyBlock. The problem came from the fact that I was using m_CurrentLowestFreeBlock to determine the starting block and element for searching the free space list before entering the outer loop, rather than initializing the loop indices in the for statements. This worked properly on the first time through the outer loop, which steps through all the blocks, but when all the elements of the first block had been read and the outer loop index was incremented to refer to the next block, the inner index was left unchanged rather than being reset to 0 to address the first element of the new block. This would have showed itself in some unpleasant way after the first 1024 blocks were allocated to objects, but luckily I found it by examination before that occurred.

Assembly Instructions Included

After the main functionality of the demonstration program for the new quantum file implementation was finished, I used the Turbo Profiler™ to find hot spots that might be cooled off by some assembly language assistance. As indicated by the profiling results, I wrote the routines `BlockMove`, `AdjustOffset`, `FindUnusedItem`, and `FindBuffer`, which are displayed in listing 7.11.[123]

Let's take a look at these routines that take up so much of the CPU time, starting with `BlockMove`, (lines 8–52), which an inspection of the figure indicates is rendered in C/C++ as just a call to `memmove`. You may be surprised to find that such a basic function can be significantly improved upon; the key here is the use of the i386 instruction `rep movsd`.[124] For those of you who aren't Intel assembly language programmers, this instruction moves `dwords` (i.e., four-byte memory doublewords) from the address pointed to by the source register pair (`ds:si`) to the address pointed to by the destination pair (`es:di`) until the count in cx is used up. Since this instruction is not available on processors below the i386, many run time libraries don't use it, so they will be compatible with lesser processors. However, it can provide a significant performance boost for programs that do a large number of big block transfers, since it takes no longer per repetition than the two-byte version `rep movsw` but executes only half as many repetitions. Therefore, it should run approximately twice as fast as the standard library function `memmove`, for a block long enough to make the start-up overhead unimportant.

Although this analysis seemed obvious enough, I prefer to check such projections against reality. When I did so, I was quite surprised to discover that the relative speeds of `BlockMove` and `memmove`, for a constant block size, varied significantly from the expected 2:1 ratio, depending on some characteristic(s) of the source and destination addresses. In some cases, the ratio was indeed 2:1, but other cases showed a ratio of 1.5 to 1, and yet others came out to almost 3:1! Especially to a high-level language programmer, it may not be obvious why the addresses of the source and destination memory blocks would have any effect at all on the time taken to copy data from one to the other. This is due to the effects of memory alignment, as will be evident in due course.[125]

---

123. Of course, I have provided versions of these routines written in C and compatible with C++, for those of you who want to run this code in a different environment; the assembly language versions are designed to work under DOS, using Borland C++ version 3.1 in a memory model that has large data pointers, although they should be fairly easily adapted to other Intel 80x86 processor environments.

124. Interestingly enough this instruction isn't in the repertoire of the in-line assembler in BC++ 3.1. Lines 41 and 80 are the literal bytes that represent that instruction in the i386 instruction set.

125. If you already understand how block transfers of memory work, you might want to skip to the discussion on page 309.

The Top and the Bottom

Let's start from the beginning: suppose we want to move some bytes from one location in memory to another, and we don't want to use the library function **memmove**. Figure 7.8 shows a C program to do that simple task.

Of course, this is very inefficient, but that's not what I want to point out. This **MoveMem** function will work correctly as called in the main program shown in figure 7.8. But what if the program looks like figure 7.9?

If you were to compile and run the program in figure 7.9, you would find that its output consists of ten zeros. The reason, of course, is that on the first time through the loop in **MoveMem**, we copy a character from location 0 in the **source** array to location 1 in the same array. Therefore, when we pick up the character from location 1 in the **source** array, so that we can move it to the next location, it has already

---

Figure 7.8 *Dangerous memory move code*

```
#include "stdio.h"

#define COUNT 10

int MoveMem(char *Destination, char *Source, int count);

main()
{
    char dest[COUNT];
    char source[COUNT];
    int i;

    for (i = 0; i < COUNT; i ++)
        source[i] = i;

    MoveMem(dest,source,COUNT);

    for (i = 0; i < COUNT; i ++)
        printf("%d ",dest[i]);

}

int MoveMem(char *Destination, char *Source, int
count)
{
    int i;

    for (i = 0; i < count; i ++)
        Destination[i] = Source[i];

    return count;
}
```

---

been overwritten. Happily, this is easy to solve, by applying the following rule: if the destination address is higher than the source, start the move at the end of the respective arrays; otherwise, start the move at the beginning of the arrays. While this is necessary only if the two memory blocks overlap, it's easier to follow the rule all the time than to figure out whether there is an overlap. The program in figure 7.10 handles these cases correctly.

This digression was necessary because the same rules apply even when we are writing an assembly language program to move a block of memory much faster than the C version ever could; that is, we need separate code to handle the cases of "move higher" and "move lower". Although there doesn't seem to be any reason why one of these cases should execute noticeably faster than the other one, my first routine executed "move higher" considerably more slowly than "move lower", as was also true of the Borland run time library function `memmove`.

Figure 7.9 *Dangerous memory move code, second example*

```
#include "stdio.h"

#define COUNT 10

int MoveMem(char *Destination, char *Source, int count);

main()
{
    char dest[COUNT];
    char source[COUNT];
    int i;

    for (i = 0; i < COUNT; i ++)
        source[i] = i;

    MoveMem(source+1,source,COUNT-1);

    for (i = 0; i < COUNT; i ++)
        printf("%d ",source[i]);

}

int MoveMem(char *Destination, char *Source, int count)
{
    int i;

    for (i = 0; i < count; i ++)
        Destination[i] = Source[i];

    return count;
}
```

Figure 7.10 *Safe memory move code*

```c
#include "stdio.h"

#define COUNT 10

int MoveMem(char *Destination, char *Source, int count);

main()
{
    char dest[COUNT];
    char source[COUNT];
    int i;

    for (i = 0; i < COUNT; i ++)
        source[i] = i;

    MoveMem(dest,source,COUNT);
    MoveMem(source+1,source,COUNT-1);
    MoveMem(dest,dest+1,COUNT-1);

    for (i = 0; i < COUNT; i ++)
        printf("%d ",source[i]);

    printf("\n");

    for (i = 0; i < COUNT; i ++)
        printf("%d ",dest[i]);

}

int MoveMem(char *Destination, char *Source, int count)
{
    int i;

    if (Destination > Source)
        {
        for (i = count - 1; i >= 0; i —)
            Destination[i] = Source[i];
        }
    else
        {
        for (i = 0; i < count; i ++)
            Destination[i] = Source[i];
        }

    return count;
}
```

Where the Wild Goose Goes

My first hypothesis was that loading and storing memory words (or doublewords) at successively lower addresses was being handled in a suboptimal manner by the i486 caching hardware. This was probably a reasonable guess, given the results of an early version of my test program, "testasm.cpp", with the original version of BlockMove. The timings for this test are in figure 7.11.

However, my hypothesis turned out not to be true; after much experimentation and exploration, I discovered that the slow execution of my BlockMove "move higher" algorithm was actually caused by improper memory alignment. You see, the destination address that I selected to test the "move higher" was an odd memory address, whereas the "move lower" test moved data to an address divisible by four. Why does this matter? Because the memory in i386 and higher Intel processors is physically organized as doublewords on aligned memory boundaries: that is, each doubleword starts at an address divisible by four. In order to write a doubleword at an address not divisible by four, the processor has to fetch the two doublewords that will contain portions of the memory operand, combine the operand with the remaining bytes of the two doublewords fetched from memory, and then store the two modified doublewords back into memory. This takes far longer than simply storing a doubleword operand at an aligned boundary, which requires no reads and only one write.

Perhaps the diagram in figure 7.12 will make this clearer. The double lines indicate the natural organization of memory, while the single lines separate bytes. The speed degradation caused by writing misaligned memory operands is due to the requirement to read and write two physical doublewords to store four bytes at an odd address. Let's say our program stores the doubleword in the line labeled "Misaligned doubleword to be stored" into the physical memory at address 1. First, the processor

Figure 7.11 *First* BlockMove *algorithm: 10000 moves of 2000 bytes each on a 486/66DX2*

Destination Address	Routine	
	memmove	BlockMove
Lower	23	12
Higher	35	22

Figure 7.12 *Misaligned and aligned memory accesses*

	0	1	2	3	4	5	6	7
Byte addresses	0	1	2	3	4	5	6	7
Physical memory organization	3	1	4	1	5	9	2	6
Misaligned doubleword to be stored		2	7	2	8			
		1	2	3	4			
Aligned doubleword to be stored	1	4	9	3				
	0	1	2	3				

retrieves the doubleword starting at 0. Then it replaces bytes 1–3 in that word with "272" and stores that doubleword back at location 0. Next it retrieves the doubleword starting at address 4 and replaces its first byte with the "8" from the misaligned operand. Finally, it stores the resulting doubleword starting at location 4. Contrast this with the simplicity of storing the doubleword labeled "Aligned doubleword to be stored"; in this case, the processor just stores the new value into the doubleword starting at location 0, as only that one memory doubleword is affected.

Assuming that the incentive to fix this problem is now evident, what can we do about it? After all, the memory addresses at which the operands are stored aren't under our control in the general case, so it seems that we're stuck with the misalignment penalty. Happily, this is not the case.

Odd Man Out

To illustrate how we can eliminate the misalignment penalty, an example should help clarify matters. Let's suppose that we need to move 15 bytes from address 1002 to address 1021. The situation is illustrated in figure 7.13, where "x" means "don't care".

We know that we don't want to just start fetching doublewords starting at 1002 and storing them starting at 1021, because that would cause the misalignment penalty described above. However, there is something else we can do; we can move the three bytes starting at 1002 to bytes 1021–1023, leaving us with the situation in figure 7.14, where "x" still means "don't care" and "*" means "already moved".

Now we can do the rest of the move by loading doublewords starting at 1005 and storing them starting at 1024. However, it might not be obvious that we've gained anything; aren't we still doing misaligned accesses?

On i386 machines, which don't have internal caches, misaligned reads are penalized in much the same way that writes are, so we're not home free; however, it never hurts to make sure that at least the writes are aligned. As you can see from figures

Figure 7.13 *The alignment problem, part 1*

Address	Data
1000	x x 3 1
1004	4 1 5 9
1008	2 6 5 3
1012	5 8 9 7
1016	9 x x x
1020	x x x x
1024	x x x x
1028	x x x x
1032	x x x x

7.15 and 7.16, the performance of `BlockMove` is usually much higher than that of `memmove` and can hold its own under any scenario.

The biggest payoff, however, comes with the i486 processor, whose internal cache effectively eliminates the penalty for reading misaligned doublewords but can't do anything about misaligned writes. But before we get to the results, let's take a look at the extra coding needed to deliver optimum performance.

Figure 7.14 *The alignment problem, part 2*

Address	Data
1000	x x * *
1004	* 1 5 9
1008	2 6 5 3
1012	5 8 9 7
1016	9 x x x
1020	x 3 1 4
1024	x x x x
1028	x x x x
1032	x x x x

Figure 7.15 *Fast* `BlockMove` *algorithm: 10,000 doubleword-aligned moves of 2000 bytes each on a 386/33*

Destination Address	Routine	
	memmove	BlockMove
Lower	41	21
Higher	84	21

Figure 7.16 *Fast* `BlockMove` *algorithm: 10,000 misaligned moves of 2000 bytes each on a 386/33*

Source Alignment	Destination Alignment	Routine	
		memmove	BlockMove
1	0	58	39
0	1	67	39
3	1	41	39
1	3	85	39

The Code

The code needed to do the alignment of the destination operand turns out not to be too difficult. There's no need to describe the adjustment for both "move lower" and "move higher", because they're very similar; since "move higher" is slightly more complicated, I'll describe that one. This code is in listing 7.11, starting at line 54. The first thing we have to do is to determine whether there are at least four bytes to move; if not, the adjustment code might overrun the number of bytes to be moved, so we don't execute it. Next, at line 58, we test whether the destination is already aligned, by testing the low two bits for zero and proceeding to the main loop if the test succeeds. Now we're up to line 61, where we start a loop that decrements the source and destination pointers, gets a byte from the source, moves it to the destination, decrements the counter, and then checks whether the destination pointer is aligned. If it is, we exit the alignment loop and set up for the main loop by adjusting the source and destination pointers to point to the starting addresses of the doublewords that will be accessed by the rep movsd instruction.

The payoff for this slight extra complication is shown in figures 7.17 and 7.18.

As we expect, the aligned moves were unaffected by these changes, but there's no longer any penalty for misaligned moves. By the way, tests on other machines, including one with a Pentium CPU, generally support the superiority of the BlockMove function over memmove; however, there are major discrepancies in the actual times on a different brand of machine with the same 486–66/DX2 processor as

Figure 7.17 *Fast* BlockMove *algorithm: 10,000 doubleword-aligned moves of 2000 bytes each on a 486/66DX2*

Destination Address	Routine memmove	Routine BlockMove
Lower	23	12
Higher	34	11

Figure 7.18 *Fast* BlockMove *algorithm: 10,000 misaligned moves of 2000 bytes each on a 486/66DX2*

Source Alignment	Destination Alignment	Routine memmove	Routine BlockMove
1	0	23	12
0	1	35	11
3	1	23	12
1	3	34	12

in my home machine! Obviously, the design of the cache and memory architecture can greatly affect performance at this low level; interestingly enough, the i486 machine whose times were approximately twice as fast as my home machine on this test is MUCH slower in actual use, due to its lack of a local bus architecture. This merely illustrates the well-known fact that low-level benchmarks are often misleading as an index of application-level performance.

One more point of interest: as you will note from these figures, the Borland C++ memmove doesn't perform as well when moving data to higher addresses, whether aligned or misaligned. I don't know the reason for this discrepancy; however, that's their problem rather than mine!

Other Assembly Routines

The other assembly language routines are much more straightforward. Let's go over them briefly, paying attention to their individual quirks of implementation. First, we have AdjustOffset (listing 7.11, lines 94–126), which is used to update the elements in the ItemIndex in a quantum after an item has been increased or decreased in size. This routine retrieves each element of the item index, extracts its offset part, updates the offset, and merges the result back into the element in the index. This routine obviously is quite dependent on the structure of an item index element, but could be updated fairly easily if that were to change.

The next assembly routine is FindUnusedItem (lines 129–181), which searches an ItemIndex for an item that is currently marked as unused and can therefore be reused for a new item. As with AdjustOffset, this routine has no notable characteristics other than its dependence on the format of an ItemIndex entry and could be easily updated if the format changed.

Finally, we have FindBuffer (lines 184–223), which searches a list of block numbers to find a given block number. This routine would require a bit more work than the previous ones if a block number were to increase in size beyond 16 bits, as it uses a rep scasw instruction to scan a list of words to find the block number. If we went to a 32-bit block number, the change would be a simple substitution of rep scasd, the doubleword scan instruction; however, if we were to change the block number to any other size, such as 24 bits, we'd have to write a programmed loop to search the list.

Paying the Piper

Since this is a book on writing better programs, perhaps we should take a look at the performance of the C++ version of the quantum file access method compared to the C version. The performance of the original C++ version was about one-third that of the C version; when I started optimizing the C++ version, I hoped to be able to match the C version with the aid of careful tuning, including the assembly language routines mentioned above. Unfortunately, I was unable to meet this goal; the timing of the "blocktst.cpp" test program vs. the "oldquant.cpp" program that uses the C version of the algorithm indicates that the final version of the C++ code has only about 83% of the performance of the C program. Is the extra convenience and lower memory requirement of the C++ program worth this overhead?

I think the reusability and elegance of the C++ language are worth the CPU performance overhead in most cases. As for myself, I intend to avoid C programming in the future if possible, after having exploited some of the power of object-oriented programming.

Heavenly Hash

Now that we have looked at some of the interesting implementation details of the C++ version of the quantum file access method, as well as the performance comparisons with the C version, it's time to revisit the topic of hash coding, or "hashing" for short, which we previously discussed in Chapter 2. Hashing is a way to store and retrieve large numbers of records rapidly, by calculating an address close to the one where the record is actually stored. However, we saw in that discussion that traditional disk-based methods of hashing have several deficiencies: variable-length records cannot be stored in the hash table; deleting records and reusing the space is difficult; the time needed to store and retrieve a record in a file increases greatly as the file fills up, due to overflows between previously separated areas of the file; and most serious of all, the maximum capacity of the file cannot be changed after its creation. The first of these problems can be handled by having fixed-length hash records pointing to variable-length records in another file, although this increases the access time. The second problem can be overcome with some extra work in the implementation to mark deleted records for later reuse. The third problem can be alleviated significantly by the use of "last-come, first-served" hashing.[126] However, until relatively recently, the fourth problem, a fixed maximum capacity for a given file, seemed intractable.

Of course, nothing stops us from creating a new, bigger, hash table and copying the records from the old file into it, rehashing them as we go along. In fact, one of the questions at the end of Chapter 2 asks how we could handle a file that becomes full, as an off-line process, and the "suggested approaches" section in Chapter 8 proposes that exact answer.

However, this solution to the problem of a full hash table has two serious drawbacks. For one thing, we have to have two copies of the file (one old and one new) while we're doing this update, which can take up a large amount of disk space tem-

---

126. For a description of "last-come, first-served" hashing, see Patricio V. Poblete and J. Ian Munro, "Last-Come-First-Served Hashing", in *Journal of Algorithms* 10(October 1989), 228–248, or my article "Galloping Algorithms", in *Windows Tech Journal,* 2(February 1993), 40–43.

porarily. More important in many applications, this "big bang" file maintenance approach won't work for a file that has to be available all of the time. Without doing a lot of extra work, we can't update the data during this operation, which might take a long time (perhaps several hours or even days) if the file is big. Is it possible to increase the size of the file after its creation without incurring these penalties, and still gain the traditional advantages of hashing, i.e., extremely fast access to large amounts of data by key?

Until a few months ago, I would have said that it wasn't possible. Therefore, I was quite intrigued when I ran across an article describing a hashing algorithm that can dynamically resize the hash table as needed during execution, without any long pauses in execution.[127] Unfortunately, the implementation described in the article relies on the use of linked lists to hold the records pointed to by the hash slots. While this is acceptable for in-memory hash tables,[128] such an implementation is not appropriate for disk-based hash tables, where minimizing the number of disk seeks is critical to achieving good performance.

Nonetheless, it is a fascinating algorithm that obviously deserves wider use, so I decided to investigate it.

Just Another Link in the Chain

According to the the Griswold and Townsend article, Per-Ake Larson adapted an algorithm called "linear dynamic hashing", previously limited to accessing external files, to make it practical for use with in-memory tables.[129] The result, appropriately enough, is called "Larson's algorithm". How does it work?

First, let's look at the "slot" method of handling overflow used by many in-memory hash table algorithms, including Larson's algorithm. To store an element in the hash table, we might proceed as follows, assuming the element to be stored contains a "next" pointer to point to another such element:

1. The key of each element to be stored is translated into a slot number to which the element should be attached, via the hashing algorithm.
2. The "next" pointer of the element to be attached to the slot is set to the current contents of the slot's "first" pointer, which is initialized to zero when the table is created.
3. The slot's "first" pointer is set to the address of the element being attached to the slot.

127. William G. Griswold and Gregg M. Townsend, "The Design and Implementation of Dynamic Hashing for Sets and Tables in Icon". *Software Practice and Experience*, 23(April 1993), 351–367.

128. Such tables must really be in physical memory, though; having them swapped to disk in a virtual memory implementation produces terrible performance.

129. P.-A. Larson, "Dynamic Hash Tables". *Communications of the ACM*, 31(1988).

The result of this procedure is that the new element is linked into the chain attached to the slot, as its first element.

To retrieve an element, given its key, we simply use the hashing algorithm to get the slot number, and then follow the chain from that slot until we find the element. If the element isn't found by the time we get to a 0 pointer, it's not in the table.

This algorithm is easy to implement, but as written it has a performance problem: namely, with a fixed number of slots, the chains attached to each slot get longer in proportion to the number of elements in the table, which means that the retrieval time increases proportionately to the number of elements added. However, if we could increase the number of slots in proportion to the number of elements added, then the average time to find an element wouldn't change, no matter how many elements were added to the table. The problem is how we can find elements we've already added to the table if we increase the number of slots. It may not be obvious why this is a problem; for example, can't we just leave them where they are and add the new elements into the new slots?

Unfortunately, this won't work. The reason is that when we want to look up an element, we don't generally know when the element was added, so as to tell what "section" of the hash file it resides in. The only piece of information we're guaranteed to have available is the key of the element, so we had better be able to find an element given only its key. Of course, we could always rehash every element in the table to fit the new number of slots, but we've already seen that this can cause serious delays in file availability. Larson's contribution was to find an efficient way to increase the number of slots in the table without having to relocate every element when we do it.

Relocation Assistance

The basic idea is reasonably simple, as are most great ideas, once you understand them.[130] For our example, let's assume that the key is an unsigned value; we start out with 8 slots, all marked "active"; and we want to limit the average number of elements per slot to 6.

This means that in order to store an element in the table, we have to generate a number between 0 and 7, representing the number of the slot to which we will chain the new element being stored. For purposes of illustration, we'll simply divide the key by the number of slots and take the remainder.[131] For reasons which will become apparent shortly, the actual algorithm looks like this:

---

130. Of course, thinking them up in the first place is a little harder!

131. This step alone will probably not provide a good distribution of records with a number of slots that is a power of two; in such cases, it effectively discards all the high-order bits of the key. In our example program, in order to improve the distribution, we precede this step by one that uses all of the bits in the input value. However, the principle is the same.

1. Divide the key by the number of slots (8), taking the remainder. This will result in a number from 0 to the number of slots - 1, i.e., 0–7 in this case.
2. If the remainder is greater than or equal to the number of "active" slots (8), subtract one-half the number of slots (4).

You will notice that the way the parameters are currently set, the second rule will never be activated, since the remainder can't be greater than or equal to 8; we'll see the reason for the second rule shortly.

Now we're set up to handle up to 48 elements. On the 49th element, we should add another slot to keep the average number per slot from exceeding 6. What do we do to the hash function to allow us to access those elements we have already stored?

We double the number of slots, making it 16, recording that new number of slots allocated; then we increase the number of "active" slots, bringing that number to 9. The hash calculation now acts like this:

1. Divide the key by the number of slots (16), taking the remainder; the result will be between 0 and 15 inclusive.
2. If the remainder is more than the number of active slots (9), subtract one-half the number of slots (8).

This modified hashing algorithm will spread newly added elements over nine slots rather than eight, since the possible slot values now range from 0 to 8 rather than 0 to 7. This keeps the number of elements per slot from increasing as we add new elements, but how do we retrieve elements that were already in the table?

This is where the brilliance of this algorithm comes into play. Only one slot has elements that might have to be moved under the new hashing algorithm, and that is the first slot in the table! Why is this so?

The analysis isn't really very difficult. Let's look at the elements in the second slot (i.e., slot number 1). We know that their hash codes under the old algorithm were all equal to 1, or they wouldn't be in that slot. That is, the remainder after dividing their keys by 8 was always 1, which means that the binary value of the remainder always ended in 001. Now let's see what the possible hash values are under the new algorithm. We divide the key by 16 and take the remainder. This is equivalent to taking the last four bits of the remainder. However, the last three bits of the remainder after dividing by 16 and the last three bits of the remainder after dividing by 8 have to be the same.[132] Therefore, we have to examine only the fourth bit (the 8's place) of the

---

132. This may be obvious, but if it's not, here's a demonstration
1. Let's call the value to be hashed x.
2. $y = x >> 4$ [divide by 16]
3. $z = y << 4$ [multiply result by 16; result must have low four bits = 0]
4. $x \% 16 = x - z$ [definition of "remainder"; result is low four bits of x]
Obviously, an analogous result holds true for the remainder after dividing by 8; therefore, the low three bits of these two values must be the same.

remainder to calculate the new hash code. There are only two possible values of that bit, 0 and 1. If the value of that bit is 0, we have the same hash code as we had previously, so we obviously can look up the element successfully. However, if the value is 1, the second rule tells us to compare the hash code, which is 1001 binary or 9 decimal against the number of active slots (9). Since the first is greater than or equal to the second, we subtract 8, getting 1 again; therefore, the lookup will always succeed. The same considerations apply to all the other slots previously occupied in the range 2–7. There's only one where this analysis breaks down, and that's slot 0. Why is this one different?

Because slot 8 is actually available; therefore, the second rule won't apply. In this case, we do have to know whether an element is in slot 0 or 8. While this will be automatic for newly added elements using the new hash code, we still have the old elements in slot 0 to contend with; on the average, half of them will need to be moved to slot 8. This is easy to fix; all we have to do is to retrieve each element from slot 0 and recalculate its hash value with the new parameters. If the result is 0, we put it back in slot 0; if the result is 8, we move it to slot 8.

Now we're okay until we have to add the 57th element to the hash table; we're going to have to add another slot to keep the average chain length to 6. Happily, all we have to do is to increase the number of active slots by 1 (to 10) and rehash the elements in slot 1. It works just like the example above; none of the slots 2–7 is affected by the change, because the second rule "folds" all of their hash calculations into their current slots.

When we have added a total of 96 elements, the number of "active" slots and the total number of slots will both be 16, so we will be back to a situation similar to the one we were in before we added our first expansion slot. What do we do when we have to add the 97th element? We double the total number of slots again and start over as before.[133] This can go on until the number of slots gets to be too big to fit in the size of integer in which we maintain it, or until we run out of memory, whichever comes first.

Of course, if we want to handle a lot of data, we will probably run out of memory before we run out of slot numbers.[134] Since the ability to retrieve any record in any size table in constant time, on the average, would certainly be very valuable when dealing with very large databases, I considered that it was worth trying to adapt this algorithm to disk-based hash tables. All that was missing was a way to store the chains of records using a storage method appropriate for disk files.

---

133. As it turns out, there's no reason to actually allocate storage for all the new slots when we double the current maximum count, because the only one that's immediately needed is the first new one created. Accordingly, Larson's algorithm allocates them in blocks of a fixed size as they're needed, which is effectively the way my adaptation works as well.

134. In case you're thinking that the availability of virtual memory will solve this problem, you may be surprised to discover that the performance of such an algorithm in virtual memory is likely to be extremely poor. I provide an example of this phenomenon in my previously cited article "Galloping Algorithms".

Making a Quantum Leap

Upon further consideration, I realized that the quantum file access method could be used to store a variable-length "storage element" pointed to by each hash slot, with the rest of the algorithm implemented pretty much as it was in the article. This would make it possible to store a very large number of strings by key and get back any of them with an average of a little more than one disk access, without having to know how big the file would be when we created it. This algorithm also has the pleasant effect of making deletions fairly simple to implement, with the file storage of deleted elements automatically reclaimed as they are removed.

Contrary to my usual practice elsewhere in this book, I have not developed a sample "application" program, but have instead opted to write a test program to validate the algorithm. This was very useful to me during the development of the algorithm; after all, this implementation of dynamic hashing is supposed to be able to handle hundreds of thousands of records while maintaining rapid access, so it is very helpful to be able to demonstrate that it can indeed do that. The test program is "hashtest.cpp" (listing 7.1); it stores and retrieves strings by a nine-digit key, stored as an unsigned long value. In order to be able to store more entries than the 64K indexing limit of our 16-bit implementation, all strings having the same hash code are combined into one "storage element" in the quantum file system; each storage element is addressed by one "hash slot". The current version of the dynamic hashing algorithm used by hashtest.exe allocates one hash slot for every six strings in the file; since the average individual string length is about 60 characters, and there are six bytes of overhead for each string in a storage element (two bytes for the length and four bytes for the key value), this means that the average storage element will be approximately 400 characters long. A larger element packing factor than six strings per element would produce a smaller hash table and would therefore be more space efficient. However, the current implementation of the dynamic hashing algorithm does not have any provision for a storage element to be split into two quantum file elements; therefore, to minimize the probability of any element becoming too large to fit into a quantum, I experimented with a few values, finally picking 6 as a reasonably safe compromise between space efficiency and the chance of an excessively long storage element. Using this packing factor, I have been able to load 250,000 strings into a quantum file without any of the storage elements exceeding the length of a quantum.

Of course, in order to run meaningful tests, we have to do more than store records in the hash file; we also have to retrieve what has been stored, which means that we have to store the keys someplace so that we can use them again to retrieve records corresponding to those keys. However, even if we limit our test to 100,000 records, we will probably run out of memory on a DOS machine trying to save 100,000 keys of four bytes each in memory; in addition, keeping the stored keys in RAM means that they will have to be read from the input file on each run. In early versions of hashtest.cpp, I kept only every tenth record's key in memory, in order not to run out of space, but this partial solution still required reading the input file to get the keys again every time we want to retrieve data from the hash file; clearly, it would be better to save all the keys where we could access them efficiently. So I decided to use the quantum file storage to implement a persistent array of unsigned long values, and store the keys in such an array.

Persistence Pays Off

It was surprisingly easy to implement a persistent array of unsigned long values, for which I defined a typedef of Ulong, mostly to save typing.[135]   As you can see from the listings of "persist.h" and "persist.cpp" (listings 7.6 and 7.7, respectively), not too much code is involved, and most of that code is fairly straightforward. However, we get a lot out of these relatively few lines of code; these arrays are not only persistent, but they also automatically expand to any size up to and including the maximum size of a quantum file; with the current maximum of 32 MB, a maximum size PersistentArrayUlong could contain approximately 8,000,000 elements! Of course, we don't store each element directly in a separate addressable entry within a main object, as this would be inappropriate for two reasons: first, we can only have 64K elements in a main object; and, second, the space overhead per item is 6 bytes, which is larger than the Ulongs we want to store! Instead, we employ a two-level system similar to the one used in the dynamic hashing algorithm; the quantum file system stores "segments" of data, each one containing as many Ulongs as will fit in a quantum. To store or retrieve an element, we determine which segment the element belongs to and access the element by its offset in that segment, as you will see in the code for StoreElement and GetElement.

Before we can use a PersistentArrayUlong, we have to construct it. The default constructor (listing 7.7, lines 8–11) doesn't actually create a usable array; it is only there to allow us to declare a PersistentArrayUlong before we want to use it. When we really want to construct a usable array (lines 17–30), we provide a pointer to the quantum file in which it is to be stored, along with a name for the array. The object directory of that quantum file is searched for a main object with the name specified in the constructor; if it is found, the construction is complete. Otherwise, a new object is created with one element, expandable to fill up the entire file system if necessary.

To store an element in the array we have created, we can use StoreElement (lines 32–62). You will notice from this routine's prototype that the element number, p_Index, is a Ulong, rather than an unsigned short, so that we can address the potentially large number of elements contained in a PersistentArrayUlong. This routine first calculates which segment of the array contains the element we need to retrieve, and the element number within that segment. Then, if we are running the "debugging" version (i.e., asserts are enabled), it checks whether the segment number is within the maximum range we set up when we created the array. This test should never fail unless there is something wrong with the calling routine (or its callers), so

---

135. Given the quantum file access method, that is!

that the element number passed in is absurdly large. As discussed above, with all such conditional checks, we have to try to make sure that our testing is good enough to find any errors that might cause this to happen; with a "release" version of the program, this would be a fatal error.

Next, we check whether the segment number we need is already allocated to the array; if not, we increase the number of segments as needed by calling `GrowMainObject`, but don't actually initialize any new segments until they're accessed, so that "sparse" arrays won't take up as much room as ones that are filled in completely. Next, we get a copy of the segment containing the element to be updated; if it's of zero length, we have to allocate a new segment and fill it with zeros. At this point, we are ready to create an `AccessVector` called `TempUlongVector` of type `Ulong` and use it as a "template" (no pun intended) to allow access to the element we want to modify.[136] Since `AccessVector` has the semantics of an array, we can simply set the `ElementNumberth` element of `TempUlongVector` to the value of the input argument `p_Element`; the result of this is to place the new element value into the correct place in the `TempVector` array. Finally, we store `TempVector` back into the main object, replacing the old copy of the segment.

Retrieving an element via `GetElement` (lines 64–78) is considerably simpler, as you might expect. First, we calculate the segment number and element number, and check (via `qfassert`) whether the segment number is within the range of allocated segments; if it isn't, we have committed the programming error of accessing an uninitialized value. Assuming this test is passed, we retrieve the segment, set up the temporary vector `TempUlongVector` to allow access to the segment as an array of `Ulongs`, and return the value in the `ElementNumberth` element of the array.

All this is very well if we want to write things like "`Y.Put(100,100000L)`" or "`X = Y.Get(100)`", to store or retrieve the 100th element of the `Y` "array", respectively. But wouldn't it be much nicer to be able to write "`Y[100] = 100000L`" or "`X = Y[100]`" instead?

In Resplendent Array

Clearly, that would be a big improvement in the syntax; as it happens, it's not hard to make such references possible, with the addition of only a few lines of code.[137] Unfortunately, this code is not the most straightforward, but the syntactic improve-

---

136. As its name is intended to suggest, an `AccessVector` is a means of accessing a prealлоcated area of memory. The basic notion is to be able to access the data as an array in much the same manner as with a regular `Vector`; the difference is that with an `AccessVector`, the data are in some fixed location such as a buffer, rather than being assigned during a copy or create. As a result, the copy constructor is defaulted, as is assignment and the destructor, and there is no `SetSize` function such as exists for "regular" `Vectors`. The code for this template class is in listing 7.14, lines 157–209.

137. This is also from James Coplien's book, mentioned earlier.

ment that it provides is worth the trouble. The key is the implementation of `operator[ ]` (lines 96–99), which returns a temporary value of a type that behaves differently in the context of an "lvalue" reference (i.e., a "write") than it does when referenced as an "rvalue" (i.e, a "read"). In order to follow how this process works, let's use the example in figure 7.19.

The first question to be answered is how the compiler decodes the following line:

```
Save[1000000L] = 1234567L;
```

According to the definition of `PersistentArrayUlong::operator[ ]`, this operator returns a `PersistentArrayUlongRef` that is constructed with the two parameters `*this` and `p_Index`, where the former is the `PersistentArrayUlong` object for which `operator[ ]` was called (i.e., Save), and the latter is the value inside the `[ ]`, which in this case is 1000000L. What is this return value? To answer this question, we have to look at lines 80–83. What this constructor does is set `m_PAU` to a reference to `p_PAU` and `m_Index` to the value of `p_Index`, so the resulting object that will be returned from the `operator[ ]` call will be a `PersistentArrayUlongRef` with those values. Therefore, the compiler-generated code looks something like this, so far:

```
PersistentArrayUlongRef T(Save,1000000L);
T = 1234567L;
```

Figure 7.19 *Persistent array example*

```
/*TITLE persistent array example program*/

/****keyword-flag*** "%v %f %n" */
/* "4 8-Mar-94,21:50:10 ASMFUNC.CPP" */

/****revision-history****/
/****revision-history****/

#include "common.h"

main()
{
    PersistentArrayUlong Save;
    QuantumFile QF;
    Ulong TestValue;

    QF.Open("testx.qnt",100);
    Save = PersistentArrayUlong(&QF,"Save");
    Save[1000000L] = 1234567L;
    TestValue = Save[1000000L];
    printf("%lu\n",TestValue);
}
```

where T is an arbitrary name for a temporary object. The second of these lines is then translated into a call to `PersistentArrayUlongRef::operator=` (lines 85–89), which will do the assignment operation. The generated code now looks something like this:

```
PersistentArrayUlongRef T(Save,1000000L);
T.operator=(1234567L);
```

The `operator=` code, as you can see from the listing, calls the `StoreElement` operation of `m_PAU`, which as we noted above is a reference to the original object `Save`; the arguments to that call are `m_Index`, a copy of the index supplied in the original `operator[]` call, and `p_Element`, which is the value specified in the `operator=` call. Thus, the result is the same as calling `Save.StoreElement(1000000L,1234567L)`, while the notation is that of a "normal" array access.

However, we've only handled the case where we're updating an element of the array. We also need to be able to retrieve values once they've been stored. To see how that works, let's follow the translation of the following line:

```
TestValue = Save[1000000L];
```

The process is fairly similar to what we've already done. The definition of `PersistentArrayUlong::operator[]` causes the compiler to generate code somewhat like the following:

```
PersistentArrayUlongRef T(Save,1000000L);
TestValue = T;
```

This time, however, rather than translating the second line into a call to `PersistentArrayUlongRef::operator=`, the compiler translates it into a call to `PersistentArrayUlongRef::operator Ulong`, a "conversion function" that allows a `PersistentArrayUlongRef` to be used where a `Ulong` is expected (lines 85–89). Therefore, the final generated code comes out something like this:

```
PersistentArrayUlongRef T(Save,1000000L);
TestValue = Ulong(T);
```

As should be evident by looking at the code for that conversion function, it merely calls the `GetElement` operation of `m_PAU`, which as we noted above is a reference to the original object `Save`, with the argument `m_Index`, which is a copy of the original element index. Thus, the result is the same as the statement `TestValue = Save.GetElement(1000000L)`, while the notation is that of a "normal" array access."

Before we move on to our next topic, I have a word of warning for you. If you use these "synthetic arrays" frequently, you may be tempted to inline the definitions of these auxiliary functions that make the array notation possible. I recommend that you don't do it, at least not without a lot of testing to make sure it works correctly. In the case of Borland C++ 3.1, the result appears to work but generates terrible memory leaks; as far as I can determine, the memory that isn't being freed is that belonging to the temporary objects that are created during the operation of these functions.

Some Fine Details

Now that we have solved the problem of storing all of the keys needed to read the records back, let's look at some of the other implementation details and problems I encountered in the process of getting the dynamic hashing algorithm and the "hashtest.cpp" test program to work.

During development of the test program, I discovered that running the tests on large numbers of records took a great deal of time; to generate a quantum file with 250,000 records in it might take four or five hours! Although this is actually pretty fast when one considers the amount of data being processed, I still didn't want to have to execute such a long-running program very many times. Therefore, the test program needed to have the capability of incrementally adding records to a preexisting quantum file. However, this meant that the test program had to be able to start somewhere in the middle of the input file, since adding the same records again and again wouldn't work; to prevent the list of records for each hash slot from growing too large for a quantum, duplicates had to be screened out.

As the test program is implemented, only two pieces of information need to be saved between runs in order to allow the addition of previously unused records to the quantum file: the index number in the **Save** array where the next key should be saved, and the offset into the input file where the next record begins. We don't have to save the name of the input file or the ASCII output file, since those are compiled into the program; of course, if the input file could change from one run to the next, the information as to where we stopped when reading records wouldn't be of much use. Since both of the data items that need to be preserved happen to be representable by an **unsigned long** value, I decided to use the beginning of the **Save** array to save them between runs. As you can see from listing 7.7, lines 8–11, the only difference between starting a new quantum file and adding records to an existing file is that when we start a new quantum file, the offset in the input file and the starting position for keys to be added to the **Save** array have to be reset to their initial values.

This ability to build on a previously created quantum file turned out to be quite useful in fixing an interesting bug that I ran into during capacity testing. The theoretical capacity of a quantum file with the current size parameters, when used to support the dynamic hashing algorithm, can be calculated as 64K (maximum hash slots) * 6 (average records per hash slot), or 393,216. Although I didn't necessarily need to demonstrate that this exact number of records could actually be stored and retrieved successfully, especially in view of the number of hours that my machine would be doing continual random disk accesses, I felt that it was important to check that a very large number of records could be accommodated. I selected 250,000 as a nice round number that wouldn't take quite so long to test, and started to run tests for every multiple of 50,000 records up to 250,000.[138] As each test was finished, I copied the resulting quantum file to a new name to continue the testing to the next higher multiple of 50,000 records.

Everything went along very nicely through the test that created a 150,000 record quantum file. Since adding 50,000 records takes about 45 minutes, I started the next test, which should have generated a 200,000 record file, and went away to do some chores. Imagine my surprise when I came back and found that the program had aborted somewhere between elements 196,000 and 197,000 due to the failure of an assert (listing 7.9, line 218). This assert checks that all the records in a hash slot that is being split have the correct hash code to be put into either the old slot or the new slot. Upon investigating the reason for this bug, I discovered that the problem was that `m_CurrentMaxSlotCount`, which is used in `DynamicHashArray::CalculateHash` to calculate the hash code according to Larson's algorithm (see lines 170–182), was an `unsigned` rather than an `unsigned long`. As a result, when 32K slots were occupied and it was time to double the value of `m_CurrentMaxSlotCount`, its new value, which should have been 64K, was 0. This caused the hashing function to generate incorrect values and thus caused the assert to fail. Changing the type of `m_CurrentMaxSlotCount` to `unsigned long` solved the problem.

However, there was one other place where the code had to change to implement this solution, and that was in the destructor for `DynamicHashArray`. The reason for this change is that the dynamic hashing algorithm needs to store some state information in a persistent form. To be specific, we need to keep track of the number of active slots, the current maximum slot number, and the number of elements remaining before the next slot is to be activated. With these data items saved in the file, the next time we open the file, we're ready to add more records while keeping the previously stored ones accessible.

Unfortunately, we don't have a convenient persistent numeric array to save these values in, and it doesn't make much sense to create one just for three values. However, we do have a persistent string array, which we're using to store the hashed records, and we can use the first element of that array to store ASCII representations of the three values that must be maintained in the file.[139] The normal constructor of the `DynamicHashArray` type (lines 140–168) retrieves these values from the first

---

138. You may wonder where I got such a large number of records to test with. They are extracted from a telephone directory on CD-ROM; unfortunately, I can't distribute them for your use, since I don't have permission to do so.

139. In order to hide this implementation detail from the rest of the dynamic hashing algorithm, the `GetString` and `PutString` functions increment the element index before using it. Thus, the request to read or update element 0 is translated into an operation on element 1, and so forth. To access element 0, the index is specified as -1.

element of the array if it has already been created, and the destructor (lines 127–138) stores them into the first element of the array; after the change to the type of m_CurrentMaxSlotCount, the sprintf format parameter for that type also had to change, to "%6lu" from "%6u", so that the whole value of the variable would be used. If I hadn't made this change, the data would have been written to the parameter string incorrectly, and the parameters wouldn't have been read back in correctly the next time the file was opened.

Bigger and Better

While nearly 400,000 records is a pretty big file, there are certainly applications for which it is not sufficient. Thus we come to the interesting question of how we can increase the maximum capacity of a dynamic hashing array significantly, preferably without having to make massive changes in the program. As it happens, there are two parameters of the quantum file access method that we can adjust without affecting the implementation very much: BlockSize, which specifies how large each quantum is, and the size of the m_QuantumNumber part of an ItemReference object. In the current implementation, BlockSize is set to 2048, which means we need 11 bits to specify the location of an item in a quantum. Since an ItemIndex (listing 7.2, lines 35–45) uses one 16- bit word to hold both the offset and the type of the item, the type currently takes up 5 bits. There are only six values of ObjectType defined at present, so 3 bits would be sufficient; that would allow a BlockSize to be increased to 8192, with a corresponding increase in the offset field to 13 bits. Let's take a look at the advantages and disadvantages of increasing the quantum size.

Suppose we increase the size of each quantum, for example, to 4K bytes from 2K. It's easy to see that this would double the maximum capacity of the file for dynamic hashing use, by allowing us to double the average number of records in each storage element without increasing the risk of generating a storage element that would be too large to fit in a quantum. What may not be so obvious is that this change would also decrease the memory requirements for efficient file access via dynamic hashing, for a given number of records in the file! To see why this is so, we have to look at the typical usage of disk buffers when looking up a string by key in the dynamic hashing algorithm.

Suppose we want to find the string that has the key 609643342. The algorithm calculates which hash slot points to the storage element in which a string with that key would be stored. It then calls the quantum file access routine GetModifiableElement to retrieve that storage element. GetModifiableElement retrieves the big pointer array block for the array that the storage elements are kept in; then it retrieves the little pointer array block for the correct storage element; and finally it gets the block where the storage element is stored, retrieves it from the block, and returns it. The dynamic hashing algorithm then searches the storage element to find the key we specified and, if it is found, extracts the string we want.

So a total of three blocks are accessed for each retrieval of a string: the big pointer array block, a little pointer array block, and the final "leaf" block. The first of these blocks is referenced on every string retrieval, so it is almost certain to be in memory. The "leaf" block, on the other hand, is not very likely to be in memory, since the purpose of the hashing algorithm is to distribute the data as evenly as possible over the file: with a reasonably large file, most "leaf" accesses aren't going to be to one of the relatively few blocks we can keep in memory.

Fortunately, this pessimistic outlook does not apply to the second block retrieved, the little pointer array block. If we have 150,000 strings in our file, there are 25,000 storage elements that the quantum file algorithm has to deal with. With a 2K-byte block, 674 little pointer elements fit in each little pointer block, so with about 40 buffers for little pointer blocks, it would be very likely that the one we needed would be in memory when we needed it.

Let's look at the situation if we go to 4K-byte blocks. If we double the number of strings in the average storage element to 12, then the number of little pointer array elements needed to access a given number of records is halved; in addition, the number of little pointer array elements that fit in each little pointer block is doubled.[140] This means that to be fairly sure that the little pointer block we need will be present in memory, instead of 40 blocks taking up 80K of memory, we need only about 10 blocks taking up 40K of memory!

In the case of dynamic hashing, this effect greatly alleviates the primary drawback of increasing the block size, which is that the number of blocks that can be held in a given amount of memory is inversely proportional to the size of each block. In the general case, however, this reduction in the number of buffers can hurt the performance of the program; the system can "thrash" if the working set of data needed at any given time needs more buffers than are available.

The only other apparent drawback of increasing the size of the quanta is that the free space codes become less accurate, since the code remains fixed in size at one byte; with an 8K block, each increment in the size code represents 32 bytes. I doubt that this will cause any significant problems with space utilization.

The More, the Merrier

The other fairly simple way to increase the capacity of the system is to increase the number of blocks that can be addressed. The `ItemReference` class (listing 7.2, lines 47–69) defines objects that take up three bytes each, 14 bits for the `m_QuantumNumber` field, and 10 bits for the `m_RelativeItemNumber` field. If we wanted to increase the number of quanta from its current 16K, we could increase the size of `m_QuantumNumber` to 15 or 16 bits; to avoid an increase in the object size,

---

140. Of course, having a larger block size also makes the algorithm more suitable to other applications with larger data items.

we'd have to reduce the number of items that could be held in each quantum correspondingly, to either 512 or 256. What are the drawbacks of this approach?

I don't see any real downside to reducing the number of items per quantum to 512, at least if the quantum size stays at 2K; after all, each item has 4 bytes of overhead for its corresponding `ItemIndex` entry, so the `ItemIndex` for 512 items would occupy the entire quantum, leaving no room for the items themselves. Even an index limited to 256 items per quantum would still leave room for only 4 bytes of data per item on the average in a 2K quantum with a full `ItemIndex`; those would be very small items. Certainly there would be no problem in the current program, since the dynamic hashing implementation is set up to average about five elements per block. Even in a more typical case, such as a word processor that stores each line as a separate item, the average size would probably be closer to 40 than 4 bytes per item.

The limitation on the number of items per block is probably more important if the block size is increased; with 8K blocks, 256 items per block would mean that the average item size would have to be about 28 bytes in order to avoid wasting space by running out of items before the block gets full. Even that doesn't sound like too serious a limitation, though.

Another drawback of increasing the maximum block count is that the free space list gets bigger; however, if our application needs so much data that a 32-MB maximum file size is too small, the extra 96K taken up by a free space list for 64K blocks probably isn't an obstacle.

In the present application, however, there's a more serious drawback to increasing the number of blocks; such an increase alone would not have any effect on the maximum number of records we could store in one dynamic hashing array, due to the 64K indexing limit in the 16-bit implementation of the quantum file access method. The maximum number of records stored by key in a dynamic hashing array is equal to 64K multiplied by the number of records stored in one "storage element"; with a 2K block, the latter is currently set to 6, so that the maximum count is slightly less than 400,000, as mentioned above. Increasing the quantum size to 8K would proportionately increase that number to a bit more than 1.5 million records, by allowing us to increase the "packing factor" from 6 to 24, but increasing the maximum number of blocks in the file wouldn't have any effect in the number of records that could be stored, since 64K storage elements would still use only about 13,000 blocks. Only a change in the algorithm, or a 32-bit implementation, would make it possible to use more blocks.

Summary

In this chapter, we have recast the quantum file access method in C++, and used the result as the base for a disk-based variant of Larson's dynamic hashing. This algorithm provides efficient hash-coded access by key to a very large amount of variable-length textual data, while eliminating the traditional drawbacks of hashing, especially the need to specify the maximum size of the file in advance.

In the final chapter, we will summarize the algorithms we have covered in this book and discuss some other resources we can use to improve the efficiency of our programs.

Problems

1. What modifications to the dynamic hashing implementation would be needed to add the following capabilities?

   a. Deleting records and shrinking the file;
   b. Handling "storage elements" that overflow one quantum;
   c. Storing and retrieving records with duplicate keys.
   d. Adding a "mass load mode" to facilitate the addition of large numbers of records by reducing the free space list search time.

2. How could the `PersistentArrayUlong` class be generalized to other data types?

3. What changes to the "Directory" facility would make it generally useful?

(You can find suggested approaches to problems in Chapter 8).

Listing 7.1 *hashtest.cpp: test program for block classes*

```
 1
 2   /****keyword-flag*** "%v %f %n" */
 3   /* "22 20-Aug-94,19:50:22 HASHTEST.CPP" */
 4
 5   /****keyword-flag*** "%v %f %n" */
 6   char HashtestVersionInfo[] = "22 20-Aug-94,19:50:22 HASHTEST.CPP";
 7
 8
 9   #include "common.h"
10   extern "C" {
11   #include <time.h>
12   }
13
14   extern unsigned _stklen = 16384U;
15
16   int main(int argc, char *argv[])
17   {
18     QuantumFile QF;
19     MainObjectArrayPtr MOA;
20     ModifiableElement Element;
21     ArrayIndex ElementSize;
22     FILE *infile;
23     FILE *outfile;
24     long ilong;
25     ArrayIndex i;
26     ArrayIndex j;
27     ArrayIndex count;
28     char *result;
29     ArrayIndex TestMainObjectIndex;
30     ModifiableElement TestName;
31     String Command;
32     clock_t StartAdd;
33     clock_t StartRead;
34     clock_t End;
35     clock_t CurrentTicks;
36     clock_t PreviousTicks;
37     FlexArray TestArray;
38     AccountNumber AcctNum;
39     ModifiableElement TempElement;
40     DynamicHashArray DHArray;
41     long Dup = 0;
42     long Unique;
43     PersistentArrayUlong Save;
44     char buf[1000];
45     char *KeyPtr = &buf[0];
46     char *DataPtr = &buf[10];
47     long TotalKeys = 100000L;
48     ArrayIndex nbuf = 20;
49     long CurrentReadCount;
50     long PreviousReadCount;
51     long CurrentWriteCount;
```

Listing 7.1 *hashtest.cpp: test program for block classes (continued)*

```
52      long PreviousWriteCount;
53      String TestFile = "testx.qnt";
54      ModifiableElement Key;
55      FILE *StatsFile;
56      long ReadCount;
57      long AddCount;
58      long AddIndex;
59      const int KeyOffset = 10;
60      long CurrentTotalKeys;
61      long PreviousTotalKeys;
62      long StartingElement;
63      int NewKeyAdded;
64      PrintStat Statistics;
65
66      if (argc == 1)
67          {
68          printf("Syntax: hashtest command buffers qfile total-keys [starting-element] \n");
69          printf("Where 'command' is one of the following:\n");
70          printf("%s\n%s\n%s\n",
71          "a (add elements to existing file)",
72          "i (import new file)",
73          "r (read and export elements from existing file);");
74          printf("'buffers' is the number of buffers to allocate;\n");
75          printf("'qfile' is the name of the quantum file;\n");
76          printf("for 'a' or 'i' commands,\n"
77          "'total-keys' is the number of keys the file should contain after the run;\n");
78          printf("for 'r' commands, 'total-keys' is the number of keys to read\n"
79             "and 'starting-element' is the key number to start with.\n");
80          exit(1);
81          }
82
83      Command = argv[1];
84      if (Command.GetSize() > 2)
85          {
86          printf("Only one command at a time, please!\n");
87          exit(1);
88          }
89
90      if (argc > 2)
91          nbuf = atoi(argv[2]);
92
93      if (argc > 3)
94          TestFile = argv[3];
95
96      if (argc > 4)
97          TotalKeys = atol(argv[4]);
98
99      if (argc > 5)
100         StartingElement = atol(argv[5]);
101
102     strcpy(buf," ");
```

Listing 7.1 *hashtest.cpp: test program for block classes (continued)*

```
103     for (i = 1; i < argc; i ++)
104         {
105         strcat(buf,argv[i]);
106         strcat(buf," ");
107         }
108
109     Statistics.Init("stats.out");
110     Statistics.Write("\n\n%s\nArguments:%s\n",HashtestVersionInfo,buf);
111
112     if (Command == "i")
113         remove(TestFile);
114
115     TestName = ModifiableElement("Test");
116
117     infile = fopen("names.in","rb");
118     setvbuf(infile,NULL,_IOFBF,16384);
119     outfile = fopen("names.out","wb");
120     setvbuf(outfile,NULL,_IOFBF,16384);
121
122     QF.Open(TestFile,nbuf);
123
124     Save = PersistentArrayUlong(&QF,"Save");
125
126     DHArray = DynamicHashArray(&QF,"Test");
127
128     Element = "";
129
130     Statistics.Write("\nSetup\n");
131     CurrentReadCount = QF.GetReadCount();
132     CurrentWriteCount = QF.GetWriteCount();
133     CurrentTicks = clock();
134     Statistics.Write("%lu:%lu:%lu\n",
135     CurrentTicks,
136     CurrentReadCount,
137     CurrentWriteCount);
138     PreviousTicks = CurrentTicks;
139     PreviousReadCount = CurrentReadCount;
140     PreviousWriteCount = CurrentWriteCount;
141
142     StartAdd = clock();
143
144     if (Command == "i")
145         {
146         Save[0] = KeyOffset; // start storing keys here
147         Save[1] = 0L; // offset in input file
148         Command = "a"; // now it's the same as appending
149         }
150
151     CurrentTotalKeys = Save[0] - KeyOffset;
152     PreviousTotalKeys = CurrentTotalKeys;
153     Statistics.Write("\nPrevious keys stored: %lu",CurrentTotalKeys);
```

Listing 7.1 *hashtest.cpp: test program for block classes (continued)*

```
154
155     if (Command == "a")
156         {
157         Statistics.Write("\nWrite");
158
159         fseek(infile,Save[1],SEEK_SET); // skip used input lines
160
161         Statistics.Write("\n%6lu: ",CurrentTotalKeys);
162
163         NewKeyAdded = FALSE;
164         while (CurrentTotalKeys < TotalKeys)
165             {
166             if (CurrentTotalKeys % 4000 == 0 && NewKeyAdded == TRUE)
167                 {
168                 NewKeyAdded = FALSE;
169                 Statistics.Write("\n%6lu: ",CurrentTotalKeys);
170                 }
171             if (CurrentTotalKeys % 1000 == 999 && NewKeyAdded == TRUE)
172                 {
173                 NewKeyAdded = FALSE;
174                 CurrentReadCount = QF.GetReadCount();
175                 CurrentWriteCount = QF.GetWriteCount();
176                 CurrentTicks = clock();
177                 Statistics.Write("%lu:%lu:%lu ",
178                 CurrentTicks-PreviousTicks,
179                 CurrentReadCount-PreviousReadCount,
180                 CurrentWriteCount-PreviousWriteCount);
181                 PreviousTicks = CurrentTicks;
182                 PreviousReadCount = CurrentReadCount;
183                 PreviousWriteCount = CurrentWriteCount;
184                 }
185             result = fgets(buf, 1000, infile);
186             if (result == NULL)
187                 break;
188
189             Key = ModifiableElement(10,KeyPtr); // get account number and blank
190             AcctNum = atol(Key);
191             Element = ModifiableElement(strlen(DataPtr),DataPtr);
192             TempElement = DHArray[AcctNum];
193             if (TempElement.GetSize() == 0)
194                 {
195                 DHArray[AcctNum] = Element;
196                 Save[CurrentTotalKeys+KeyOffset] = AcctNum;
197                 CurrentTotalKeys++;
198                 NewKeyAdded = TRUE;
199                 }
200             else
201                 Dup++;
202             }
203         Save[0] = CurrentTotalKeys+KeyOffset; // set to next available place
204         Save[1] = ftell(infile); // where to start the next time we add stuff
```

Listing 7.1 *hashtest.cpp: test program for block classes* *(continued)*

```
205            }
206
207    StartRead = clock();
208    PreviousTicks = StartRead;
209
210    if (Command == "r")
211            {
212        Statistics.Write("\nRead");
213        if (StartingElement % 4000 != 0)
214                Statistics.Write("\n%6lu: ", StartingElement);
215
216        for (ilong = StartingElement; ilong < TotalKeys; ilong ++)
217                {
218            if (ilong % 4000 == 0)
219                    Statistics.Write("\n%6lu: ",ilong);
220            if (ilong % 1000 == 999)
221                    {
222                    CurrentReadCount = QF.GetReadCount();
223                    CurrentWriteCount = QF.GetWriteCount();
224                    CurrentTicks = clock();
225                    Statistics.Write("%lu:%lu:%lu ",
226                    CurrentTicks-PreviousTicks,
227                    CurrentReadCount-PreviousReadCount,
228                    CurrentWriteCount-PreviousWriteCount);
229                    PreviousTicks = CurrentTicks;
230                    PreviousReadCount = CurrentReadCount;
231                    PreviousWriteCount = CurrentWriteCount;
232                    }
233            AcctNum = Save[ilong+KeyOffset];
234            if (AcctNum == 0L)
235                    break;
236            Element = DHArray[AcctNum];
237            sprintf(buf,"%lu ",AcctNum);
238            strncat(buf,Element,Element.GetSize());
239            Element = buf;
240            fwrite(Element,Element.GetSize()-1,1,outfile);
241                }
242        ReadCount = ilong - StartingElement;
243            }
244
245    QF.Flush();
246    Statistics.Write("\n");
247    CurrentReadCount = QF.GetReadCount();
248    CurrentWriteCount = QF.GetWriteCount();
249
250    End = clock();
251
252    fclose(infile);
253    fclose(outfile);
254
255    if (Command == "a")
```

Listing 7.1 *hashtest.cpp: test program for block classes (continued)*

```
256            {
257            Statistics.Write("\nTimer ticks to add %lu elements: %lu\n",
258                CurrentTotalKeys-PreviousTotalKeys,StartRead-StartAdd);
259            Statistics.Write("%lu duplicates found\n",Dup);
260            }
261
262     if (Command == "r")
263         Statistics.Write("\nTimer ticks to read %lu elements: %lu\n",ReadCount,End-
StartRead);
264
265     Statistics.Write("\nTotal ticks: %lu, total reads: %lu, total writes: %lu\n",
266     End,CurrentReadCount, CurrentWriteCount);
267
268     if (Command == "a" || Command == "i")
269         Statistics.Write("\nTotal number of keys stored: %lu\n",CurrentTotalKeys);
270
271     return(0);
272     };
273
274
275
```

Listing 7.2 *block.h: declarations for block classes*

```
 1
 2    /****keyword-flag*** "%v %f %n" */
 3    /* "31 26-Apr-94,19:58:04 BLOCK.H" */
 4
 5
 6    typedef unsigned char FreeSpaceCode;
 7    typedef unsigned char ObjectNumber;
 8    typedef unsigned short ItemSize;
 9    typedef unsigned short QuantumIndex;
10    typedef unsigned short QuantumNumber;
11    typedef unsigned short BlockNumber;
12    typedef unsigned short RelativeItemNumber;
13    typedef unsigned short SlotNumber;
14    typedef unsigned short MainObjectEntry;
15    typedef long FileOffset;
16    typedef AccessVector<QuantumNumber> BigPointerArray;
17    typedef Vector<char> ModifiableElement;
18
19    enum ObjectType {UNUSED_ITEM=1,VARIABLE_LENGTH_STRING,LITTLE_POINTER_ARRAY,
20    BIG_POINTER_ARRAY,LEAF_NODE,BIG_ARRAY_HEADER};
21
22    enum StatusType {OKAY,ERROR};
23
24    struct FreeSpaceEntry
25    {
26    FreeSpaceCode m_FreeSpaceCode;
27    ObjectNumber m_ObjectNumber;
28    };
29
30    /* The following must be considered when changing the block size */
31    const ArrayIndex BlockSize=2048;
32    const ArrayIndex FreeSpaceConversion = BlockSize/256; // granularity of free space
33    const RelativeItemNumber NoItem = 1023; // a larger value won't fit in the ItemReference
34
35    struct ItemIndex
36      {
37    // Note: must change the next two items if changing block size
38    // m_Type must be at least 3 to accommodate the types that are
39    // currently defined; this limits the possible size of m_Offset
40    // to 13 bits (i.e., block size of 8192), assuming that we
41    // don't want the ItemIndex to get larger.
42      unsigned m_Offset:11;
43      unsigned m_Type:5;
44      ArrayIndex m_Index;
45      };
46
47    class ItemReference
48      {
49    protected:
50    // The size of the m_QuantumNumber field limits the number
51    // of quanta that can exist in one file.  If we don't want
```

Listing 7.2 *block.h: declarations for block classes (continued)*

```
52    // to increase the size of an ItemReference object, then
53    // we can't increase this number without simultaneously
54    // lowering the number of items in a block.
55      unsigned m_QuantumNumber:14;
56      unsigned m_RelativeItemNumber:10;
57    public:
58      IsReference() { return m_RelativeItemNumber != NoItem; }
59      GetItemNumber() {return m_RelativeItemNumber;}
60      GetQuantumNumber() {return m_QuantumNumber;}
61      void SetItemNumber(ArrayIndex p_ItemNumber)
62          {
63          m_RelativeItemNumber = p_ItemNumber;
64          }
65      void SetQuantumNumber(QuantumNumber p_QuantumNumber)
66          {
67          m_QuantumNumber = p_QuantumNumber;
68          }
69      };
70
71
72    /* The above must be considered when changing the block size */
73
74    const ArrayIndex Margin = 10;
75    const ArrayIndex AvailableQuantum = 0xff;
76    const MainObjectEntry NoObject = 0;
77    const QuantumNumber NoQuantum = 65535;
78    const ArrayIndex DefaultBufferCount = 20;
79    const ArrayIndex MainObjectIndexCount = 256;
80    const ArrayIndex MaxFileQuantumCount = 16384;
81    const ArrayIndex BadArrayIndex = (ArrayIndex)-1;
82    const ArrayIndex MainNameObject = 1;
83
84    class BaseBlockPtr;
85    class FreeSpaceBlockPtr;
86    class FreeSpaceBlock;
87    class MainObjectBlock;
88    class MainObjectBlockPtr;
89    class QuantumBlock;
90    class FreeSpaceArrayPtr;
91    class MainObjectArrayPtr;
92    class BigPointerBlock;
93    class BigPointerBlockPtr;
94    class LittlePointerBlock;
95    class LittlePointerBlockPtr;
96    class LeafBlock;
97    class LeafBlockPtr;
98    struct QuantumFileHeaderStruct
99        {
100       char quantum_version_info[64];
101       FILE *dos_file_ptr;
102       char *file_name;
```

Listing 7.2 *block.h: declarations for block classes (continued)*

```
103     ArrayIndex main_object_index_count;
104     ArrayIndex free_space_list_count;
105     ArrayIndex memory_resident_quantum_count;
106     int filler0;
107     void *filler1;
108     void *filler2;
109     void *filler3;
110     void *filler4;
111     void *filler5;
112     void *filler6;
113     void *filler7;
114     FileOffset main_object_index_offset;
115     FileOffset free_space_list_offset;
116     FileOffset starting_quantum_offset;
117     };
118
119   struct BigArrayHeader
120     {
121     ArrayIndex m_ElementCount;
122     ArrayIndex m_MaxElementCount;
123     QuantumNumber m_LastQuantumAddedTo;
124     };
125
126   const unsigned BadBlockNumber = unsigned(-1);
127
128   struct QuantumBlockHeader
129     {
130       ObjectType m_QuantumType;
131       ObjectNumber m_MainObjectNumber;
132       ArrayIndex m_ItemCount;
133     };
134
135   struct QuantumBlockStruct
136     {
137       QuantumBlockHeader m_QuantumBlockHeader;
138       ItemIndex m_ItemIndex[1]; // place holder for item index array
139     };
140
141   const ArrayIndex ItemReferencesPerBlock =
142   (BlockSize - (sizeof(QuantumBlockHeader) + 16))
143   / sizeof(ItemReference);
144
145   const ArrayIndex MaxItemSize = BlockSize - (sizeof(QuantumBlockHeader) + Margin);
146
147   typedef AccessVector<ItemReference> LittlePointerArray;
148
149   const ArrayIndex FreeSpaceEntriesPerBlock = BlockSize/sizeof(FreeSpaceEntry);
150   const ArrayIndex MainObjectEntriesPerBlock = BlockSize/sizeof(MainObjectEntry);
151
152   union Block
153     {
```

Listing 7.2 *block.h: declarations for block classes (continued)*

```
154     char m_Data[BlockSize];
155     char m_QuantumVersionInfo[64];
156     FreeSpaceEntry m_FreeSpaceData[FreeSpaceEntriesPerBlock];
157     MainObjectEntry m_MainObjectData[MainObjectEntriesPerBlock];
158     QuantumBlockStruct m_QuantumBlockData;
159   };
160
161   class QuantumFile
162   {
163   protected:
164   Vector<Block *> m_Block;
165   Vector<ArrayIndex> m_BlockNumber;
166   Vector<char> m_BufferModified;
167   Vector<ArrayIndex> m_TimeStamp;
168   String m_FileName;
169   FILE * m_DosFilePtr;
170   BlockNumber m_CurrentLowestFreeBlock;
171   BlockNumber m_MainObjectStartingBlock;
172   BlockNumber m_FreeSpaceListStartingBlock;
173   BlockNumber m_QuantumStartingBlock;
174   ArrayIndex m_MainObjectCount;
175   ArrayIndex m_FreeSpaceListCount;
176   ArrayIndex m_Counter;
177   FreeSpaceArrayPtr *m_FreeSpaceArray;
178   MainObjectArrayPtr *m_MainObjectArray;
179   long m_ReadCount;
180   long m_WriteCount;
181
182   void Position(ArrayIndex p_BlockNumber);
183   void Write(ArrayIndex p_BlockNumber);
184   void Read(ArrayIndex p_BlockNumber);
185   QuantumFile(const QuantumFile&);
186   QuantumFile& operator=(const QuantumFile&);
187
188   public:
189   ~QuantumFile();
190   QuantumFile();
191   void Open(String p_FileName="", ArrayIndex p_BufferCount=DefaultBufferCount);
192    FreeSpaceBlockPtr MakeFreeSpaceBlockPtr(ArrayIndex p_Index);
193    MainObjectBlockPtr MakeMainObjectBlockPtr(ArrayIndex p_Index);
194    BigPointerBlockPtr MakeBigPointerBlockPtr(ArrayIndex p_Index);
195    LittlePointerBlockPtr MakeLittlePointerBlockPtr(ArrayIndex p_Index);
196    LeafBlockPtr MakeLeafBlockPtr(ArrayIndex p_Index);
197   Block *MakeBlockResident(ArrayIndex p_BlockNumber);
198   void SetModified(ArrayIndex p_BlockNumber);
199   void Flush();
200   void Close();
201    ArrayIndex GetMainObjectCount() {return m_MainObjectCount;}
202    ArrayIndex GetMainObjectBlockCount()
203     {return (m_MainObjectCount-1) / MainObjectEntriesPerBlock + 1;}
204    ArrayIndex GetFreeSpaceListCount() {return m_FreeSpaceListCount;}
```

Listing 7.2 *block.h: declarations for block classes (continued)*

```
205   ArrayIndex GetFreeSpaceListBlockCount()
206     {return (m_FreeSpaceListCount-1) / FreeSpaceEntriesPerBlock+1;}
207   void SetFreeSpace(ArrayIndex p_QuantumNumber, FreeSpaceEntry p_FreeSpaceEntry);
208   FreeSpaceEntry GetFreeSpace(ArrayIndex p_QuantumNumber);
209   QuantumNumber FindEmptyBlock();
210   QuantumNumber FindSpaceForItem(ObjectNumber p_ObjectNumber, ArrayIndex p_ItemSize);
211   ArrayIndex GetQuantumNumberAdjustment() {return m_QuantumStartingBlock-1;}
212   long GetReadCount() {return m_ReadCount;}
213   long GetWriteCount() { return m_WriteCount;}
214   };
215
216   class BaseBlockPtr
217   {
218   protected:
219   Block *m_Block;
220   ArrayIndex m_BlockNumber;
221   QuantumFile *m_BlockManager;
222   BaseBlockPtr();
223   };
224
225   class FreeSpaceBlockPtr
226   {
227   class FreeSpaceBlock : public BaseBlockPtr
228   {
229   friend FreeSpaceBlockPtr;
230   public:
231   FreeSpaceBlock();
232   FreeSpaceBlock(ArrayIndex p_BlockNumber, QuantumFile *p_BlockManager);
233   FreeSpaceEntry Get(ArrayIndex p_Index);
234   void Set(ArrayIndex p_Index, FreeSpaceEntry p_Value);
235   ArrayIndex FindEmpty();
236   LeafBlockPtr MakeLeafBlockPtr(ArrayIndex p_Index);
237   };
238   protected:
239   FreeSpaceBlock m_FreeSpaceBlock;
240   public:
241   FreeSpaceBlockPtr();
242   FreeSpaceBlockPtr(ArrayIndex p_BlockNumber, QuantumFile *p_BlockManager);
243   FreeSpaceBlock *operator->();
244   };
245
246   class MainObjectBlockPtr
247   {
248   class MainObjectBlock : public BaseBlockPtr
249   {
250   friend MainObjectBlockPtr;
251   public:
252   MainObjectBlock();
253   MainObjectBlock(ArrayIndex p_BlockNumber, QuantumFile *p_BlockManager);
254   MainObjectEntry Get(ArrayIndex p_Index);
255   void Set(ArrayIndex p_Index, MainObjectEntry p_Value);
256   };
```

Listing 7.2 *block.h: declarations for block classes (continued)*

```
257   protected:
258   MainObjectBlock m_MainObjectBlock;
259   public:
260   MainObjectBlockPtr();
261   MainObjectBlockPtr(ArrayIndex p_BlockNumber, QuantumFile *p_BlockManager);
262   MainObjectBlock *operator->();
263   };
264
265   class QuantumBlock : public BaseBlockPtr
266   {
267   protected:
268   ItemIndex *m_ItemIndex;
269   QuantumBlock();
270   QuantumBlock(ArrayIndex p_BlockNumber, QuantumFile *p_BlockManager);
271   public:
272    void SetItemCount(ArrayIndex p_NewItemCount);
273    void SetQuantumType(ObjectType p_QuantumType);
274    void SetMainObjectNumber(ObjectNumber p_MainObjectNumber);
275    ArrayIndex GetMainObjectNumber();
276    ArrayIndex GetItemCount();
277   ModifiableElement GetModifiableItem(ArrayIndex p_ItemNumber);
278    void DeleteItem(ArrayIndex p_ItemNumber);
279    ArrayIndex AddItem(ModifiableElement p_Element, ObjectType p_Type, ArrayIndex p_Index);
280   ArrayIndex AddItem(void *p_Element, ArrayIndex p_ElementSize, ObjectType p_Type, ArrayIndex p_Index);
281    void UpdateFreeSpace();
282   ArrayIndex CalculateFreeSpace();
283    void SetModified();
284    void Clear();
285   };
286
287   class BigPointerBlock : public QuantumBlock
288   {
289   friend BigPointerBlockPtr;
290   protected:
291   BigArrayHeader *m_BigArrayHeader;
292   BigPointerArray m_BigPointerArray;
293   BigPointerBlock();
294   public:
295    BigPointerArray &GetBigPointerArray(){return m_BigPointerArray;};
296    void SetBigArrayHeader();
297    void SetBigPointerArray();
298    ArrayIndex GetBigArrayElementCount();
299    void SetBigArrayElementCount(ArrayIndex p_ElementCount);
300    ArrayIndex GetBigArrayMaxElementCount();
301    QuantumNumber GetBigArrayElement(ArrayIndex p_Index);
302    void SetBigArrayElement(ArrayIndex p_Index, QuantumNumber p_Element);
303    QuantumNumber GetLastQuantumAddedTo();
304    void SetLastQuantumAddedTo(QuantumNumber p_QuantumNumber);
305   };
306
307   class LittlePointerBlock : public QuantumBlock
308   {
```

Listing 7.2 *block.h: declarations for block classes (continued)*

```
309   friend LittlePointerBlockPtr;
310   protected:
311   LittlePointerArray m_LittlePointerArray;
312   LittlePointerBlock();
313   public:
314    void SetLittlePointerArray();
315    void ClearLittleArray();
316    ItemReference GetLittleArrayElement(ArrayIndex p_Index);
317    void SetLittleArrayElement(ArrayIndex p_Index, ItemReference p_ItemReference);
318    ArrayIndex GetLittleArraySize();
319   };
320
321   class LeafBlock : public QuantumBlock
322   {
323   friend LeafBlockPtr;
324   protected:
325   LeafBlock();
326   public:
327   void PutStringItem(ArrayIndex p_ItemNumber, String p_Value);
328   };
329
330   class BigPointerBlockPtr
331   {
332   protected:
333   BigPointerBlock m_BigPointerBlock;
334   public:
335   BigPointerBlockPtr(ArrayIndex p_BlockNumber, QuantumFile *p_BlockManager);
336   BigPointerBlockPtr();
337   BigPointerBlock *operator->();
338   };
339
340   class LittlePointerBlockPtr
341   {
342   protected:
343   LittlePointerBlock m_LittlePointerBlock;
344   public:
345   LittlePointerBlockPtr(ArrayIndex p_BlockNumber, QuantumFile *p_BlockManager);
346   LittlePointerBlockPtr();
347   LittlePointerBlock *operator->();
348   };
349
350   class LeafBlockPtr
351   {
352   protected:
353   LeafBlock m_LeafBlock;
354   public:
355   LeafBlockPtr(ArrayIndex p_BlockNumber, QuantumFile *p_BlockManager);
356   LeafBlockPtr();
357   LeafBlock *operator->();
358   };
359
```

Listing 7.3 *block.cpp: implementation of block classes*

```
1
2    /****keyword-flag*** "%v %f %n" */
3    /* "57 18-May-94,22:11:46 BLOCK.CPP" */
4
5    /****keyword-flag*** "%v %f %n" */
6    char program_version_info[] = "57 18-May-94,22:11:46 BLOCK.CPP";
7
8
9    #include "common.h"
10
11   #define INLINE
12
13   //QuantumFile member functions
14
15   void QuantumFile::SetModified(ArrayIndex p_BlockNumber)
16   {
17     int BufferNumber;
18
19     BufferNumber = FindBuffer(p_BlockNumber,(ArrayIndex *)m_BlockNumber.GetDataAddress(),
20         m_BlockNumber.GetSize());
21     qfassert(BufferNumber != -1);
22
23     m_BufferModified[BufferNumber] = TRUE;
24   }
25
26   Block *QuantumFile::MakeBlockResident(ArrayIndex p_BlockNumber)
27   {
28     ArrayIndex TimeStamp;
29     ArrayIndex i;
30     ArrayIndex EarliestStamp;
31     int BufferNumber;
32
33     m_Counter ++;
34     if (m_Counter == 0)  // thrash prevention
35         {
36         for (i = 0; i < m_BlockNumber.GetSize(); i ++)
37             m_TimeStamp[i] = 0;
38         }
39
40     BufferNumber = FindBuffer(p_BlockNumber,(ArrayIndex *)m_BlockNumber.GetDataAddress(),
41         m_BlockNumber.GetSize());
42     if (BufferNumber != -1)
43         {
44         m_TimeStamp[BufferNumber] = m_Counter;
45         return m_Block[BufferNumber];
46         }
47
48     TimeStamp = ULONG_MAX;
49     EarliestStamp = 0; // in case we don't find anything to boot
50     for (i = 0; i < m_TimeStamp.GetSize(); i ++)
51         {
```

Listing 7.3 *block.cpp: implementation of block classes (continued)*

```
52              if (m_TimeStamp[i] < TimeStamp) // find the earliest timestamp
53                  {
54                  TimeStamp = m_TimeStamp[i];
55                  EarliestStamp = i;
56                  }
57          }
58
59      if (m_BufferModified[EarliestStamp]) /* it needs to be written out */
60          Write(EarliestStamp);
61
62      m_BlockNumber[EarliestStamp] = p_BlockNumber; // set block number of new occupant
63      m_BufferModified[EarliestStamp] = FALSE; // not modified yet
64      m_TimeStamp[EarliestStamp] = m_Counter;
65      Read(EarliestStamp);
66
67      return m_Block[EarliestStamp];
68  }
69
70  void QuantumFile::Open(String p_FileName, ArrayIndex p_BufferCount)
71  {
72      QuantumFileHeaderStruct QFHS;
73      char *TempBlock;
74      QuantumNumber *TempMainObjectBlock;
75      FreeSpaceEntry *TempFreeSpaceBlock;
76      ArrayIndex i;
77      ArrayIndex j;
78      int FileCreation;
79      QuantumNumber NewQuantum;
80      FreeSpaceEntry TempFreeSpaceEntry;
81      int ProgramVersion;
82      int FileVersion;
83
84      m_ReadCount = 0;
85      m_WriteCount = 0;
86      m_Block.SetSize(p_BufferCount);
87      m_BlockNumber.SetSize(p_BufferCount);
88      m_BufferModified.SetSize(p_BufferCount);
89      m_TimeStamp.SetSize(p_BufferCount);
90
91      if (p_FileName == "")
92          {
93          m_DosFilePtr = 0;
94          return;
95          }
96
97      m_DosFilePtr = fopen(p_FileName,"r+b");
98
99      if (m_DosFilePtr == NULL) /* file does not exist */
100         {
101         FileCreation = TRUE;
102         m_DosFilePtr = fopen(p_FileName,"w+b"); /* create it */
```

Listing 7.3 *block.cpp: implementation of block classes (continued)*

```
103
104              TempBlock = new char[BlockSize];
105              TempMainObjectBlock = (QuantumNumber *)TempBlock;
106              TempFreeSpaceBlock = (FreeSpaceEntry *)TempBlock;
107
108              memset((void *)&QFHS,0,sizeof(QuantumFileHeaderStruct));
109              QFHS.main_object_index_count = MainObjectIndexCount;
110              QFHS.free_space_list_count = MaxFileQuantumCount;
111              strcpy(QFHS.quantum_version_info,program_version_info);
112              QFHS.main_object_index_offset = BlockSize;
113              QFHS.free_space_list_offset = QFHS.main_object_index_offset+
114                  BlockSize*((MainObjectIndexCount-1)/MainObjectEntriesPerBlock+1);
115              QFHS.starting_quantum_offset = QFHS.free_space_list_offset+
116                  BlockSize*((MaxFileQuantumCount-1)/FreeSpaceEntriesPerBlock+1);
117
118              fseek(m_DosFilePtr,0,SEEK_SET);
119              memset(TempBlock,0,BlockSize);
120              fwrite(TempBlock,1,BlockSize,m_DosFilePtr); // clear block 0
121
122              fseek(m_DosFilePtr,0,SEEK_SET);
123              fwrite(&QFHS,1,sizeof(QuantumFileHeaderStruct), m_DosFilePtr);
124
125              /* clear the main object index */
126              memset(TempMainObjectBlock,0,BlockSize);
127              TempMainObjectBlock[0] = NoQuantum;
128              fseek(m_DosFilePtr,QFHS.main_object_index_offset, SEEK_SET);
129              fwrite(TempMainObjectBlock,BlockSize,1,m_DosFilePtr);
130
131              /* clear the free space list */
132              TempFreeSpaceEntry.m_FreeSpaceCode = AvailableQuantum;
133              TempFreeSpaceEntry.m_ObjectNumber = 0;
134              for (i = 0; i < FreeSpaceEntriesPerBlock; i ++)
135                  TempFreeSpaceBlock[i] = TempFreeSpaceEntry;
136              TempFreeSpaceBlock[0].m_FreeSpaceCode = 0; /* Q #0 doesn't exist */
137              for (i = 0; i < QFHS.free_space_list_count / FreeSpaceEntriesPerBlock; i ++)
138                  {
139                  fseek(m_DosFilePtr,QFHS.free_space_list_offset+i*BlockSize,SEEK_SET);
140                  fwrite(TempFreeSpaceBlock,sizeof(FreeSpaceEntry),
141                  FreeSpaceEntriesPerBlock,m_DosFilePtr);
142                  TempFreeSpaceBlock[0].m_FreeSpaceCode = AvailableQuantum;
143                  }
144          delete [] TempBlock;
145          }
146      else
147          {
148          FileCreation = FALSE;
149          fread(&QFHS,1,sizeof(QuantumFileHeaderStruct),m_DosFilePtr);
150          ProgramVersion = atoi(program_version_info);
151          FileVersion = atoi(QFHS.quantum_version_info);
152          if (ProgramVersion != FileVersion)
```

Listing 7.3 *block.cpp: implementation of block classes (continued)*

```
153                 {
154                         printf("Program version %d does not match file version %d.\n",
155                         ProgramVersion,FileVersion);
156                         exit(1);   // file is newer than program, so forget it
157                 }
158         }
159
160     m_MainObjectStartingBlock = QFHS.main_object_index_offset / BlockSize;
161     m_FreeSpaceListStartingBlock = QFHS.free_space_list_offset / BlockSize;
162     m_QuantumStartingBlock = QFHS.starting_quantum_offset / BlockSize;
163     m_MainObjectCount = QFHS.main_object_index_count;
164     m_FreeSpaceListCount = QFHS.free_space_list_count;
165
166     for (i = 0; i < p_BufferCount; i ++)
167         {
168         m_Block[i] = new Block;
169         m_BlockNumber[i] = BadBlockNumber;
170         m_BufferModified[i] = FALSE;
171         m_TimeStamp[i] = 0;
172         }
173
174     m_FreeSpaceArray = new FreeSpaceArrayPtr(this);
175     m_MainObjectArray = new MainObjectArrayPtr(this);
176
177     if (FileCreation == TRUE) // set up main object name object
178         (*m_MainObjectArray)->CreateMainObject("Directory", MainObjectDirectory,
179             MainObjectIndexCount);
180 }
181
182 QuantumFile::QuantumFile():
183 m_Block((unsigned short)0),
184 m_BlockNumber((unsigned short)0),
185 m_BufferModified((unsigned short)(0)),
186 m_TimeStamp((unsigned short)0),
187 m_FileName(""),
188 m_DosFilePtr(0),
189 m_CurrentLowestFreeBlock(0),
190 m_MainObjectStartingBlock(0),
191 m_FreeSpaceListStartingBlock(0),
192 m_QuantumStartingBlock(0),
193 m_MainObjectCount(0),
194 m_FreeSpaceListCount(0),
195 m_Counter(0),
196 m_FreeSpaceArray(0),
197 m_MainObjectArray(0)
198 {
199 }
200
201 QuantumFile::~QuantumFile()
202 {
203    if (m_DosFilePtr)
```

Listing 7.3 *block.cpp: implementation of block classes (continued)*

```
204              {
205              for (ArrayIndex i=0; i < m_Block.GetSize(); i ++)
206                  {
207                  if (m_BufferModified[i])
208                      Write(i);
209                  }
210
211              fclose(m_DosFilePtr);
212              m_DosFilePtr = 0;
213              for (i = 0; i < m_Block.GetSize(); i ++)
214                  delete m_Block[i];
215              }
216      }
217
218      void QuantumFile::Close()
219      {
220        if (m_DosFilePtr)
221              {
222              for (ArrayIndex i=0; i < m_Block.GetSize(); i ++)
223                  {
224                  if (m_BufferModified[i])
225                      Write(i);
226                  }
227
228              fclose(m_DosFilePtr);
229              m_DosFilePtr = 0;
230              }
231      }
232
233      void QuantumFile::Flush()
234      {
235        if (m_DosFilePtr)
236              {
237              for (ArrayIndex i=0; i < m_Block.GetSize(); i ++)
238                  {
239                  if (m_BufferModified[i])
240                      Write(i);
241                  }
242              }
243      }
244
245      void QuantumFile::Read(ArrayIndex p_BufferNumber)
246      {
247        Position(m_BlockNumber[p_BufferNumber]); // position the file
248
249        fread((char *)m_Block[p_BufferNumber],1,BlockSize,m_DosFilePtr);
250
251        m_BufferModified[p_BufferNumber] = FALSE;
252
253        m_ReadCount ++;
254      };
```

Listing 7.3 *block.cpp: implementation of block classes (continued)*

```
255
256    void QuantumFile::Write(ArrayIndex p_BufferNumber)
257    {
258      Position(m_BlockNumber[p_BufferNumber]); // position the file
259
260      fwrite((char *)m_Block[p_BufferNumber],1,BlockSize,m_DosFilePtr);
261
262      m_BufferModified[p_BufferNumber] = FALSE;
263
264      m_WriteCount ++;
265    };
266
267    void QuantumFile::Position(ArrayIndex p_BlockNumber)
268    {
269      long DesiredPosition;
270
271      DesiredPosition = (p_BlockNumber)*(long)BlockSize;
272
273      fseek(m_DosFilePtr,DesiredPosition,SEEK_SET);
274    };
275
276
277
278    //FreeSpaceBlock member functions
279
280    LeafBlockPtr FreeSpaceBlockPtr::FreeSpaceBlock::MakeLeafBlockPtr(ArrayIndex p_Index)
281    {
282      return m_BlockManager->MakeLeafBlockPtr(p_Index);
283    }
284
285    ArrayIndex FreeSpaceBlockPtr::FreeSpaceBlock::FindEmpty()
286    {
287      ArrayIndex i;
288      FreeSpaceEntry TempFreeSpaceEntry;
289
290      for (i = 0; i < FreeSpaceEntriesPerBlock; i ++)
291          {
292          TempFreeSpaceEntry = m_Block->m_FreeSpaceData[i];
293          if (TempFreeSpaceEntry.m_FreeSpaceCode == AvailableQuantum)
294              return i;
295          }
296
297      return BadBlockNumber;
298    }
299
300    //MainObjectBlock member functions
301
302    MainObjectBlockPtr::MainObjectBlock *MainObjectBlockPtr::operator->()
303    {
304      m_MainObjectBlock.m_Block =
305      m_MainObjectBlock.m_BlockManager->MakeBlockResident(
```

Listing 7.3 *block.cpp: implementation of block classes* (continued)

```
306        m_MainObjectBlock.m_BlockNumber);
307
308      return &m_MainObjectBlock;
309    }
310
311    //LittlePointerBlockPtr member functions
312
313    LittlePointerBlock *LittlePointerBlockPtr::operator->()
314    {
315      m_LittlePointerBlock.m_Block =
316      m_LittlePointerBlock.m_BlockManager->MakeBlockResident(
317      m_LittlePointerBlock.m_BlockNumber);
318
319      m_LittlePointerBlock.m_ItemIndex =
320      &m_LittlePointerBlock.m_Block->m_QuantumBlockData.m_ItemIndex[0];
321
322      m_LittlePointerBlock.SetLittlePointerArray();
323
324      return &m_LittlePointerBlock;
325    }
326
327
328    //LeafBlockPtr member functions
329
330    LeafBlock *LeafBlockPtr::operator->()
331    {
332      m_LeafBlock.m_Block =
333      m_LeafBlock.m_BlockManager->MakeBlockResident(
334      m_LeafBlock.m_BlockNumber);
335
336      m_LeafBlock.m_ItemIndex =
337      &m_LeafBlock.m_Block->m_QuantumBlockData.m_ItemIndex[0];
338
339      return &m_LeafBlock;
340    }
341
342
343    ArrayIndex QuantumBlock::AddItem(void *p_ItemAddress, ArrayIndex p_ElementSize, ObjectType p_Type,
344      ArrayIndex p_Index)
345    {
346      ArrayIndex StartingOffset;
347      ArrayIndex Length;
348      char *StartingLocation;
349      ArrayIndex LastItemOffset;
350      char *DataFrom;
351      char *DataTo;
352      ArrayIndex DataLength;
353      ItemIndex TempItemIndex;
354      int ItemFound;
355      ArrayIndex ItemNumber;
356
```

Listing 7.3 *block.cpp: implementation of block classes (continued)*

```cpp
357     SetModified();
358
359     ItemFound = FindUnusedItem(&m_ItemIndex[0], GetItemCount());
360     TempItemIndex = m_ItemIndex[ItemFound];
361
362     qfassert(CalculateFreeSpace() > p_ElementSize);
363
364     if (ItemFound >= 0) // we can reuse an item
365         {
366         TempItemIndex.m_Type = p_Type;
367         TempItemIndex.m_Index = p_Index;
368         m_ItemIndex[ItemFound] = TempItemIndex;
369
370         StartingOffset = m_ItemIndex[ItemFound].m_Offset;
371         LastItemOffset = m_ItemIndex[GetItemCount()-1].m_Offset;
372         DataFrom = m_Block->m_Data + BlockSize - LastItemOffset;
373         DataTo = DataFrom - p_ElementSize;
374         DataLength = LastItemOffset - StartingOffset;
375         BlockMove(DataTo,DataFrom,DataLength);
376
377         AdjustOffset(&m_ItemIndex[ItemFound],GetItemCount()-ItemFound, p_ElementSize);
378
379         DataTo = m_Block->m_Data + BlockSize - m_ItemIndex[ItemFound].m_Offset;
380         BlockMove(DataTo,p_ItemAddress,p_ElementSize);
381         ItemNumber = ItemFound + 1;
382         }
383     else // must make a new item
384         {
385         if (GetItemCount() == 0)
386             TempItemIndex.m_Offset = p_ElementSize;
387         else
388             {
389             LastItemOffset = m_ItemIndex[GetItemCount()-1].m_Offset;
390             TempItemIndex.m_Offset = LastItemOffset + p_ElementSize;
391             }
392         DataTo = m_Block->m_Data + BlockSize - TempItemIndex.m_Offset;
393         BlockMove(DataTo,p_ItemAddress,p_ElementSize);
394         TempItemIndex.m_Type = p_Type;
395         TempItemIndex.m_Index = p_Index;
396         m_ItemIndex[GetItemCount()] = TempItemIndex;
397         SetItemCount(GetItemCount()+1);
398         ItemNumber = GetItemCount(); // 1-based
399         }
400     UpdateFreeSpace();
401     return ItemNumber;
402 }
403
404 void QuantumBlock::DeleteItem(ArrayIndex p_ItemNumber)
405 {
406     ModifiableElement TempItem;
407     ArrayIndex StartingOffset;
```

Listing 7.3 *block.cpp: implementation of block classes (continued)*

```
408        ArrayIndex Length;
409        char *StartingLocation;
410        int i; // must be signed for termination condition
411        ArrayIndex LastItemOffset;
412        char *DataFrom;
413        char *DataTo;
414        ArrayIndex DataLength;
415
416        SetModified();
417        qfassert (p_ItemNumber > 0 && p_ItemNumber <= GetItemCount());
418        p_ItemNumber --; /* make it zero-based */
419        if (p_ItemNumber == GetItemCount() - 1) // it's the last one
420            {
421            m_ItemIndex[p_ItemNumber].m_Type = UNUSED_ITEM;
422            for (i = GetItemCount() - 1; i >= 0; i --)
423                {
424                if (m_ItemIndex[i].m_Type == UNUSED_ITEM)
425                    {
426                    m_ItemIndex[i].m_Offset = 0;
427                    m_ItemIndex[i].m_Index = 0;
428                    m_ItemIndex[i].m_Type = 0;
429                    }
430                else
431                    break;
432                }
433            SetItemCount(i+1);
434            if (i == -1) // we've cleared out the whole block
435                Clear();
436            UpdateFreeSpace();
437            return;
438            }
439
440        StartingOffset = m_ItemIndex[p_ItemNumber].m_Offset;
441        if (p_ItemNumber == 0) /* the first one goes to the end of the block */
442            Length = StartingOffset;
443        else
444            Length = StartingOffset - m_ItemIndex[p_ItemNumber-1].m_Offset;
445
446        LastItemOffset = m_ItemIndex[GetItemCount()-1].m_Offset;
447        DataFrom = m_Block->m_Data + BlockSize - LastItemOffset;
448        DataTo = DataFrom + Length;
449        DataLength = LastItemOffset - StartingOffset;
450        BlockMove(DataTo,DataFrom,DataLength);
451
452        AdjustOffset(&m_ItemIndex[p_ItemNumber+1],GetItemCount()-(p_ItemNumber+1), -Length);
453
454        m_ItemIndex[p_ItemNumber].m_Type = UNUSED_ITEM;
455
456        //Must set up correct offset for length calculation of next item
457        if (p_ItemNumber == 0)
458            m_ItemIndex[p_ItemNumber].m_Offset = 0;
```

Listing 7.3 *block.cpp: implementation of block classes (continued)*

```
459     else
460         m_ItemIndex[p_ItemNumber].m_Offset = m_ItemIndex[p_ItemNumber-1].m_Offset;
461
462     UpdateFreeSpace();
463   }
464
465
466   ModifiableElement QuantumBlock::GetModifiableItem(ArrayIndex p_ItemNumber)
467   {
468     ModifiableElement TempItem;
469     ArrayIndex StartingOffset;
470     ArrayIndex Length;
471     char *StartingLocation;
472
473     qfassert (p_ItemNumber > 0 && p_ItemNumber <= GetItemCount());
474     p_ItemNumber --; /* make it zero-based */
475     StartingOffset = m_ItemIndex[p_ItemNumber].m_Offset;
476     StartingLocation = m_Block->m_Data + BlockSize - StartingOffset;
477     if (p_ItemNumber == 0) /* the first one goes to the end of the block */
478         Length = StartingOffset;
479     else
480         Length = StartingOffset - m_ItemIndex[p_ItemNumber-1].m_Offset;
481     TempItem = ModifiableElement(Length, StartingLocation);
482     return TempItem;
483   }
484
485
486   ArrayIndex QuantumBlock::CalculateFreeSpace()
487   {
488     int FreeSpace;
489     ArrayIndex LastItemOffset;
490
491     FreeSpace = BlockSize - (Margin + sizeof(QuantumBlockHeader));
492
493     if (GetItemCount() == 0)
494       return(BlockSize - 1);
495
496     LastItemOffset = m_ItemIndex[GetItemCount()-1].m_Offset;
497
498     FreeSpace -= sizeof(m_ItemIndex) * GetItemCount();
499     FreeSpace -= LastItemOffset;
500
501     if (FreeSpace < 0)
502       FreeSpace = 0;
503
504     return(ArrayIndex(FreeSpace));
505   }
506
507
508   FreeSpaceBlockPtr::FreeSpaceBlockPtr(ArrayIndex p_BlockNumber,
509   QuantumFile *p_BlockManager)
```

Listing 7.3 *block.cpp: implementation of block classes (continued)*

```
510   {
511     m_FreeSpaceBlock.m_BlockNumber = p_BlockNumber;
512     m_FreeSpaceBlock.m_BlockManager = p_BlockManager;
513     m_FreeSpaceBlock.m_Block = 0;
514   }
515
516   FreeSpaceBlockPtr::FreeSpaceBlock::FreeSpaceBlock(ArrayIndex p_BlockNumber,
517   QuantumFile *p_BlockManager)
518   {
519     m_BlockNumber = p_BlockNumber;
520     m_BlockManager = p_BlockManager;
521     m_Block = 0;
522   }
523
524   MainObjectBlockPtr::MainObjectBlockPtr(ArrayIndex p_BlockNumber,
525   QuantumFile *p_BlockManager)
526   {
527     m_MainObjectBlock.m_BlockNumber = p_BlockNumber;
528     m_MainObjectBlock.m_BlockManager = p_BlockManager;
529     m_MainObjectBlock.m_Block = 0;
530   }
531
532
533   MainObjectBlockPtr::MainObjectBlock::MainObjectBlock(ArrayIndex p_BlockNumber,
534   QuantumFile *p_BlockManager)
535   {
536     m_BlockNumber = p_BlockNumber;
537     m_BlockManager = p_BlockManager;
538     m_Block = 0;
539   }
540
541   BigPointerBlockPtr::BigPointerBlockPtr(ArrayIndex p_BlockNumber, QuantumFile *p_BlockManager)
542   {
543     m_BigPointerBlock.m_BlockNumber = p_BlockNumber;
544     m_BigPointerBlock.m_BlockManager = p_BlockManager;
545     m_BigPointerBlock.m_Block = 0;
546   }
547
548   LittlePointerBlockPtr::LittlePointerBlockPtr(ArrayIndex p_BlockNumber, QuantumFile *p_BlockManager)
549   {
550     m_LittlePointerBlock.m_BlockNumber = p_BlockNumber;
551     m_LittlePointerBlock.m_BlockManager = p_BlockManager;
552     m_LittlePointerBlock.m_Block = 0;
553   }
554
555   LeafBlockPtr::LeafBlockPtr(ArrayIndex p_BlockNumber, QuantumFile *p_BlockManager)
556   {
557     m_LeafBlock.m_BlockNumber = p_BlockNumber;
558     m_LeafBlock.m_BlockManager = p_BlockManager;
559     m_LeafBlock.m_Block = 0;
560   }
```

Listing 7.3 *block.cpp: implementation of block classes (continued)*

```
561
562    void BigPointerBlock::SetBigArrayHeader()
563    {
564      BigArrayHeader *TempItem;
565      ArrayIndex StartingOffset;
566      ArrayIndex Length;
567      char *StartingLocation;
568
569      StartingOffset = m_ItemIndex[0].m_Offset;
570      StartingLocation = m_Block->m_Data + BlockSize - StartingOffset;
571      m_BigArrayHeader = (BigArrayHeader *)(StartingLocation);
572    }
573
574    void BigPointerBlock::SetBigPointerArray()
575    {
576      BigPointerArray *TempItem;
577      ArrayIndex StartingOffset;
578      ArrayIndex Length;
579      char *StartingLocation;
580      ArrayIndex ElementCount;
581
582      StartingOffset = m_ItemIndex[1].m_Offset;
583      StartingLocation = m_Block->m_Data + BlockSize - StartingOffset;
584      Length = StartingOffset - m_ItemIndex[0].m_Offset;
585      ElementCount = Length/sizeof(QuantumNumber);
586      m_BigPointerArray = BigPointerArray(ElementCount,(QuantumNumber *)StartingLocation);
587    }
588
589    void LittlePointerBlock::SetLittlePointerArray()
590    {
591      LittlePointerArray *TempItem;
592      ArrayIndex StartingOffset;
593      ArrayIndex Length;
594      char *StartingLocation;
595      ArrayIndex ElementCount;
596
597      StartingOffset = m_ItemIndex[0].m_Offset;
598      StartingLocation = m_Block->m_Data + BlockSize - StartingOffset;
599      Length = StartingOffset;
600      ElementCount = Length/sizeof(ItemReference);
601      m_LittlePointerArray = LittlePointerArray(ElementCount,(ItemReference *)StartingLocation);
602    }
603
604
605    INLINE FreeSpaceBlockPtr QuantumFile::MakeFreeSpaceBlockPtr(ArrayIndex p_Index)
606    {
607      return FreeSpaceBlockPtr(p_Index+m_FreeSpaceListStartingBlock, this);
608    };
609
610    INLINE MainObjectBlockPtr QuantumFile::MakeMainObjectBlockPtr(ArrayIndex p_Index)
611    {
```

Listing 7.3 *block.cpp: implementation of block classes (continued)*

```
612       return MainObjectBlockPtr(p_Index+m_MainObjectStartingBlock, this);
613   };
614
615   INLINE LittlePointerBlockPtr QuantumFile::MakeLittlePointerBlockPtr(ArrayIndex p_Index)
616   {
617   // note: there is no quantum number 0, so we must correct the index
618     return LittlePointerBlockPtr(p_Index+m_QuantumStartingBlock-1, this);
619   };
620
621   INLINE BigPointerBlockPtr QuantumFile::MakeBigPointerBlockPtr(ArrayIndex p_Index)
622   {
623   // note: there is no quantum number 0, so we must correct the index
624     return BigPointerBlockPtr(p_Index+m_QuantumStartingBlock-1, this);
625   };
626
627   INLINE LeafBlockPtr QuantumFile::MakeLeafBlockPtr(ArrayIndex p_Index)
628   {
629   // note: there is no quantum number 0, so we must correct the index
630     return LeafBlockPtr(p_Index+m_QuantumStartingBlock-1, this);
631   };
632
633   INLINE void QuantumFile::SetFreeSpace(ArrayIndex p_QuantumNumber,
                      FreeSpaceEntry p_FreeSpaceEntry)
634   {
635     (*m_FreeSpaceArray)->Set(p_QuantumNumber, p_FreeSpaceEntry);
636   }
637
638   INLINE FreeSpaceEntry QuantumFile::GetFreeSpace(ArrayIndex p_QuantumNumber)
639   {
640     return (*m_FreeSpaceArray)->Get(p_QuantumNumber);
641   }
642
643   INLINE QuantumNumber QuantumFile::FindEmptyBlock()
644   {
645     return (*m_FreeSpaceArray)->FindEmptyBlock();
646   }
647
648
649   INLINE QuantumNumber QuantumFile::FindSpaceForItem(ObjectNumber p_ObjectNumber,
650     ArrayIndex p_ItemSize)
651   {
652     return (*m_FreeSpaceArray)->FindSpaceForItem(p_ObjectNumber, p_ItemSize);
653   }
654
655
656   INLINE FreeSpaceBlockPtr::FreeSpaceBlockPtr()
657   {
658   }
659
660   INLINE FreeSpaceBlockPtr::FreeSpaceBlock::FreeSpaceBlock()
661   {
```

Listing 7.3 *block.cpp: implementation of block classes (continued)*

```
662      m_Block = 0;
663    }
664
665    INLINE FreeSpaceEntry FreeSpaceBlockPtr::FreeSpaceBlock::Get(ArrayIndex p_Index)
666    {
667      return m_Block->m_FreeSpaceData[p_Index];
668    }
669
670    INLINE void FreeSpaceBlockPtr::FreeSpaceBlock::Set(ArrayIndex p_Index,
                       FreeSpaceEntry p_Value)
671    {
672      m_BlockManager->SetModified(m_BlockNumber);
673      m_Block->m_FreeSpaceData[p_Index] = p_Value;
674    }
675
676
677    INLINE MainObjectBlockPtr::MainObjectBlockPtr()
678    {
679    }
680
681    INLINE MainObjectBlockPtr::MainObjectBlock::MainObjectBlock()
682    {
683      m_Block = 0;
684    }
685
686    INLINE MainObjectEntry MainObjectBlockPtr::MainObjectBlock::Get(ArrayIndex p_Index)
687    {
688      return m_Block->m_MainObjectData[p_Index];
689    }
690
691    INLINE void MainObjectBlockPtr::MainObjectBlock::Set(ArrayIndex p_Index, MainObjectEntry p_Value)
692    {
693      m_BlockManager->SetModified(m_BlockNumber);
694      m_Block->m_MainObjectData[p_Index] = p_Value;
695    }
696
697
698    INLINE BigPointerBlockPtr::BigPointerBlockPtr()
699    {
700    }
701
702    INLINE LittlePointerBlockPtr::LittlePointerBlockPtr()
703    {
704    }
705
706    INLINE LeafBlockPtr::LeafBlockPtr()
707    {
708    }
709
710
711    INLINE BigPointerBlock::BigPointerBlock()
```

Listing 7.3 *block.cpp: implementation of block classes (continued)*

```
712    {
713    }
714
715    INLINE ArrayIndex BigPointerBlock::GetBigArrayMaxElementCount()
716    {
717      return m_BigArrayHeader->m_MaxElementCount;
718    }
719
720    INLINE ArrayIndex BigPointerBlock::GetBigArrayElementCount()
721    {
722      return m_BigArrayHeader->m_ElementCount;
723    }
724
725    INLINE void BigPointerBlock::SetBigArrayElementCount(ArrayIndex p_ElementCount)
726    {
727      if (m_BigArrayHeader->m_ElementCount != p_ElementCount)
728          {
729          m_BigArrayHeader->m_ElementCount = p_ElementCount;
730          SetModified();
731          }
732    }
733    INLINE QuantumNumber BigPointerBlock::GetBigArrayElement(ArrayIndex p_Index)
734    {
735      return m_BigPointerArray[p_Index];
736    }
737
738    INLINE void BigPointerBlock::SetBigArrayElement(ArrayIndex p_Index, QuantumNumber p_Element)
739    {
740      m_BigPointerArray[p_Index] = p_Element;
741    }
742
743    INLINE QuantumNumber BigPointerBlock::GetLastQuantumAddedTo()
744    {
745      return m_BigArrayHeader->m_LastQuantumAddedTo;
746    }
747
748    INLINE void BigPointerBlock::SetLastQuantumAddedTo(QuantumNumber p_QuantumNumber)
749    {
750      if (m_BigArrayHeader->m_LastQuantumAddedTo != p_QuantumNumber)
751          {
752          m_BigArrayHeader->m_LastQuantumAddedTo = p_QuantumNumber;
753          SetModified();
754          }
755    }
756
757
758    void LittlePointerBlock::ClearLittleArray()
759    {
760      ItemReference NullItemReference;
761      ArrayIndex i;
762
```

Listing 7.3 *block.cpp: implementation of block classes (continued)*

```
763        NullItemReference.SetItemNumber(NoItem);
764        NullItemReference.SetQuantumNumber(NoQuantum);
765        for (i = 0; i < GetLittleArraySize(); i ++)
766              m_LittlePointerArray[i] = NullItemReference;
767    }
768
769
770    INLINE void QuantumBlock::SetModified()
771    {
772       m_BlockManager->SetModified(m_BlockNumber);
773    }
774
775    INLINE ArrayIndex QuantumBlock::AddItem(ModifiableElement p_Element, ObjectType p_Type,
776       ArrayIndex p_Index)
777    {
778       ArrayIndex ItemSize = p_Element.GetSize();
779       void *ItemAddress = p_Element.GetDataAddress();
780
781       return AddItem(ItemAddress, ItemSize, p_Type, p_Index);
782    }
783
784    INLINE void QuantumBlock::SetItemCount(ArrayIndex p_NewItemCount)
785    {
786       m_Block->m_QuantumBlockData.m_QuantumBlockHeader.m_ItemCount = p_NewItemCount;
787    }
788
789    INLINE void QuantumBlock::SetQuantumType(ObjectType p_QuantumType)
790    {
791       m_Block->m_QuantumBlockData.m_QuantumBlockHeader.m_QuantumType = p_QuantumType;
792    }
793
794    INLINE void QuantumBlock::SetMainObjectNumber(ObjectNumber p_MainObjectNumber)
795    {
796       m_Block->m_QuantumBlockData.m_QuantumBlockHeader.m_MainObjectNumber = p_MainObjectNumber;
797    }
798
799    INLINE void QuantumBlock::UpdateFreeSpace()
800    {
801       FreeSpaceEntry SpaceAvailable;
802
803       SpaceAvailable.m_ObjectNumber = GetMainObjectNumber();
804       SpaceAvailable.m_FreeSpaceCode = CalculateFreeSpace()/FreeSpaceConversion;
805       m_BlockManager->SetFreeSpace(m_BlockNumber-m_BlockManager->GetQuantumNumberAdjustment(),
806              SpaceAvailable);
807    }
808
809    INLINE ArrayIndex QuantumBlock::GetMainObjectNumber()
810    {
811       return m_Block->m_QuantumBlockData.m_QuantumBlockHeader.m_MainObjectNumber;
812    }
813
```

Listing 7.3 *block.cpp: implementation of block classes (continued)*

```
814
815    INLINE void QuantumBlock::Clear()
816    {
817      memset(m_Block,0,BlockSize);
818      SetModified();
819    }
820
821    INLINE ItemReference LittlePointerBlock::GetLittleArrayElement(ArrayIndex p_Index)
822    {
823      return m_LittlePointerArray[p_Index];
824    }
825
826    INLINE void LittlePointerBlock::SetLittleArrayElement(ArrayIndex p_Index,
827      ItemReference p_ItemReference)
828    {
829      m_BlockManager->SetModified(m_BlockNumber);
830      m_LittlePointerArray[p_Index] = p_ItemReference;
831    }
832
```

Listing 7.4 *newquant.h: declarations for logical layer classes*

```
1
2   /****keyword-flag*** "%v %f %n" */
3   /* "17 24-Mar-94,8:32:32 NEWQUANT.H" */
4
5
6   class FreeSpaceArrayPtr
7   {
8   protected:
9   class FreeSpaceArray
10  {
11  friend FreeSpaceArrayPtr;
12  protected:
13  Vector<FreeSpaceBlockPtr> m_BlockPtr;
14  ArrayIndex m_FreeSpaceListCount;
15  ArrayIndex m_FreeSpaceListBlockCount;
16  ArrayIndex m_CurrentLowestFreeBlock;
17  ArrayIndex m_QuantumBlockNumberAdjustment;
18  int m_ReferenceCount;
19
20  public:
21    FreeSpaceArray();
22    FreeSpaceArray(QuantumFile *p_QuantumFile);
23    ~FreeSpaceArray();
24  FreeSpaceEntry Get(ArrayIndex p_Index);
25  void Set(ArrayIndex p_Index, FreeSpaceEntry p_Entry);
26  QuantumNumber FindEmptyBlock();
27  QuantumNumber FindSpaceForItem(ObjectNumber p_ObjectNumber, ArrayIndex p_ItemSize);
28  ArrayIndex GetFreeSpaceListCount() {return m_FreeSpaceListCount;}
29  };
30  FreeSpaceArray *m_FSA;
31
32  public:
33  FreeSpaceArrayPtr();
34  FreeSpaceArrayPtr(const FreeSpaceArrayPtr& p_FSAP);
35  FreeSpaceArrayPtr(QuantumFile *p_QuantumFile);
36  FreeSpaceArray *operator->();
37  FreeSpaceArrayPtr& operator=(const FreeSpaceArrayPtr& p_FSAP);
38  ~FreeSpaceArrayPtr();
39  };
40
41  class MainObjectArrayPtr
42  {
43  protected:
44  class MainObjectArray
45  {
46  friend MainObjectArrayPtr;
47  protected:
48  QuantumFile *m_QuantumFile;
49  Vector<MainObjectBlockPtr> m_BlockPtr;
50  ArrayIndex m_MainObjectCount;
51  ArrayIndex m_MainObjectBlockCount;
```

Listing 7.4 *newquant.h: declarations for logical layer classes (continued)*

```
52   ArrayIndex m_CurrentLowestFreeObject;
53   int m_ReferenceCount;
54
55   public:
56   MainObjectArray();
57   MainObjectArray(QuantumFile *p_QuantumFile);
58   ~MainObjectArray();
59   MainObjectEntry Get(ArrayIndex p_Index);
60   void Set(ArrayIndex p_Index, MainObjectEntry p_Entry);
61   ArrayIndex FindAvailableObject();
62   ArrayIndex GetMainObjectCount() {return m_MainObjectCount;}
63   ModifiableElement GetModifiableElement(ArrayIndex p_MainObjectNumber,
64      ArrayIndex p_ElementIndex);
65   int PutElement(ArrayIndex p_MainObjectNumber,
66      ArrayIndex p_ElementIndex, ModifiableElement p_Element);
67   void CreateMainObject(ModifiableElement p_ObjectName,
68      ArrayIndex p_ObjectNumber, ArrayIndex p_ElementCount=100,
69      ArrayIndex p_MaxElementCount=unsigned(-1));
70   ArrayIndex GetMainObjectElementCount(ArrayIndex p_MainObjectNumber);
71   ArrayIndex GetMainObjectMaxElementCount(ArrayIndex p_MainObjectNumber);
72   ArrayIndex FindObjectByName(ModifiableElement p_ObjectName);
73   ArrayIndex GrowMainObject(ArrayIndex p_ObjectNumber, ArrayIndex p_NewElementCount);
74   };
75
76   MainObjectArray *m_MOA;
77
78   public:
79   MainObjectArrayPtr();
80   MainObjectArrayPtr(const MainObjectArrayPtr& p_MOAP);
81   MainObjectArrayPtr(QuantumFile *p_QuantumFile);
82   MainObjectArray *operator->();
83   MainObjectArrayPtr& operator=(const MainObjectArrayPtr& p_MOAP);
84   ~MainObjectArrayPtr();
85   };
86
87
88   class FlexArrayRef
89   {
90   private:
91     MainObjectArrayPtr &m_MOA;
92     ArrayIndex m_MOAIndex;
93     ArrayIndex m_ElementIndex;
94   public:
95     FlexArrayRef(MainObjectArrayPtr &p_MOA, ArrayIndex p_MOAIndex, ArrayIndex p_ElementIndex);
96     FlexArrayRef &operator=(ModifiableElement p_ROE);
97     operator ModifiableElement();
98   };
99
100  class FlexArray
101  {
102  protected:
```

Listing 7.4 *newquant.h: declarations for logical layer classes (continued)*

```
103      MainObjectArrayPtr m_MOA;
104      ArrayIndex m_MOAIndex;
105      ArrayIndex m_ElementCount;
106      ArrayIndex m_MaxElementCount;
107    public:
108      FlexArray();
109      FlexArray(MainObjectArrayPtr p_MOA, ArrayIndex p_MOAIndex);
110      FlexArrayRef operator[](ArrayIndex p_ElementIndex);
111    };
112
```

Listing 7.5 *newquant.cpp: implementation of logical layer classes*

```
1
2    /****keyword-flag*** "%v %f %n" */
3    /* "31 26-Apr-94,19:58:06 NEWQUANT.CPP" */
4
5
6    #include "common.h"
7
8    #define INLINE
9
10   FreeSpaceArrayPtr::FreeSpaceArrayPtr()
11   {
12     m_FSA = new FreeSpaceArray;
13     m_FSA->m_ReferenceCount = 1;
14   }
15
16   FreeSpaceArrayPtr::FreeSpaceArrayPtr(QuantumFile *p_QuantumFile)
17   {
18     m_FSA = new FreeSpaceArray(p_QuantumFile);
19     m_FSA->m_ReferenceCount = 1;
20   }
21
22
23   FreeSpaceArrayPtr::FreeSpaceArrayPtr(const FreeSpaceArrayPtr& p_FSAP)
24   {
25     m_FSA = p_FSAP.m_FSA;
26     m_FSA->m_ReferenceCount++;
27   }
28
29
30   FreeSpaceArrayPtr::FreeSpaceArray *FreeSpaceArrayPtr::operator->()
31   {
32     return m_FSA;
33   }
34
35   FreeSpaceArrayPtr& FreeSpaceArrayPtr::operator=(const FreeSpaceArrayPtr& p_FSAP)
36   {
37     m_FSA->m_ReferenceCount--;
38     if (m_FSA->m_ReferenceCount <= 0 && m_FSA != p_FSAP.m_FSA)
39         delete m_FSA;
40     m_FSA = p_FSAP.m_FSA;
41     m_FSA->m_ReferenceCount ++;
42     return *this;
43   }
44
45   FreeSpaceArrayPtr::~FreeSpaceArrayPtr()
46   {
47     m_FSA->m_ReferenceCount --;
48     if (m_FSA->m_ReferenceCount <= 0)
49         delete m_FSA;
50   }
51
```

Listing 7.5 *newquant.cpp: implementation of logical layer classes (continued)*

```
52    FreeSpaceArrayPtr::FreeSpaceArray::FreeSpaceArray():
53    m_FreeSpaceListCount(0),
54    m_FreeSpaceListBlockCount(0),
55    m_CurrentLowestFreeBlock(0),
56    m_QuantumBlockNumberAdjustment(0)
57    {
58    };
59
60    FreeSpaceArrayPtr::FreeSpaceArray::~FreeSpaceArray()
61    {
62    }
63
64    FreeSpaceArrayPtr::FreeSpaceArray::FreeSpaceArray(QuantumFile *p_MRU)
65    {
66      ArrayIndex i;
67
68      m_FreeSpaceListCount = p_MRU->GetFreeSpaceListCount();
69      m_FreeSpaceListBlockCount = p_MRU->GetFreeSpaceListBlockCount();
70      m_CurrentLowestFreeBlock = 0;
71      m_QuantumBlockNumberAdjustment = p_MRU->GetQuantumNumberAdjustment();
72      m_BlockPtr.SetSize(p_MRU->GetFreeSpaceListBlockCount());
73      for (i = 0; i < m_BlockPtr.GetSize(); i ++)
74          m_BlockPtr[i] = p_MRU->MakeFreeSpaceBlockPtr(i);
75    }
76
77    FreeSpaceEntry FreeSpaceArrayPtr::FreeSpaceArray::Get(ArrayIndex p_Index)
78    {
79      ArrayIndex Block;
80      ArrayIndex Element;
81      FreeSpaceEntry Result;
82
83      if (p_Index >= m_FreeSpaceListCount)
84          {
85          Result.m_ObjectNumber = 0;
86          Result.m_FreeSpaceCode = 0;
87          return Result;
88          }
89
90      Block = p_Index / FreeSpaceEntriesPerBlock;
91      Element = p_Index % FreeSpaceEntriesPerBlock;
92      Result = m_BlockPtr[Block]->Get(Element);
93
94      return Result;
95    }
96
97    void FreeSpaceArrayPtr::FreeSpaceArray::Set(ArrayIndex p_Index, FreeSpaceEntry p_Entry)
98    {
99      ArrayIndex Block;
100     ArrayIndex Element;
101     FreeSpaceEntry Result;
102
```

Listing 7.5 *newquant.cpp: implementation of logical layer classes (continued)*

```
103     if (p_Index >= m_FreeSpaceListCount)
104         return; // can't store off the end
105
106     Block = p_Index / FreeSpaceEntriesPerBlock;
107     Element = p_Index % FreeSpaceEntriesPerBlock;
108     m_BlockPtr[Block]->Set(Element, p_Entry);
109     if ((p_Entry.m_FreeSpaceCode == AvailableQuantum) && (p_Index < m_CurrentLowestFreeBlock))
110         m_CurrentLowestFreeBlock = p_Index;
111
112     return;
113   }
114
115   QuantumNumber FreeSpaceArrayPtr::FreeSpaceArray::FindEmptyBlock()
116   {
117     ArrayIndex Block;
118     ArrayIndex Element;
119     ArrayIndex Result = (unsigned)-1;
120
121     Block = m_CurrentLowestFreeBlock / FreeSpaceEntriesPerBlock;
122     Element = m_CurrentLowestFreeBlock % FreeSpaceEntriesPerBlock;
123     for (; Block < m_FreeSpaceListBlockCount; Block ++)
124         {
125         for (; Element < FreeSpaceEntriesPerBlock; Element ++)
126             {
127             if (m_BlockPtr[Block]->Get(Element).m_FreeSpaceCode == AvailableQuantum)
128                 {
129                 Result = Block * FreeSpaceEntriesPerBlock + Element;
130                 break;
131                 }
132             }
133         if (Result != (unsigned)-1)
134             break;
135         Element = 0;
136         }
137
138     m_CurrentLowestFreeBlock = Result;
139
140     return Result;
141   }
142
143
144   QuantumNumber FreeSpaceArrayPtr::FreeSpaceArray::FindSpaceForItem(ObjectNumber p_ObjectNumber,
145     ArrayIndex p_ItemSize)
146   {
147     ArrayIndex Block;
148     ArrayIndex Element;
149     ArrayIndex Result = BadArrayIndex;
150     ArrayIndex ItemSizeCode = p_ItemSize / FreeSpaceConversion;
151     FreeSpaceEntry TempFreeSpaceEntry;
152     LeafBlockPtr TempLeafBlockPtr;
153
```

Listing 7.5 *newquant.cpp: implementation of logical layer classes (continued)*

```
154      for (Block = 0; Block < m_FreeSpaceListBlockCount; Block ++)
155          {
156          for (Element = 0; Element < FreeSpaceEntriesPerBlock; Element ++)
157              {
158              TempFreeSpaceEntry = m_BlockPtr[Block]->Get(Element);
159              if (TempFreeSpaceEntry.m_FreeSpaceCode == AvailableQuantum)
160                  {
161                  TempFreeSpaceEntry.m_ObjectNumber = p_ObjectNumber;
162                  m_BlockPtr[Block]->Set(Element,TempFreeSpaceEntry);
163                  Result = Block * FreeSpaceEntriesPerBlock + Element;
164                  TempLeafBlockPtr = m_BlockPtr[Block]->MakeLeafBlockPtr(Result);
165                  TempLeafBlockPtr->Clear();
166                  TempLeafBlockPtr->SetQuantumType(LEAF_NODE);
167                  TempLeafBlockPtr->SetMainObjectNumber(p_ObjectNumber);
168                  break;
169                  }
170              if (TempFreeSpaceEntry.m_ObjectNumber == p_ObjectNumber &&
171                  TempFreeSpaceEntry.m_FreeSpaceCode > ItemSizeCode)
172                  {
173                  Result = Block * FreeSpaceEntriesPerBlock + Element;
174                  TempLeafBlockPtr = m_BlockPtr[Block]->MakeLeafBlockPtr(Result);
175                  if (TempLeafBlockPtr->CalculateFreeSpace() > p_ItemSize)
176                      break;
177                  else
178                      Result = BadArrayIndex;
179                  }
180              }
181          if (Result != BadArrayIndex)
182              break;
183          }
184
185      return Result;
186  }
187
188  MainObjectArrayPtr::MainObjectArrayPtr()
189  {
190    m_MOA = new MainObjectArray;
191    m_MOA->m_ReferenceCount = 1;
192  }
193
194
195  MainObjectArrayPtr::MainObjectArrayPtr(QuantumFile *p_QuantumFile)
196  {
197    m_MOA = new MainObjectArray(p_QuantumFile);
198    m_MOA->m_ReferenceCount = 1;
199  }
200
201
202  MainObjectArrayPtr::MainObjectArrayPtr(const MainObjectArrayPtr& p_MOAP)
203  {
204    m_MOA = p_MOAP.m_MOA;
```

Listing 7.5 *newquant.cpp: implementation of logical layer classes (continued)*

```
205     m_MOA->m_ReferenceCount++;
206   }
207
208
209   MainObjectArrayPtr::MainObjectArray *MainObjectArrayPtr::operator->()
210   {
211     return m_MOA;
212   }
213
214   MainObjectArrayPtr&MainObjectArrayPtr::operator=(const MainObjectArrayPtr& p_MOAP)
215   {
216     m_MOA->m_ReferenceCount--;
217     if (m_MOA->m_ReferenceCount <= 0 && m_MOA != p_MOAP.m_MOA)
218         delete m_MOA;
219     m_MOA = p_MOAP.m_MOA;
220     m_MOA->m_ReferenceCount ++;
221     return *this;
222   }
223
224   MainObjectArrayPtr::~MainObjectArrayPtr()
225   {
226     m_MOA->m_ReferenceCount --;
227     if (m_MOA->m_ReferenceCount <= 0)
228         delete m_MOA;
229   }
230
231   MainObjectArrayPtr::MainObjectArray::MainObjectArray():
232   m_QuantumFile(0),
233   m_BlockPtr((unsigned short)0),
234   m_MainObjectCount(0),
235   m_MainObjectBlockCount(0),
236   m_CurrentLowestFreeObject(0)
237   {
238   };
239
240   MainObjectArrayPtr::MainObjectArray::~MainObjectArray()
241   {
242   }
243
244   MainObjectArrayPtr::MainObjectArray::MainObjectArray(QuantumFile *p_MRU)
245   {
246     ArrayIndex i;
247
248     if (p_MRU)
249         {
250         m_QuantumFile = p_MRU;
251         m_MainObjectCount = p_MRU->GetMainObjectCount();
252         m_MainObjectBlockCount = p_MRU->GetMainObjectBlockCount();
253         m_CurrentLowestFreeObject = 0;
254         m_BlockPtr.SetSize(m_MainObjectCount);
255         for (i = 0; i < m_BlockPtr.GetSize(); i ++)
```

Listing 7.5 *newquant.cpp: implementation of logical layer classes (continued)*

```
256                    m_BlockPtr[i] = p_MRU->MakeMainObjectBlockPtr(i);
257            }
258    }
259
260    MainObjectEntry MainObjectArrayPtr::MainObjectArray::Get(ArrayIndex p_Index)
261    {
262      ArrayIndex Block;
263      ArrayIndex Element;
264      MainObjectEntry Result;
265
266      if (p_Index >= m_MainObjectCount)
267          return(0); // say there's no space here
268
269      Block = p_Index / MainObjectEntriesPerBlock;
270      Element = p_Index % MainObjectEntriesPerBlock;
271      Result = m_BlockPtr[Block]->Get(Element);
272
273      return Result;
274    }
275
276    void MainObjectArrayPtr::MainObjectArray::Set(ArrayIndex p_Index, MainObjectEntry p_Entry)
277    {
278      ArrayIndex Block;
279      ArrayIndex Element;
280      MainObjectEntry Result;
281
282      if (p_Index >= m_MainObjectCount)
283          return; // can't store off the end
284
285      Block = p_Index / MainObjectEntriesPerBlock;
286      Element = p_Index % MainObjectEntriesPerBlock;
287      m_BlockPtr[Block]->Set(Element, p_Entry);
288      if ((p_Entry == NoObject) && (p_Index < m_CurrentLowestFreeObject))
289          m_CurrentLowestFreeObject = p_Index;
290
291      return;
292    }
293
294    ArrayIndex MainObjectArrayPtr::MainObjectArray::FindObjectByName(
295      ModifiableElement p_ObjectName)
296    {
297      ArrayIndex i;
298      ModifiableElement TempElement;
299
300    // note: there is no object numbered 0
301      for (i = 1; i < m_MainObjectCount; i ++)
302          {
303          TempElement = GetModifiableElement(MainObjectDirectory,i);
304          if (TempElement.GetSize() == 0)
305              return NoObject;
306          if (p_ObjectName == TempElement)
```

Listing 7.5 *newquant.cpp: implementation of logical layer classes (continued)*

```
307                return i;
308            }
309       return NoObject;
310    }
311
312
313    void MainObjectArrayPtr::MainObjectArray::CreateMainObject(
314       ModifiableElement p_ObjectName, ArrayIndex p_ObjectNumber,
315       ArrayIndex p_ElementCount, ArrayIndex p_MaxElementCount)
316    {
317       QuantumNumber NewBigPointerQuantum;
318       BigPointerBlockPtr NewBigPointerBlock;
319       LittlePointerBlockPtr NewLittlePointerBlock;
320       BigArrayHeader NewBigArrayHeader;
321       Vector<QuantumNumber> NewBigPointerArray;
322       Vector<ItemReference> NewLittlePointerArray;
323       ArrayIndex LittlePointerBlockCount;
324       ArrayIndex i;
325       ArrayIndex j;
326       ArrayIndex NewQuantum;
327       FreeSpaceEntry TempFreeSpaceEntry;
328
329       if (p_ElementCount == 0)
330            p_ElementCount = 1;   // this is the simplest handling for 0-length arrays
331
332       NewBigPointerQuantum = m_QuantumFile->FindEmptyBlock();
333       NewBigPointerBlock = m_QuantumFile->MakeBigPointerBlockPtr(NewBigPointerQuantum);
334       TempFreeSpaceEntry.m_ObjectNumber = p_ObjectNumber;
335       TempFreeSpaceEntry.m_FreeSpaceCode = 0;
336       NewBigPointerBlock->Clear();
337       NewBigPointerBlock->SetQuantumType(BIG_POINTER_ARRAY);
338       NewBigPointerBlock->SetMainObjectNumber(p_ObjectNumber);
339       NewBigArrayHeader.m_ElementCount = p_ElementCount;
340       NewBigArrayHeader.m_MaxElementCount = p_MaxElementCount;
341       NewBigArrayHeader.m_LastQuantumAddedTo = NoQuantum;
342       NewBigPointerBlock->AddItem(&NewBigArrayHeader,
343            sizeof(BigArrayHeader), BIG_ARRAY_HEADER, 0);
344
345       LittlePointerBlockCount = (p_ElementCount-1)/ItemReferencesPerBlock + 1;
346       NewBigPointerArray = Vector<QuantumNumber>(LittlePointerBlockCount);
347       NewLittlePointerArray = Vector<ItemReference>(ItemReferencesPerBlock);
348       for (i = 0; i < LittlePointerBlockCount; i ++)
349            {
350            NewQuantum = m_QuantumFile->FindEmptyBlock();
351            m_QuantumFile->SetFreeSpace(NewQuantum,TempFreeSpaceEntry);
352            NewBigPointerArray[i] = NewQuantum;
353            NewLittlePointerBlock = m_QuantumFile->MakeLittlePointerBlockPtr(NewQuantum);
354            NewLittlePointerBlock->Clear();
355            NewLittlePointerBlock->SetQuantumType(LITTLE_POINTER_ARRAY);
356            NewLittlePointerBlock->SetMainObjectNumber(p_ObjectNumber);
357            NewLittlePointerBlock->AddItem(NewLittlePointerArray.GetDataAddress(),
```

```
358            NewLittlePointerArray.GetSize()*sizeof(ItemReference),
359              LITTLE_POINTER_ARRAY,0);
360          NewLittlePointerBlock->ClearLittleArray();
361          m_QuantumFile->SetFreeSpace(NewQuantum,TempFreeSpaceEntry);
362          }
363      NewBigPointerBlock->AddItem(NewBigPointerArray.GetDataAddress(),
364          NewBigPointerArray.GetSize()*sizeof(QuantumNumber),
365          BIG_POINTER_ARRAY,0);
366      m_QuantumFile->SetFreeSpace(NewBigPointerQuantum,TempFreeSpaceEntry);
367      Set(p_ObjectNumber,NewBigPointerQuantum);
368      PutElement(MainObjectDirectory, p_ObjectNumber, p_ObjectName);
369  }
370
371
372  ArrayIndex MainObjectArrayPtr::MainObjectArray::GrowMainObject(
373      ArrayIndex p_ObjectNumber, ArrayIndex p_NewElementCount)
374  {
375      MainObjectEntry BigPointerArrayQuantumNumber;
376      BigPointerBlockPtr BigPointerBlock;
377      LittlePointerBlockPtr NewLittlePointerBlock;
378      Vector<ItemReference> NewLittlePointerArray;
379      BigPointerArray OldBigPointerArray;
380      Vector<QuantumNumber> NewBigPointerArray;
381      ArrayIndex NewLittlePointerBlockCount;
382      ArrayIndex OldLittlePointerBlockCount;
383      ArrayIndex i;
384      ArrayIndex j;
385      ArrayIndex NewQuantum;
386      FreeSpaceEntry TempFreeSpaceEntry;
387      ArrayIndex UpdatedElementCount;
388
389      BigPointerArrayQuantumNumber = Get(p_ObjectNumber);
390      BigPointerBlock = m_QuantumFile->MakeBigPointerBlockPtr(BigPointerArrayQuantumNumber);
391      OldBigPointerArray = BigPointerBlock->GetBigPointerArray(); // big pointer array
392      NewBigPointerArray = OldBigPointerArray;
393
394      NewLittlePointerBlockCount = (p_NewElementCount-1)/ItemReferencesPerBlock + 1;
395      UpdatedElementCount = NewLittlePointerBlockCount * ItemReferencesPerBlock;
396      OldLittlePointerBlockCount = NewBigPointerArray.GetSize();
397      if (NewLittlePointerBlockCount == OldLittlePointerBlockCount) // first overflow
398          {
399          BigPointerBlock->SetBigArrayElementCount(UpdatedElementCount);
400          return UpdatedElementCount;
401          }
402
403      NewBigPointerArray.SetSize(NewLittlePointerBlockCount);
404      BigPointerBlock->SetBigArrayElementCount(UpdatedElementCount);
405
406      TempFreeSpaceEntry.m_ObjectNumber = p_ObjectNumber;
407      TempFreeSpaceEntry.m_FreeSpaceCode = 0;
408
```

Listing 7.5 *newquant.cpp: implementation of logical layer classes (continued)*

```
409     NewLittlePointerArray = Vector<ItemReference>(ItemReferencesPerBlock);
410     for (i = OldLittlePointerBlockCount; i < NewLittlePointerBlockCount; i ++)
411         {
412         NewQuantum = m_QuantumFile->FindEmptyBlock();
413         m_QuantumFile->SetFreeSpace(NewQuantum,TempFreeSpaceEntry);
414         NewBigPointerArray[i] = NewQuantum;
415         NewLittlePointerBlock = m_QuantumFile->MakeLittlePointerBlockPtr(NewQuantum);
416         NewLittlePointerBlock->Clear();
417         NewLittlePointerBlock->SetQuantumType(LITTLE_POINTER_ARRAY);
418         NewLittlePointerBlock->SetMainObjectNumber(p_ObjectNumber);
419         NewLittlePointerBlock->AddItem(NewLittlePointerArray.GetDataAddress(),
420             NewLittlePointerArray.GetSize()*sizeof(ItemReference),
421             LITTLE_POINTER_ARRAY,0);
422         NewLittlePointerBlock->ClearLittleArray();
423         m_QuantumFile->SetFreeSpace(NewQuantum,TempFreeSpaceEntry);
424         }
425     BigPointerBlock->DeleteItem(2); // big pointer array
426     BigPointerBlock->AddItem(NewBigPointerArray.GetDataAddress(),
427         NewBigPointerArray.GetSize()*sizeof(QuantumNumber),
428         BIG_POINTER_ARRAY,0);
429     m_QuantumFile->SetFreeSpace(BigPointerArrayQuantumNumber,TempFreeSpaceEntry);
430     return UpdatedElementCount;
431  }
432
433
434  ArrayIndex MainObjectArrayPtr::MainObjectArray::FindAvailableObject()
435  {
436    ArrayIndex Block;
437    ArrayIndex Element;
438    ArrayIndex Result = (unsigned)-1;
439
440    Block = m_CurrentLowestFreeObject / MainObjectEntriesPerBlock;
441    Element = m_CurrentLowestFreeObject % MainObjectEntriesPerBlock;
442    for (; Block < m_MainObjectBlockCount; Block ++)
443        {
444        for (; Element < MainObjectEntriesPerBlock; Element ++)
445            {
446            if (m_BlockPtr[Block]->Get(Element) == NoObject)
447                {
448                Result = Block * MainObjectEntriesPerBlock + Element;
449                break;
450                }
451            }
452        if (Result != (unsigned)-1)
453            break;
454        }
455    m_CurrentLowestFreeObject = Result;
456
457    return Result;
458  }
459
```

Listing 7.5 *newquant.cpp: implementation of logical layer classes (continued)*

```
460    ModifiableElement MainObjectArrayPtr::MainObjectArray::GetModifiableElement(
461        ArrayIndex p_MainObjectNumber, ArrayIndex p_ElementIndex)
462    {
463        MainObjectEntry BigPointerArrayQuantumNumber;
464        BigPointerBlockPtr BigPointerBlock;
465        LittlePointerBlockPtr LittlePointerBlock;
466        LeafBlockPtr ElementBlock;
467        ArrayIndex BigPointerIndex;
468        ArrayIndex LittlePointerIndex;
469        QuantumNumber LittlePointerArrayQuantumNumber;
470        ItemReference ElementReference;
471        ModifiableElement Element;
472
473        BigPointerArrayQuantumNumber = Get(p_MainObjectNumber);
474
475        BigPointerBlock = m_QuantumFile->MakeBigPointerBlockPtr(BigPointerArrayQuantumNumber);
476
477        BigPointerIndex = p_ElementIndex / ItemReferencesPerBlock;
478        LittlePointerArrayQuantumNumber = BigPointerBlock->GetBigArrayElement(BigPointerIndex);
479
480        LittlePointerBlock =
                    m_QuantumFile->MakeLittlePointerBlockPtr(LittlePointerArrayQuantumNumber);
481        LittlePointerIndex = p_ElementIndex % ItemReferencesPerBlock;
482        ElementReference = LittlePointerBlock->GetLittleArrayElement(LittlePointerIndex);
483
484        if (ElementReference.IsReference())
485            {
486            ElementBlock = m_QuantumFile->MakeLeafBlockPtr(ElementReference.GetQuantumNumber());
487            Element = ElementBlock->GetModifiableItem(ElementReference.GetItemNumber());
488            }
489        else
490            Element = ModifiableElement(0,0);
491
492        return Element;
493    }
494
495    int MainObjectArrayPtr::MainObjectArray::PutElement(ArrayIndex p_MainObjectNumber,
496        ArrayIndex p_ElementIndex, ModifiableElement p_Element)
497    {
498        MainObjectEntry BigPointerArrayQuantumNumber;
499        BigPointerBlockPtr BigPointerBlock;
500        LittlePointerBlockPtr LittlePointerBlock;
501        LeafBlockPtr ElementBlock;
502        ArrayIndex BigPointerIndex;
503        ArrayIndex LittlePointerIndex;
504        QuantumNumber LittlePointerArrayQuantumNumber;
505        ItemReference ElementReference;
506        ItemReference NewElementReference;
507        ModifiableElement Element;
508        FreeSpaceEntry SpaceAvailable;
509        QuantumNumber NewQuantum;
```

Listing 7.5 *newquant.cpp: implementation of logical layer classes (continued)*

```
510    QuantumNumber PossibleQuantum;
511    LeafBlockPtr NewElementBlock;
512    ArrayIndex FreeSpace;
513    ArrayIndex ActualFreeSpace;
514    ArrayIndex i;
515    ArrayIndex NewItemNumber;
516
517    qfassert (p_Element.GetSize() < MaxItemSize);
518
519    BigPointerArrayQuantumNumber = Get(p_MainObjectNumber);
520
521    BigPointerBlock = m_QuantumFile->MakeBigPointerBlockPtr(BigPointerArrayQuantumNumber);
522
523    BigPointerIndex = p_ElementIndex / ItemReferencesPerBlock;
524    LittlePointerArrayQuantumNumber = BigPointerBlock->GetBigArrayElement(BigPointerIndex);
525
526   LittlePointerBlock = m_QuantumFile->MakeLittlePointerBlockPtr(LittlePointerArrayQuantumNumber);
527    LittlePointerIndex = p_ElementIndex % ItemReferencesPerBlock;
528    ElementReference = LittlePointerBlock->GetLittleArrayElement(LittlePointerIndex);
529
530    if (ElementReference.IsReference())
531        {
532        ElementBlock = m_QuantumFile->MakeLeafBlockPtr(ElementReference.GetQuantumNumber());
533        ElementBlock->DeleteItem(ElementReference.GetItemNumber());
534        }
535
536    if (p_Element.GetSize() == 0) // nothing to store
537        {
538        ElementReference.SetQuantumNumber(NoQuantum);
539        ElementReference.SetItemNumber(NoItem);
540        LittlePointerBlock->SetLittleArrayElement(LittlePointerIndex,ElementReference);
541        return 0;
542        }
543
544    NewQuantum = NoQuantum;
545    PossibleQuantum = BigPointerBlock->GetLastQuantumAddedTo();
546    SpaceAvailable = m_QuantumFile->GetFreeSpace(PossibleQuantum);
547    FreeSpace = SpaceAvailable.m_FreeSpaceCode * FreeSpaceConversion;
548    if (FreeSpace > p_Element.GetSize())
549        {
550        NewElementBlock = m_QuantumFile->MakeLeafBlockPtr(PossibleQuantum);
551        ActualFreeSpace = NewElementBlock->CalculateFreeSpace();
552        if (ActualFreeSpace > p_Element.GetSize())
553            NewQuantum = PossibleQuantum;
554        }
555
556    if (NewQuantum == NoQuantum)
557        {
558        NewQuantum = m_QuantumFile->FindSpaceForItem(p_MainObjectNumber, p_Element.GetSize());
559        NewElementBlock = m_QuantumFile->MakeLeafBlockPtr(NewQuantum);
560        }
```

Listing 7.5 *newquant.cpp: implementation of logical layer classes (continued)*

```
561
562    BigPointerBlock->SetLastQuantumAddedTo(NewQuantum);
563    NewElementReference.SetQuantumNumber(NewQuantum);
564    NewItemNumber = NewElementBlock->AddItem(p_Element, VARIABLE_LENGTH_STRING, p_ElementIndex);
565    NewElementReference.SetItemNumber(NewItemNumber);
566
567    LittlePointerBlock->SetLittleArrayElement(LittlePointerIndex,NewElementReference);
568
569    return 0;
570  }
571
572  ArrayIndex MainObjectArrayPtr::MainObjectArray::GetMainObjectElementCount(
573    ArrayIndex p_MainObjectNumber)
574  {
575    MainObjectEntry BigPointerArrayQuantumNumber;
576    BigPointerBlockPtr BigPointerBlock;
577
578    BigPointerArrayQuantumNumber = Get(p_MainObjectNumber);
579    BigPointerBlock = m_QuantumFile->MakeBigPointerBlockPtr(BigPointerArrayQuantumNumber);
580    return BigPointerBlock->GetBigArrayElementCount();
581  }
582
583  ArrayIndex MainObjectArrayPtr::MainObjectArray::GetMainObjectMaxElementCount(
584    ArrayIndex p_MainObjectNumber)
585  {
586    MainObjectEntry BigPointerArrayQuantumNumber;
587    BigPointerBlockPtr BigPointerBlock;
588
589    BigPointerArrayQuantumNumber = Get(p_MainObjectNumber);
590    BigPointerBlock = m_QuantumFile->MakeBigPointerBlockPtr(BigPointerArrayQuantumNumber);
591    return BigPointerBlock->GetBigArrayMaxElementCount();
592  }
593
594  FlexArray::FlexArray()
595  {
596    m_MOAIndex = 0;
597  }
598
599  FlexArray::FlexArray(MainObjectArrayPtr p_MOA, ArrayIndex p_MOAIndex)
600  {
601    m_MOA = p_MOA;
602    m_MOAIndex = p_MOAIndex;
603    m_ElementCount = m_MOA->GetMainObjectElementCount(m_MOAIndex);
604    m_MaxElementCount = m_MOA->GetMainObjectMaxElementCount(m_MOAIndex);
605  }
606
607  FlexArrayRef::FlexArrayRef(MainObjectArrayPtr &p_MOA, ArrayIndex p_MOAIndex,
608    ArrayIndex p_ElementIndex)
609    :    m_MOA(p_MOA), m_MOAIndex(p_MOAIndex), m_ElementIndex(p_ElementIndex)
610  {
611  }
```

Listing 7.5 *newquant.cpp: implementation of logical layer classes (continued)*

```
612
613   FlexArrayRef& FlexArrayRef::operator=(ModifiableElement p_ROE)
614   {
615     m_MOA->PutElement(m_MOAIndex, m_ElementIndex, p_ROE);
616     return *this;
617   }
618
619   FlexArrayRef::operator ModifiableElement()
620   {
621     return m_MOA->GetModifiableElement(m_MOAIndex, m_ElementIndex);
622   }
623
624   FlexArrayRef FlexArray::operator[](ArrayIndex p_ElementIndex)
625   {
626     qfassert(p_ElementIndex < m_MaxElementCount);
627     if (p_ElementIndex >= m_ElementCount)
628         m_ElementCount = m_MOA->GrowMainObject(m_MOAIndex,p_ElementIndex+1);
629
630     return FlexArrayRef(m_MOA, m_MOAIndex, p_ElementIndex);
631   }
632
```

Listing 7.6 *persist.h: persistent array class declarations*

```
1
2    /****keyword-flag*** "%v %f %n" */
3    /* "3 20-Apr-94,17:59:26 PERSIST.H" */
4
5
6    const ArrayIndex UlongEntriesPerBlock = MaxItemSize / sizeof(Ulong);
7
8    class PersistentArrayUlong;
9
10   class PersistentArrayUlongRef
11   {
12   private:
13     PersistentArrayUlong &m_PAU;
14     Ulong m_Index;
15   public:
16     PersistentArrayUlongRef(PersistentArrayUlong &p_PAU, Ulong p_Index);
17     PersistentArrayUlongRef &operator=(Ulong p_Element);
18     operator Ulong();
19   };
20
21   class PersistentArrayUlong
22   {
23   protected:
24     ModifiableElement m_ArrayName;
25     QuantumFile *m_QF;
26     MainObjectArrayPtr m_MOA;
27     ArrayIndex m_ObjectNumber;
28   public:
29     PersistentArrayUlong();
30     ~PersistentArrayUlong();
31     PersistentArrayUlong(QuantumFile *p_QF, ModifiableElement p_ArrayName);
32     void StoreElement(Ulong p_Index, Ulong p_Element);
33     Ulong GetElement(Ulong p_Index);
34     PersistentArrayUlongRef operator[](Ulong p_Index);
35   };
```

Listing 7.7 *persist.cpp: persistent array class implementation*

```
1
2    /****keyword-flag*** "%v %f %n" */
3    /* "3 26-Apr-94,19:29:20 PERSIST.CPP" */
4
5
6    #include "common.h"
7
8    PersistentArrayUlong::PersistentArrayUlong()
9    {
10     m_ObjectNumber = 0;
11   }
12
13   PersistentArrayUlong::~PersistentArrayUlong()
14   {
15   }
16
17   PersistentArrayUlong::PersistentArrayUlong(QuantumFile *p_QF, ModifiableElement p_ArrayName)
18   {
19     m_ArrayName = p_ArrayName;
20     m_QF = p_QF;
21     m_MOA = MainObjectArrayPtr(m_QF);
22
23     m_ObjectNumber = m_MOA->FindObjectByName(m_ArrayName);
24     if (m_ObjectNumber == NoObject)
25         {
26         m_ObjectNumber = m_MOA->FindAvailableObject();
27         m_MOA->CreateMainObject(m_ArrayName,m_ObjectNumber,1,
28             MaxFileQuantumCount);
29         }
30   }
31
32   void PersistentArrayUlong::StoreElement(Ulong p_Index, Ulong p_Element)
33   {
34     ArrayIndex SegmentNumber;
35     ArrayIndex ElementNumber;
36     ModifiableElement TempVector;
37     AccessVector<Ulong> TempUlongVector;
38     ArrayIndex OldSegmentCount;
39     ArrayIndex RequiredSegmentCount;
40     ArrayIndex i;
41
42     SegmentNumber = p_Index / UlongEntriesPerBlock;
43     ElementNumber = p_Index % UlongEntriesPerBlock;
44
45     qfassert(SegmentNumber < m_MOA->GetMainObjectMaxElementCount(m_ObjectNumber));
46     OldSegmentCount = m_MOA->GetMainObjectElementCount(m_ObjectNumber);
47     RequiredSegmentCount = SegmentNumber+1;
48     if (RequiredSegmentCount > OldSegmentCount)
49         m_MOA->GrowMainObject(m_ObjectNumber,RequiredSegmentCount);
50
51     TempVector = m_MOA->GetModifiableElement(m_ObjectNumber,SegmentNumber);
```

Listing 7.7 *persist.cpp: persistent array class implementation (continued)*

```
52      if (TempVector.GetSize() == 0)
53          {
54          TempVector = ModifiableElement(UlongEntriesPerBlock*sizeof(Ulong));
55          memset(TempVector.GetDataAddress(),0,TempVector.GetSize());
56          }
57
58    TempUlongVector = AccessVector<Ulong>(UlongEntriesPerBlock,(Ulong *)TempVector.GetDataAddress());
59    TempUlongVector[ElementNumber] = p_Element;
60
61    m_MOA->PutElement(m_ObjectNumber,SegmentNumber,TempVector);
62  }
63
64  Ulong PersistentArrayUlong::GetElement(Ulong p_Index)
65  {
66    ArrayIndex SegmentNumber;
67    ArrayIndex ElementNumber;
68    ModifiableElement TempVector;
69    AccessVector<Ulong> TempUlongVector;
70
71    SegmentNumber = p_Index / UlongEntriesPerBlock;
72    ElementNumber = p_Index % UlongEntriesPerBlock;
73
74    qfassert(SegmentNumber < m_MOA->GetMainObjectElementCount(m_ObjectNumber));
75    TempVector = m_MOA->GetModifiableElement(m_ObjectNumber,SegmentNumber);
76    TempUlongVector = AccessVector<Ulong>(UlongEntriesPerBlock,(Ulong *)TempVector.GetDataAddress());
77    return TempUlongVector[ElementNumber];
78  }
79
80  PersistentArrayUlongRef::PersistentArrayUlongRef(PersistentArrayUlong &p_PAU,
81  Ulong p_Index) : m_PAU(p_PAU), m_Index(p_Index)
82  {
83  }
84
85  PersistentArrayUlongRef &PersistentArrayUlongRef::operator=(Ulong p_Element)
86  {
87    m_PAU.StoreElement(m_Index,p_Element);
88    return *this;
89  }
90
91  PersistentArrayUlongRef::operator Ulong()
92  {
93    return m_PAU.GetElement(m_Index);
94  }
95
96  PersistentArrayUlongRef PersistentArrayUlong::operator[](Ulong p_Index)
97  {
98    return PersistentArrayUlongRef(*this, p_Index);
99  }
```

Listing 7.8 *dynhash.h: dynamic hashing class declarations*

```
1
2    /****keyword-flag*** "%v %f %n" */
3    /* "8 2-Apr-94,7:15:00 DYNHASH.H" */
4
5
6    class DynamicHashArray;
7
8    class DynamicHashString
9    {
10   friend DynamicHashArray;
11   protected:
12     ArrayIndex m_Count;
13     Vector<AccountNumber> m_Key;
14     Vector<ArrayIndex> m_Offset;
15     ModifiableElement m_Data;
16   public:
17     DynamicHashString();
18     DynamicHashString(ModifiableElement p_Element);
19     void AddElement(AccountNumber p_Key, ModifiableElement p_Element);
20     ModifiableElement FindElement(AccountNumber p_Key);
21     operator ModifiableElement();
22     ModifiableElement GetSubString(ArrayIndex p_Index);
23   };
24
25   class DynamicHashArrayRef
26   {
27   private:
28     DynamicHashArray &m_DHA;
29     AccountNumber m_DHAIndex;
30   public:
31     DynamicHashArrayRef(DynamicHashArray &p_DHA, AccountNumber p_DHAIndex);
32     DynamicHashArrayRef &operator=(ModifiableElement p_ME);
33     operator ModifiableElement();
34   };
35
36   static const ArrayIndex InitCurrentSlotCount = 8;
37   static const Ulong InitCurrentMaxSlotCount = 8;
38   static const ArrayIndex ElementsPerSlot = 6;
39
40   class DynamicHashArray
41   {
42   protected:
43
44     ModifiableElement m_ArrayName;
45     QuantumFile *m_QF;
46     MainObjectArrayPtr m_MOA;
47     ArrayIndex m_ObjectNumber;
48     ArrayIndex m_CurrentSlotCount;
49     Ulong m_CurrentMaxSlotCount;
50     ArrayIndex m_ElementsBeforeExpansion;
51   public:
```

Listing 7.8 *dynhash.h: dynamic hashing class declarations (continued)*

```
52       DynamicHashArray();
53       ~DynamicHashArray();
54       DynamicHashArray(QuantumFile *p_QF, ModifiableElement p_ArrayName);
55       void AddElement(AccountNumber p_Key, ModifiableElement p_Element);
56       ModifiableElement FindElement(AccountNumber p_Key);
57       ArrayIndex CalculateHash(AccountNumber p_Key);
58       void PutString(ArrayIndex p_Index, ModifiableElement p_Element);
59       ModifiableElement GetString(ArrayIndex p_Index);
60       DynamicHashArrayRef operator[](AccountNumber p_AccountNumber);
61   };
```

Listing 7.9 *dynhash.cpp: dynamic hashing class implementation*

```
1
2    /****keyword-flag*** "%v %f %n" */
3    /* "10 23-Apr-94,16:24:54 DYNHASH.CPP" */
4
5
6    #include "common.h"
7
8    DynamicHashString::DynamicHashString()
9    {
10     m_Count = 0;
11   }
12
13   DynamicHashString::DynamicHashString(ModifiableElement p_Element)
14   {
15     ArrayIndex i;
16     char *ElementPtr = (char *)p_Element.GetDataAddress();
17     char *StartingAddress;
18     ArrayIndex TotalDataLength;
19     ArrayIndex HeaderLength;
20
21     if (p_Element.GetSize() == 0)
22         {
23         m_Count = 0;
24         return;
25         }
26
27     m_Count = *(ArrayIndex *)ElementPtr;
28     if (m_Count == 0)
29         return;
30
31     HeaderLength = sizeof(m_Count) + m_Count *
32         (sizeof(AccountNumber) + sizeof(ArrayIndex));
33     StartingAddress = ElementPtr + HeaderLength;
34     ElementPtr += sizeof(m_Count);
35     TotalDataLength = p_Element.GetSize()-HeaderLength;
36
37     m_Key = Vector<AccountNumber>(m_Count, (AccountNumber *)ElementPtr);
38     ElementPtr += m_Count * sizeof(AccountNumber);
39
40     m_Offset = Vector<ArrayIndex>(m_Count, (ArrayIndex *)ElementPtr);
41
42     m_Data = ModifiableElement(TotalDataLength,StartingAddress);
43   }
44
45
46   DynamicHashString::operator ModifiableElement()
47   {
48     ArrayIndex i;
49     ArrayIndex HeaderLength;
50     ArrayIndex DataLength = 0;
51     ModifiableElement TempValue;
```

Listing 7.9 *dynhash.cpp: dynamic hashing class implementation (continued)*

```
52      char *TempPtr;
53
54      HeaderLength = sizeof(m_Count) + m_Count *
55          (sizeof(AccountNumber) + sizeof(ArrayIndex));
56
57      DataLength = m_Data.GetSize();
58
59      TempValue.SetSize(HeaderLength+DataLength);
60      TempPtr = (char *)TempValue.GetDataAddress();
61      *(ArrayIndex *)TempPtr = m_Count;
62      TempPtr += sizeof(m_Count);
63
64      memcpy(TempPtr,m_Key.GetDataAddress(),m_Count * sizeof(AccountNumber));
65      TempPtr += m_Count * sizeof(AccountNumber);
66
67      memcpy(TempPtr,m_Offset.GetDataAddress(),m_Count * sizeof(ArrayIndex));
68      TempPtr += m_Count * sizeof(ArrayIndex);
69
70      memcpy(TempPtr,m_Data.GetDataAddress(),m_Data.GetSize());
71
72      return ModifiableElement(TempValue.GetSize(),(char *)TempValue.GetDataAddress());
73  }
74
75
76  void DynamicHashString::AddElement(AccountNumber p_Key, ModifiableElement p_Element)
77  {
78      ArrayIndex OldSize;
79      ArrayIndex NewElementSize;
80
81      m_Count ++;
82
83      m_Key.SetSize(m_Count);
84      m_Key[m_Count-1] = p_Key;
85
86      OldSize = m_Data.GetSize();
87
88      m_Offset.SetSize(m_Count);
89      m_Offset[m_Count-1] = OldSize;
90
91      NewElementSize = p_Element.GetSize();
92      m_Data.SetSize(OldSize+NewElementSize);
93      memcpy((char *)m_Data.GetDataAddress()+OldSize,p_Element.GetDataAddress(),
94      NewElementSize);
95  }
96
97  ModifiableElement DynamicHashString::GetSubString(ArrayIndex p_Index)
98  {
99      if (p_Index < m_Count - 1)
100         return m_Data.Mid(m_Offset[p_Index],m_Offset[p_Index+1]-m_Offset[p_Index]);
101     else
102         return m_Data.Mid(m_Offset[p_Index],m_Data.GetSize()-m_Offset[p_Index]);
```

Listing 7.9 *dynhash.cpp: dynamic hashing class implementation (continued)*

```
103   }
104
105   ModifiableElement DynamicHashString::FindElement(AccountNumber p_Key)
106   {
107     ArrayIndex i;
108     ModifiableElement TempString;
109
110     for (i = 0; i < m_Count; i ++)
111         {
112         if (m_Key[i] == p_Key)
113             return GetSubString(i);
114         }
115
116     return ModifiableElement();
117   }
118
119   DynamicHashArray::DynamicHashArray()
120   {
121     m_ObjectNumber = 0;
122     m_CurrentSlotCount = 0;
123     m_CurrentMaxSlotCount = 0;
124     m_ElementsBeforeExpansion = 0;
125   }
126
127   DynamicHashArray::~DynamicHashArray()
128   {
129     ModifiableElement TempString;
130     ModifiableElement OldString;
131     char buf[30];
132
133     OldString = GetString(-1);
134    sprintf(buf,"%6u %6lu %6u",m_CurrentSlotCount, m_CurrentMaxSlotCount, m_ElementsBeforeExpansion);
135     TempString = buf;
136     if (OldString != TempString)
137         PutString(-1,TempString);
138   }
139
140   DynamicHashArray::DynamicHashArray(QuantumFile *p_QF, ModifiableElement p_ArrayName)
141   {
142     ArrayIndex i;
143     ModifiableElement TempString;
144
145     m_ArrayName = p_ArrayName;
146     m_QF = p_QF;
147     m_MOA = MainObjectArrayPtr(m_QF);
148
149     m_ObjectNumber = m_MOA->FindObjectByName(m_ArrayName);
150     if (m_ObjectNumber == NoObject)
151         {
152         m_ObjectNumber = m_MOA->FindAvailableObject();
153         m_MOA->CreateMainObject(m_ArrayName,m_ObjectNumber);
```

Listing 7.9 *dynhash.cpp: dynamic hashing class implementation (continued)*

```
154            m_CurrentSlotCount = InitCurrentSlotCount;
155            m_CurrentMaxSlotCount = InitCurrentMaxSlotCount;
156            m_ElementsBeforeExpansion = ElementsPerSlot * InitCurrentSlotCount;
157            for (i = 0; i < m_CurrentSlotCount; i ++)
158                 PutString(i,TempString);
159            PutString(-1,""); // clear parameter string
160            }
161    else
162        {
163        TempString = GetString(-1); // get parameter string
164        m_CurrentSlotCount = (ArrayIndex)atol(TempString);
165        m_CurrentMaxSlotCount = (Ulong)atol(TempString.Mid(7,7));
166        m_ElementsBeforeExpansion = (ArrayIndex)atol(TempString.Mid(14,7));
167        }
168    }
169
170    ArrayIndex DynamicHashArray::CalculateHash(AccountNumber p_Key)
171    {
172      ArrayIndex Result;
173      ArrayIndex HashNumber;
174
175      HashNumber = (314159L*p_Key) % 1048583L;
176
177      Result = HashNumber & (m_CurrentMaxSlotCount-1);
178      if (Result >= m_CurrentSlotCount)
179          Result -= m_CurrentMaxSlotCount/2;
180
181      return Result;
182    }
183
184    void DynamicHashArray::AddElement(AccountNumber p_Key, ModifiableElement p_Element)
185    {
186      ArrayIndex SlotNumber;
187      DynamicHashString DHString;
188      DynamicHashString BuddyString;
189      DynamicHashString NewSlotString;
190      ArrayIndex i;
191      ArrayIndex BuddySlotNumber;
192      ArrayIndex NewSlotNumber;
193      AccountNumber AcctNumber;
194      ModifiableElement Data;
195      DynamicHashString TempString;
196
197      if (m_ElementsBeforeExpansion == 0)
198          {
199          if (m_CurrentSlotCount == UINT_MAX)
200              exit(1); // should be an exception, but not yet
201          if (m_CurrentSlotCount == m_CurrentMaxSlotCount)
202              m_CurrentMaxSlotCount *= 2;
203          PutString(m_CurrentSlotCount,ModifiableElement());
204          BuddySlotNumber = m_CurrentSlotCount - m_CurrentMaxSlotCount/2;
```

Listing 7.9 dynhash.cpp: dynamic hashing class implementation (continued)

```
205              NewSlotNumber = m_CurrentSlotCount;
206              m_CurrentSlotCount ++;
207              TempString = DynamicHashString(GetString(BuddySlotNumber));
208              PutString(BuddySlotNumber,ModifiableElement());
209              for (i = 0; i < TempString.m_Count; i ++)
210                  {
211                  AcctNumber = TempString.m_Key[i];
212                  SlotNumber = CalculateHash(AcctNumber);
213                  if (SlotNumber == BuddySlotNumber)
214                      BuddyString.AddElement(AcctNumber, TempString.GetSubString(i));
215                  else if (SlotNumber == NewSlotNumber)
216                      NewSlotString.AddElement(AcctNumber, TempString.GetSubString(i));
217                  else
218                      qfassert(0); // should never happen
219                  }
220              PutString(NewSlotNumber,NewSlotString);
221              PutString(BuddySlotNumber,BuddyString);
222              m_ElementsBeforeExpansion = ElementsPerSlot;
223              }
224
225      SlotNumber = CalculateHash(p_Key);
226      DHString = DynamicHashString(GetString(SlotNumber));
227      DHString.AddElement(p_Key, p_Element);
228      PutString(SlotNumber,DHString);
229      m_ElementsBeforeExpansion --;
230  }
231
232  void DynamicHashArray::PutString(ArrayIndex p_Index, ModifiableElement p_Element)
233  {
234      p_Index ++;
235      qfassert(p_Index < m_MOA->GetMainObjectMaxElementCount(m_ObjectNumber));
236      if (p_Index >= m_MOA->GetMainObjectElementCount(m_ObjectNumber))
237          m_MOA->GrowMainObject(m_ObjectNumber,p_Index+1);
238
239      m_MOA->PutElement(m_ObjectNumber,p_Index,p_Element);
240  }
241
242  ModifiableElement DynamicHashArray::GetString(ArrayIndex p_Index)
243  {
244      p_Index ++;
245      qfassert(p_Index < m_MOA->GetMainObjectElementCount(m_ObjectNumber));
246      return m_MOA->GetModifiableElement(m_ObjectNumber,p_Index);
247  }
248
249  ModifiableElement DynamicHashArray::FindElement(AccountNumber p_Key)
250  {
251      ArrayIndex SlotNumber;
252      DynamicHashString DHString;
253
254      SlotNumber = CalculateHash(p_Key);
```

Listing 7.9 *dynhash.cpp: dynamic hashing class implementation (continued)*

```
255      DHString = DynamicHashString(GetString(SlotNumber));
256      return DHString.FindElement(p_Key);
257    }
258
259    DynamicHashArrayRef::DynamicHashArrayRef(DynamicHashArray &p_DHA, AccountNumber p_DHAIndex)
260      : m_DHA(p_DHA), m_DHAIndex(p_DHAIndex)
261    {
262    }
263
264    DynamicHashArrayRef &DynamicHashArrayRef::operator=(ModifiableElement p_ME)
265    {
266      m_DHA.AddElement(m_DHAIndex,p_ME);
267      return *this;
268    }
269
270    DynamicHashArrayRef::operator ModifiableElement()
271    {
272      return m_DHA.FindElement(m_DHAIndex);
273    }
274
275    DynamicHashArrayRef DynamicHashArray::operator[](AccountNumber p_AccountNumber)
276    {
277      return DynamicHashArrayRef(*this, p_AccountNumber);
278    }
```

Listing 7.10 *asmfunc.h: assembly routine declarations*

```
1
2    /****keyword-flag*** "%v %f %n" */
3    /* "3 8-Mar-94,7:46:28 ASMFUNC.H" */
4
5
6    void BlockMove(void *dest, const void *src, size_t n);
7    void AdjustOffset(ItemIndex *Item, int Count, int Adjustment);
8    int FindUnusedItem(ItemIndex *Item, int Count);
9    int FindBuffer(ArrayIndex BlockNumber, ArrayIndex *BlockNumberList, int Count);
```

Listing 7.11 *asmfunc.cpp: assembly routines for speed*

```
 1
 2   /****keyword-flag*** "%v %f %n" */
 3   /* "9 10-Apr-94,13:13:54 ASMFUNC.CPP" */
 4
 5
 6   #include "common.h"
 7
 8   void BlockMove(void *dest, const void *src, size_t n)
 9   {
10   #ifndef USEASM386
11     memmove(dest,src,n);
12   #else
13     if ((void huge *)src < (void huge *)dest)
14   asm        jmp endfirst
15
16   frontfirst:
17   asm    push ds
18   asm    lds  si,src    // get source address
19   asm    les  di,dest   // get destination address
20   asm    mov  cx,n // number of bytes to move
21   asm    cmp  cx,4 // if we don't have at least this many, forget opts
22   asm    jc   frontok   // since it doesn't matter anyway
23
24   asm    test di,3// if destination is aligned,
25   asm    jz   frontok   // do it
26
27   frontalign:
28   asm    mov  al,[si]   // otherwise, get a byte
29   asm    mov  es:[di],al// and store it
30   asm    inc  si        // next source
31   asm    inc  di        // next dest
32   asm    dec  cx        // reduce count
33   asm    test di,3// when this gets to be 0, we're ready
34   asm    jnz  frontalign// until then, keep it up
35
36   frontok:          // do it
37   asm    mov  ax,cx     // copy for termination handling
38   asm    and  ax,3 // leftover byte count at end
39   asm    shr  cx,2 // number of dwords to move
40
41   asm    db   0f3h, 66h, 0a5h    // these bytes represent "rep movsd"
42   asm    mov  cx,ax     // do rest of bytes
43   asm    rep  movsb     // if any are needed
44   asm    jmp  done // exit normally
45
46   endfirst:
47   asm    push ds
48   asm    lds  si,src    // get source address
49   asm    les  di,dest   // get destination address
50   asm    mov  bx,n // get count
51   asm    add  si,bx     // fix source
```

Listing 7.11 *asmfunc.cpp: assembly routines for speed (continued)*

```
52    asm    add  di,bx      // and destination
53
54    asm    mov  cx,n // number of bytes to move
55    asm    cmp  cx,4 // if we don't have more than this, forget opts
56    asm    jc   endok      // since it doesn't matter anyway
57
58    asm    test di,3 // if this produces 0, destination is aligned already
59    asm    jz   endok      // if it's the best we can do, do it
60
61    endalign:
62    asm    dec  si         // must predecrement
63    asm    dec  di         // since we're already off the end
64    asm    mov  al,[si]    // get a byte
65    asm    mov  es:[di],al// and store it
66    asm    dec  cx         // reduce count
67    asm    test di,3// when this gets to be 0, we're ready
68    asm    jnz  endalign// until then, keep it up
69
70    endok:
71    asm    sub  si,4 // offsets are of the lowest
72    asm    sub  di,4 // byte to be moved, so adjust them
73
74    asm    mov  ax,cx      // copy for termination handling
75    asm    and  ax,3 // leftover byte count at end
76    asm    shr  cx,2 // number of dwords to move
77
78    asm    std             // move from high to low
79
80    asm    db   0f3h, 66h, 0a5h     // these bytes represent "rep movsd"
81    asm    mov  cx,ax      // odd bytes, if any
82    asm    add  si,3 // fix source for last bytes
83    asm    add  di,3 // fix dest
84    asm    rep  movsb      // do it
85    asm    cld             // set direction flag back to forward
86
87    done:
88    asm    pop  ds
89
90    #endif
91    }
92
93
94    void AdjustOffset(ItemIndex *Item, int Count, int Adjustment)
95    {
96    #ifndef USEASM386
97      int i;
98
99      for (i = 0; i < Count; i ++)
100          Item[i].m_Offset += Adjustment;
101   #else
102     int ItemSize = sizeof(ItemIndex);
```

Listing 7.11 *asmfunc.cpp: assembly routines for speed (continued)*

```
103
104    asm      push ds
105    asm      lds  si,Item
106    asm      mov  cx,Count
107    asm      mov  ax,Adjustment
108    asm      jcxz eloop           // if nothing to do
109
110    sloop:
111    asm      mov  bx,[si]         // get value from table
112    asm      mov  dx,bx          // copy for merge
113    asm      and  bx,BlockSize-1 // clear rest of word
114    asm      add  bx,ax          // add adjustment to current offset
115    asm      and  dx,-(BlockSize) // clear offset in result
116    asm      add  dx,bx          // add new offset
117    asm      mov  [si],dx        // and put it back
118    asm      add  si,ItemSize    // update ptr
119    asm      dec  cx             // check if more to do
120    asm      jnz  sloop          // and continue if so
121
122    eloop:
123    asm      pop  ds
124
125    #endif
126    }
127
128
129    int FindUnusedItem(ItemIndex *Item, int Count)
130    {
131    #ifndef USEASM386
132
133      int i;
134      ItemIndex TempItemIndex;
135      int ItemFound;
136
137      ItemFound = -1;
138
139      for (i = 0; i < Count; i ++)
140          {
141          TempItemIndex = Item[i];
142          if (TempItemIndex.m_Type == UNUSED_ITEM)
143              {
144              ItemFound = i;
145              break;
146              }
147          }
148
149      return ItemFound;
150
151    #else
152      int ItemSize = sizeof(ItemIndex);
153      unsigned UnusedItem = UNUSED_ITEM * BlockSize;
```

Listing 7.11 *asmfunc.cpp: assembly routines for speed (continued)*

```
154     qfassert(Count >= 0);
155
156   asm     push ds
157   asm     lds  si,Item
158   asm     mov  cx,Count
159   asm     mov  ax,0xffff      // not found yet
160   asm     xor  dx,dx          // up count
161   asm     jcxz eloop          // if nothing to do
162
163   sloop:
164   asm     mov  bx,[si]        // get value from table
165   asm     and  bx,-(BlockSize) // get type
166   asm     cmp  bx,UnusedItem  // see if it matches
167   asm     jnz  cloop          // if not, keep going
168   asm     mov  ax,dx          // if so, set value
169   asm     jmp  eloop          // and go
170
171   cloop:
172   asm     add  si,ItemSize    // point to next item
173   asm     inc  dx             // do again if needed
174   asm     cmp  dx,cx          // more to do?
175   asm     jnz  sloop          // if so, do it
176
177   eloop:
178   asm     pop  ds
179
180   #endif
181   }
182
183
184   int FindBuffer(ArrayIndex BlockNumber, ArrayIndex *BlockNumberList, int Count)
185   {
186   #ifndef USEASM386
187
188     int i;
189     int ItemFound;
190
191     ItemFound = -1;
192
193     for (i = 0; i < Count; i ++)
194         {
195         if (BlockNumber == BlockNumberList[i])
196             {
197             ItemFound = i;
198             break;
199             }
200         }
201
202     return ItemFound;
203
204   #else
```

Listing 7.11 *asmfunc.cpp: assembly routines for speed (continued)*

```
205
206    asm    les    di,BlockNumberList // where to start
207    asm    mov    cx,Count           // how many to search
208    asm    mov    ax,BlockNumber // what to look for
209    asm    jcxz   notfound           // if nothing to do
210
211    asm    repne scasw               // search for block number
212    asm    jnz    notfound           // if not found, say so
213    asm    mov    ax,Count           // get slot count
214    asm    sub    ax,cx              // subtract where we are
215    asm    dec    ax                 // and adjust for postdecrement
216    asm    jmp    done               // we have the answer
217
218    notfound:
219    asm    mov    ax,-1              // not found
220
221    done:
222    #endif
223    }
```

Listing 7.12 *qfassert.h: quantum file assert header file*

```
1
2    /****keyword-flag*** "%v %f %n" */
3    /* "3 23-Apr-94,11:18:34 QFASSERT.H" */
4
5
6    #ifndef QFASSERT_H
7    #define QFASSERT_H
8
9    #ifdef DEBUG
10   #define qfassert(p) ((p) ? (void)0 : (void) QFAssertFail( \
11     "Assertion failed: %s, file %s, line %d\n", \
12     #p, __FILE__, __LINE__ ) )
13   #else
14   #define qfassert(p)
15   #endif
16
17   int QFAssertFail(char *p_FormatString, char *p_Message,
18     char *p_FileName, unsigned p_LineNumber);
19
20   #endif
```

Listing 7.13 *qfassert.cpp: implementation of quantum file asserts*

```
1
2    /****keyword-flag*** "%v %f %n" */
3    /* "4 26-Apr-94,19:58:04 QFASSERT.CPP" */
4
5
6    #include "common.h"
7
8    int QFAssertFail(char *p_FormatString, char *p_Message,
9      char *p_FileName, unsigned p_LineNumber)
10   {
11     printf(p_FormatString, p_Message, p_FileName, p_LineNumber);
12     asm int 3;
13     return 0;
14   }
```

Listing 7.14 *vector.h: vector definition*

```
 1
 2   /****keyword-flag*** "%v %f %n" */
 3   /* "20 31-Mar-94,22:55:52 VECTOR.H" */
 4
 5
 6   #include "common.h"
 7
 8
 9   template <class T> class AccessVector;
10
11   template <class T>
12   class Vector
13   {
14   protected:
15     T *m_Data;
16     ArrayIndex m_Count;
17   public:
18     Vector();
19     Vector(ArrayIndex p_Count);
20     Vector(ArrayIndex p_Count, T *p_Data);
21     Vector(char *p_Data);
22     Vector(const Vector& p_Vector);
23     Vector(AccessVector<T>& p_AccessVector);
24   operator char *() const {return (char *)m_Data;};
25   int operator==(char *p_Data);
26   int    operator==(const Vector& p_Vector);
27   void *GetDataAddress(){return (void *)m_Data;}
28   Vector& operator =( const Vector& p_Vector);
29   T& operator[](ArrayIndex p_ArrayIndex)
30   {
31   qfassert (this && (p_ArrayIndex < m_Count));
32   return m_Data[p_ArrayIndex];
33   }
34   ArrayIndex GetSize() {return m_Count;}
35   void    SetSize(ArrayIndex p_NewCount);
36     ~Vector() {delete [] m_Data;}
37   };
38
39   template <class T>
40   Vector<T>::Vector()
41   {
42     m_Data = new T[0];
43     m_Count = 0;
44   };
45
46   template <class T>
47   Vector<T>::Vector(ArrayIndex p_Count)
48   {
49     m_Data = new T[p_Count];
50     m_Count = p_Count;
51   };
```

Listing 7.14 *vector.h: vector definition (continued)*

```
52
53   template <class T>
54   Vector<T>::Vector(ArrayIndex p_Count, T *p_Data)
55   {
56     m_Data = new T[p_Count];
57     m_Count = p_Count;
58     for (ArrayIndex i = 0; i < m_Count; i ++)
59         m_Data[i] = p_Data[i];
60   };
61
62   template <class T>
63   Vector<T>::Vector(char *p_Data)
64   {
65     m_Count = strlen(p_Data);
66     m_Data = new T[m_Count];
67     memcpy((void *)m_Data,p_Data,m_Count);
68   };
69
70   template <class T>
71   Vector<T>::Vector(const Vector<T>& p_Vector)
72   {
73     if (this == &p_Vector)
74         return;
75
76     m_Count = p_Vector.m_Count;
77     m_Data = new T[m_Count];
78     for (ArrayIndex i = 0; i < m_Count; i ++)
79         m_Data[i] = p_Vector.m_Data[i];
80   };
81
82
83   template <class T>
84   Vector<T>::Vector(AccessVector<T>& p_AccessVector)
85   {
86     m_Count = p_AccessVector.GetSize();
87     m_Data = new T[m_Count];
88     for (ArrayIndex i = 0; i < m_Count; i ++)
89         m_Data[i] = p_AccessVector[i];
90   };
91
92
93   template <class T>
94   Vector<T>& Vector<T>::operator=(const Vector<T>& p_Vector)
95   {
96     if (this == &p_Vector)
97         return *this;
98
99     delete [] m_Data;
100    m_Count = p_Vector.m_Count;
101    m_Data = new T[m_Count];
102    for (ArrayIndex i = 0; i < m_Count; i ++)
```

Listing 7.14 *vector.h: vector definition (continued)*

```
103          m_Data[i] = p_Vector.m_Data[i];
104     return *this;
105   };
106
107
108   template <class T>
109   int Vector<T>::operator==(const Vector<T>& p_Vector)
110   {
111     if (this == &p_Vector)
112         return 1;
113     if (m_Count != p_Vector.m_Count)
114         return 0;
115     if (m_Count == 0)
116         return 1;
117     if (memcmp(m_Data,p_Vector.m_Data,m_Count*sizeof(T)) == 0)
118         return 1;
119     return 0;
120   };
121
122
123   template <class T>
124   int Vector<T>::operator==(char *p_Data)
125   {
126     int CompareLength = strlen(p_Data);
127
128     if (CompareLength != m_Count)
129         return 0;
130
131     if (memcmp((void *)m_Data,(void *)p_Data, strlen(p_Data)) == 0)
132         return 1;
133
134     return 0;
135   };
136
137
138   template <class T>
139   void Vector<T>::SetSize(ArrayIndex p_NewCount)
140   {
141     T *TempPtr;
142     ArrayIndex i;
143     ArrayIndex Smaller;
144
145     Smaller = min(p_NewCount, m_Count);
146
147     TempPtr = new T[p_NewCount];
148     for (i = 0; i < Smaller; i ++)
149         TempPtr[i] = m_Data[i];
150
151     delete [] m_Data;
152     m_Count = p_NewCount;
153     m_Data = TempPtr;
```

Listing 7.14 *vector.h: vector definition (continued)*

```
154    };
155
156
157    template <class T>
158    class AccessVector
159    {
160    protected:
161      T *m_Data;
162      ArrayIndex m_Count;
163    public:
164      AccessVector();
165      AccessVector(ArrayIndex p_Count, T *p_Data);
166      AccessVector(char *p_Data);
167    void *GetDataAddress(){return (void *)m_Data;}
168    int    operator==(const AccessVector& p_AccessVector);
169    T& operator[](ArrayIndex p_ArrayIndex)
170    {
171    qfassert (p_ArrayIndex < m_Count);
172    return m_Data[p_ArrayIndex];
173    }
174    ArrayIndex GetSize() {return m_Count;}
175    };
176
177    template <class T>
178    AccessVector<T>::AccessVector()
179    {
180      m_Data = 0;
181      m_Count = 0;
182    };
183
184    template <class T>
185    AccessVector<T>::AccessVector(ArrayIndex p_Count, T *p_Data)
186    {
187      m_Data = p_Data;
188      m_Count = p_Count;
189    };
190
191    template <class T>
192    AccessVector<T>::AccessVector(char *p_Data)
193    {
194      m_Data = (T *)p_Data;
195      m_Count = strlen(p_Data);
196    };
197
198    template <class T>
199    int AccessVector<T>::operator==(const AccessVector<T>& p_AccessVector)
200    {
201      if (this == &p_AccessVector)
202          return 1;
203      if (m_Count != p_AccessVector.m_Count)
204          return 0;
```

Listing 7.14 *vector.h: vector definition (continued)*

```
205     if (memcmp(m_Data,p_AccessVector.m_Data,m_Count*sizeof(T)) == 0)
206         return 1;
207     return 0;
208  };
209
210
211  class VectorCharRep;
212
213  class Vector<char>
214  {
215  protected:
216    VectorCharRep *m_Rep;
217  public:
218    Vector<char>();
219    Vector<char>(ArrayIndex p_Count);
220    Vector<char>(ArrayIndex p_Count, char *p_Data);
221    Vector<char>(char *p_Data);
222    Vector<char>(const Vector<char>& p_Vector);
223  operator char *() const;
224  int operator==(char *p_Data);
225  int    operator==(const Vector<char>& p_Vector);
226  int operator!=(char *p_Data);
227  int    operator!=(const Vector<char>& p_Vector);
228  void *GetDataAddress();
229  Vector<char>& operator =( const Vector<char>& p_Vector);
230  char& operator[](ArrayIndex p_ArrayIndex);
231  ArrayIndex GetSize();
232  void    SetSize(ArrayIndex p_NewCount);
233  ~Vector();
234  Vector<char> Mid(ArrayIndex p_Start, ArrayIndex p_Length);
235  };
236
237  class VectorCharRep
238  {
239  friend Vector<char>;
240  protected:
241    char *m_Data;
242    ArrayIndex m_Count;
243    int m_RefCount;
244  };
245
246
247  typedef Vector<char> String;
248
```

CHAPTER 8

Mozart, No. Would
You Believe Gershwin?

Introduction

In this final chapter we will summarize the characteristics of the algorithms we have encountered in previous chapters (figures 8.1-8.5), discuss the future of the art of optimization, and examine approaches to the problems posed in previous chapters.

Figure 8.1 *Characteristics of file access time reduction techniques*

- **Standard disk-based hashing[141] (Chapter 2)**
  - Excellent time efficiency
  - Extra storage needed to handle collisions (usually 25% extra is enough)
  - Appropriate for tables of a few hundred or more entries
  - Data can be accessed by a unique key which can be assigned arbitrarily

- **Dynamic hashing (Chapter 7)**
  - Excellent time efficiency
  - Table expands as needed
  - Appropriate for tables of almost unlimited size
  - Data can be accessed by a unique key which can be assigned arbitrarily

- **Caching[142] (Chapter 2)**
  - Excellent time efficiency
  - Memory utilization can be adjusted according to availability
  - Useful when the same data are read repeatedly

- **Strip files (Chapter 3)**
  - Good time efficiency
  - Useful when a particular subset of the data in every record is accessed frequently

---

141. Hash coding can also be used to eliminate binary or linear searches through tables in memory.

142. Caching can also be used to reduce processor time during searches of tables in memory, as the most recently or most frequently referenced items from the table can be kept in a cache.

Summary of Characteristics

Figure 8.2 *Characteristics of quantum file access method*

C implementation (Chapter 6)
Excellent time efficiency
Memory utilization can be adjusted according to availability
Allows random access to records whose length can vary dynamically

C++ implementation (Chapter 7)
Excellent time efficiency
Memory utilization can be adjusted according to availability
Allows random access to records whose length can vary dynamically
Provides array notation for ease of integration

Figure 8.3 *Characteristics of threaded-interpretive languages*

Token-threaded interpreters (Chapter 5)
- Excellent time efficiency
- Extremely compact code
- Expert assembly language programmer required to create

Figure 8.4 *Characteristics of data compression techniques*

o Radix40 (Chapters 1 and 2)
- Predictable output size
- Good time efficiency
- Moderate compression ratio: output size = .67 * input size
- Character set limited to 40 distinct characters

o BCD (Chapter 2)
- Predictable output size
- Good time efficiency
- Good compression ratio: output size = .5 * input size
- Character set limited to 16 distinct characters

o Bitmaps (Chapter 3)
- Predictable output size
- Good time efficiency
- Excellent compression ratio: output size = .125 * input size
- Character set limited to two distinct characters

o Arithmetic coding (Chapter 4)
- Unpredictable output size
- Fair time efficiency
- Very good compression ratio: output size typically ranges from .3 to .5 * input size
- Character set not artificially restricted

Figure 8.5 *Characteristics of processor time reduction techniques*

- Hash coding (Chapter 2)
  - See entry in figure 8.1

- Lookup tables (Chapter 1)
  - Excellent time efficiency
  - May use somewhat more memory than searching a list
  - Appropriate for tables of a few hundred or thousand items
  - Data can be accessed only by a unique index number, not an arbitrary key

- The distribution counting sort (Chapter 3)
  - Excellent time efficiency, proportional to number of keys
  - Predictable timing
  - Extra memory needed for copy of pointer array
  - Appropriate for sorting a few hundred or more keys
  - Each type of key to be sorted must be handled separately

- Assembly language enhancements (Chapters 4, 5, and 7)
  - Excellent time efficiency
  - Knowledge of underlying machine required
  - More difficult to debug than higher-level language routines

- Threaded-interpretive languages (Chapter 5)
  - See entry in figure 8.3

- Caching (Chapter 2)
  - See entry in figure 8.1

Some Thoughts on the Future

Although many managers might wish it otherwise, the writing of efficient computer programs will always be an art, not a science. This may appear to be a rash statement, but I think time will prove me correct. Of course, if I am wrong, I am following a rich tradition: according to (Arthur C.) Clarke's Law, if a distinguished elderly scientist [defined as over 30 years old] says that something is possible, he is almost always right; if he says that something is impossible, he is almost always wrong.[143]

However, I feel I am on reasonably firm ground. The main reason is that, as demonstrated by Goedel's Proof, no automatic procedure can discover all of the true statements in a consistent axiomatic system such as the behavior of a programmable

---

143. A remarkable example of such hyperconservatism is the following statement, from an otherwise fine book by Edward Yourdon: "*As a programmer, you will always be working for an employer.* Unless you are very rich and very eccentric, you will not enjoy the luxury of having a computer in your own home...". (emphasis in the original) Yourdon, E. *Techniques of Program Structure and Design.* Englewood Cliffs, New Jersey: Prentice-Hall, Inc., 1975, pp. 2-3. This clearly ranks with the worst predictions of all time.

computer.[144] This implies that the development of new algorithms will always be an adventure. A fine example of this is the optimization in Chapter 4, in which I discovered that I could replace 16-bit occurrence counts with 4-bit indexes and actually speed up the operation of the program at the same time; I'd like to see the optimizing compiler that could figure that out! Obviously, such unpredictability can be quite expensive. While other engineering professionals, such as structural engineers, routinely estimate the time and money required for their projects to within a few percent, software engineers are not nearly so accurate. In fact, overruns of hundreds of percent are not uncommon. Why is this so?

Why Johnny Can't Estimate

The answer is quite simple: once a structural engineer has built a dozen bridges (for example), the thirteenth is mostly an application of the knowledge he has already acquired. Of course, this is not to say that the expertise of the engineer is unimportant; far from it. However, experience is a great teacher, and experience gained in such a specialty is extremely valuable.

We software engineers, however, face a fundamentally different situation: once we have solved a given problem, we should never need to solve it again, as we can reuse the solution already developed. Therefore, in our development projects, we are always venturing into unexplored territory, and we all know how to identify pioneers.[145]

Actually, I find it enjoyable to have a new set of challenges with each new project. We should take pride in our work; it is fairly clear to me, at least, that large software systems are the most complex of human creations. They combine the characteristics of art and engineering: first, we conceive of and build something out of sheer thought, the most evanescent material any artist has ever used, and then it actually performs a useful function![146]

Goodbye for Now

We have reached the end of this book. I hope you have learned as much from reading this volume as I have while writing it.

---

144. An excellent explanation of this important mathematical discovery can be found in Douglas Hofstadter's book *Goedel, Escher, Bach*. New York: Vintage Books, 1979.

145. They're the ones with the arrows in their backs.

146. Interestingly enough, the previously cited passage in Yourdon's book goes on to say: "In short, you cannot be an artist, separate and aloof; it is highly unlikely that the programming community will ever generate a Michaelangelo or a Rembrandt". This is quite a difficult standard to meet: how many artists of this stature have come from any field, including sculpture and painting? While the jury is still out on this prediction, I think we will see a great artist of programming one of these days, although his or her work might be inaccessible to laymen.

Suggested Approaches to Problems

Chapter 2

1. Modifications to add capabilities to the program:

    a. To delete records, we need to invent another flag value (for example, 14 or 0xe for the first digit) indicating that the record has been used in the past, but currently is unused. This allows us to continue looking for a record that might be after the current position in the file; however, we should remember the position of this "previously owned" record, so that if the record we are seeking turns out not to be in the file, we can reuse this record rather than taking up an unused one. Of course, this solution will not prevent the file from gradually being filled up with previously used records, which will result in slower and slower access times, particularly when looking for records which are not in the file; clearly, if every record has been used at least once, we would have to search the entire file to determine that a particular record is not in the file. This can be taken care of by periodic maintenance as in the answer to the next question.

    b. In order to handle the case of a full file, or a file which has become nearly filled with deleted records, we can copy the records in the file to a larger one. This requires opening both the old new file and a new one, with the initialization of the new file set to create a larger file. Then we read every valid record in the old file and write it to the new one; since we don't copy any deleted records, the new file starts out with a clean slate. This situation illustrates why we use a `PriceFile` structure to keep track of the data for each file; this is what allows us to have both the new and old file open at once.

    c. Keeping track of the inventory of each item requires an inventory field to the `ItemRecord` structure and updating this information whenever items are sold or added to inventory.

2. Hash coding could be applied to tables in memory in much the same way as we have applied it to disk files: the main difference is that since memory is a true random-access device, we could use a different method of selecting which slot to use for overflow records, rather than having to use the next sequential slot.

3. If we wish to reduce the time needed to look up an entry in a table in memory by a key, we can maintain a cache of the most recently seen entries, employing a hash code based on the key to be looked up. Each time we find an entry, we store its key and record number in the cache entry corresponding to its hash code. Then, when we want to find a record, the first place we look is in the cache entry corresponding to its key's hash code. If the key in that cache entry matches the key of the record we are looking for, we use the record number in the cache entry to access the record; if the key doesn't match, we have to search the table as we

otherwise would have to do anyway. Since the amount of time needed to check the cache entry is small compared to the time needed to search the table, we should come out ahead in most cases.

Chapter 3

1. One way to produce output in descending rather than ascending order is to subtract each character from 256 before using it as an index.

2. In order to make only one pass through the data for each character position, rather than two as at present, we have to add the pointer for each key to the end of a linked list for characters having the ASCII code of the character at the current position in the key. For example, if the current character in the key we are processing is 'A', then the pointer to that key would be added to the 'A' list; similarly for 'B', 'C', and any other character that might occur in the key. When the pointers for all the keys have been added to the appropriate lists, the lists are concatenated into one big list, with the 'B' list attached to the end of the 'A' list, the 'C' list attached to the end of the 'B' list, and so on. Then the process starts again for the next character position. After we have made this change to the algorithm, the resulting algorithm is known as a "radix sort".

3. In order to sort integer or floating-point data rather than character data, we have to know the internal structure of the data. For example, on the Intel 80x86 machines, the low byte of a two-byte unsigned value has a lower memory address than the high byte. We can view this as a two-byte key, with the less significant part lower in memory. Since we have to sort by the less significant portion first, our outer loop index must count up from 0 to 1, rather than the other way around as it would with a two-byte string. Of course, on a Motorola or other "high end first" machine, such unsigned values would be sorted in the same order as strings. Signed values pose additional difficulty, as the high-order byte of a negative value has a greater character value than the high-order byte of a positive value: one way around this is to negate all the keys both before and after the sort. Applying the distribution sort or any other noncomparison sort to floating- point values is even more complex, as the internal representation of a floating-point value is composed of several parts with differing functions; for this reason, the algorithm must be tailored to the individual circumstances. However, the performance of the resulting algorithm makes this effort worthwhile if the number of values to be sorted is reasonably large.

4. Probably the best way to handle variable-length strings as keys is to make one pass through the key array, calling `strlen` to identify the length of each key, and then saving the result in a temporary array. Then, whenever we are ready to extract a character from the key, we first determine whether we are past the end of the key, in which case we substitute a null byte. Another possible way to sort variable-length strings is to ignore the fact that they differ in length. Since a C string is normally terminated by a null byte, two strings that are identical up to

the end of the shorter one will sort correctly if both are treated as having the length of the longer one; the null byte will make the shorter one sort before the longer one. However, this approach will not work if you are using a protected-mode operating system and you try to access bytes following the end of a short string when these bytes have not been allocated to your program; you will get a protection violation. Another aspect of this approach is that the garbage after the end of a string that is shorter than the key being sorted will be used to rearrange identical keys that should remain in the same relative position in the file. This may cause problems in applications that rely on identical keys keeping their relative orders.

Chapter 4

1. In order to use arithmetic coding where each of a number of blocks of text must be decompressed without reference to the other blocks, we must generate a table of probabilities by analyzing a file or files which have characteristics similar to those to be compressed. Then, rather than compute the probabilities on the fly when compressing or decompressing one of our text blocks, we use the precomputed probability table. This also increases the speed of compressing and decompressing, as the table does not need to be updated.

2. If the data to be compressed consists entirely of characters with ASCII codes 0 through 127 (or any other subset of the ASCII range), we can eliminate a significant amount of the storage for the probability tables by allocating only those tables needed to encode or decode the characters that can occur in the data. In the example given, we need only 128 tables of 128 elements, rather than 256 tables of 256 elements; the resulting memory requirement is approximately 8 Kbytes rather than approximately 32 Kbytes, saving about 24 Kbytes.

3. There are two excellent places to apply assembly language enhancements to the Megasort routine from Chapter 3: the instructions in the loop that counts the number of occurrences of each character; and the instructions in the loop that copies the pointers to the temporary array are executed for each character of the data to be sorted. Replacing those two loops with assembly language equivalents can increase the speed of the sort by a factor of about six.

Chapter 5

1. Given a token-threaded interpreter:

   a. To extend the number of op-codes, some number of the 256 basic op-codes could be reserved to mean "extended op-code follows". For example, if one-fourth of the "op-code space" were reserved for extensions, then the interpreter could examine the op-code to see if its top two bits are both 1; if so, the next 14 bits (i.e., the low six of the current byte and all of the next byte) would be the "extended op-code". This provides 192 one-byte base codes and 16K two-byte extended ones. Unfortunately, this will slow down the interpreter due to the extra decoding step; also, the NEXT macro will become larger. Probably a better alternative is to manage this process in the 64 op-codes reserved for extended operations; this allows the implementation of the 192 one- byte op-codes to avoid extra overhead.

b. One way to add a subroutine capability is to define subroutines as having extended op-codes as defined above; in that case, part of the dispatch logic for the extended op-codes would be to save the current value of IP on the CPU stack and reload it with the address of the beginning of the subroutine. Each subroutine would then end with an op-code that would pop the IP from the stack, so that interpretation would continue where it had left off at the subroutine call.

c. A possible way to add new data types is to create new op-codes that would handle strings, integers, etc., in much the same way that floating-point values are handled in the example. However, because the 80x86 processors do not provide stack-oriented instructions for any data type other than floats, that logic would have to be handled explicitly by the interpreter.

d. Some applications for the ability to move code around in memory during execution include: replacing code while the system is running; loading infrequently used code from disk when it is accessed; and eliminating code used only at initialization, to make room for more data at run time.

Chapter 6

1. In order to allow arrays to be extended automatically when the user stores into an element past the end of the array, we have to add code similar to that in `initialize_big_pointer_array` to `qf_store_item`, This code has to lengthen the last segment of the item reference array (IRA) and possibly add segments to the IRA, depending on the number of elements to be added. Then we initialize the new or extended IRA segments and update the big pointer array to account for this increase in size. In the case of a sparse array, which has many more unused elements than used ones, it would be possible to create only those IRA segments (small pointer arrays) that contained items in use, thus eliminating the storage required by unused IRA segments.

2. The QFIX program has the following general description. The first phase starts from the main object index, checking the validity of each main object. The big pointer array quantum is checked to see that it belongs to the object in question. Then each of the small pointer arrays is similarly checked, and then each small pointer array entry is checked as well. If all is well so far, the next main object is checked in the same manner. If a problem is found with any main object, we record its object number in a table of problem objects and continue the scan. When all entries in the main object table have been checked, we start phase two. Skipping any quanta containing the main object table, big pointer arrays, and little pointer arrays, we examine each quantum containing actual user data. For

each such quantum, we extract the object number to which that quantum belongs. If that object number is not in the list of problem objects, we continue to the next quantum. However, if it is in the list, we construct or add to a big pointer array and little pointer arrays corresponding to the data in the quantum. Since we know the index numbers of all the elements in the quantum we are examining, we have enough information to do this.

Chapter 7

1. Modifications to add capabilities to the dynamic hashing implementation:

    a. Deleting records is almost exactly the inverse of adding records. Every time the number of records decreases by the average number of records per slot, we take the storage element from the highest-numbered slot and combine it with the one from its buddy slot, placing the result back in the buddy slot. Then we decrease the active slot count by one. If the active slot count becomes equal to one-half of the allocated slot count, we halve the allocated count.

    b. One solution to the problem of storage elements that exceed the size of one quantum is to chain them together. The beginning of each storage element would have space reserved for the array index number of the next element in the chain. Of course, chasing storage elements all over the disk could get pretty slow, but that should be a rare event if the hashing algorithm is working; if it's not working, the whole system will break down anyway.

    c. The main problem with duplicate keys is that since records with the same key will always wind up in the same storage element, they make it imperative to handle the overflow problem mentioned just above. Once that is solved, handling duplicate keys is easy: once you have located all storage elements that might contain records with that key, search each of them to the end, rather than stopping when you get a match. Of course, you then have to decide which record you want to use, but that's an application-specific problem.

    d. To provide a "mass load mode", you'll have to add a function to change the behavior of `PutElement`, so that it will start a new block when the current "last added to" block doesn't have enough space. Of course, you'll also have to add a complementary function to reset its behavior when you're done with the mass load.

2. This is a wonderful application for templates. Even the name of the class is intended to suggest that it could very easily be changed to `PersistentArray<type>`.

3. The directory utility will have to be able to add and delete array names randomly. A hash-coded lookup would probably be the best solution for large numbers of arrays, although this is not critical in the current implementation, which is limited to 256 arrays per file.

Index